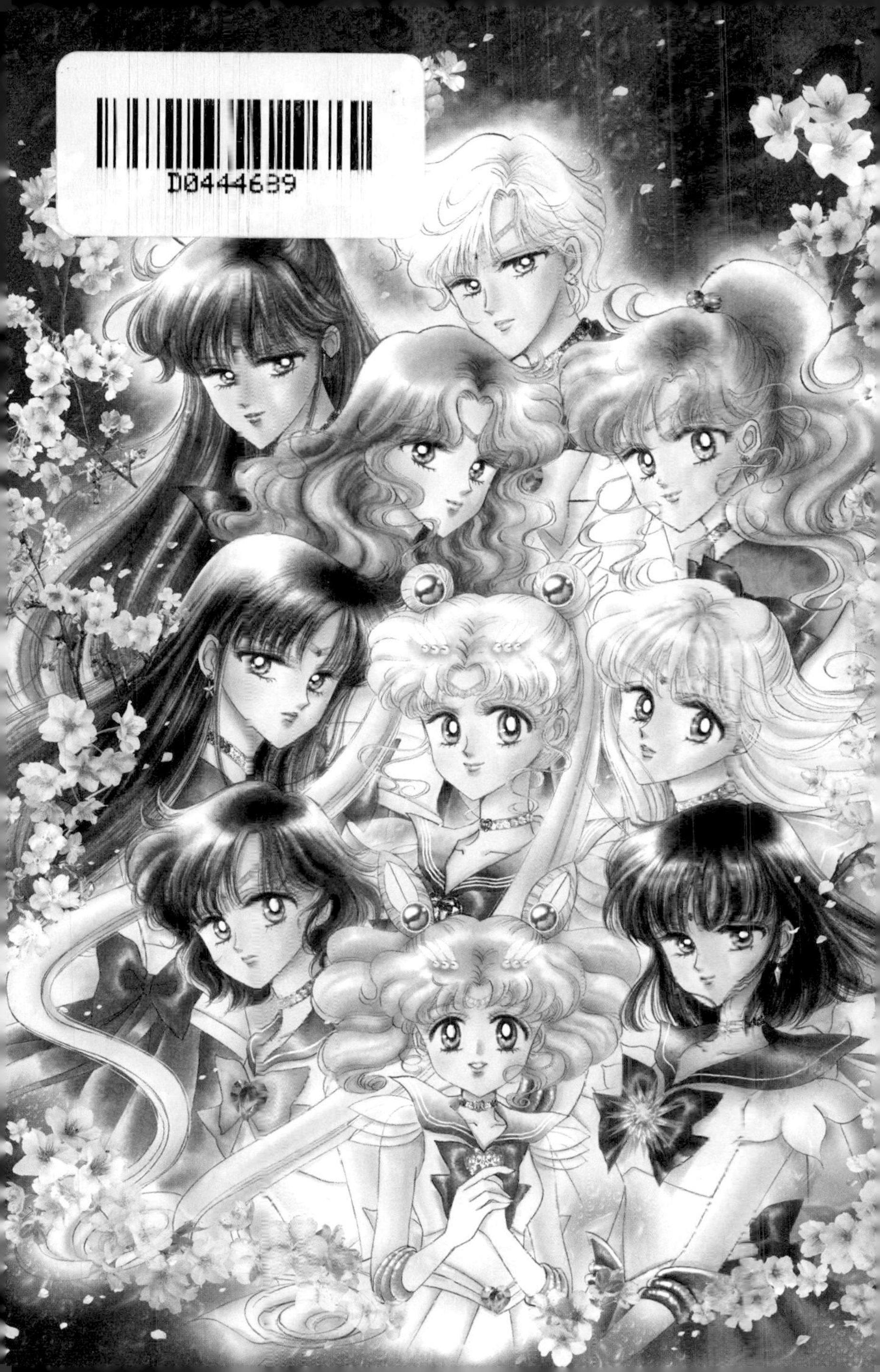

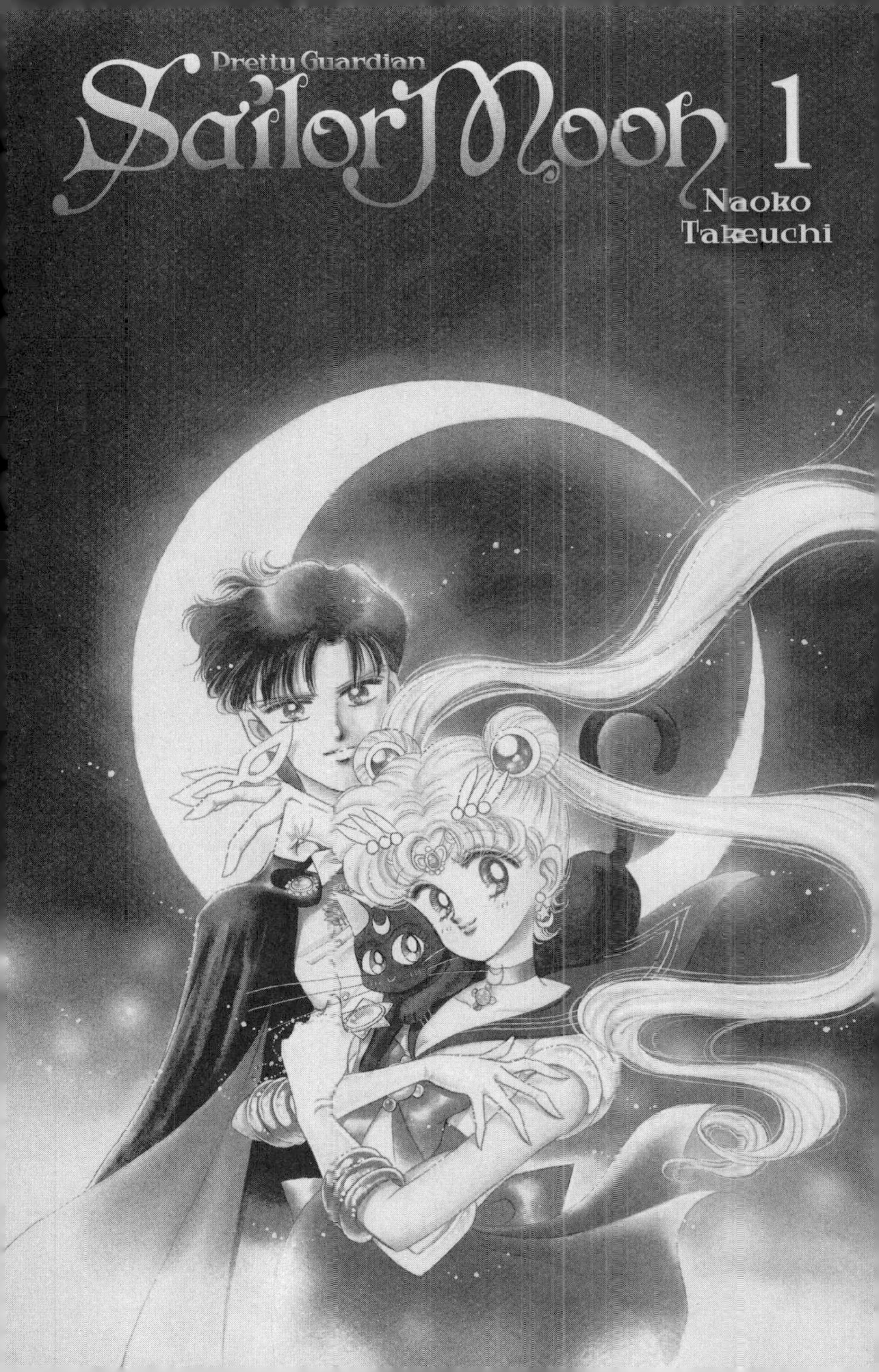
Pretty Guardian
Sailor Moon 1
Naoko
Takeuchi

CONTENTS

Pretty Guardian Sailor Moon

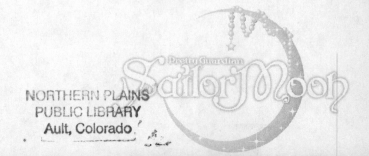

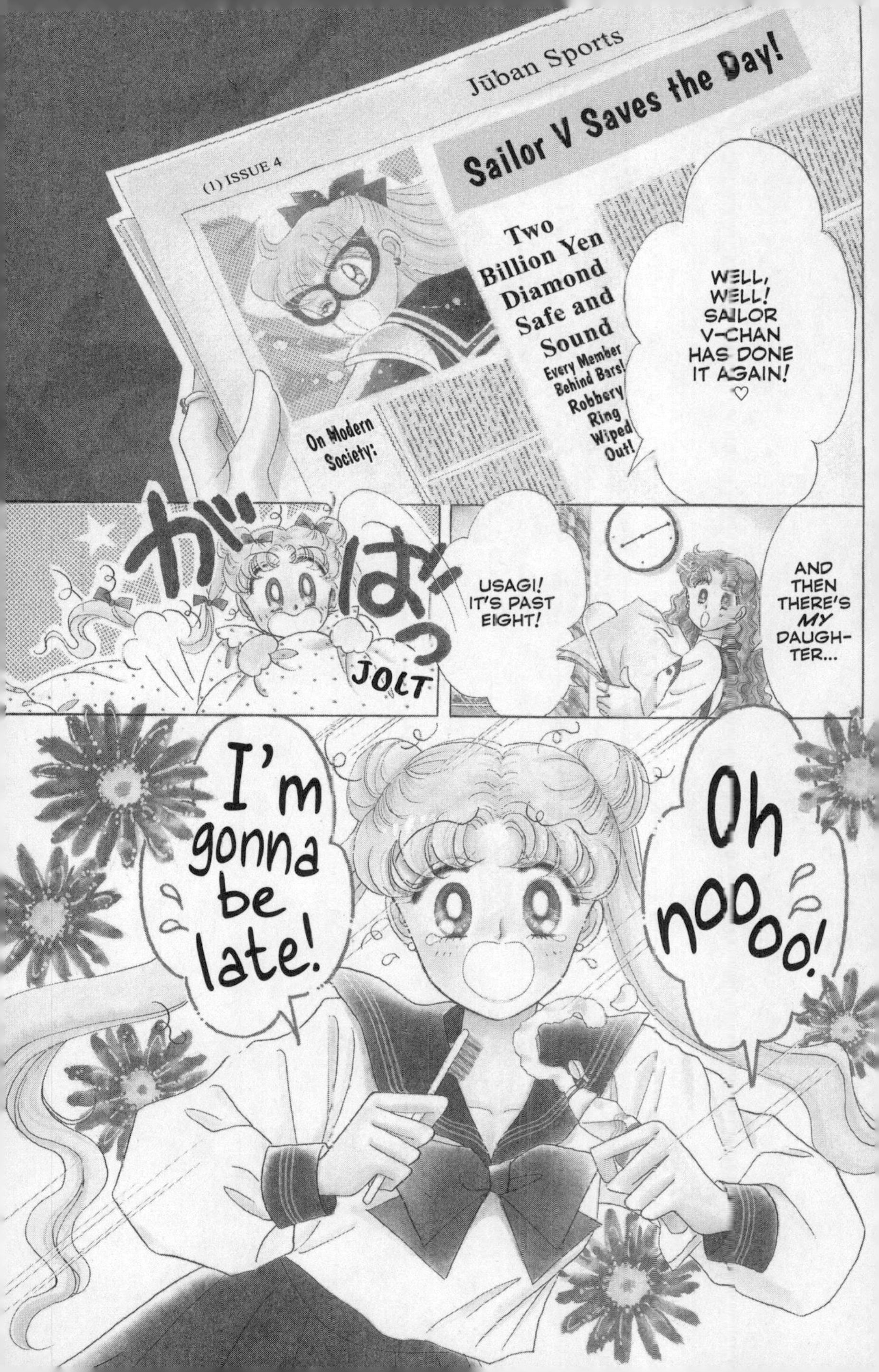
WELL, WELL! SAILOR V-CHAN HAS DONE IT AGAIN! ♡
Jūban Sports
Sailor V Saves the Day!
(1) ISSUE 4
Two Billion Yen Diamond Safe and Sound
Every Member Behind Bars! Robbery Ring Wiped Out!
On Modern Society:
AND THEN THERE'S *MY* DAUGHTER...
USAGI! IT'S PAST EIGHT!
がばっ
JOLT
Oh noooo!
I'm gonna be late!

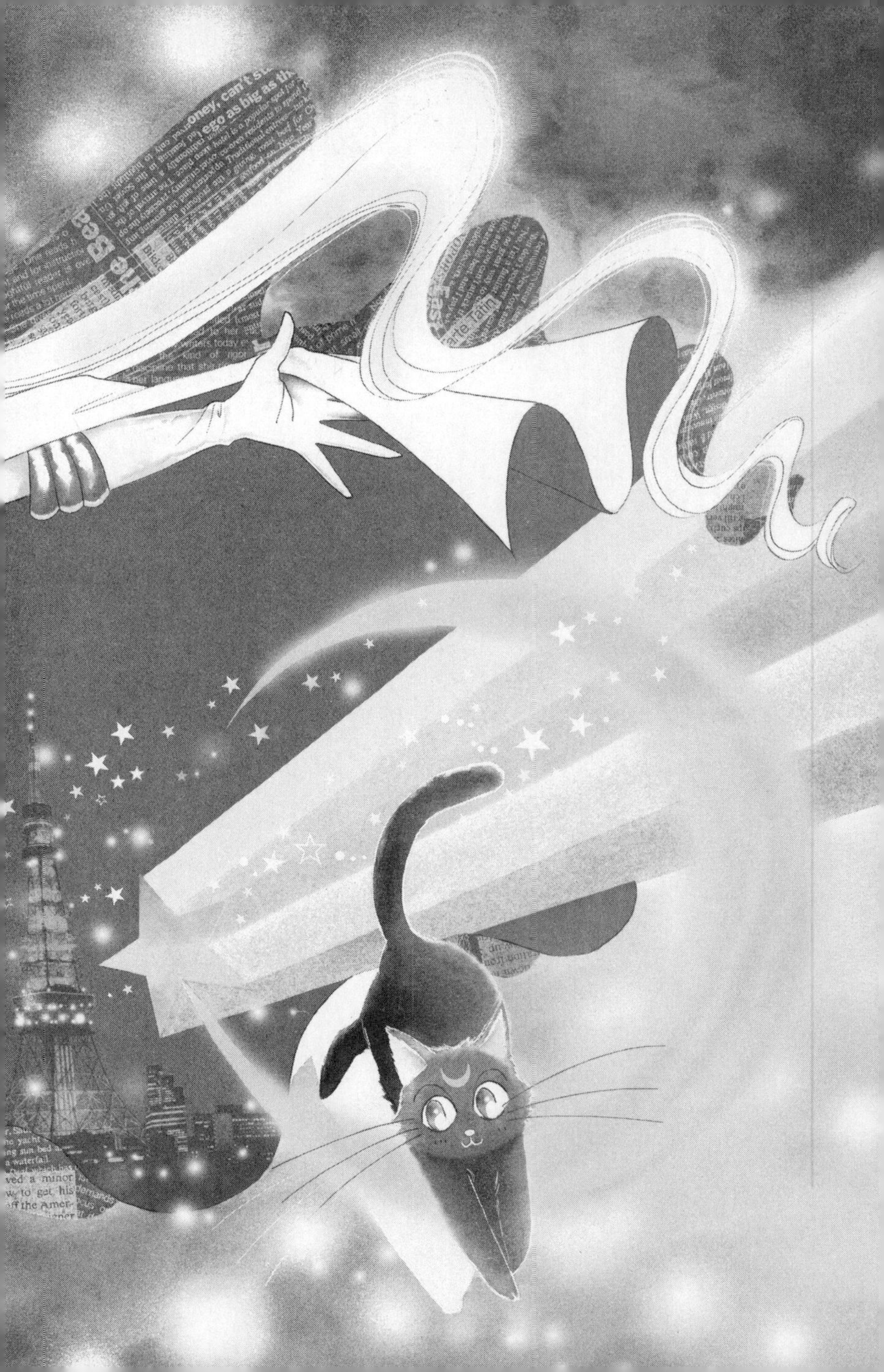

Act.1 Usagi: Sailor Moon

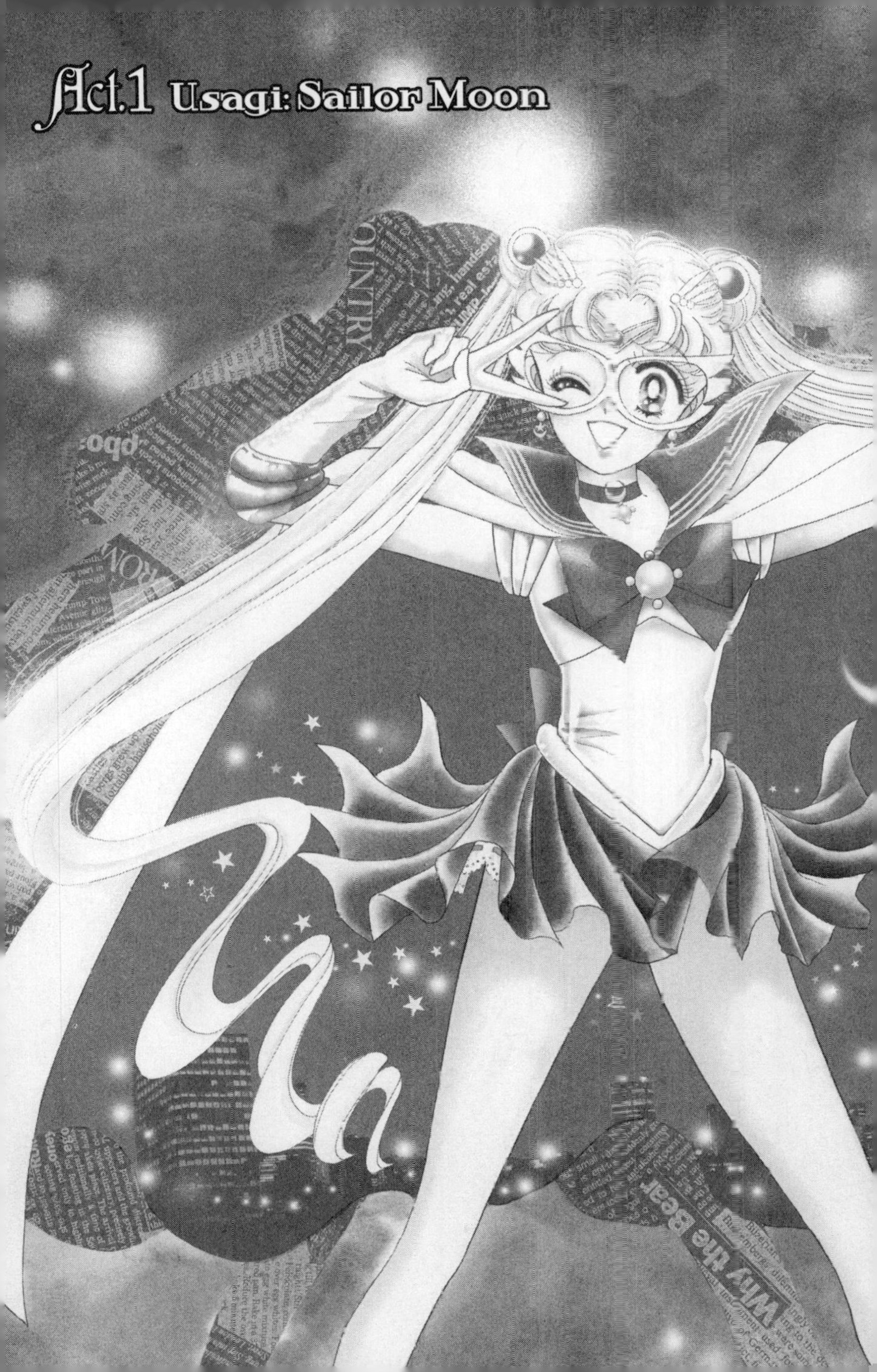

Pretty Guardian
Sailor Moon

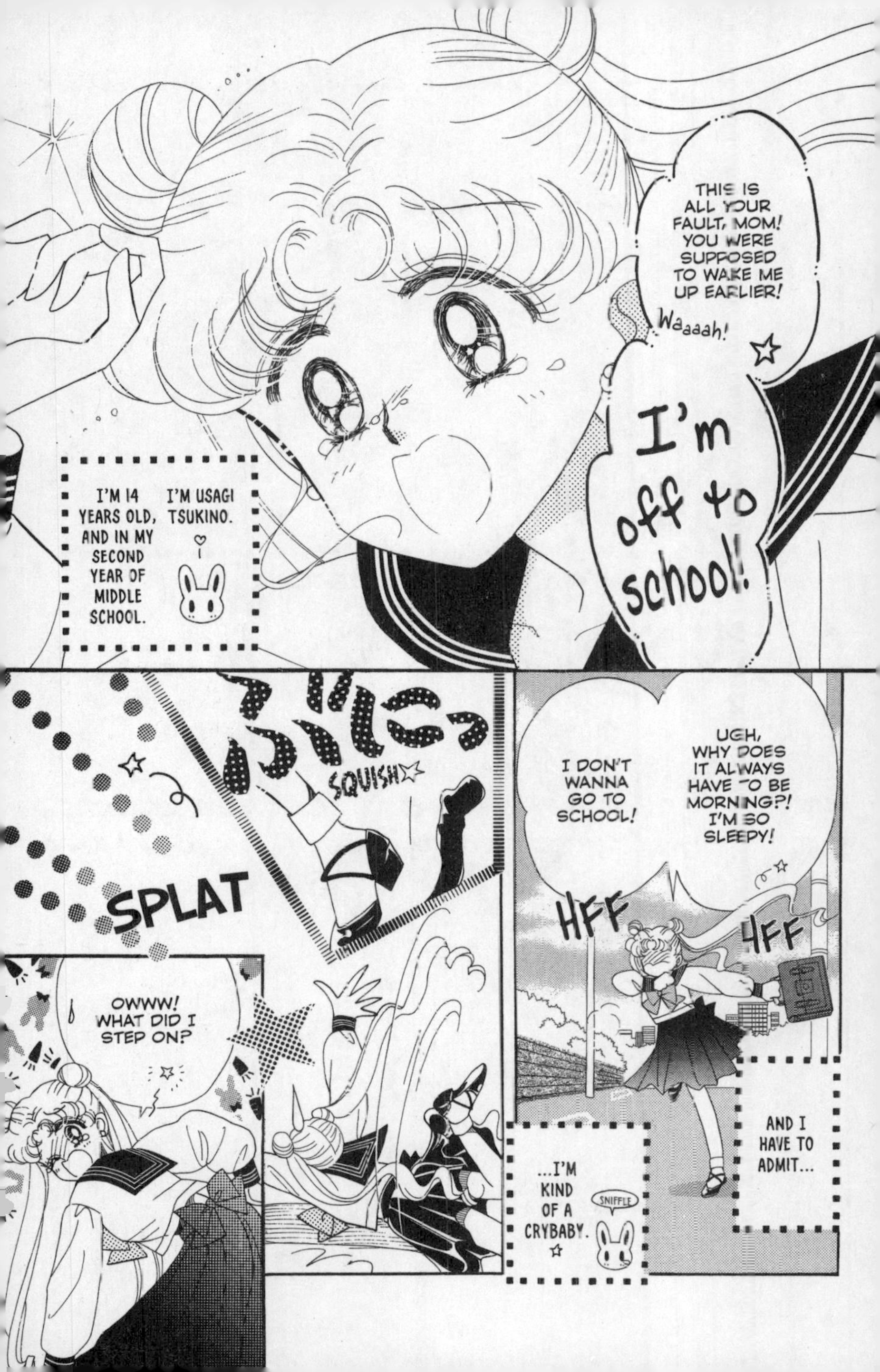
THIS IS ALL YOUR FAULT, MOM! YOU WERE SUPPOSED TO WAKE ME UP EARLIER!
Waaaah!
I'm off to school!!
I'M USAGI TSUKINO.
I'M 14 YEARS OLD, AND IN MY SECOND YEAR OF MIDDLE SCHOOL.
UGH, WHY DOES IT ALWAYS HAVE TO BE MORNING?! I'M SO SLEEPY!
I DON'T WANNA GO TO SCHOOL!
HFF
HFF
AND I HAVE TO ADMIT...
...I'M KIND OF A CRYBABY.
SNIFFLE
SQUISH
SPLAT
OWWW! WHAT DID I STEP ON?

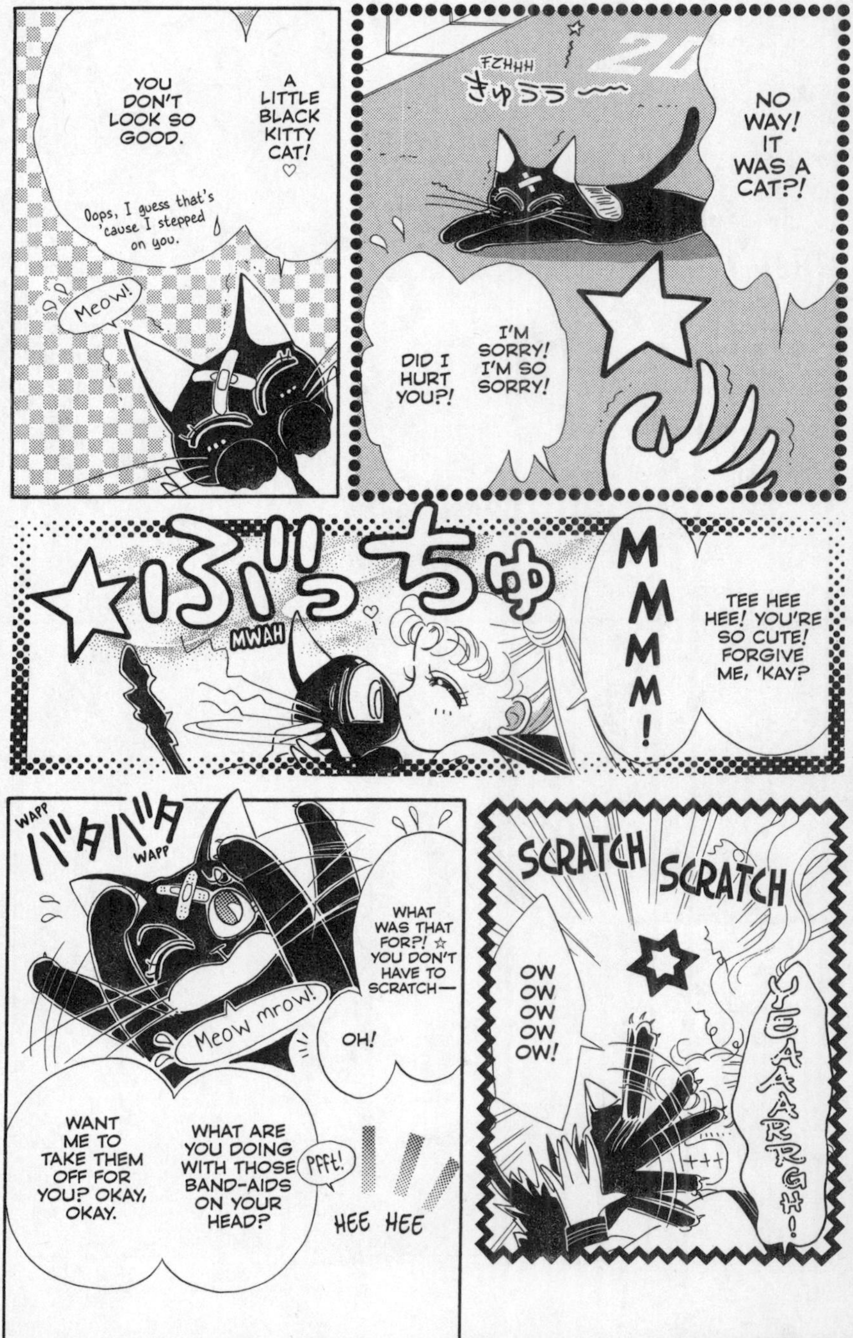
きゅうう〜〜
FZHHH
NO WAY! IT WAS A CAT?!
I'M SORRY! I'M SO SORRY!
DID I HURT YOU?!
A LITTLE BLACK KITTY CAT! ♡
YOU DON'T LOOK SO GOOD.
Oops, I guess that's 'cause I stepped on you.
Meow!
MMMMM!
TEE HEE HEE! YOU'RE SO CUTE! FORGIVE ME, 'KAY?
ぶっちゅ
MWAH
SCRATCH SCRATCH
YEAAARGH!
OW OW OW OW OW!
バタバタ
WAPP WAPP
WHAT WAS THAT FOR?! ☆ YOU DON'T HAVE TO SCRATCH—
Meow mrow!
OH!
HEE HEE
Pfft!
WHAT ARE YOU DOING WITH THOSE BAND-AIDS ON YOUR HEAD?
WANT ME TO TAKE THEM OFF FOR YOU? OKAY, OKAY.

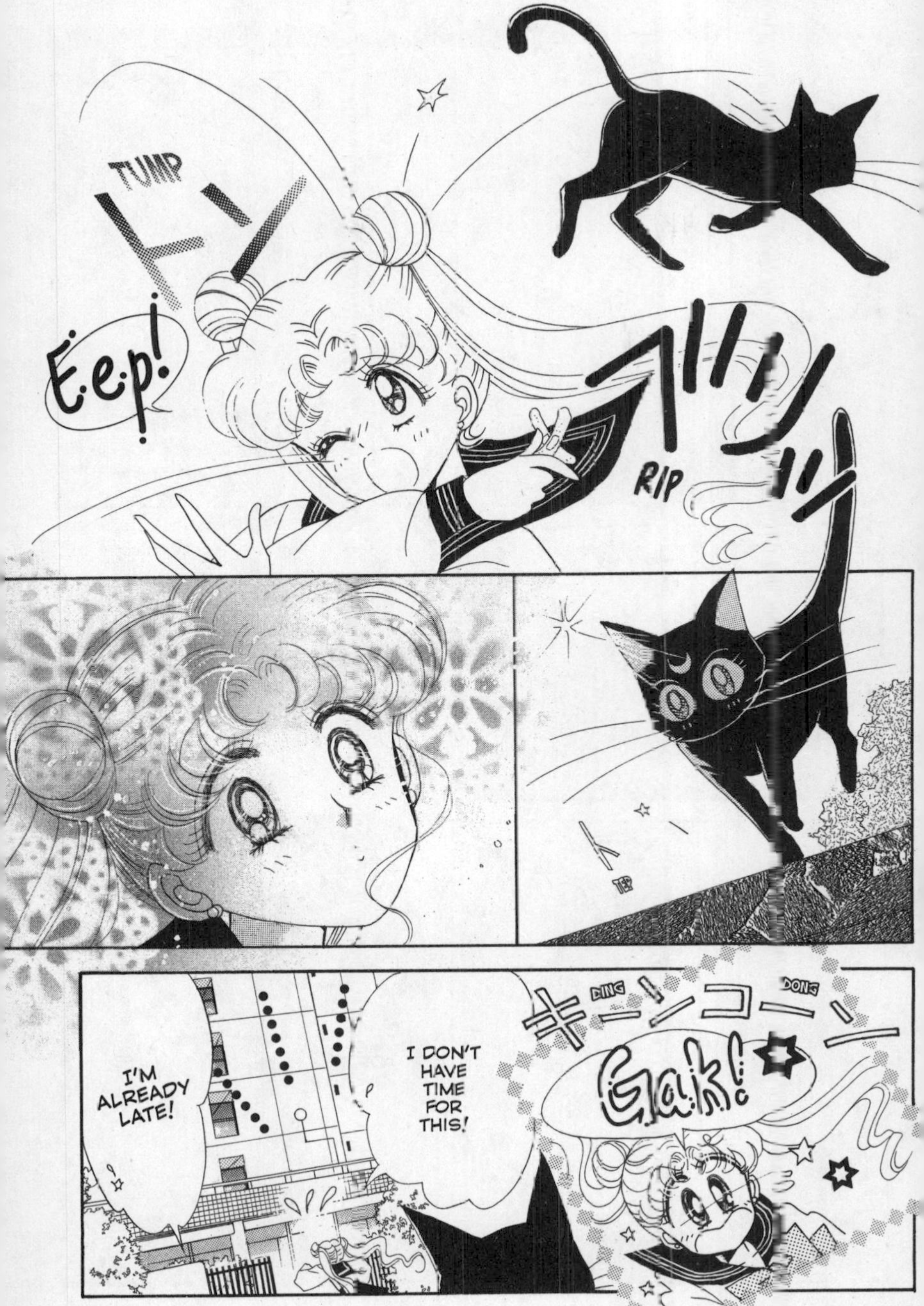
TUMP
Eep!
RIP
TEP
DING
DONG
Gak!
I DON'T HAVE TIME FOR THIS!
I'M ALREADY LATE!

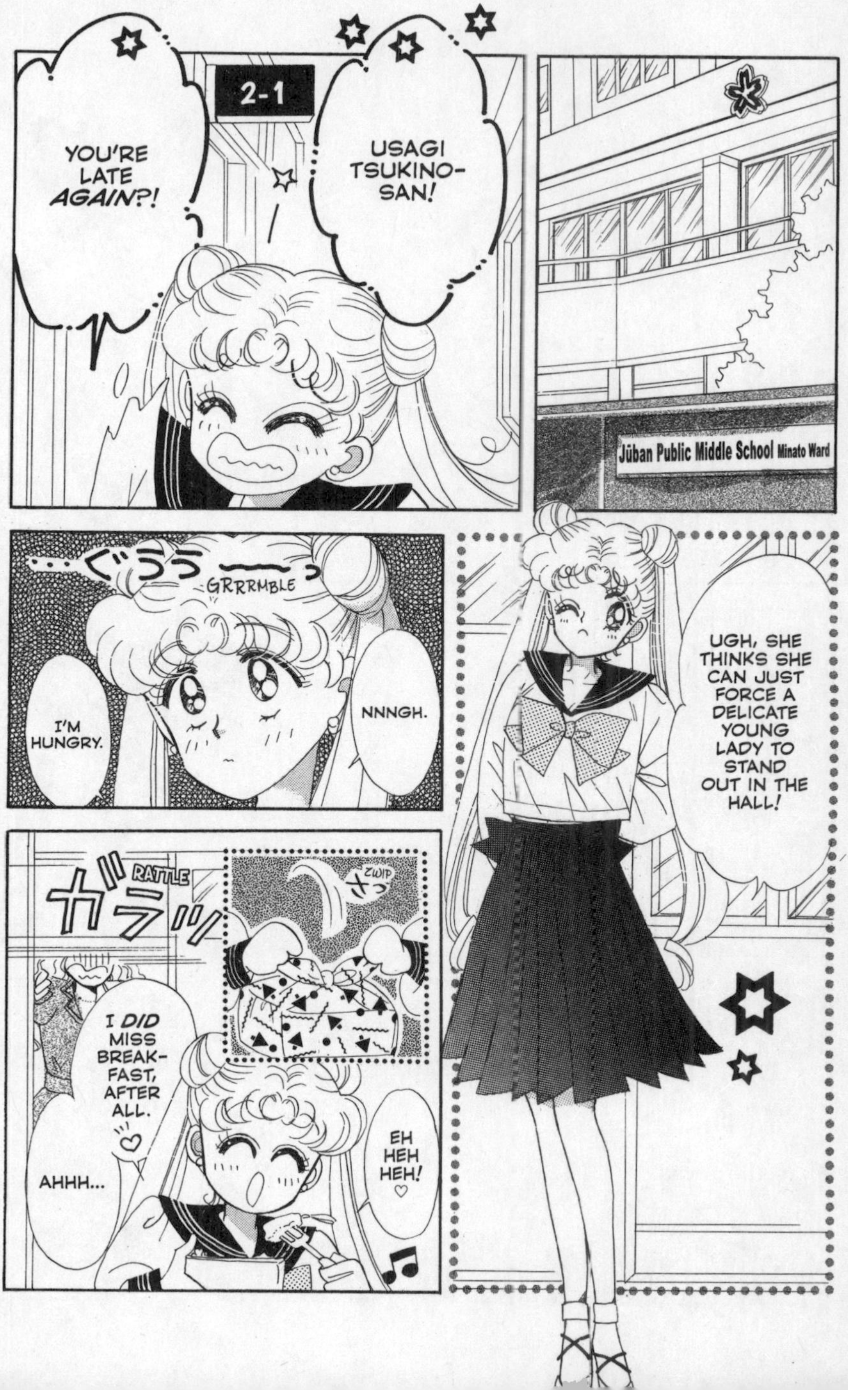
Jūban Public Middle School Minato Ward
2-1
USAGI TSUKINO-SAN!
YOU'RE LATE AGAIN?!
UGH, SHE THINKS SHE CAN JUST FORCE A DELICATE YOUNG LADY TO STAND OUT IN THE HALL!
ぐううーーっ
GRRRMBLE
NNNGH.
I'M HUNGRY.
ガラッ
RATTLE
ZWIP
EH HEH HEH! ♡
I DID MISS BREAKFAST, AFTER ALL.
AHHH...

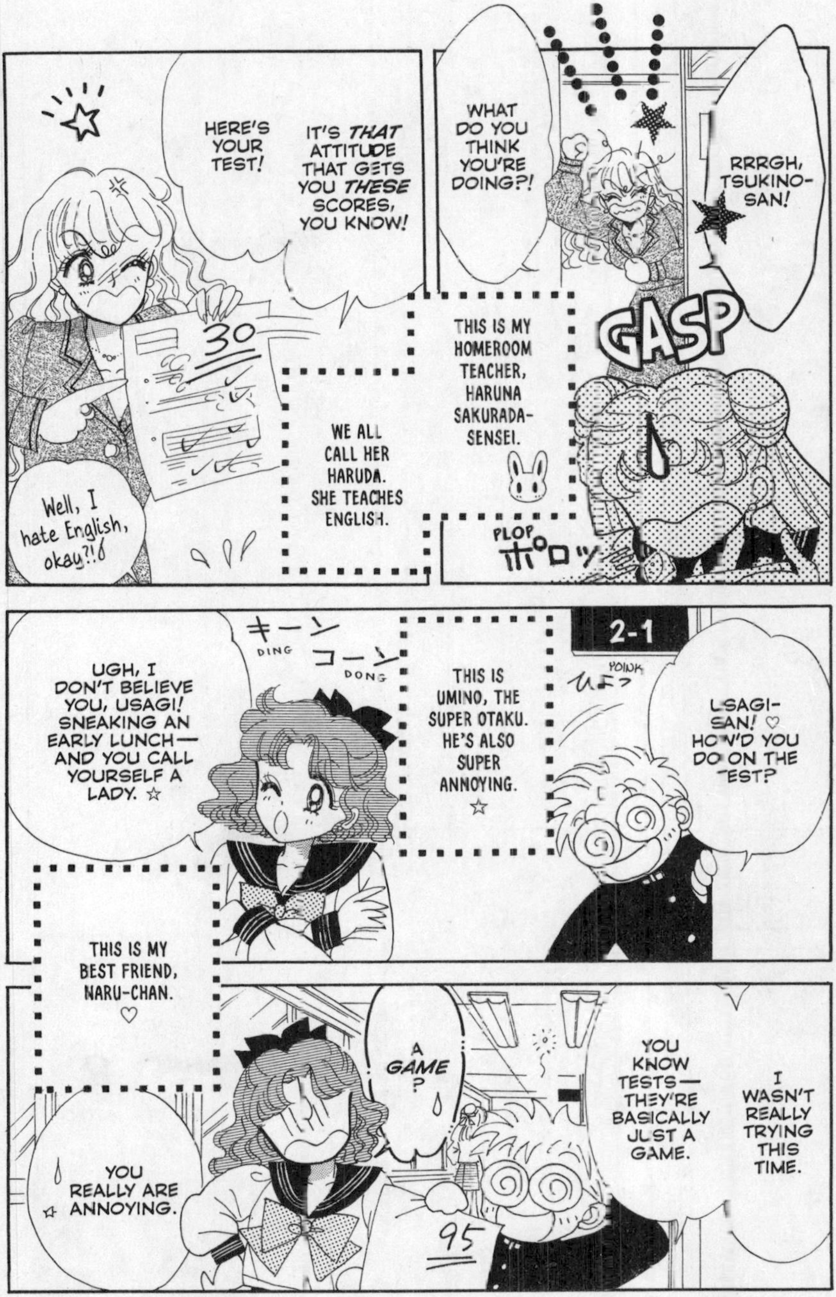
RRRGH, TSUKINO-SAN!
WHAT DO YOU THINK YOU'RE DOING?!
GASP
THIS IS MY HOMEROOM TEACHER, HARUNA SAKURADA-SENSEI.
PLOP
ポロッ
HERE'S YOUR TEST!
IT'S *THAT* ATTITUDE THAT GETS YOU *THESE* SCORES, YOU KNOW!
30
WE ALL CALL HER HARUDA. SHE TEACHES ENGLISH.
Well, I hate English, okay?!
2-1
YOINK
USAGI-SAN! ♡ HOW'D YOU DO ON THE TEST?
THIS IS UMINO, THE SUPER OTAKU. HE'S ALSO SUPER ANNOYING. ☆
キーン
DING
コーン
DONG
UGH, I DON'T BELIEVE YOU, USAGI! SNEAKING AN EARLY LUNCH—AND YOU CALL YOURSELF A LADY. ☆
THIS IS MY BEST FRIEND, NARU-CHAN. ♡
I WASN'T REALLY TRYING THIS TIME.
YOU KNOW TESTS—THEY'RE BASICALLY JUST A GAME.
A *GAME*?
95
YOU REALLY ARE ANNOYING.

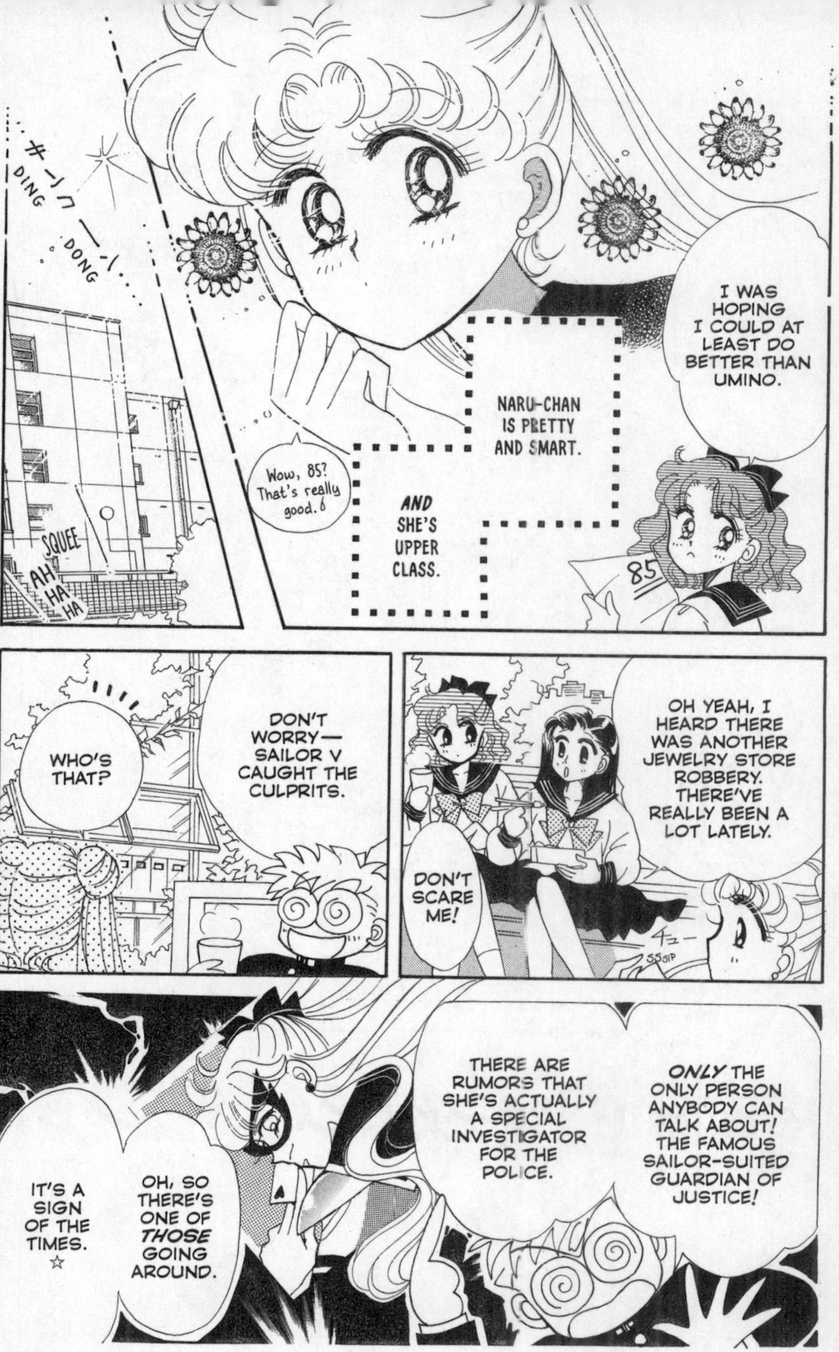
I WAS HOPING I COULD AT LEAST DO BETTER THAN UMINO.
NARU-CHAN IS PRETTY AND SMART.
85
Wow, 85? That's really good.
AND SHE'S UPPER CLASS.
キーンコーン
DING DONG
SQUEE
AH HA HA
OH YEAH, I HEARD THERE WAS ANOTHER JEWELRY STORE ROBBERY. THERE'VE REALLY BEEN A LOT LATELY.
DON'T SCARE ME!
チュー
SSSIP
DON'T WORRY— SAILOR V CAUGHT THE CULPRITS.
WHO'S THAT?
ONLY THE ONLY PERSON ANYBODY CAN TALK ABOUT! THE FAMOUS SAILOR-SUITED GUARDIAN OF JUSTICE!
THERE ARE RUMORS THAT SHE'S ACTUALLY A SPECIAL INVESTIGATOR FOR THE POLICE.
OH, SO THERE'S ONE OF THOSE GOING AROUND.
IT'S A SIGN OF THE TIMES. ☆

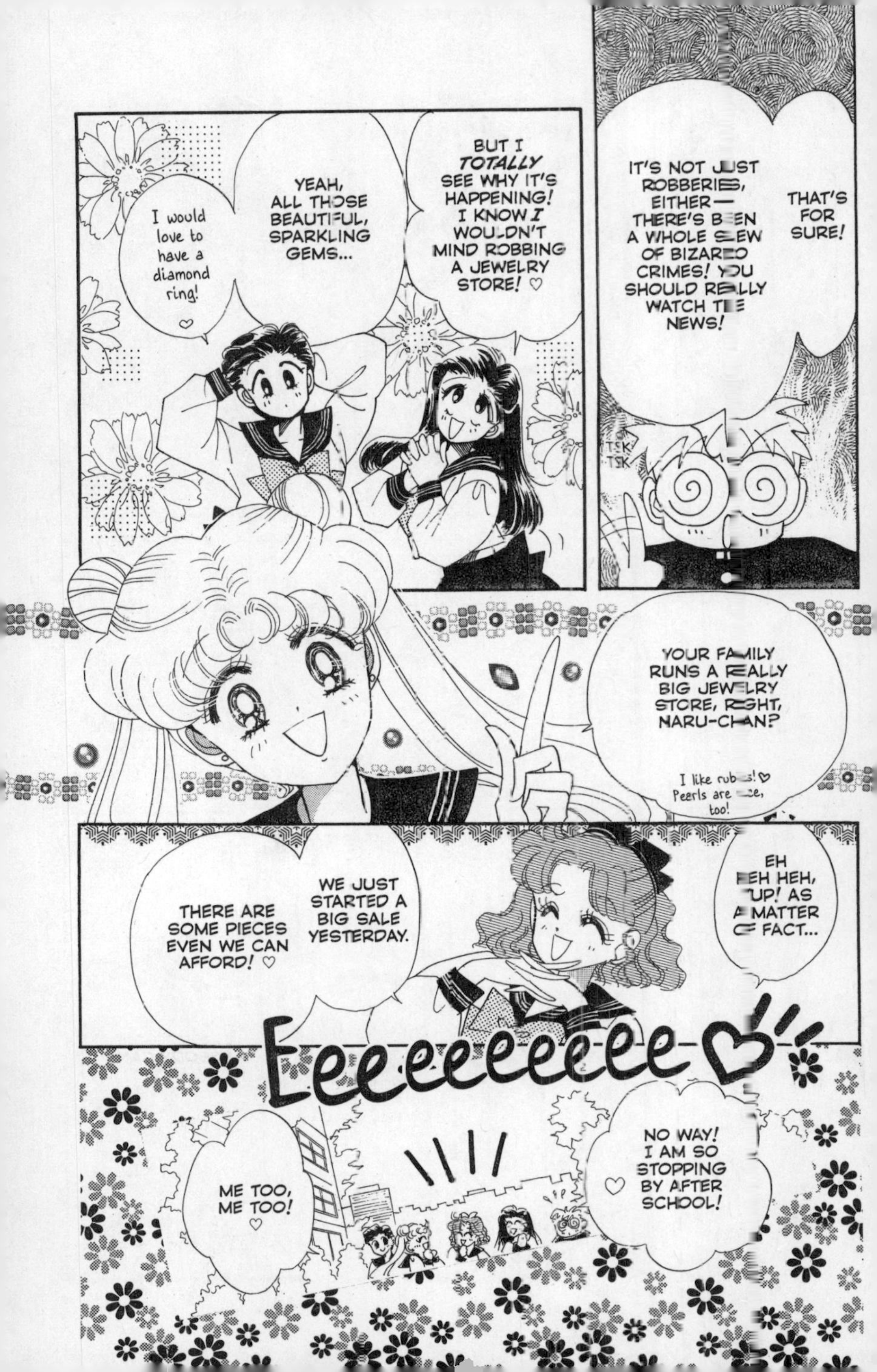
IT'S NOT JUST ROBBERIES, EITHER— THERE'S BEEN A WHOLE SLEW OF BIZARRE CRIMES! YOU SHOULD REALLY WATCH THE NEWS!
THAT'S FOR SURE!
TSK TSK
BUT I *TOTALLY* SEE WHY IT'S HAPPENING! I KNOW *I* WOULDN'T MIND ROBBING A JEWELRY STORE! ♡
YEAH, ALL THOSE BEAUTIFUL, SPARKLING GEMS...
I would love to have a diamond ring! ♡
YOUR FAMILY RUNS A REALLY BIG JEWELRY STORE, RIGHT, NARU-CHAN?
I like rubies! ♡ Pearls are nice, too!
EH HEH HEH, YUP! AS A MATTER OF FACT...
WE JUST STARTED A BIG SALE YESTERDAY.
THERE ARE SOME PIECES EVEN WE CAN AFFORD! ♡
Eeeeeeeee ♡
NO WAY! I AM SO STOPPING BY AFTER SCHOOL! ♡
ME TOO, ME TOO! ♡

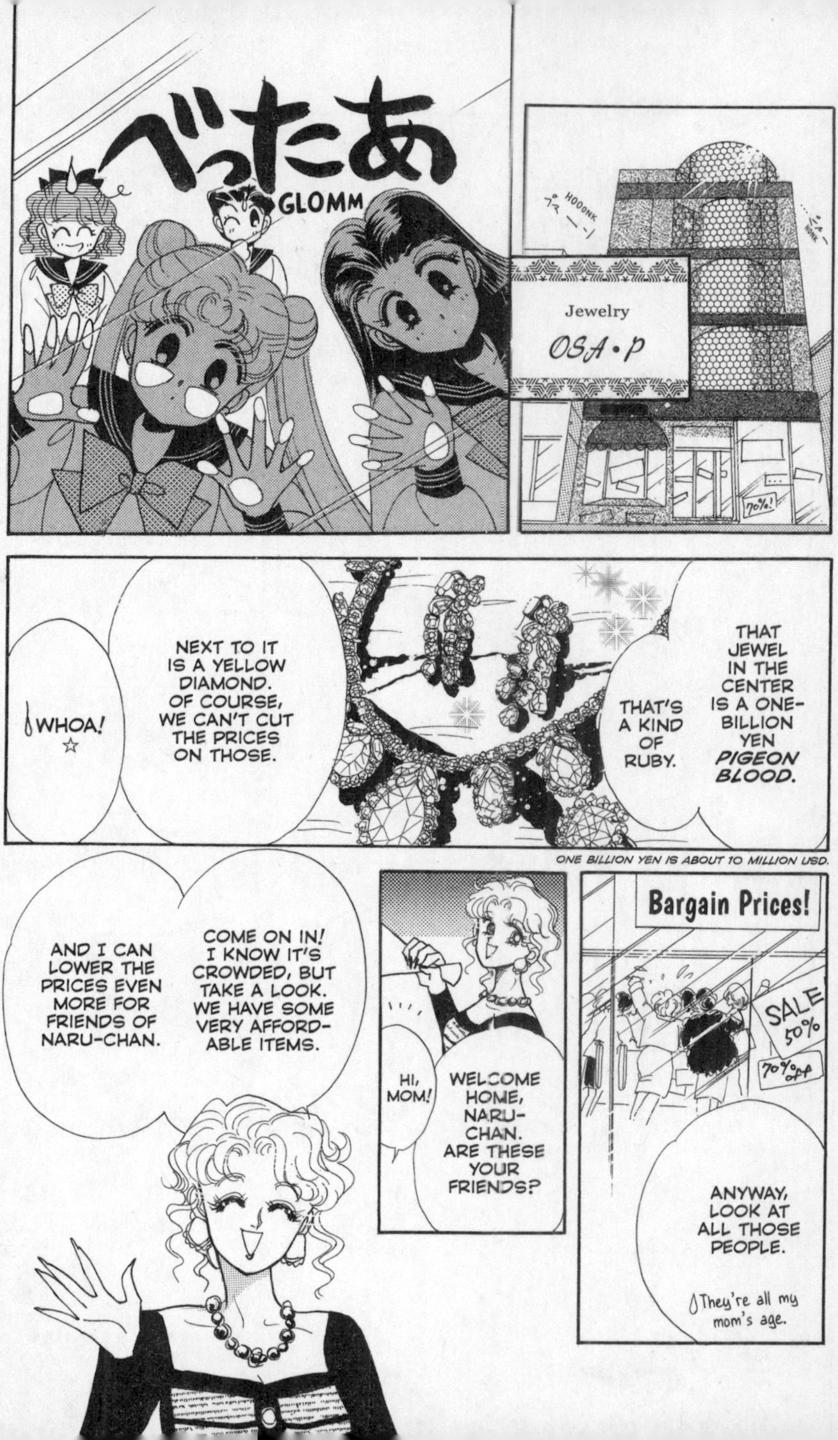
HOOONK
HONK
Jewelry
OSA • P
70%!
べったあ
GLOMM
THAT JEWEL IN THE CENTER IS A ONE-BILLION YEN *PIGEON BLOOD*.
THAT'S A KIND OF RUBY.
NEXT TO IT IS A YELLOW DIAMOND. OF COURSE, WE CAN'T CUT THE PRICES ON THOSE.
WHOA! ☆
Bargain Prices!
SALE 50%
70% off
ANYWAY, LOOK AT ALL THOSE PEOPLE.
They're all my mom's age.
WELCOME HOME, NARU-CHAN. ARE THESE YOUR FRIENDS?
HI, MOM!
COME ON IN! I KNOW IT'S CROWDED, BUT TAKE A LOOK. WE HAVE SOME VERY AFFORD-ABLE ITEMS.
AND I CAN LOWER THE PRICES EVEN MORE FOR FRIENDS OF NARU-CHAN.

ONE BILLION YEN IS ABOUT 10 MILLION USD.

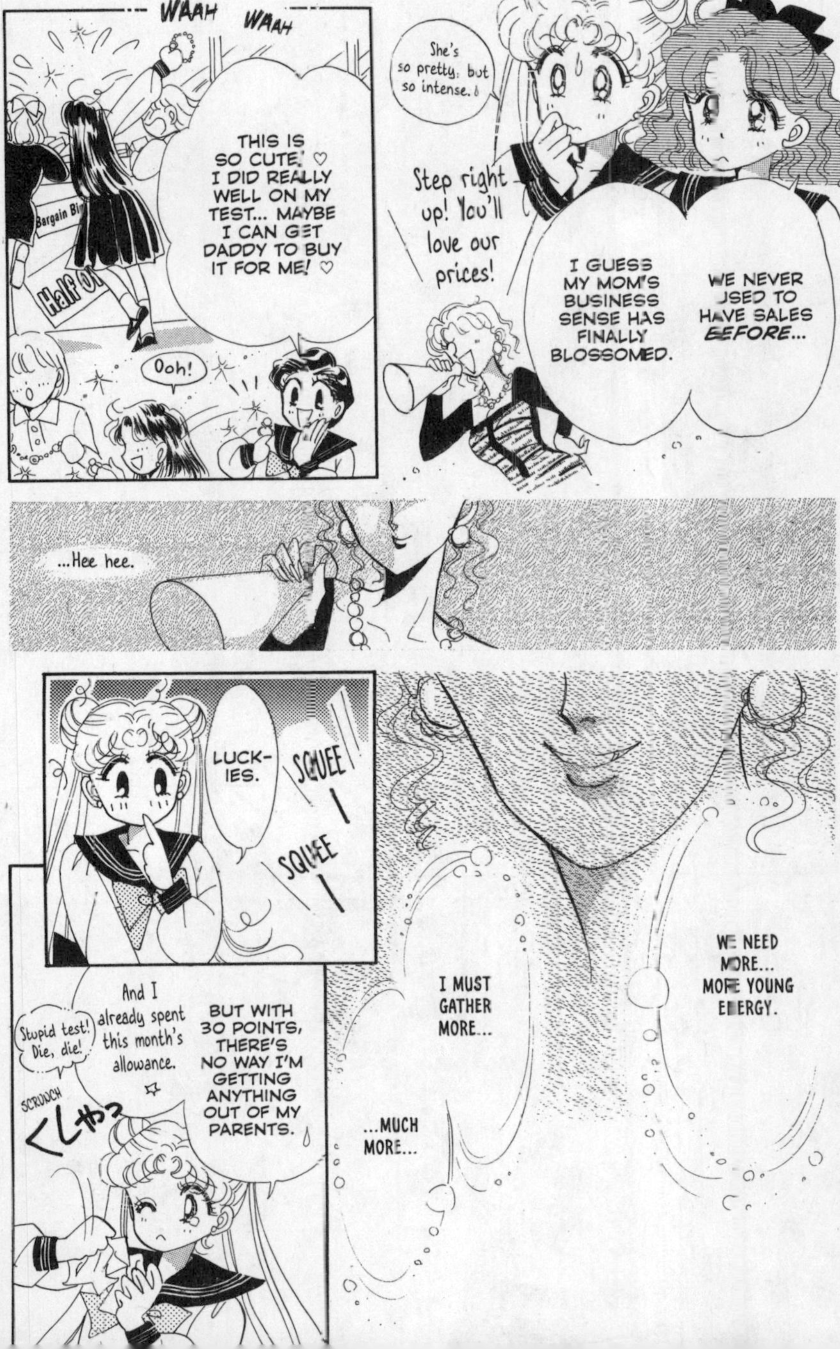
WE NEVER USED TO HAVE SALES BEFORE...
I GUESS MY MOM'S BUSINESS SENSE HAS FINALLY BLOSSOMED.
She's so pretty, but so intense.
Step right up! You'll love our prices!
WAAH WAAH
THIS IS SO CUTE! ♡ I DID REALLY WELL ON MY TEST... MAYBE I CAN GET DADDY TO BUY IT FOR ME! ♡
Bargain Bin
Ooh!
...Hee hee.
WE NEED MORE... MORE YOUNG ENERGY.
I MUST GATHER MORE...
...MUCH MORE...
LUCK-IES.
SQUEE
SQUEE
BUT WITH 30 POINTS, THERE'S NO WAY I'M GETTING ANYTHING OUT OF MY PARENTS.
And I already spent this month's allowance.
Stupid test! Die, die!
SCRUNCH
くしゃっ

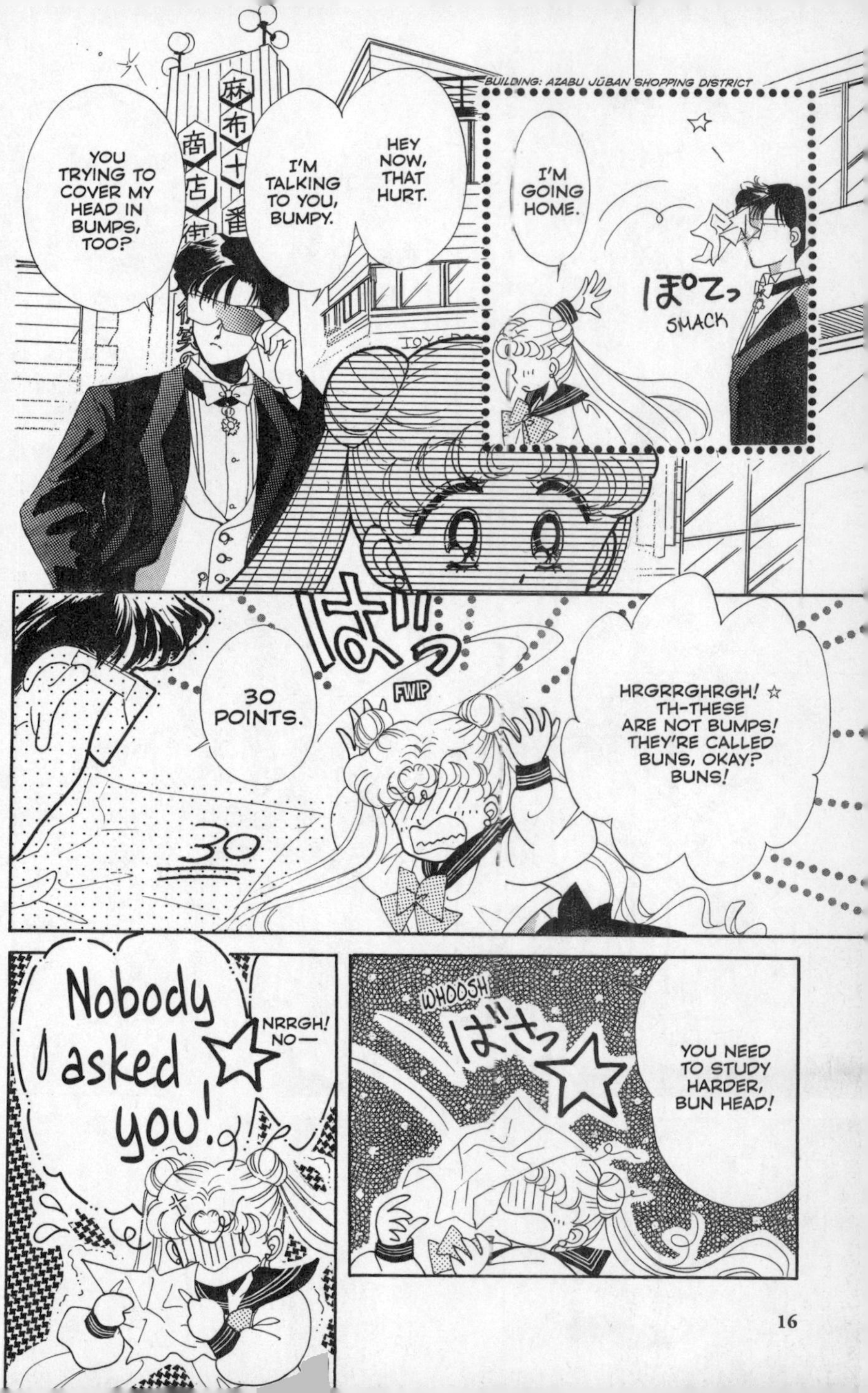
BUILDING: AZABU JŪBAN SHOPPING DISTRICT
I'M GOING HOME.
ぽてっ
SMACK
HEY NOW, THAT HURT.
I'M TALKING TO YOU, BUMPY.
麻布十番商店街
YOU TRYING TO COVER MY HEAD IN BUMPS, TOO?
HRGRRGHRGH! ☆ TH-THESE ARE NOT BUMPS! THEY'RE CALLED BUNS, OKAY? BUNS!
ばっ
FWIP
30 POINTS.
30
YOU NEED TO STUDY HARDER, BUN HEAD!
ばさっ
WHOOSH
NRRGH! NO—
Nobody asked you!

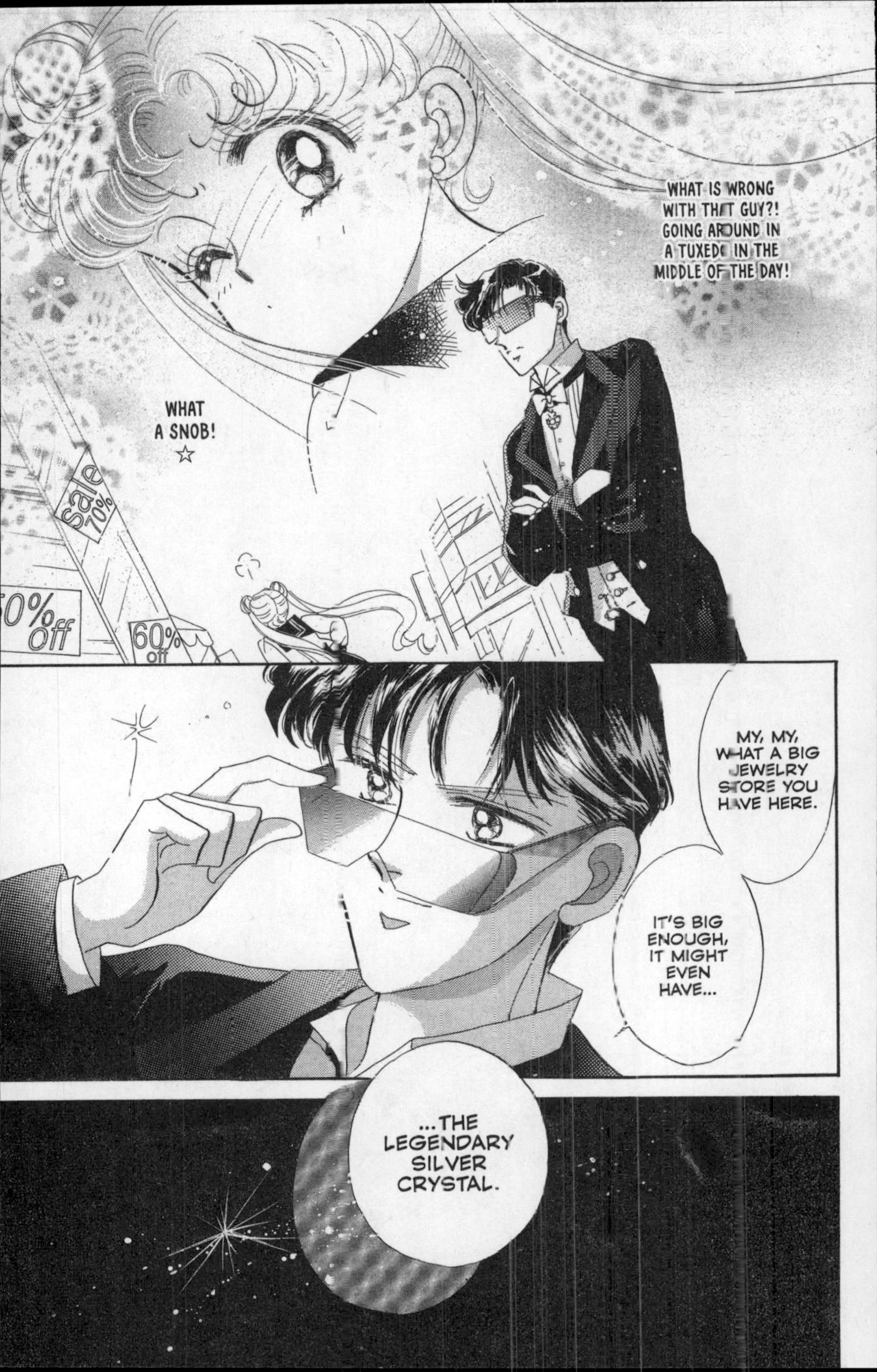
WHAT IS WRONG WITH THAT GUY?! GOING AROUND IN A TUXEDO IN THE MIDDLE OF THE DAY!
WHAT A SNOB! ☆
Sale 70%
60% off
MY, MY, WHAT A BIG JEWELRY STORE YOU HAVE HERE.
IT'S BIG ENOUGH, IT MIGHT EVEN HAVE...
...THE LEGENDARY SILVER CRYSTAL.

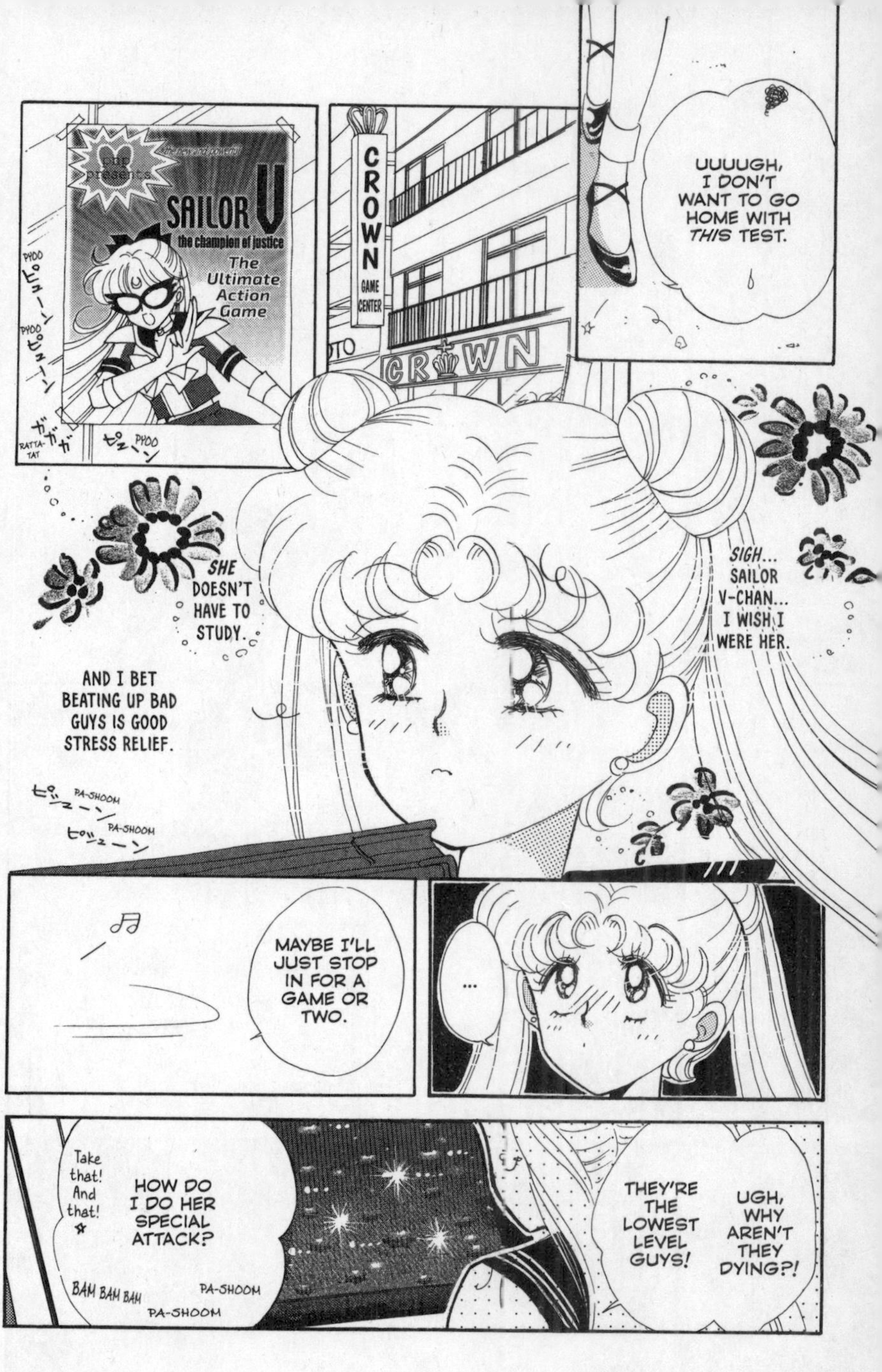

UUUUGH, I DON'T WANT TO GO HOME WITH *THIS* TEST.
CROWN GAME CENTER
CROWN
SAILOR V
the champion of justice
The Ultimate Action Game
PYOO
PYOO
RATTA-TAT
PYOO
SIGH... SAILOR V-CHAN... I WISH I WERE HER.
SHE DOESN'T HAVE TO STUDY.
AND I BET BEATING UP BAD GUYS IS GOOD STRESS RELIEF.
PA-SHOOM
PA-SHOOM
...
MAYBE I'LL JUST STOP IN FOR A GAME OR TWO.
UGH, WHY AREN'T THEY DYING?!
THEY'RE THE LOWEST LEVEL GUYS!
HOW DO I DO HER SPECIAL ATTACK?
Take that! And that!
BAM BAM BAM
PA-SHOOM
PA-SHOOM

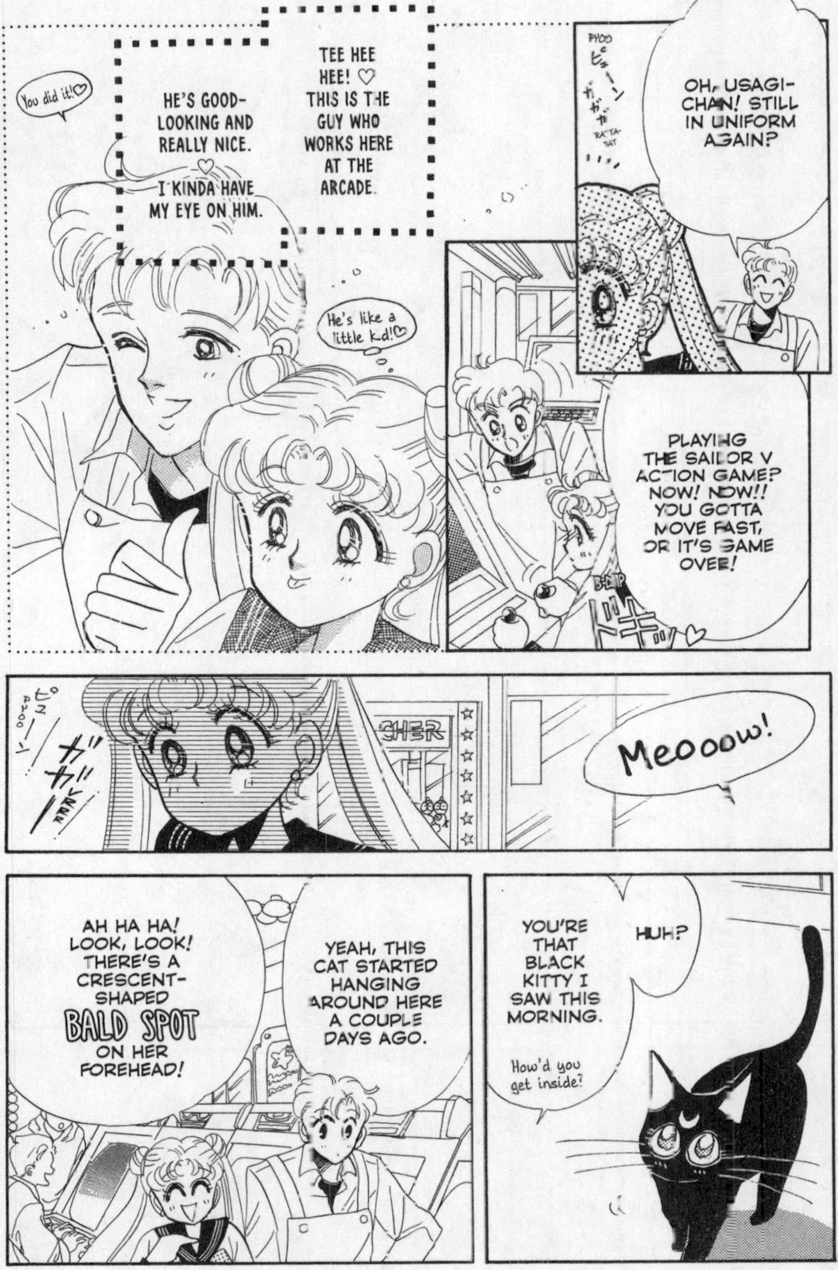
PYOO
OH, USAGI-CHAN! STILL IN UNIFORM AGAIN?
RA-TA-TAT
PLAYING THE SAILOR V ACTION GAME? NOW! NOW!! YOU GOTTA MOVE FAST, OR IT'S GAME OVER!
BEEP
TEE HEE HEE! ♡ THIS IS THE GUY WHO WORKS HERE AT THE ARCADE.
HE'S GOOD-LOOKING AND REALLY NICE. ♡ I KINDA HAVE MY EYE ON HIM.
He's like a little kid!♡
You did it!♡
Meooow!
HUH?
YOU'RE THAT BLACK KITTY I SAW THIS MORNING.
How'd you get inside?
YEAH, THIS CAT STARTED HANGING AROUND HERE A COUPLE DAYS AGO.
AH HA HA! LOOK, LOOK! THERE'S A CRESCENT-SHAPED BALD SPOT ON HER FOREHEAD!

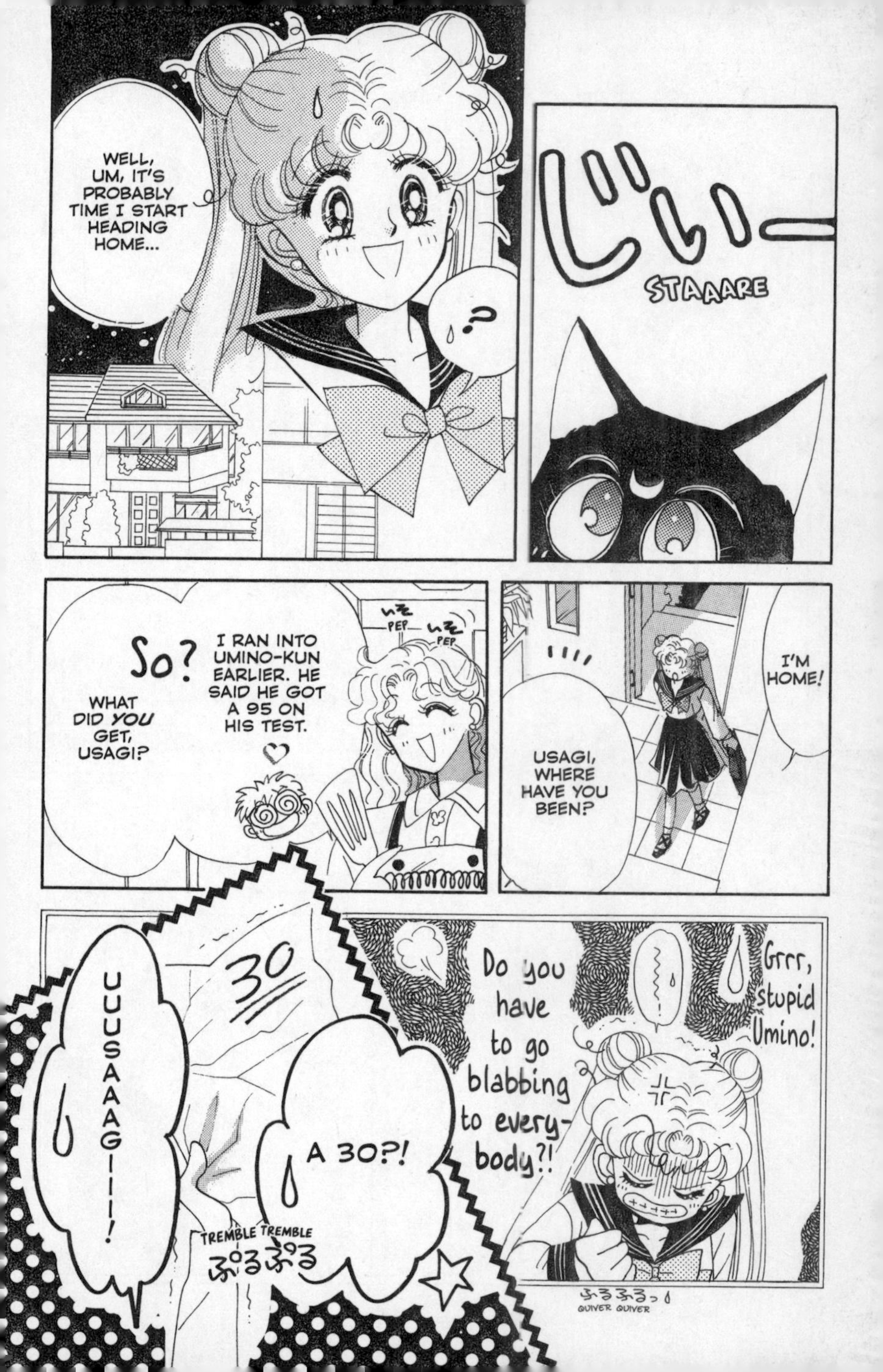
じぃー
STAAARE
?
WELL, UM, IT'S PROBABLY TIME I START HEADING HOME...
I'M HOME!
USAGI, WHERE HAVE YOU BEEN?
PEP PEP
I RAN INTO UMINO-KUN EARLIER. HE SAID HE GOT A 95 ON HIS TEST.
So?
WHAT DID *YOU* GET, USAGI?
Grrr, stupid Umino!
Do you have to go blabbing to everybody?!
ふるふるっ
QUIVER QUIVER
30
A 30?!
UUUSAAAAG...!
TREMBLE TREMBLE
ぷるぷる

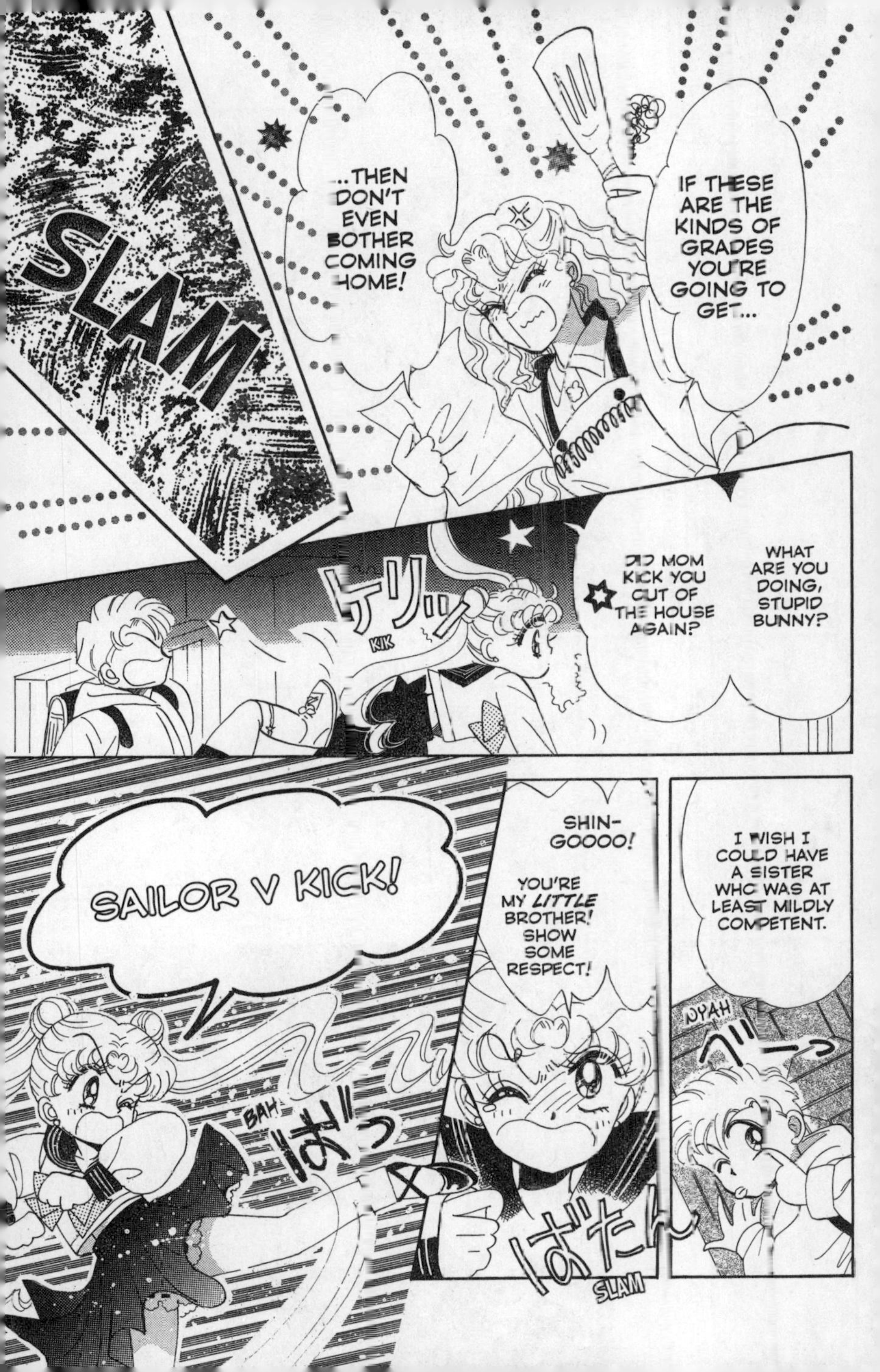
IF THESE ARE THE KINDS OF GRADES YOU'RE GOING TO GET...
...THEN DON'T EVEN BOTHER COMING HOME!
SLAM
WHAT ARE YOU DOING, STUPID BUNNY?
DID MOM KICK YOU OUT OF THE HOUSE AGAIN?
ケリッ
KIK
I WISH I COULD HAVE A SISTER WHO WAS AT LEAST MILDLY COMPETENT.
べーっ
NYAH
SHIN-GOOOO!
YOU'RE MY *LITTLE* BROTHER! SHOW SOME RESPECT!
SAILOR V KICK!
ばっ
BAH
ばたん
SLAM

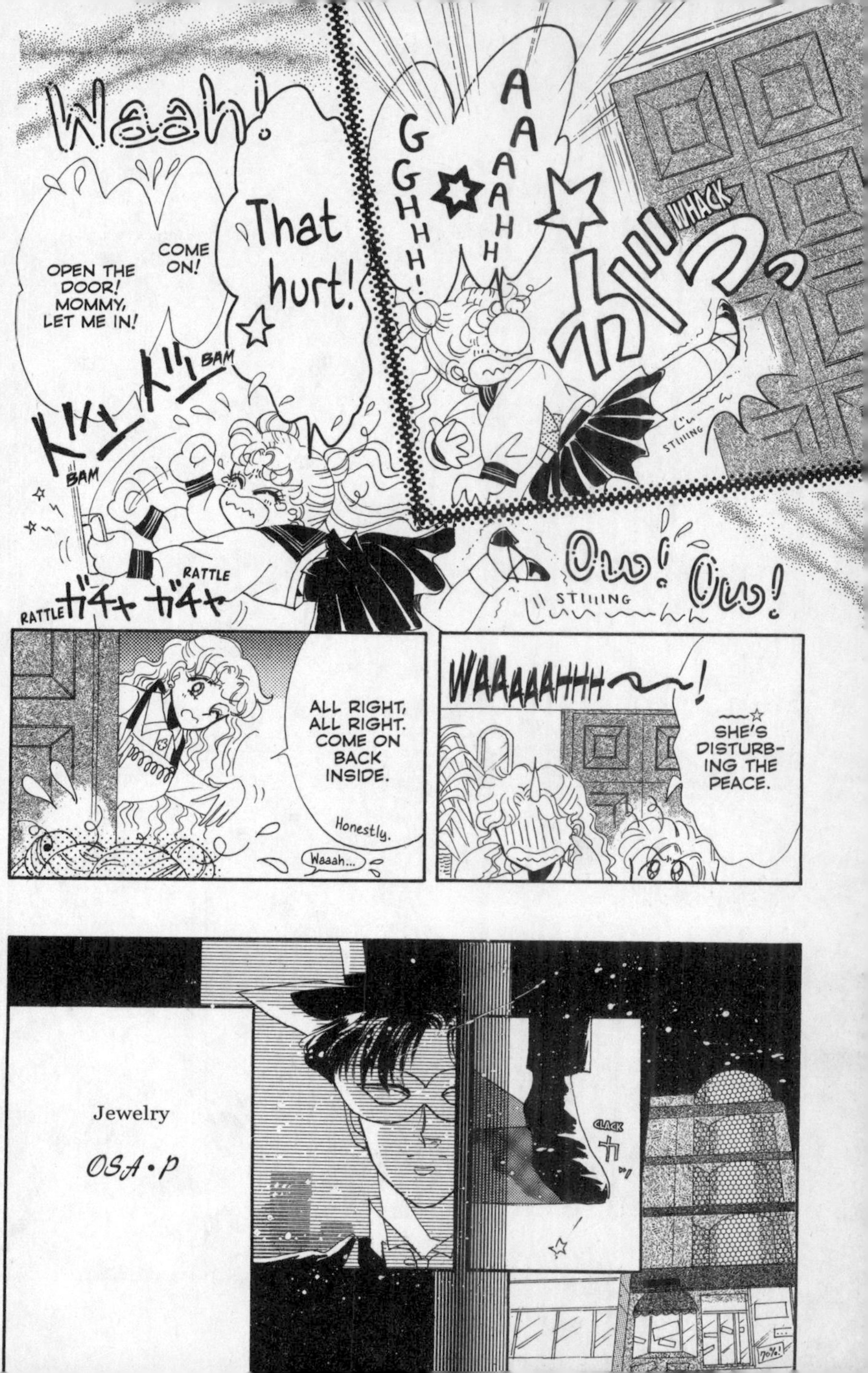

GGHHH! AAAAAAH
カッ
WHACK
じーん
STIIIING
Waaah!
That hurt!
COME ON!
OPEN THE DOOR! MOMMY, LET ME IN!
ドン ドン
BAM
BAM
ガチャ ガチャ
RATTLE
RATTLE
Ow! Ow!
STIIIING
WAAAAAHHH~~!
~~☆ SHE'S DISTURBING THE PEACE.
ALL RIGHT, ALL RIGHT. COME ON BACK INSIDE.
Honestly.
Waaah...
Jewelry
OSA•P
CLACK
70%!

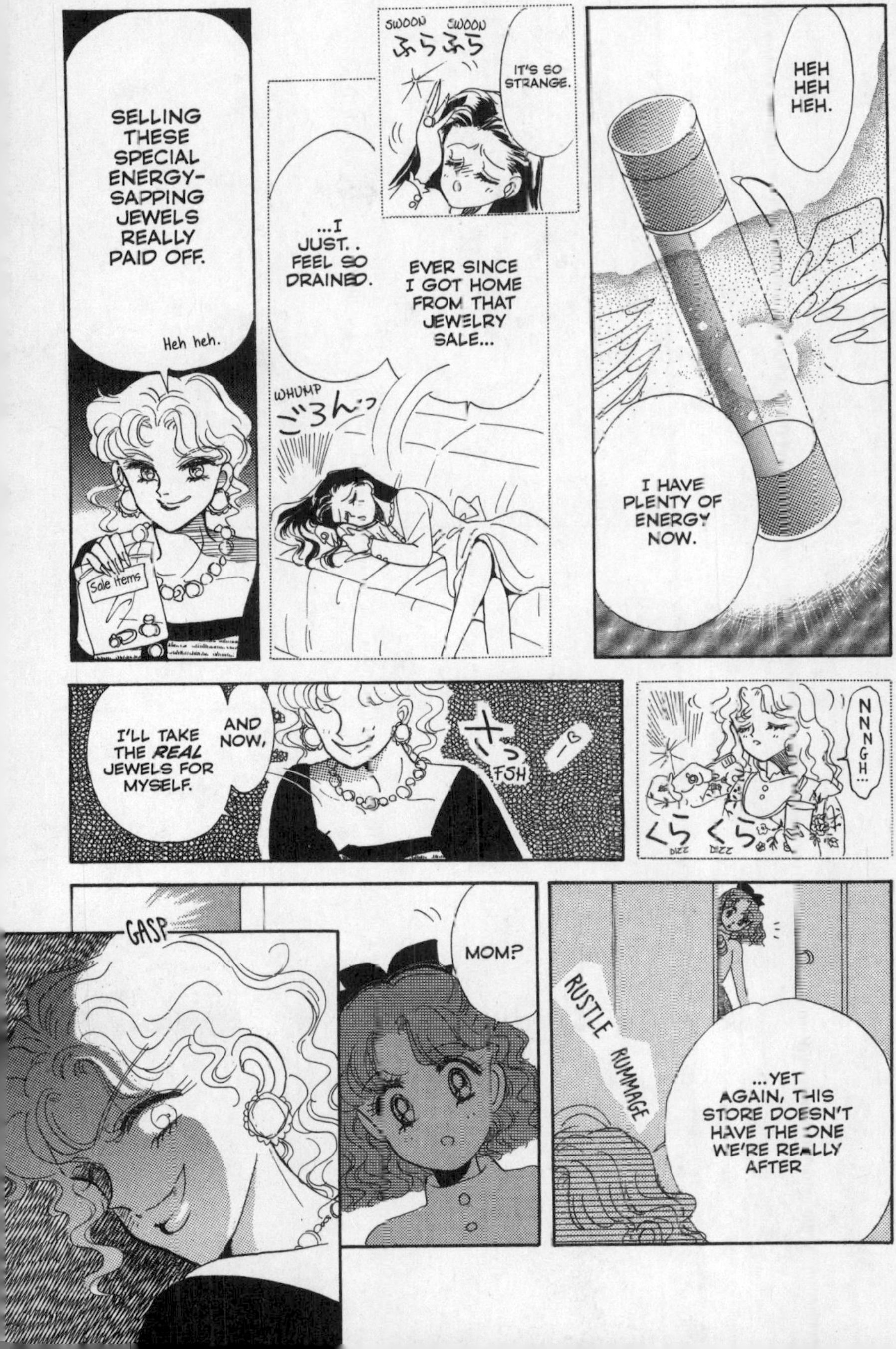
HEH HEH HEH.
I HAVE PLENTY OF ENERGY NOW.
SWOON SWOON
ふらふら
IT'S SO STRANGE.
EVER SINCE I GOT HOME FROM THAT JEWELRY SALE...
...I JUST. . FEEL SO DRAINED.
WHUMP
ごろんっ
SELLING THESE SPECIAL ENERGY-SAPPING JEWELS REALLY PAID OFF.
Heh heh.
Sale Items
NNNGH...
くら くら
DIZZ DIZZ
AND NOW,
I'LL TAKE THE *REAL* JEWELS FOR MYSELF.
さっ
FSH
RUSTLE
RUMMAGE
...YET AGAIN, THIS STORE DOESN'T HAVE THE ONE WE'RE REALLY AFTER
MOM?
GASP

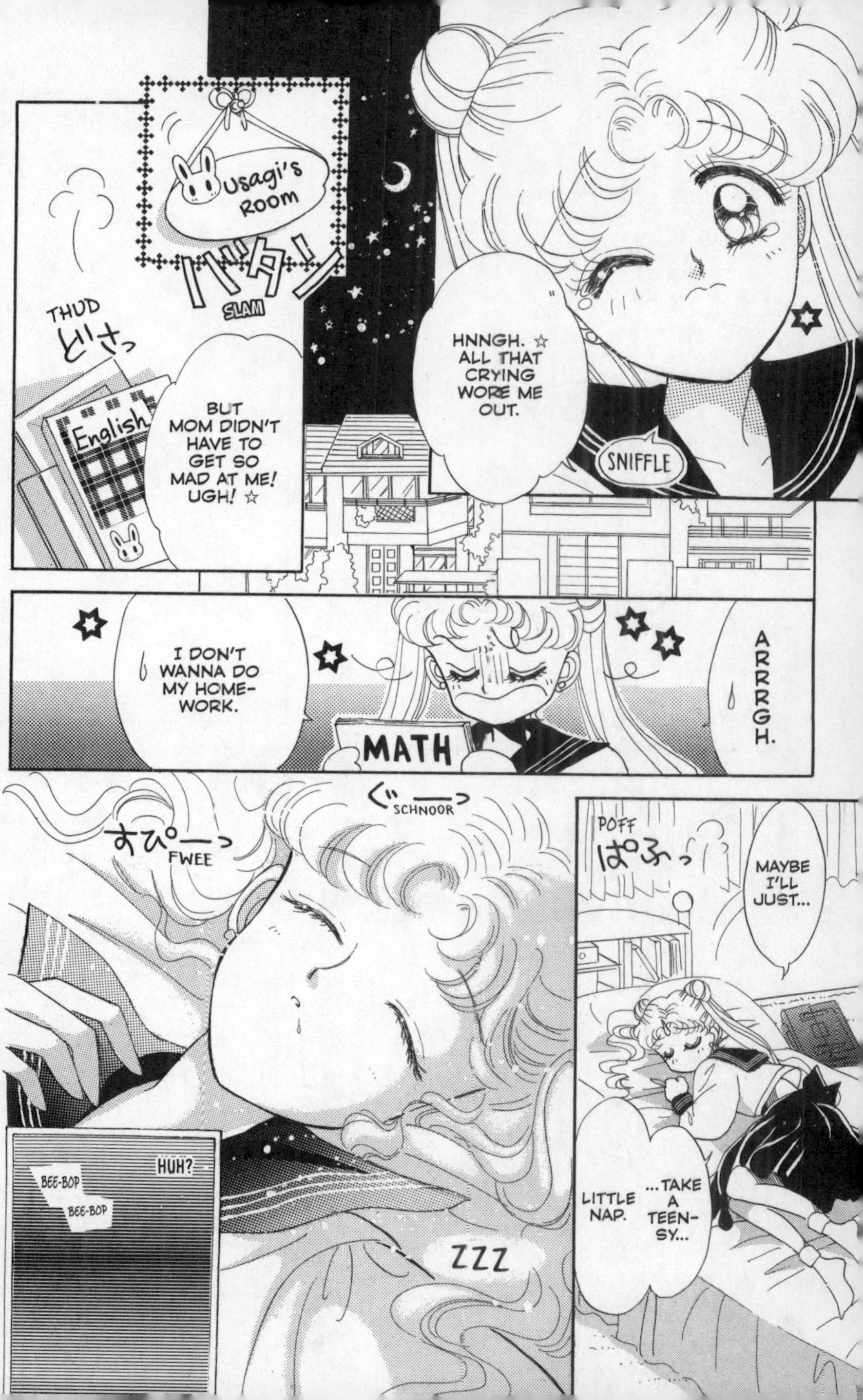
HNNGH. ☆ ALL THAT CRYING WORE ME OUT.
SNIFFLE
Usagi's Room
バタン
SLAM
THUD
どさっ
English
BUT MOM DIDN'T HAVE TO GET SO MAD AT ME! UGH! ☆
ARRRGH.
I DON'T WANNA DO MY HOME-WORK.
MATH
POFF
ぱふっ
MAYBE I'LL JUST...
...TAKE A TEENSY...
LITTLE NAP.
ぐーっ
SCHNOOR
すぴーっ
FWEE
HUH?
BEE-BOP
BEE-BOP
ZZZ

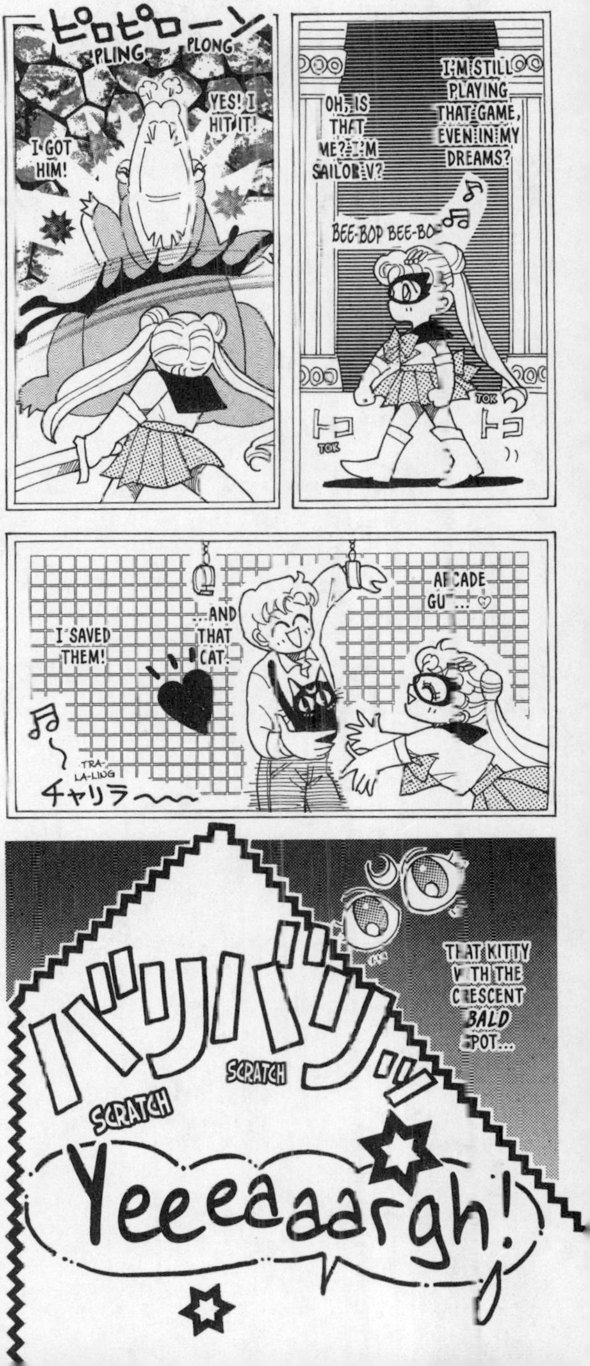
I'M STILL PLAYING THAT GAME, EVEN IN MY DREAMS?
OH, IS THAT ME? I'M SAILOR V?
BEE-BOP BEE-BO
トコ
TOK
トコ
TOK
ピロピローン
PLING PLONG
YES! I HIT IT!
I GOT HIM!
ARCADE GU… ♡
…AND THAT CAT.
I SAVED THEM!
TRA-LA-LING
チャリラ〜〜
THAT KITTY WITH THE CRESCENT BALD SPOT…
バリバリッ
SCRATCH
SCRATCH
Yeeeaaargh!

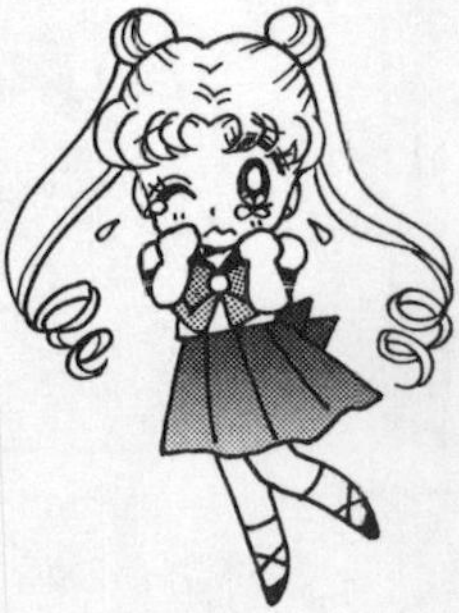

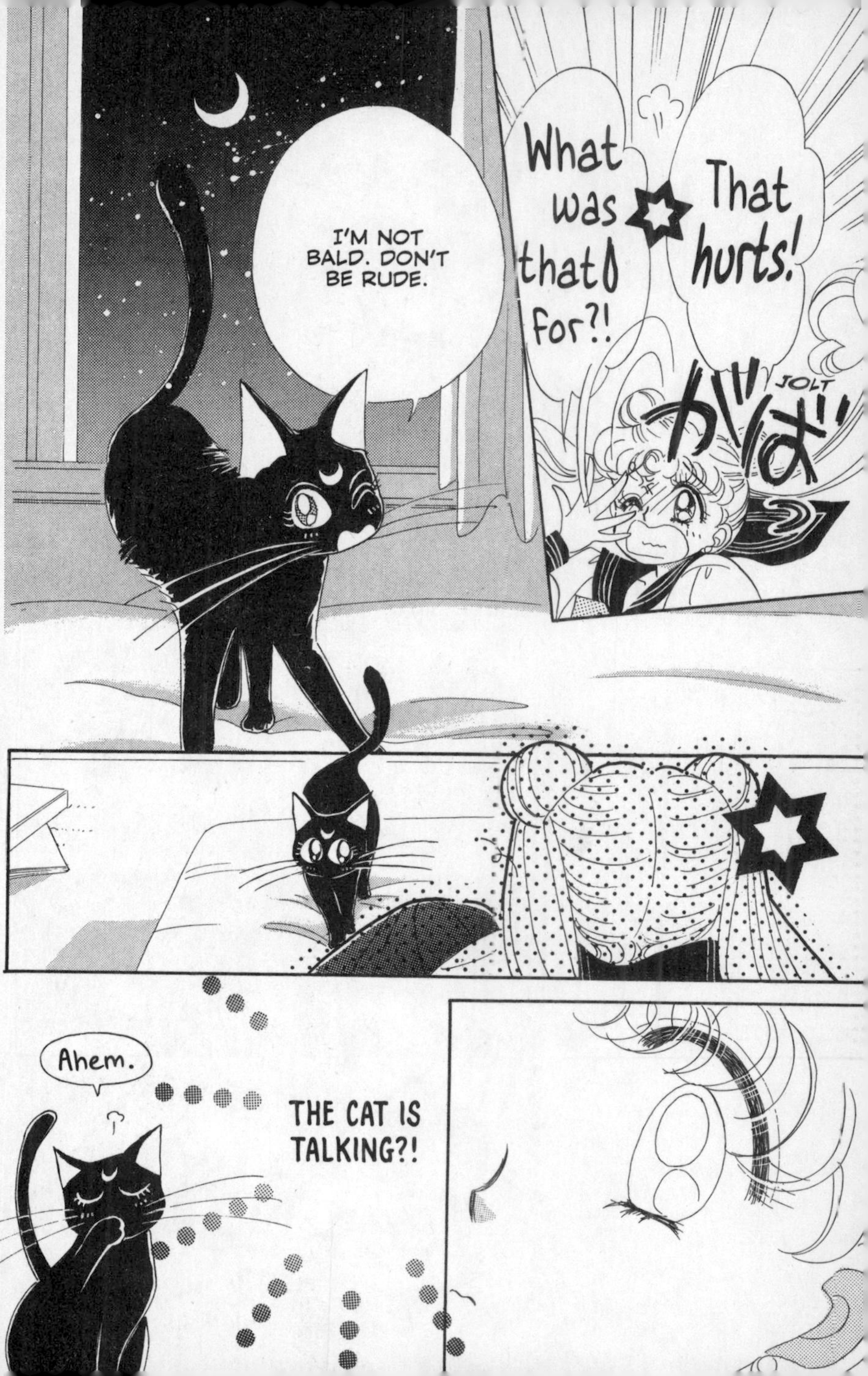

That hurts!
What was that for?!
JOLT
I'M NOT BALD. DON'T BE RUDE.
Ahem.
THE CAT IS TALKING?!

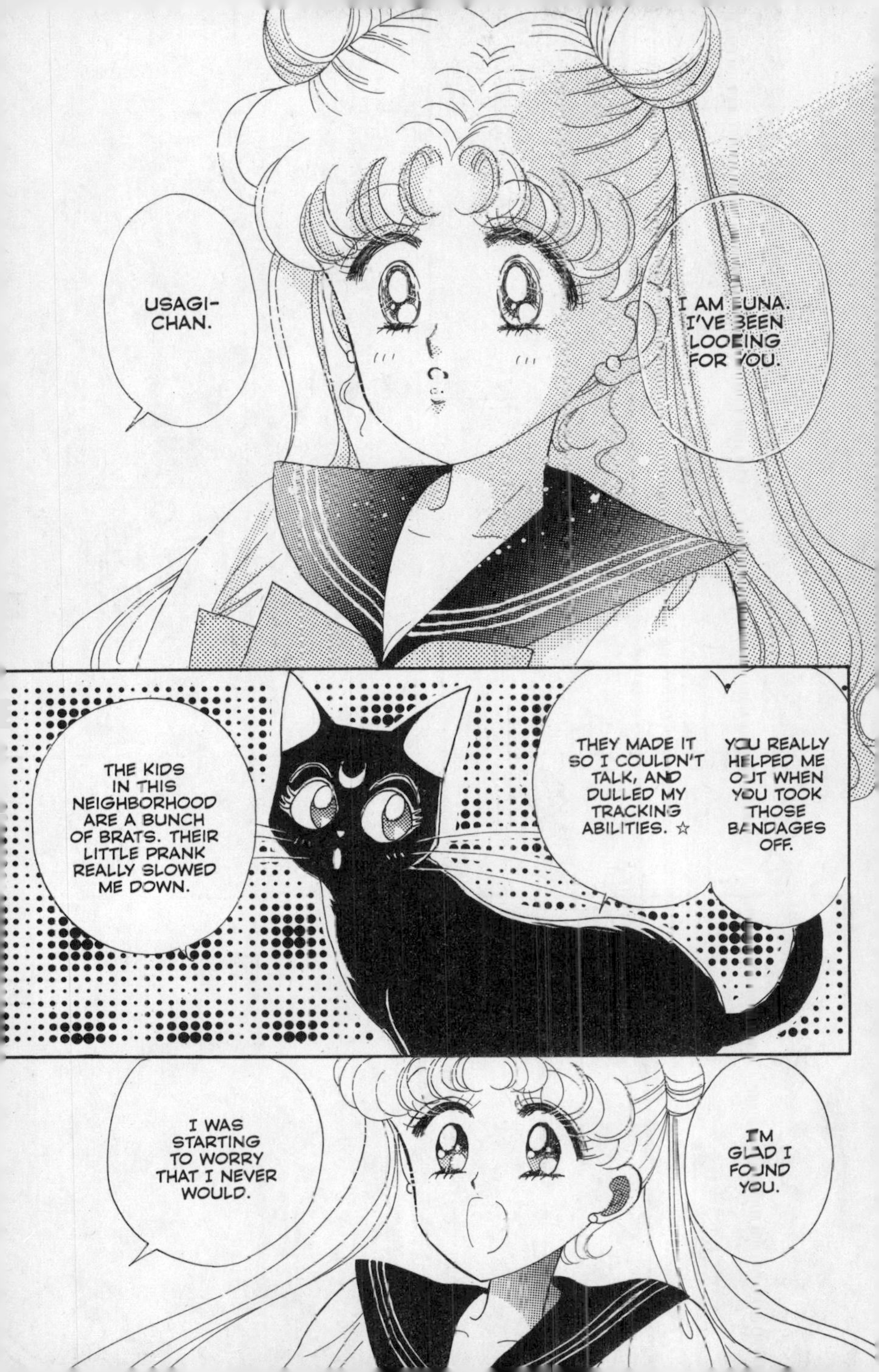
I AM LUNA. I'VE BEEN LOOKING FOR YOU.
USAGI-CHAN.
YOU REALLY HELPED ME OUT WHEN YOU TOOK THOSE BANDAGES OFF.
THEY MADE IT SO I COULDN'T TALK, AND DULLED MY TRACKING ABILITIES. ☆
THE KIDS IN THIS NEIGHBORHOOD ARE A BUNCH OF BRATS. THEIR LITTLE PRANK REALLY SLOWED ME DOWN.
I'M GLAD I FOUND YOU.
I WAS STARTING TO WORRY THAT I NEVER WOULD.

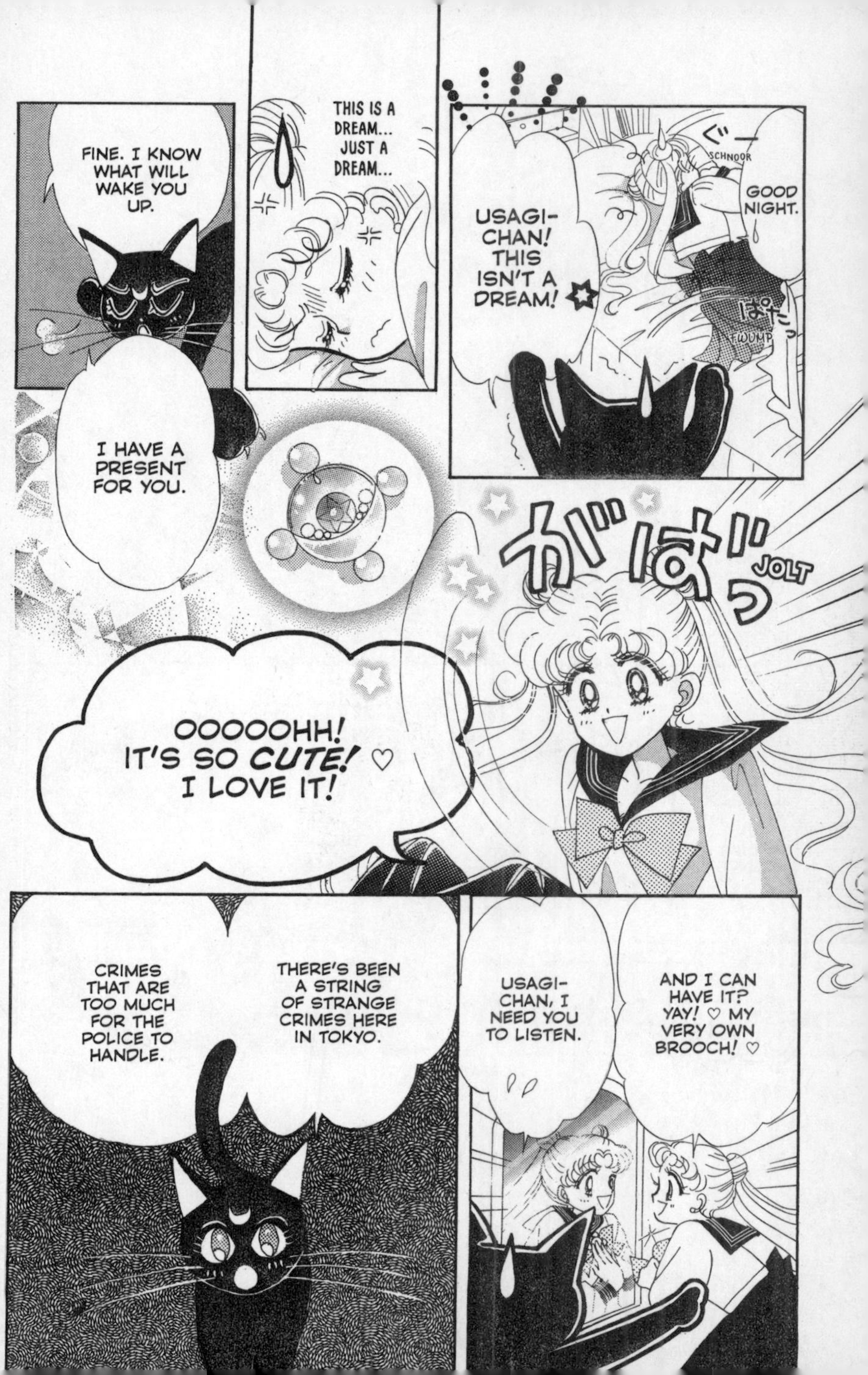
ぐー SCHNOOR
GOOD NIGHT.
USAGI-CHAN! THIS ISN'T A DREAM!
ぱたっ FWUMP
THIS IS A DREAM... JUST A DREAM...
FINE. I KNOW WHAT WILL WAKE YOU UP.
I HAVE A PRESENT FOR YOU.
がばっ JOLT
OOOOOHH! IT'S SO *CUTE!* ♡ I LOVE IT!
AND I CAN HAVE IT? YAY! ♡ MY VERY OWN BROOCH! ♡
USAGI-CHAN, I NEED YOU TO LISTEN.
THERE'S BEEN A STRING OF STRANGE CRIMES HERE IN TOKYO.
CRIMES THAT ARE TOO MUCH FOR THE POLICE TO HANDLE.

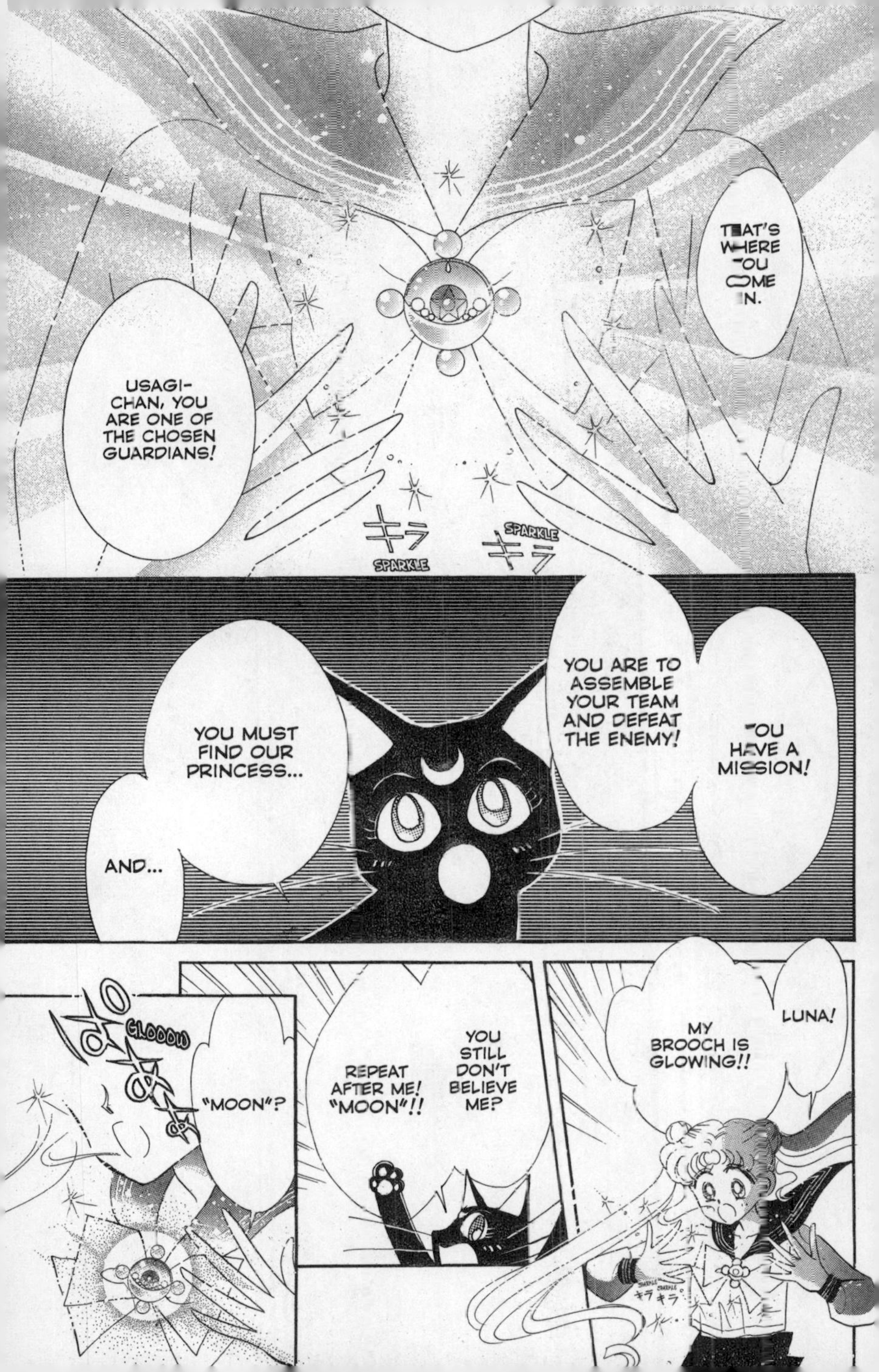
THAT'S WHERE YOU COME IN.
USAGI-CHAN, YOU ARE ONE OF THE CHOSEN GUARDIANS!
キラ SPARKLE
キラ SPARKLE
YOU HAVE A MISSION!
YOU ARE TO ASSEMBLE YOUR TEAM AND DEFEAT THE ENEMY!
YOU MUST FIND OUR PRINCESS...
AND...
LUNA!
MY BROOCH IS GLOWING!!
キラ キラ SPARKLE SPARKLE
YOU STILL DON'T BELIEVE ME?
REPEAT AFTER ME! "MOON"!!
GLOOOW
"MOON"?

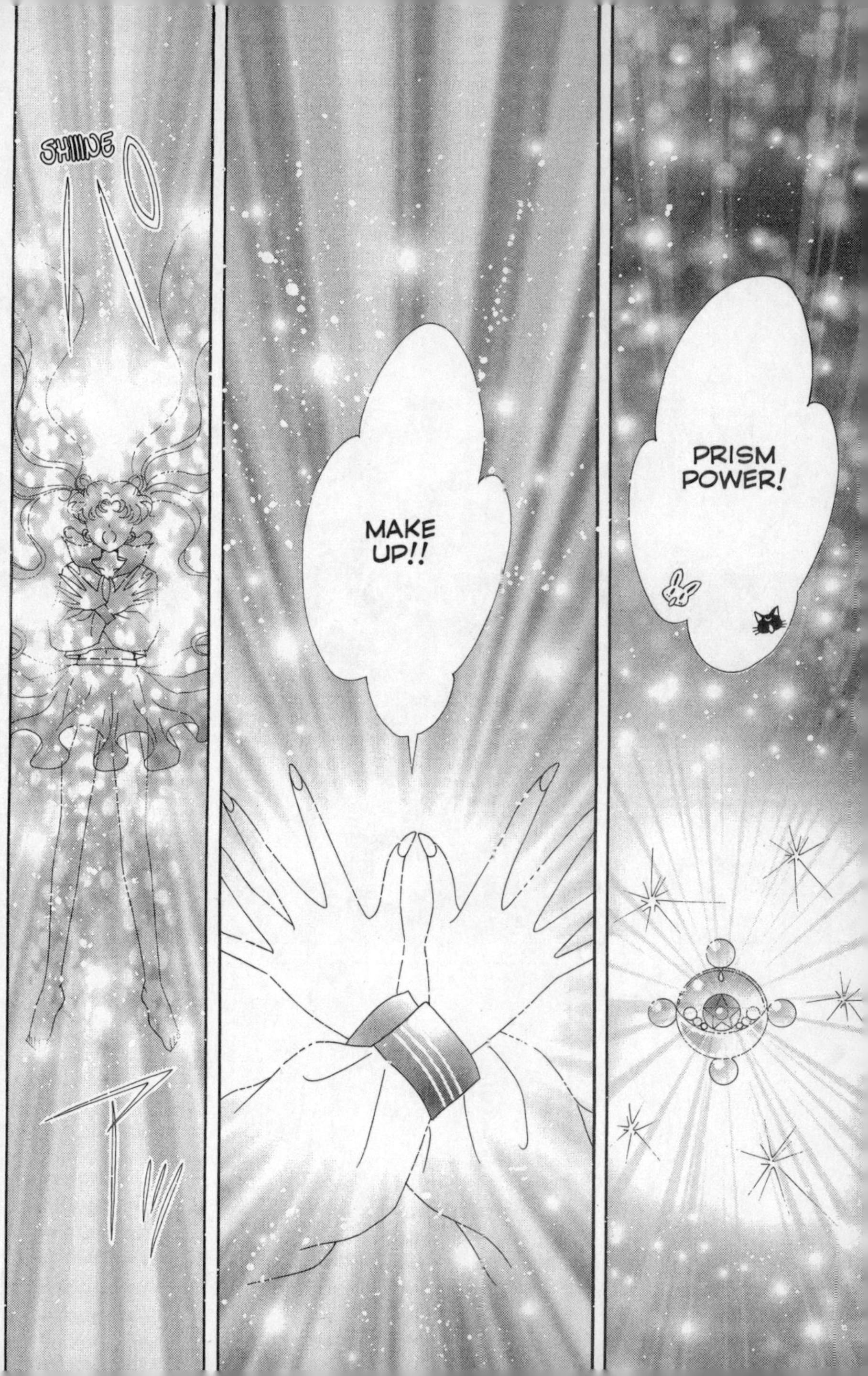
PRISM POWER!
MAKE UP!!
SHIIINE

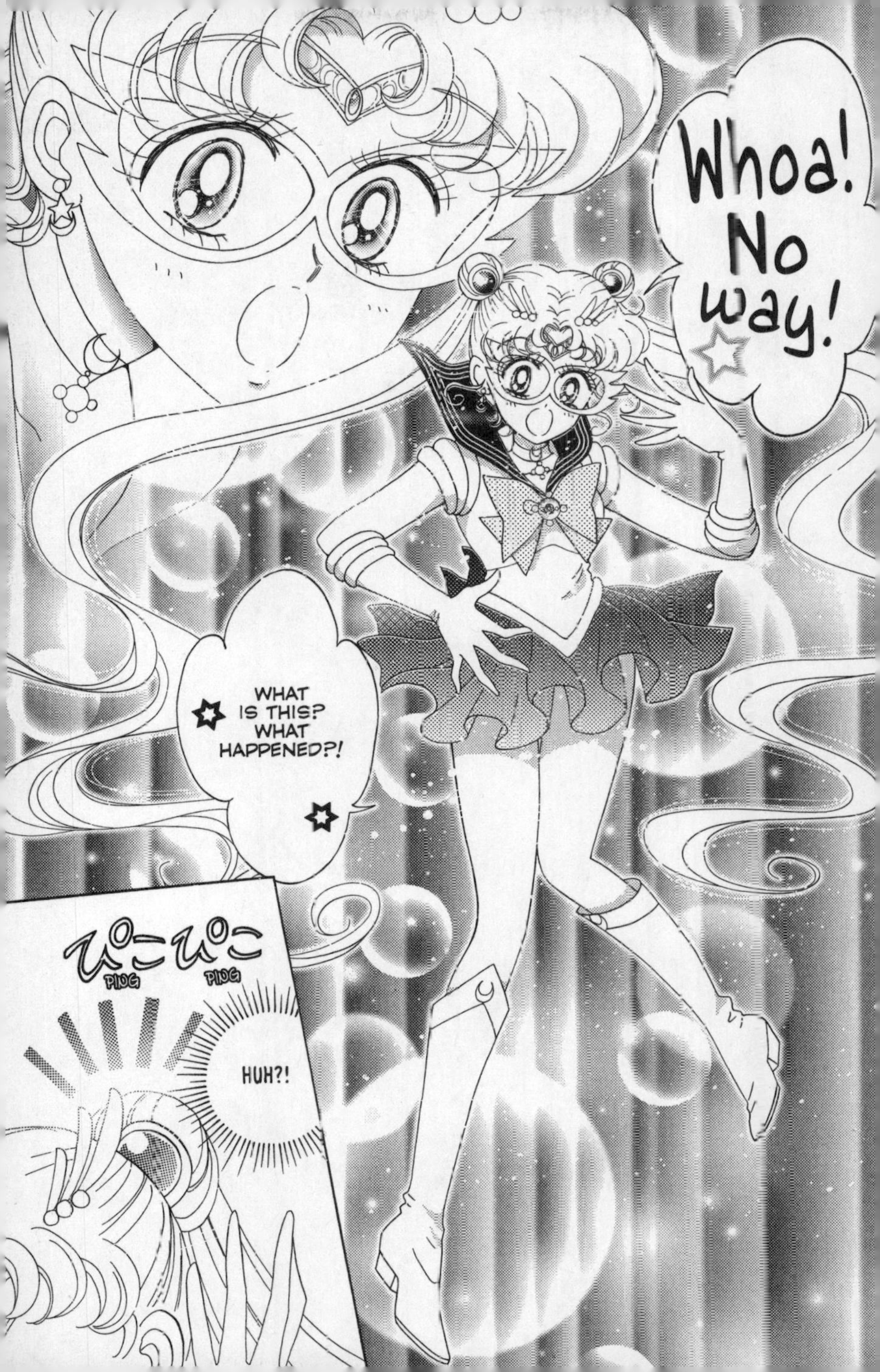
Whoa! No way!
WHAT IS THIS? WHAT HAPPENED?!
ぴこぴこ
PING PING
HUH?!

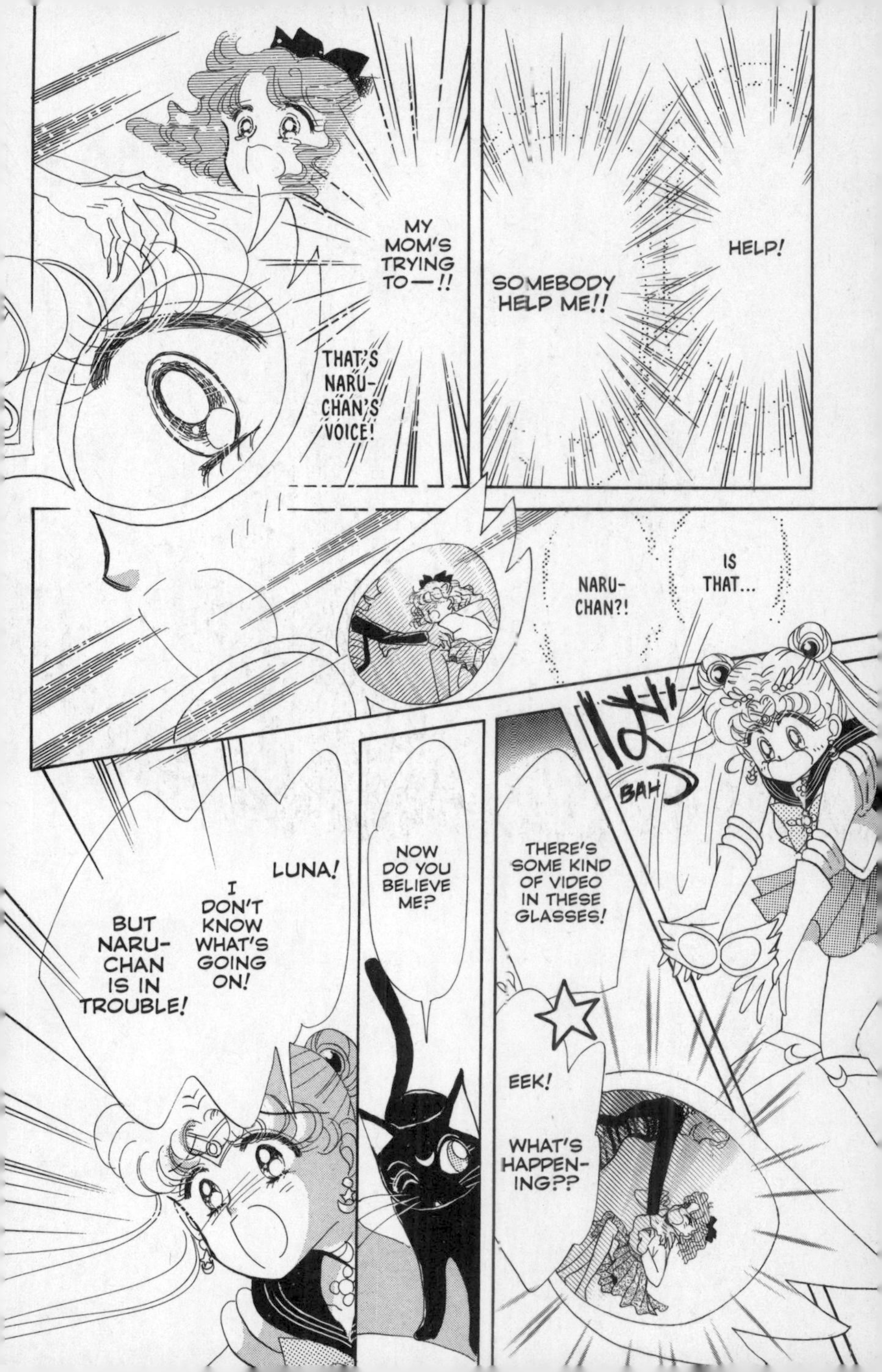
HELP!
SOMEBODY HELP ME!!
MY MOM'S TRYING TO—!!
THAT'S NARU-CHAN'S VOICE!
IS THAT...
NARU-CHAN?!
BAH
THERE'S SOME KIND OF VIDEO IN THESE GLASSES!
EEK!
WHAT'S HAPPENING??
NOW DO YOU BELIEVE ME?
LUNA!
I DON'T KNOW WHAT'S GOING ON!
BUT NARU-CHAN IS IN TROUBLE!

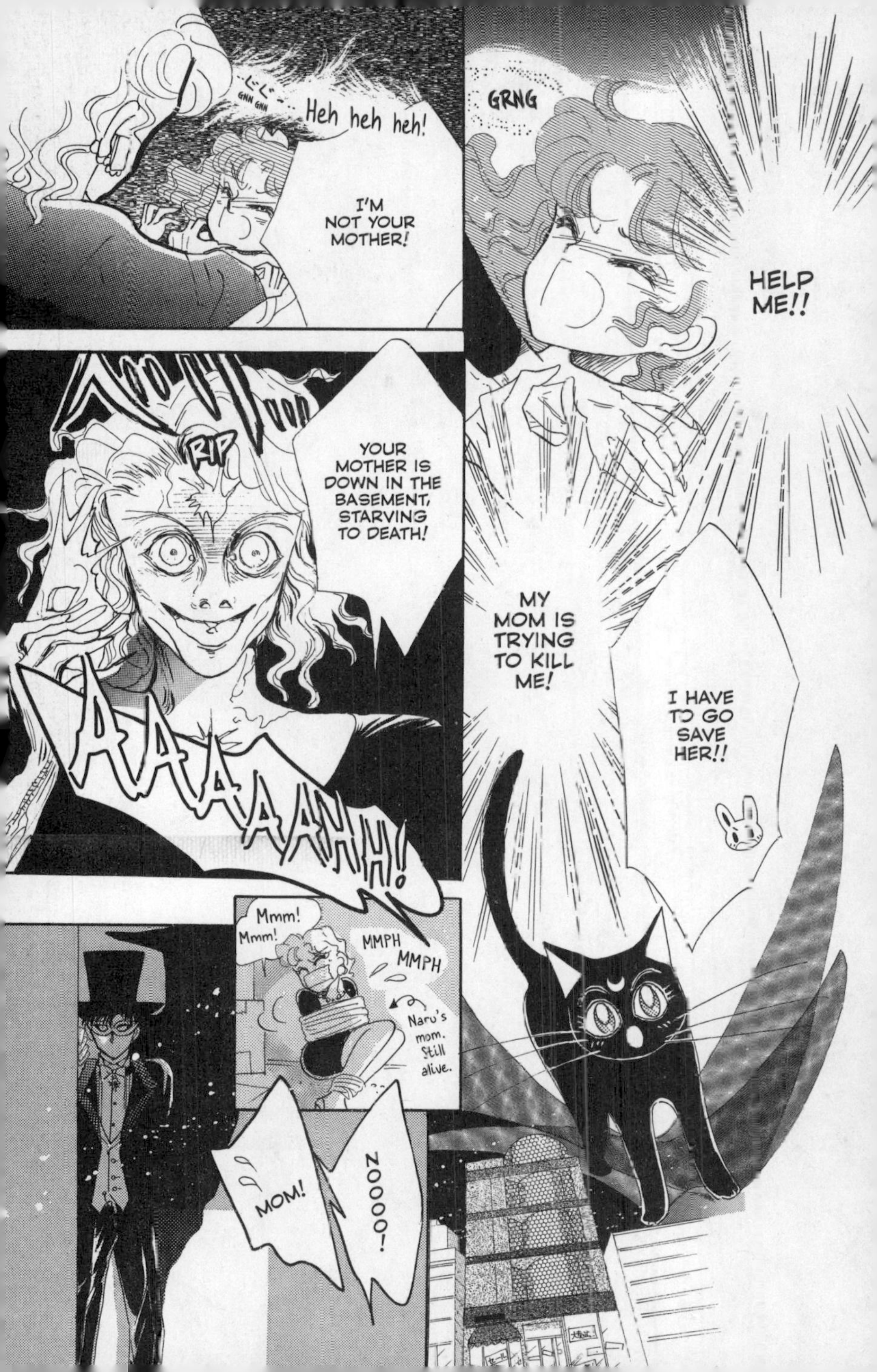
GRNG
HELP ME!!
MY MOM IS TRYING TO KILL ME!
I HAVE TO GO SAVE HER!!
GNN GNN
Heh heh heh!
I'M NOT YOUR MOTHER!
YOUR MOTHER IS DOWN IN THE BASEMENT, STARVING TO DEATH!
RIP
AAAAAHH!
Mmm! Mmm!
MMPH MMPH
Naru's mom. Still alive.
NOOOO!
MOM!

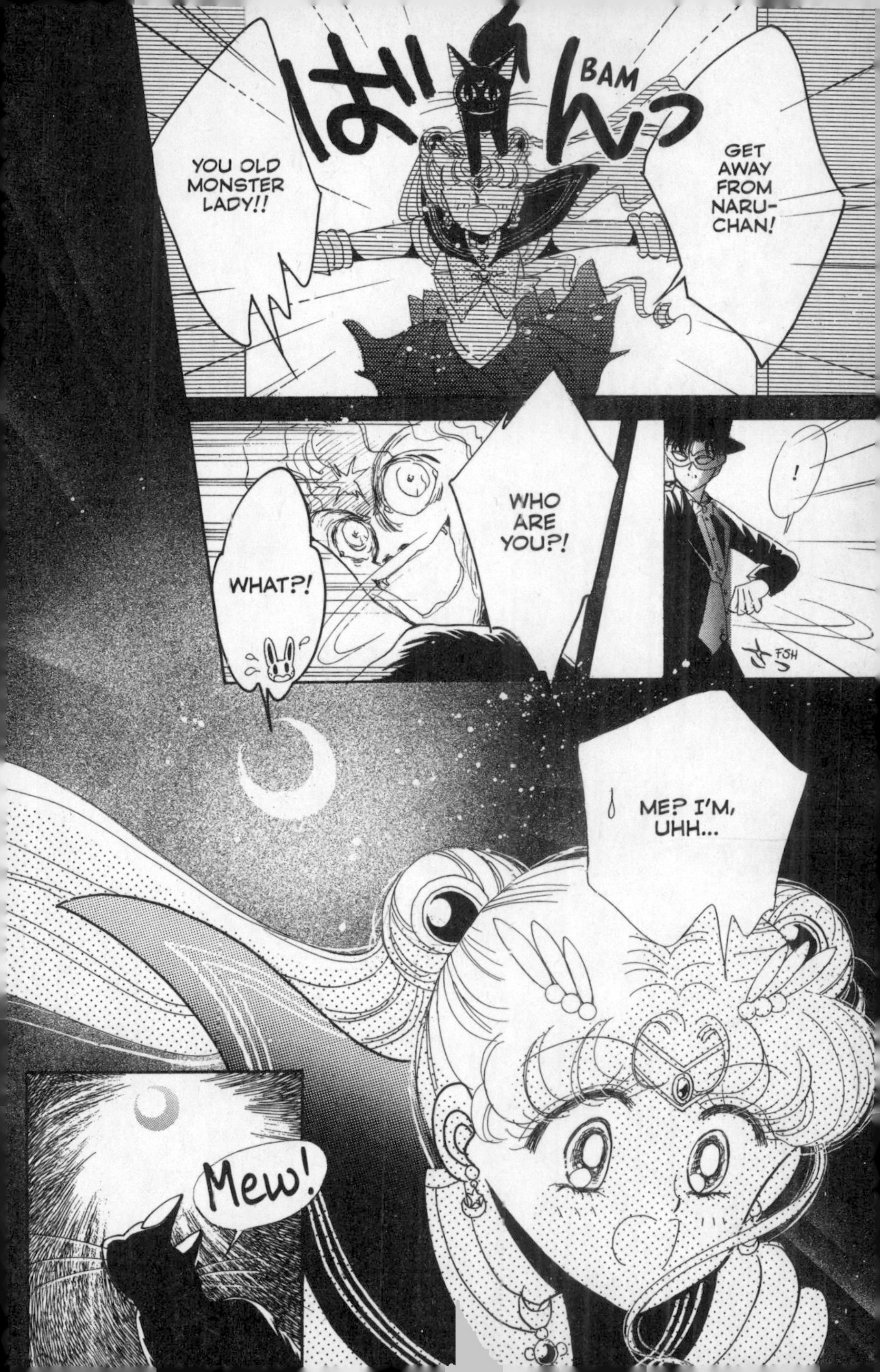
BAM
GET AWAY FROM NARU-CHAN!
YOU OLD MONSTER LADY!!
!
FSH
WHO ARE YOU?!
WHAT?!
ME? I'M, UHH...
Mew!

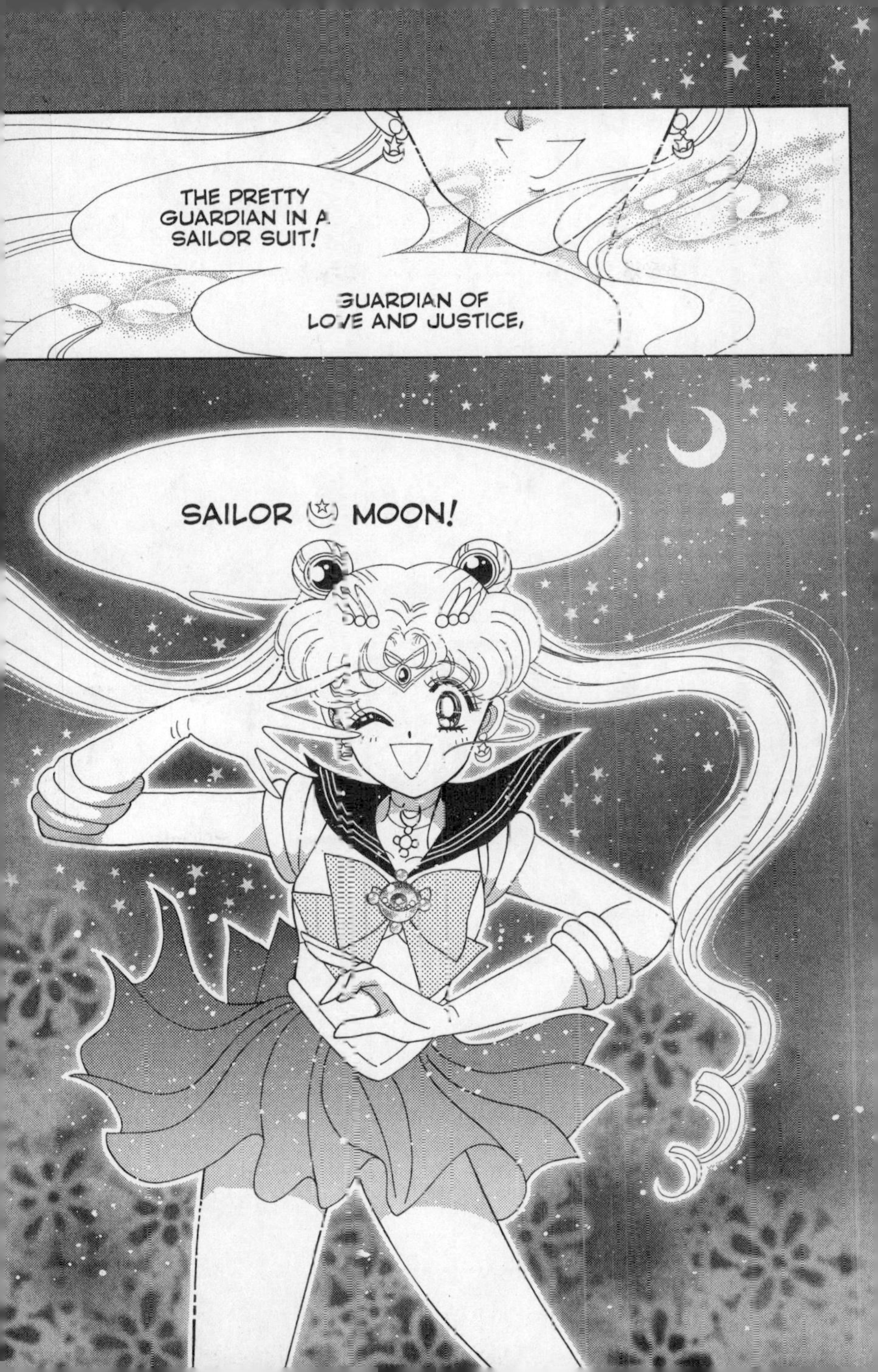
THE PRETTY GUARDIAN IN A SAILOR SUIT!
GUARDIAN OF LOVE AND JUSTICE,
SAILOR MOON!

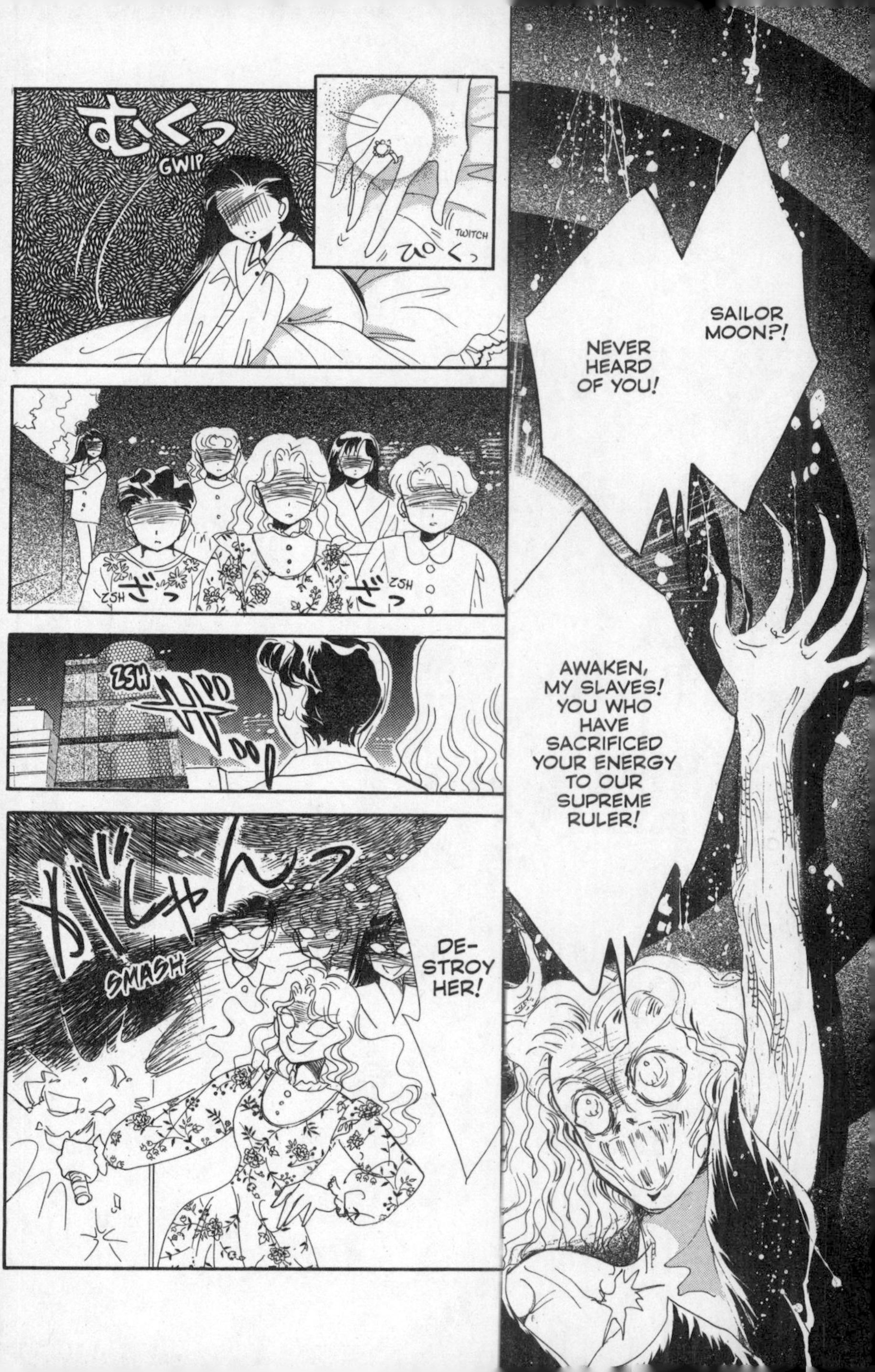
SAILOR MOON?!
NEVER HEARD OF YOU!
AWAKEN, MY SLAVES! YOU WHO HAVE SACRIFICED YOUR ENERGY TO OUR SUPREME RULER!
TWITCH
ぴくっ
むくっ
GWIP
ざっ
ZSH
ざっ
ZSH
ZSH
DE-STROY HER!
がしゃんっ
SMASH

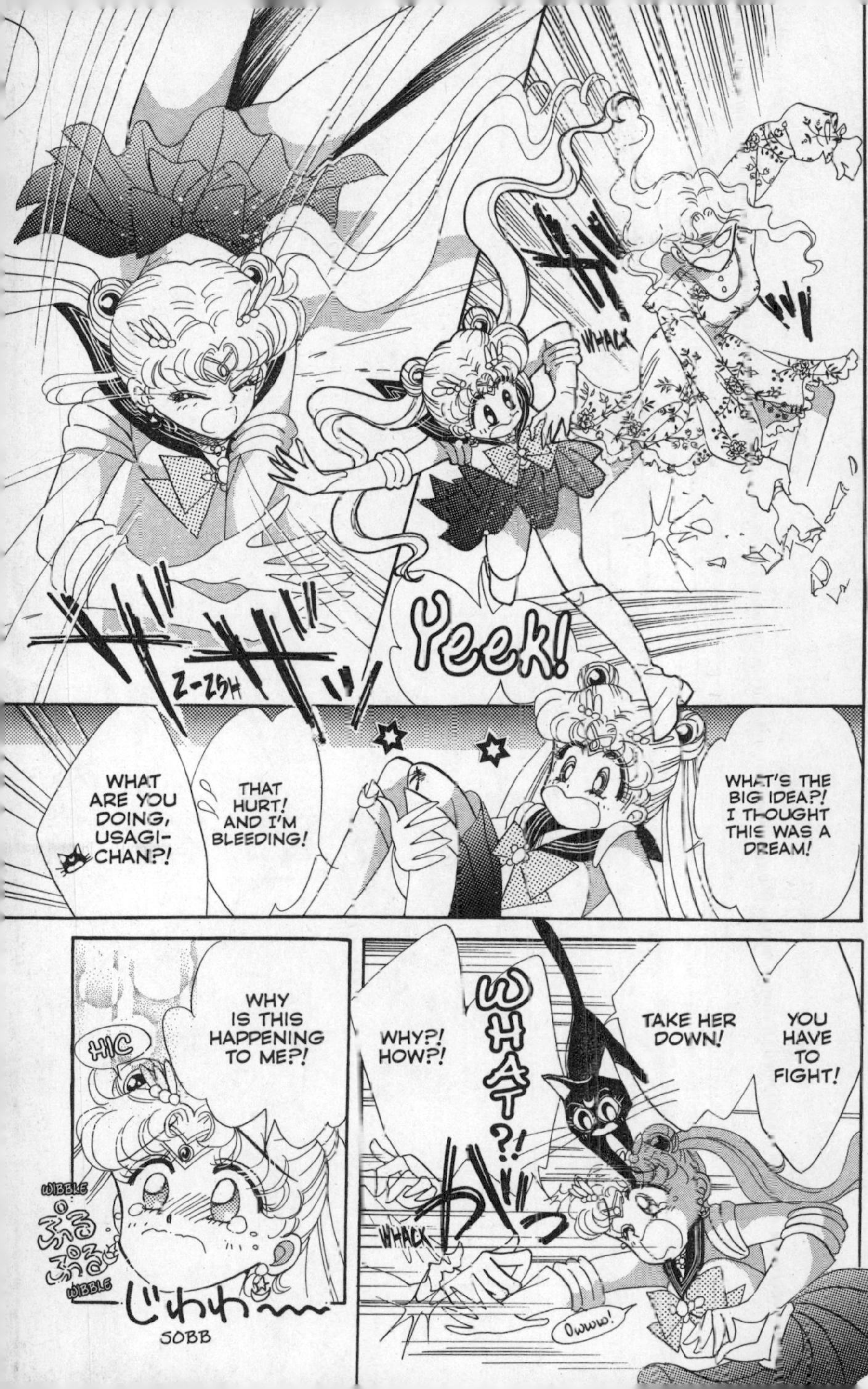
WHACK
Yeek!
Z-ZSH
WHAT'S THE BIG IDEA?! I THOUGHT THIS WAS A DREAM!
THAT HURT! AND I'M BLEEDING!
WHAT ARE YOU DOING, USAGI-CHAN?!
YOU HAVE TO FIGHT!
TAKE HER DOWN!
WHAT?!
WHY?! HOW?!
WHACK
Owww!
WHY IS THIS HAPPENING TO ME?!
HIC
WIBBLE
WIBBLE
SOBB

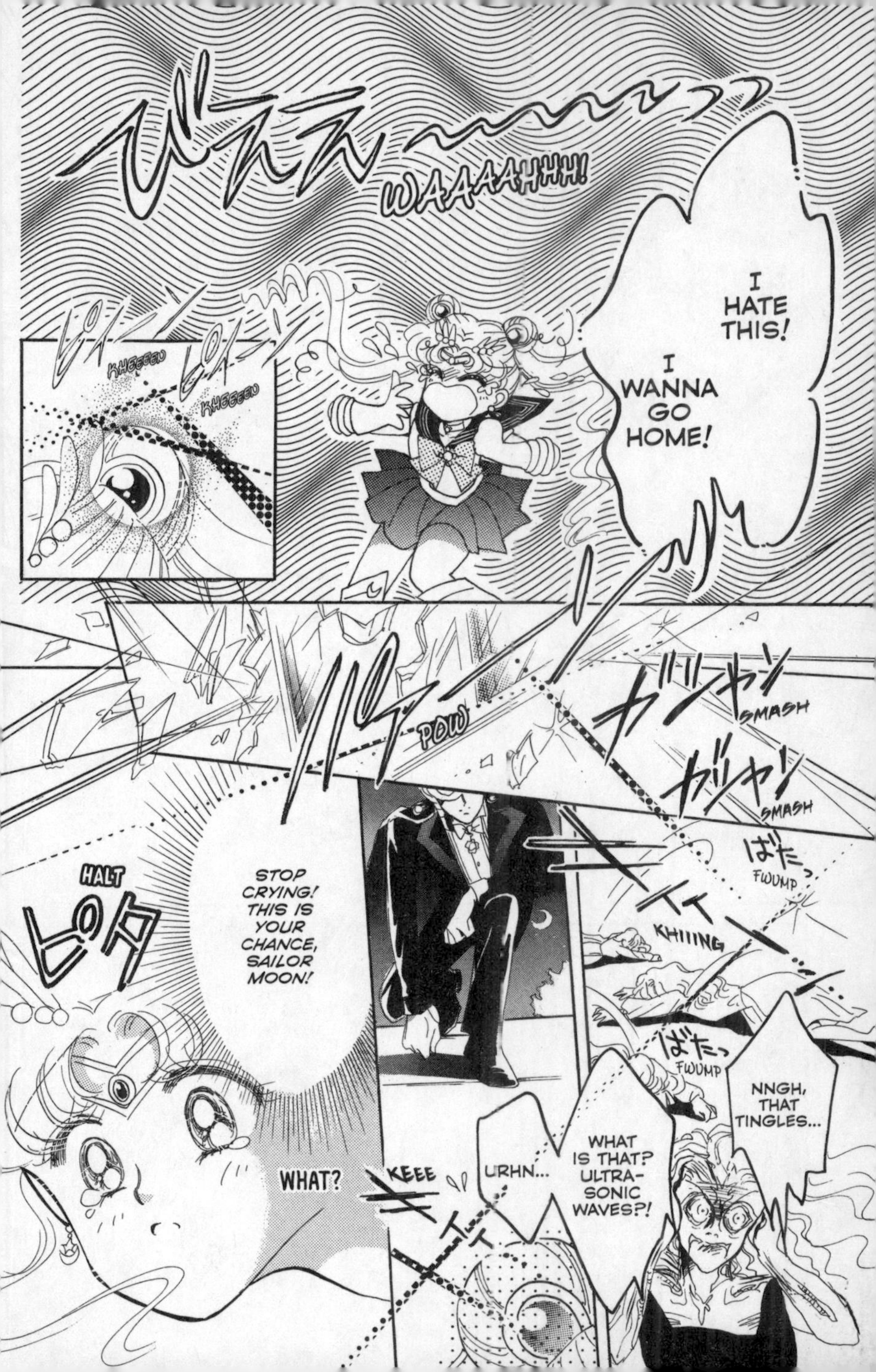

ぴええ~~っっ
WAAAAHHH!
I HATE THIS!
I WANNA GO HOME!
KHEEEEU
KHEEEEU
ガシャン
SMASH
ガシャン
SMASH
POW
ばたっ
FWUMP
KHIIING
ばたっ
FWUMP
NNGH, THAT TINGLES...
WHAT IS THAT? ULTRA-SONIC WAVES?!
URHN...
KEEE
STOP CRYING! THIS IS YOUR CHANCE, SAILOR MOON!
HALT
ピタ
WHAT?

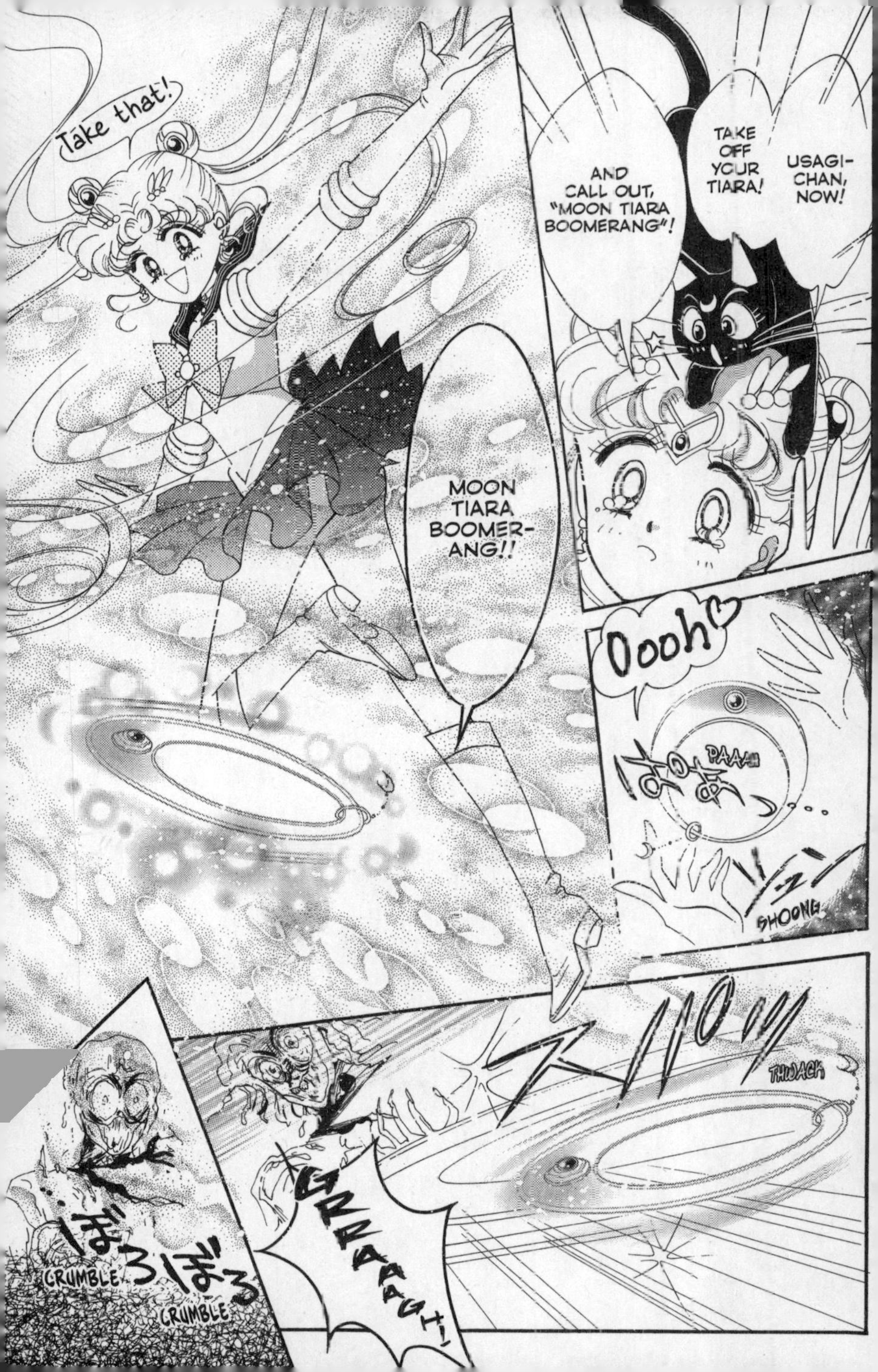
USAGI-CHAN, NOW!
TAKE OFF YOUR TIARA!
AND CALL OUT, "MOON TIARA BOOMERANG"!
Oooh♡
PAAAH
SHOONG
Take that!
MOON TIARA BOOMER-ANG!!
THWACK
GRRAAAGH!
CRUMBLE
CRUMBLE

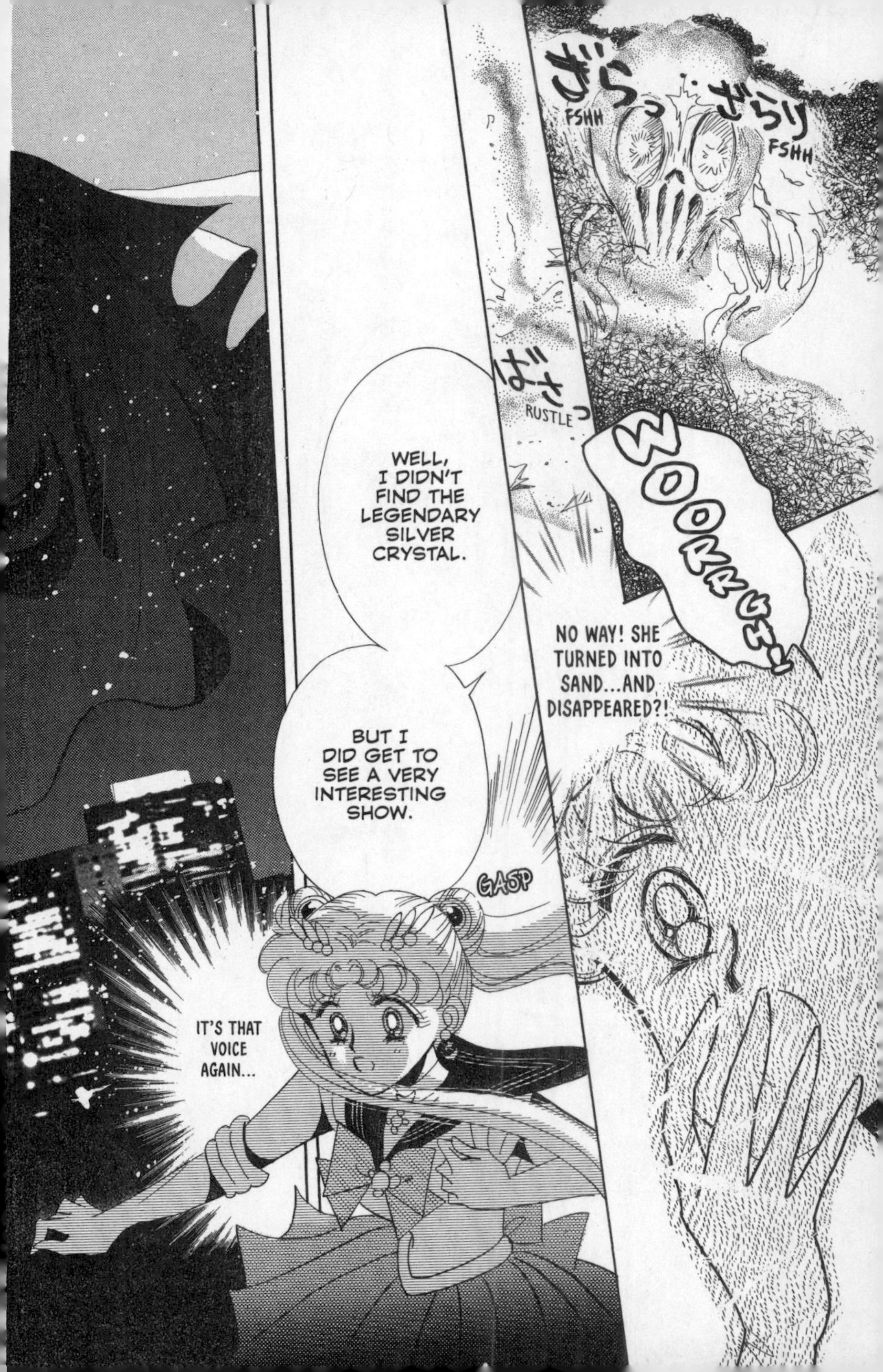
ざらっ
FSHH
ざらり
FSHH
ばさっ
RUSTLE
NO WAY! SHE TURNED INTO SAND...AND DISAPPEARED?!
WELL, I DIDN'T FIND THE LEGENDARY SILVER CRYSTAL.
BUT I DID GET TO SEE A VERY INTERESTING SHOW.
GASP
IT'S THAT VOICE AGAIN...

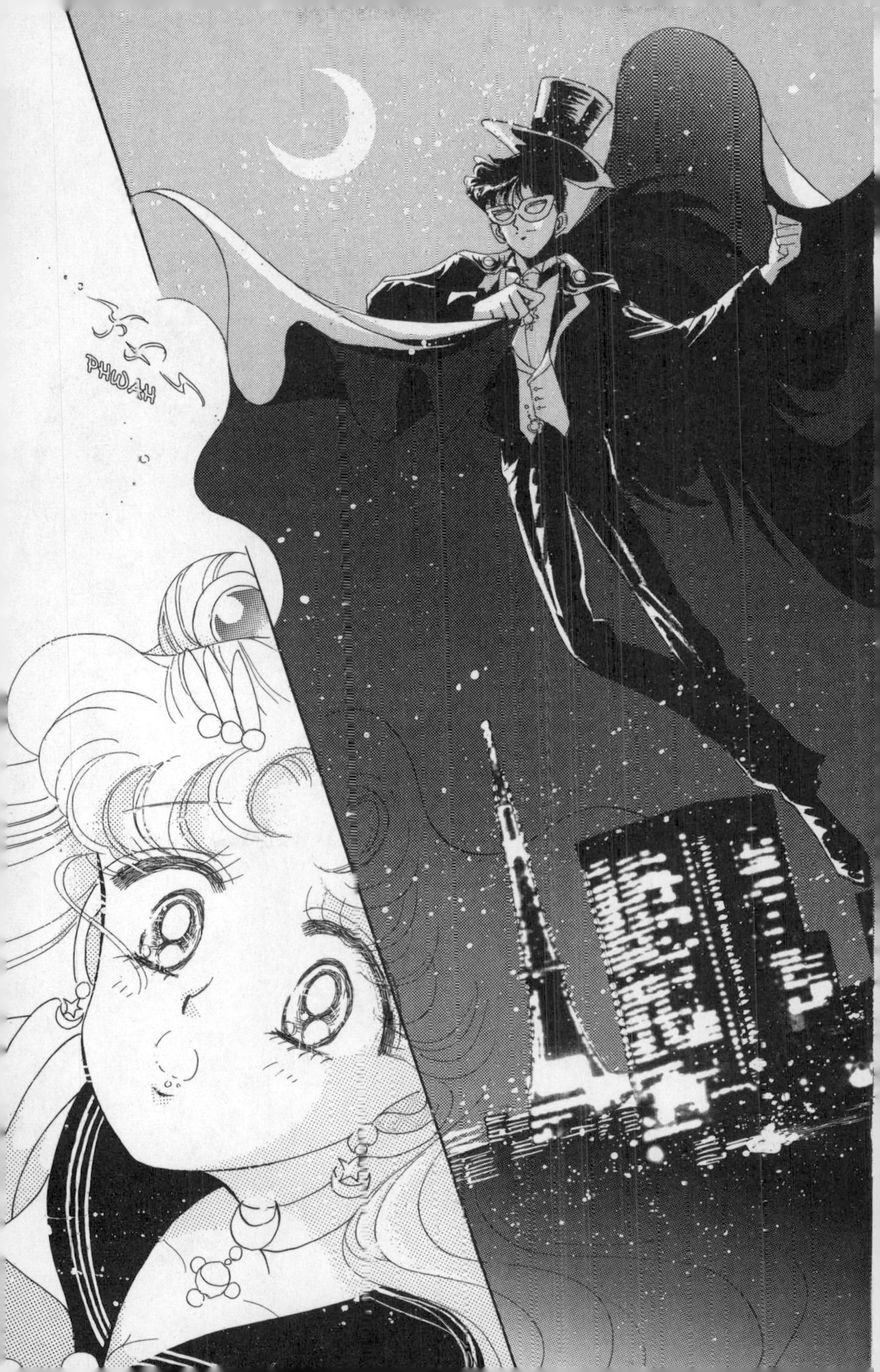
PHWAH

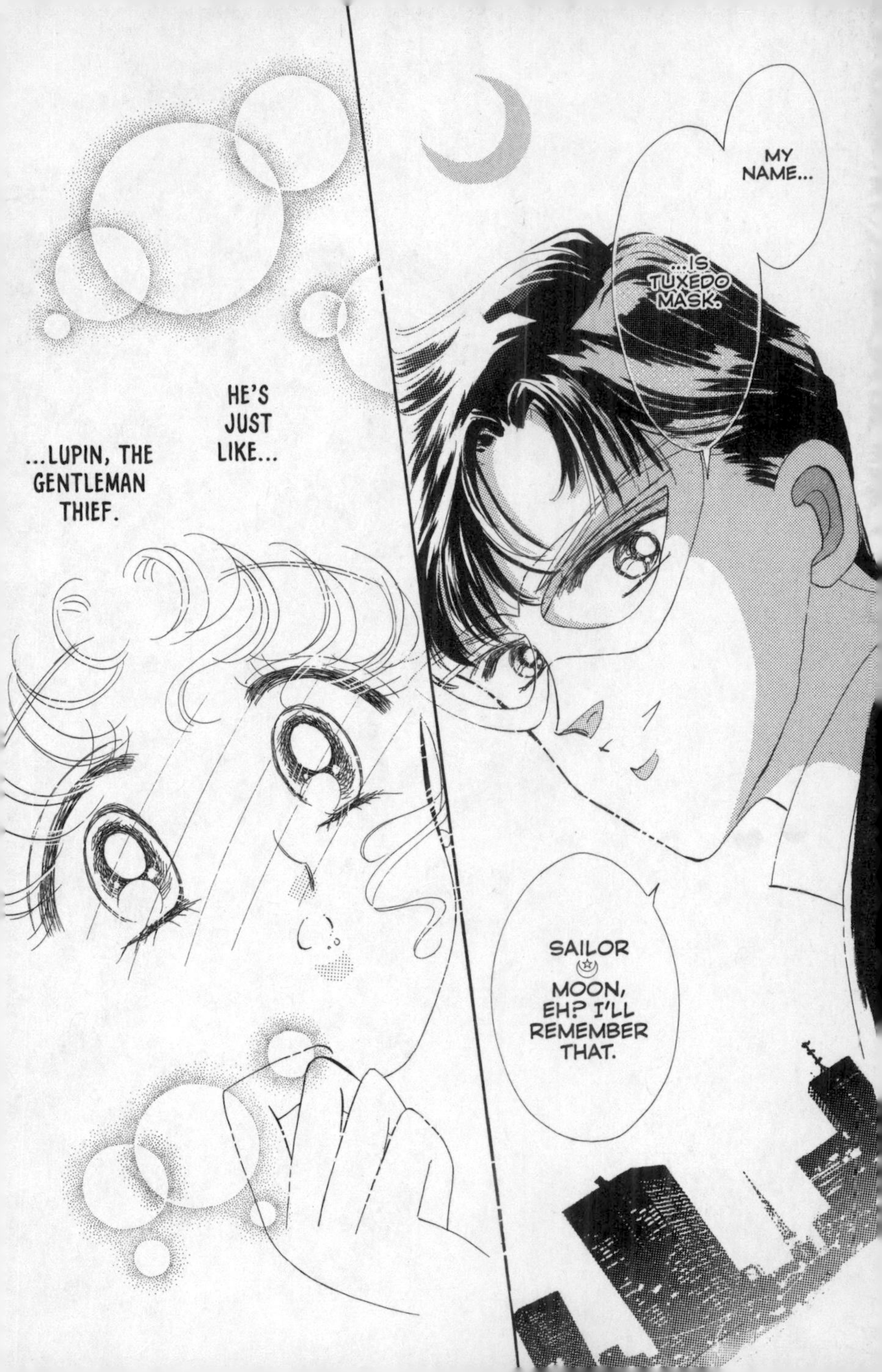
MY NAME...
...IS TUXEDO MASK.
SAILOR MOON, EH? I'LL REMEMBER THAT.
HE'S JUST LIKE...
...LUPIN, THE GENTLEMAN THIEF.

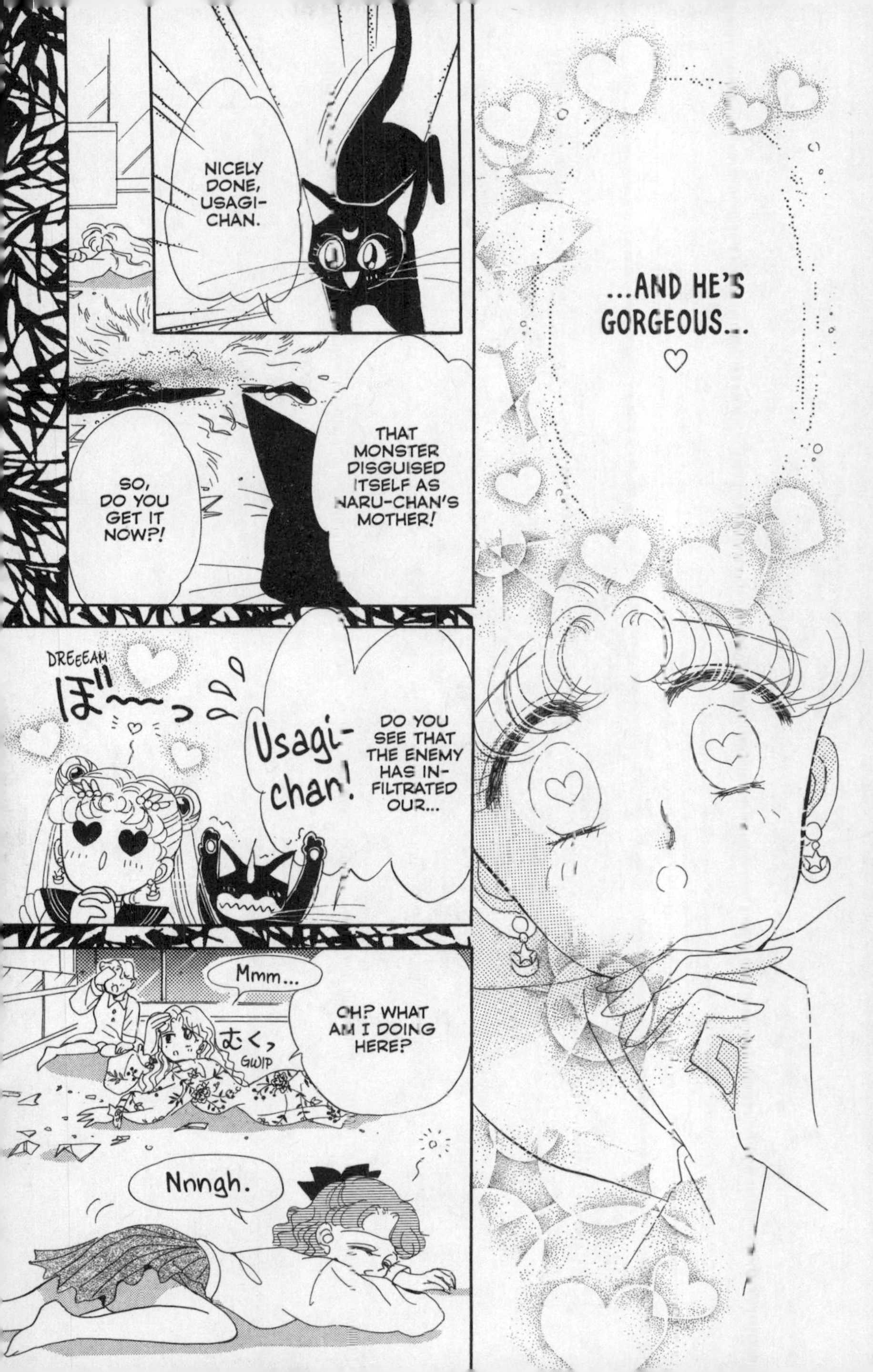
...AND HE'S GORGEOUS...
♡
NICELY DONE, USAGI-CHAN.
THAT MONSTER DISGUISED ITSELF AS NARU-CHAN'S MOTHER!
SO, DO YOU GET IT NOW?!
Usagi-chan!
DO YOU SEE THAT THE ENEMY HAS INFILTRATED OUR...
DREEEAM
ぼ~~っ
OH? WHAT AM I DOING HERE?
Mmm...
むくっ
GWIP
Nnngh.

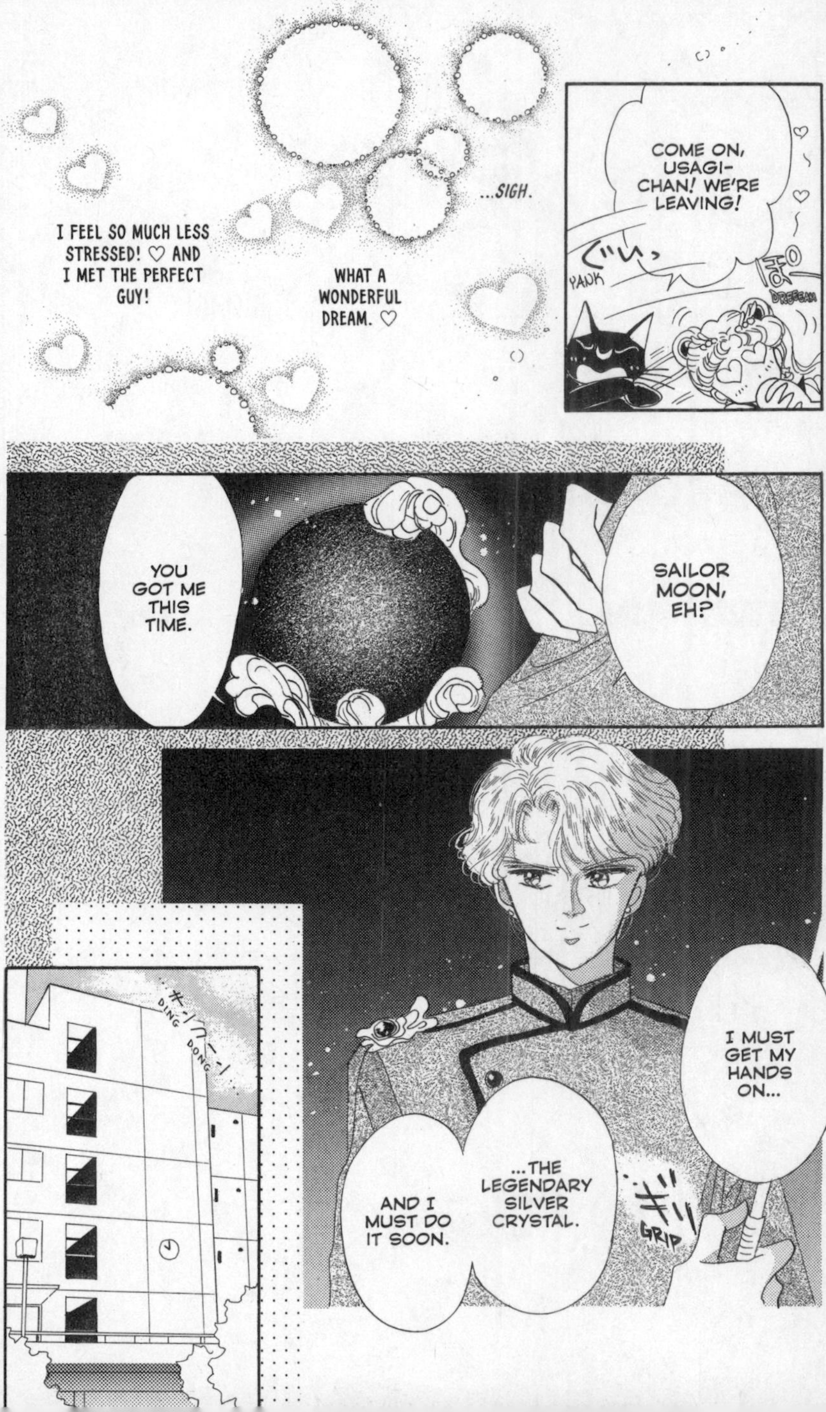

COME ON, USAGI-CHAN! WE'RE LEAVING!
YANK
DREEEAM
...SIGH.
WHAT A WONDERFUL DREAM. ♡
I FEEL SO MUCH LESS STRESSED! ♡ AND I MET THE PERFECT GUY!
SAILOR MOON, EH?
YOU GOT ME THIS TIME.
I MUST GET MY HANDS ON...
GRIP
...THE LEGENDARY SILVER CRYSTAL.
AND I MUST DO IT SOON.
DING DONG

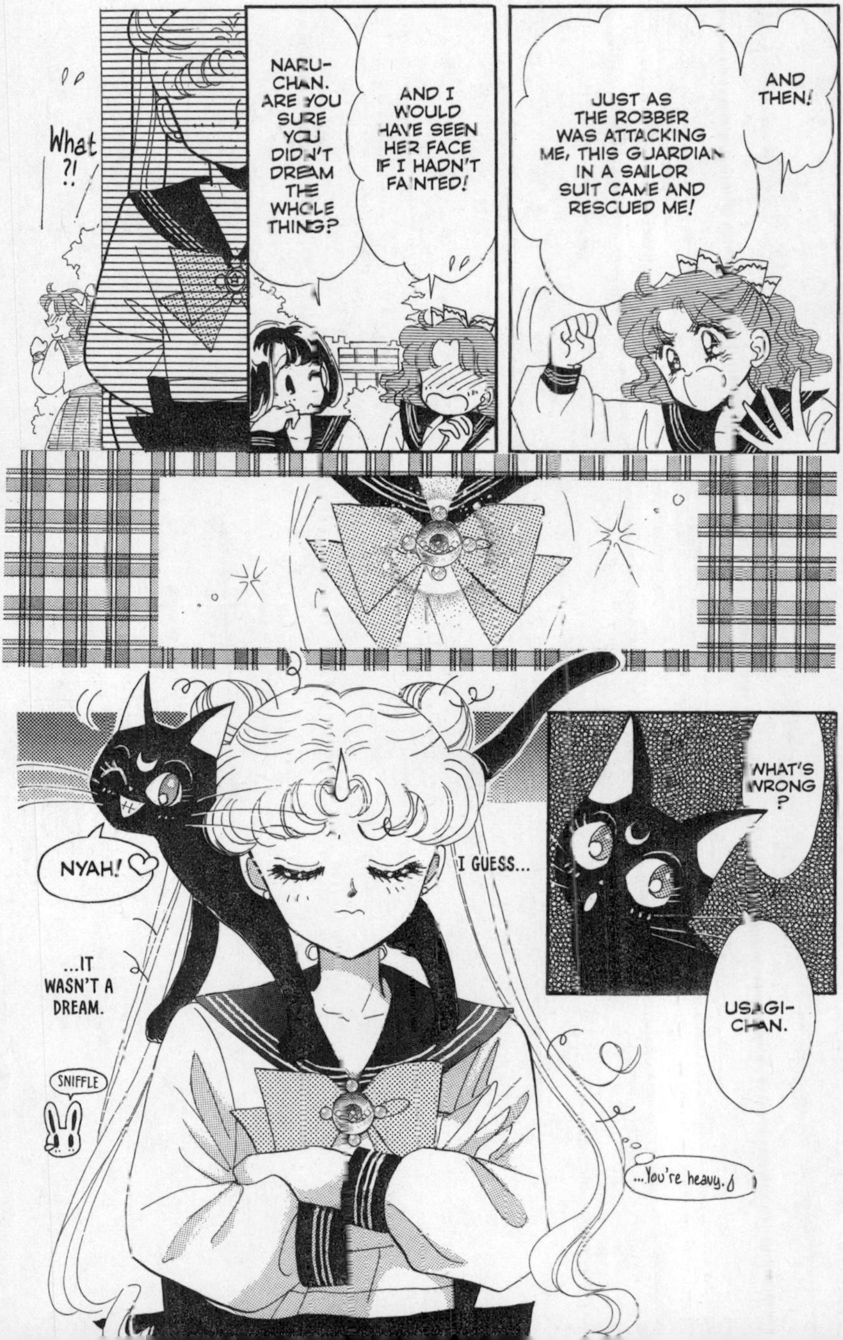
AND THEN!
JUST AS THE ROBBER WAS ATTACKING ME, THIS GUARDIAN IN A SAILOR SUIT CAME AND RESCUED ME!
AND I WOULD HAVE SEEN HER FACE IF I HADN'T FAINTED!
NARU-CHAN. ARE YOU SURE YOU DIDN'T DREAM THE WHOLE THING?
What?!
WHAT'S WRONG?
USAGI-CHAN.
I GUESS...
NYAH!
...IT WASN'T A DREAM.
...You're heavy.
SNIFFLE

Pretty Guardian Sailor Moon

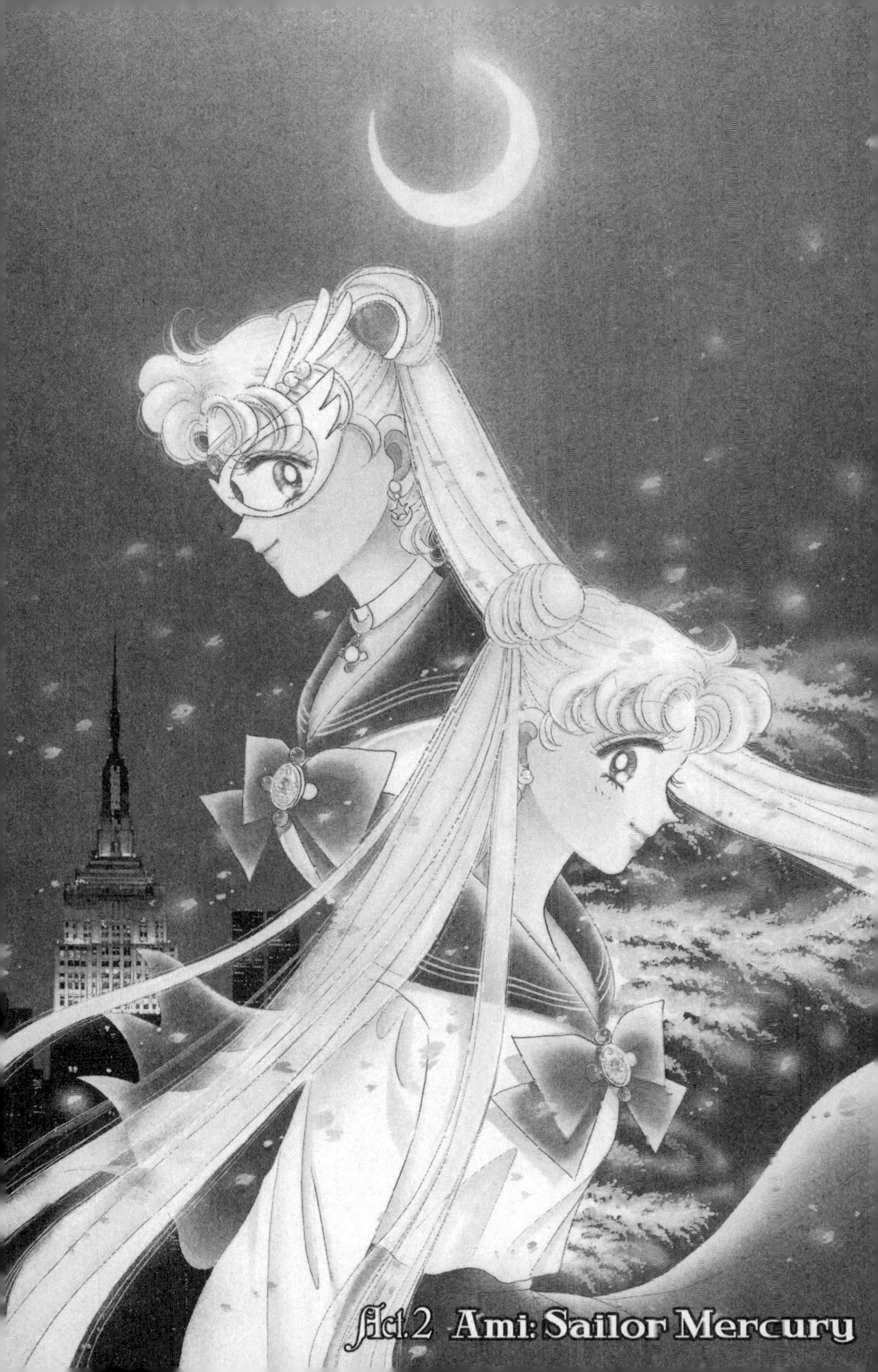
Act.2 Ami: Sailor Mercury

Pretty Guardian Sailor Moon

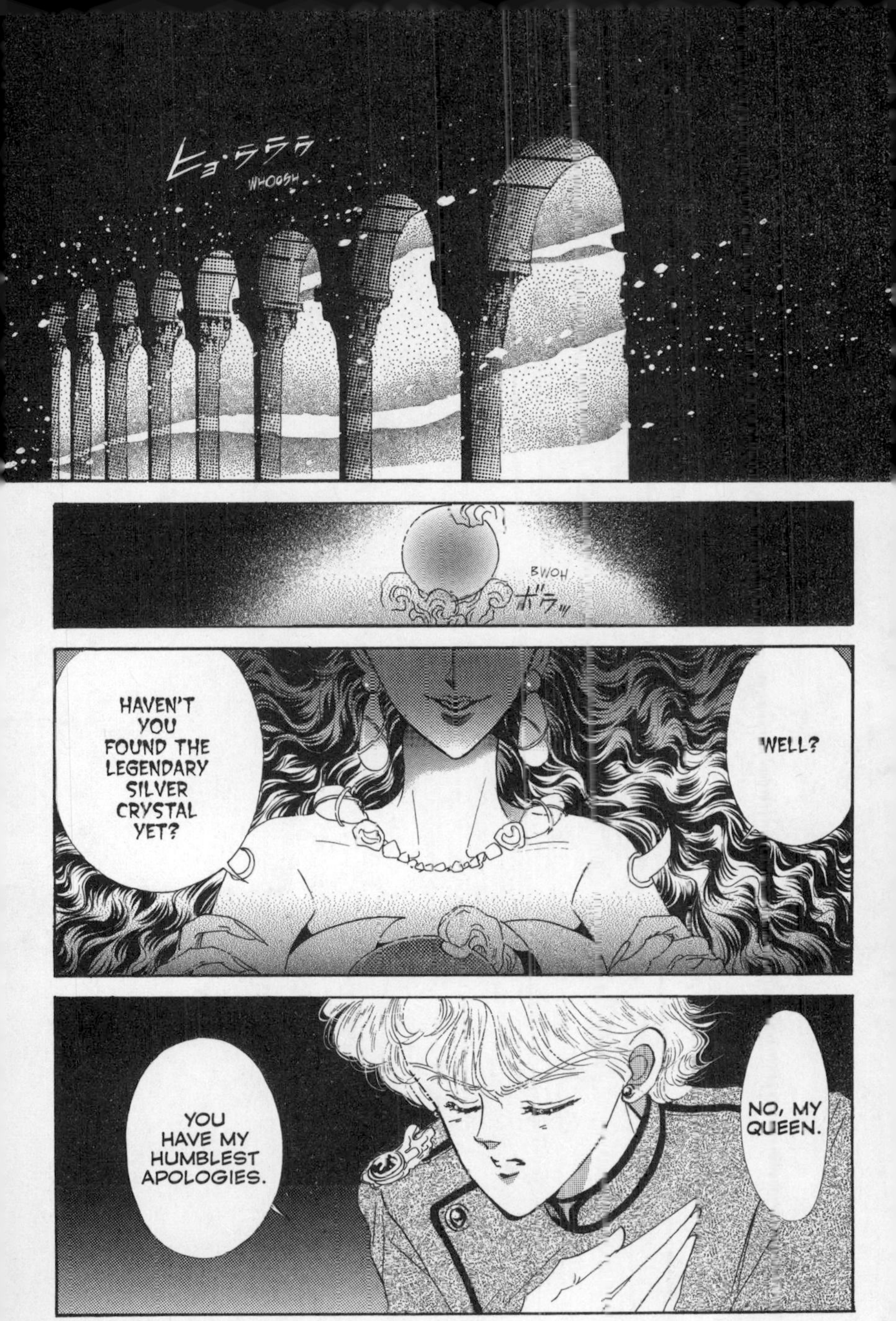
ヒョ・ラララ
WHOOSH
BWOH
ボウッ
WELL?
HAVEN'T YOU FOUND THE LEGENDARY SILVER CRYSTAL YET?
NO, MY QUEEN.
YOU HAVE MY HUMBLEST APOLOGIES.

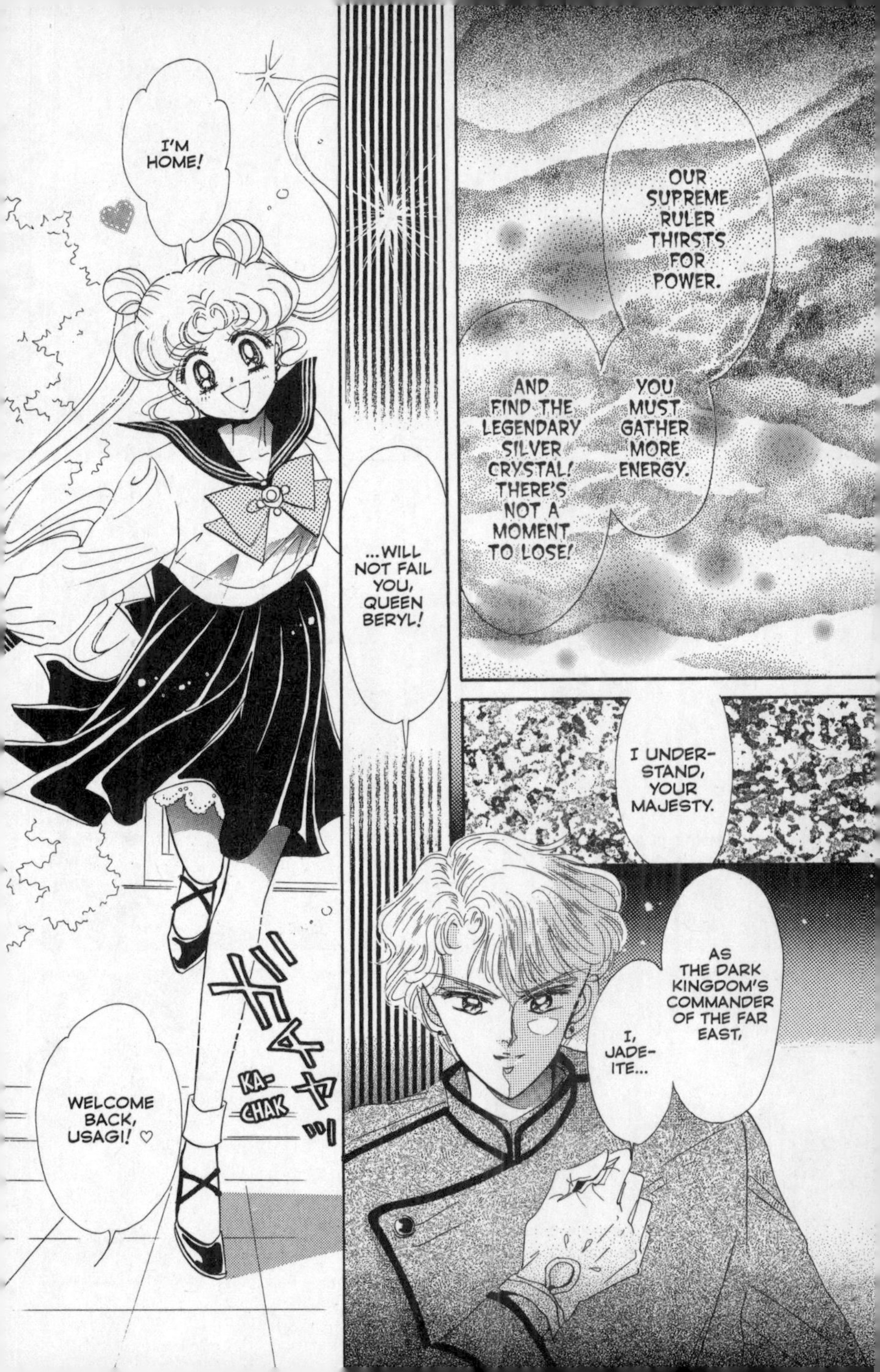
OUR SUPREME RULER THIRSTS FOR POWER.
YOU MUST GATHER MORE ENERGY.
AND FIND THE LEGENDARY SILVER CRYSTAL! THERE'S NOT A MOMENT TO LOSE!
I UNDER-STAND, YOUR MAJESTY.
AS THE DARK KINGDOM'S COMMANDER OF THE FAR EAST,
I, JADE-ITE...
...WILL NOT FAIL YOU, QUEEN BERYL!
I'M HOME!
KA-CHAK
WELCOME BACK, USAGI! ♡

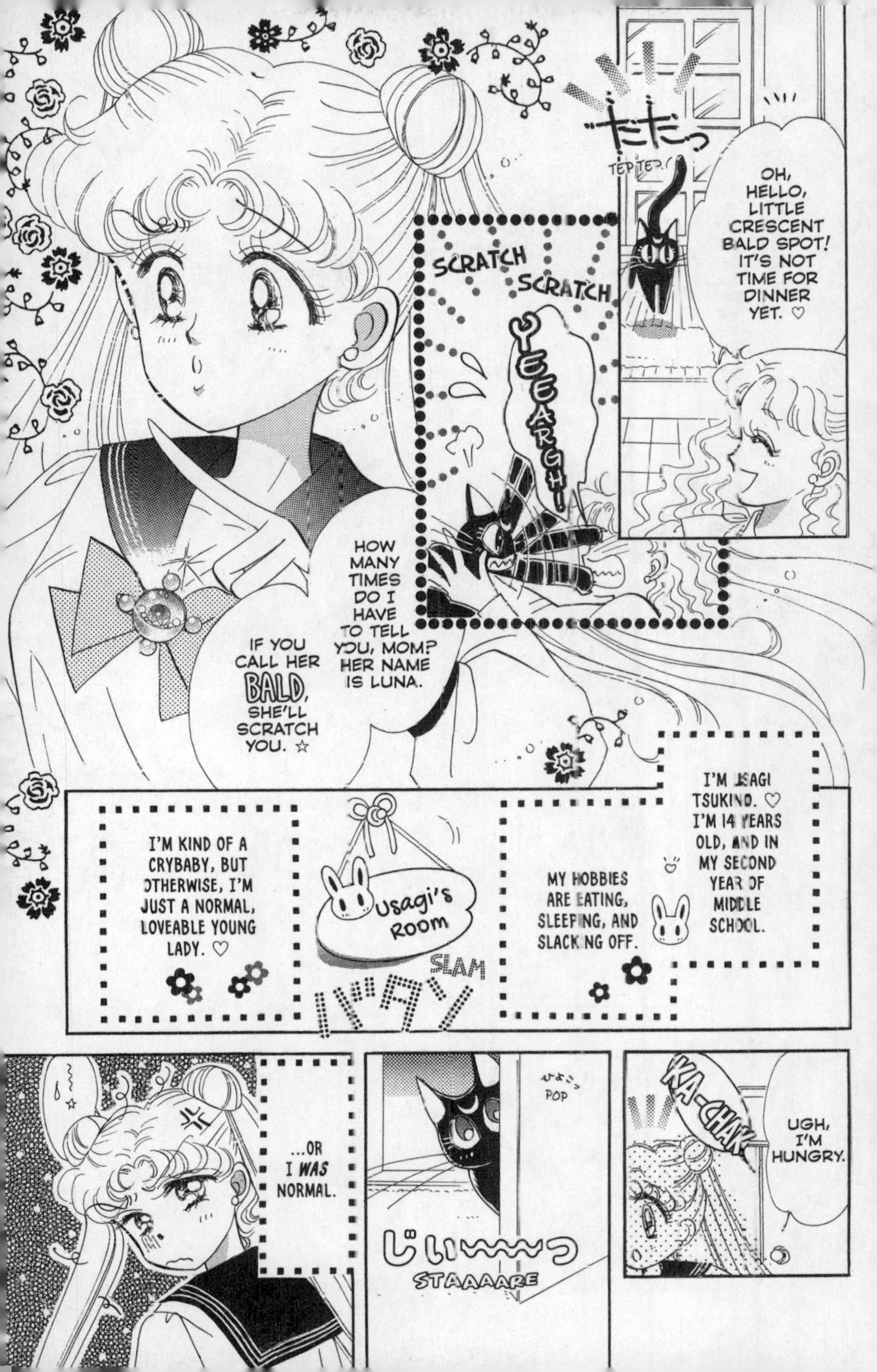
だだっ
TEP TEP
OH, HELLO, LITTLE CRESCENT BALD SPOT! IT'S NOT TIME FOR DINNER YET. ♡
SCRATCH
SCRATCH
YEEARGH!
HOW MANY TIMES DO I HAVE TO TELL YOU, MOM? HER NAME IS LUNA.
IF YOU CALL HER BALD, SHE'LL SCRATCH YOU. ☆
I'M USAGI TSUKINO. ♡ I'M 14 YEARS OLD, AND IN MY SECOND YEAR OF MIDDLE SCHOOL.
MY HOBBIES ARE EATING, SLEEPING, AND SLACKING OFF.
Usagi's Room
バタン
SLAM
I'M KIND OF A CRYBABY, BUT OTHERWISE, I'M JUST A NORMAL, LOVEABLE YOUNG LADY. ♡
KA-CHAK
UGH, I'M HUNGRY.
ぴょこっ
POP
じぃ〜〜っ
STAAAARE
...OR I *WAS* NORMAL.

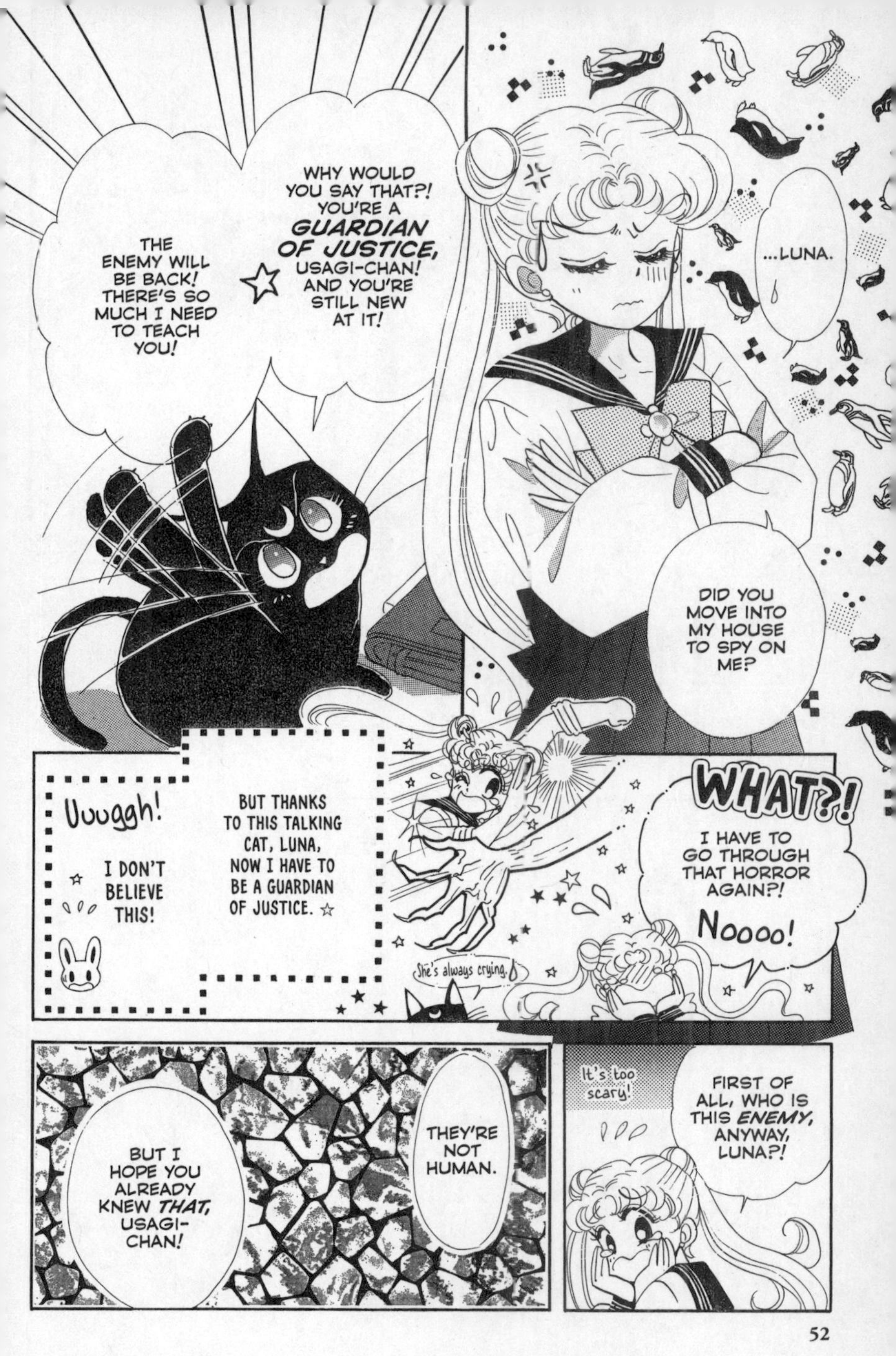
...LUNA.
DID YOU MOVE INTO MY HOUSE TO SPY ON ME?
WHY WOULD YOU SAY THAT?! YOU'RE A *GUARDIAN OF JUSTICE,* USAGI-CHAN! AND YOU'RE STILL NEW AT IT!
THE ENEMY WILL BE BACK! THERE'S SO MUCH I NEED TO TEACH YOU!
WHAT?!
I HAVE TO GO THROUGH THAT HORROR AGAIN?!
Noooo!
She's always crying.
BUT THANKS TO THIS TALKING CAT, LUNA, NOW I HAVE TO BE A GUARDIAN OF JUSTICE.
Uuuggh!
I DON'T BELIEVE THIS!
It's too scary!
FIRST OF ALL, WHO IS THIS *ENEMY,* ANYWAY, LUNA?!
THEY'RE NOT HUMAN.
BUT I HOPE YOU ALREADY KNEW *THAT,* USAGI-CHAN!

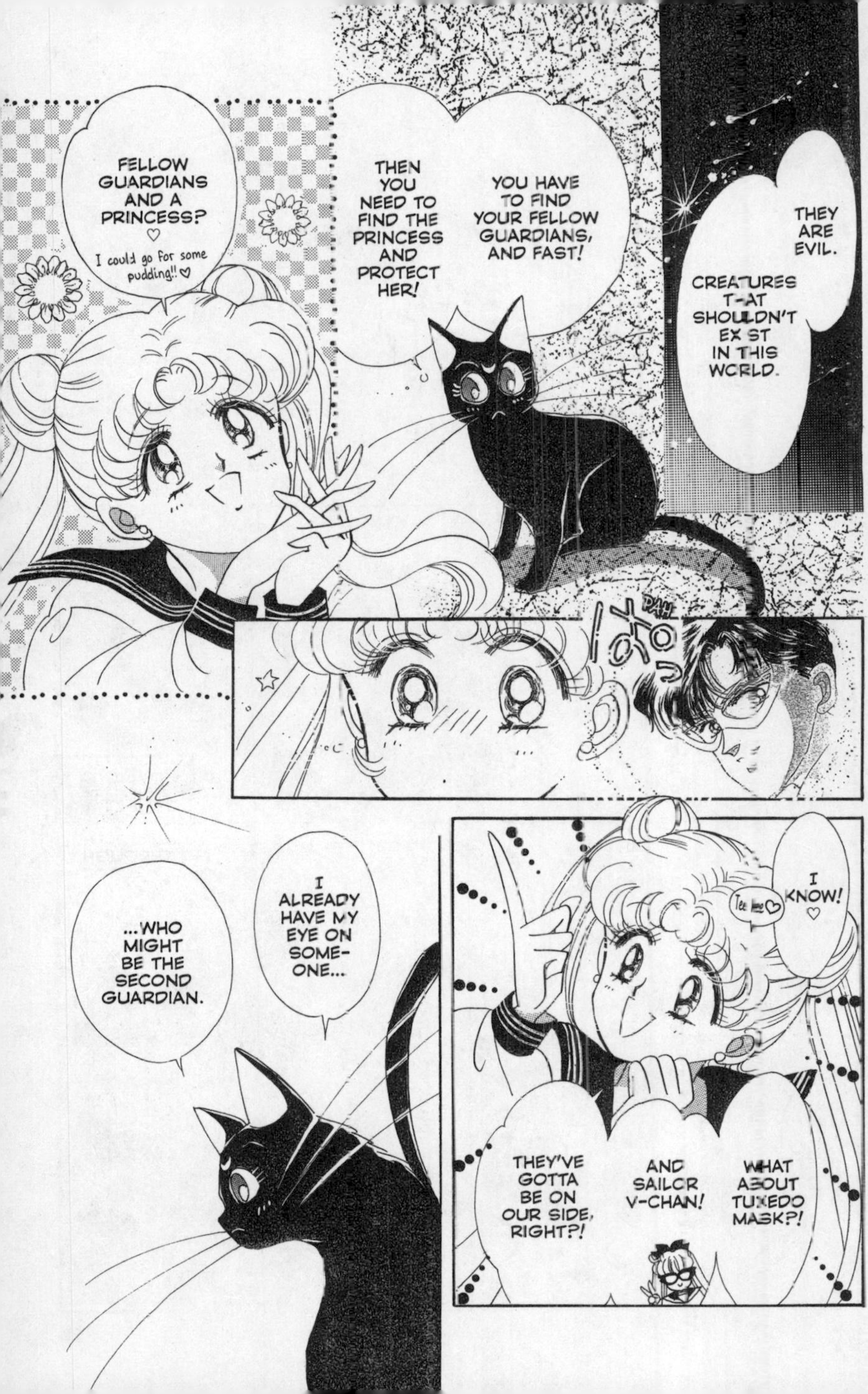
THEY ARE EVIL.
CREATURES THAT SHOULDN'T EXIST IN THIS WORLD.
YOU HAVE TO FIND YOUR FELLOW GUARDIANS, AND FAST!
THEN YOU NEED TO FIND THE PRINCESS AND PROTECT HER!
FELLOW GUARDIANS AND A PRINCESS? ♡
I could go for some pudding!! ♡
DAH
I KNOW! ♡
Tee hee ♡
WHAT ABOUT TUXEDO MASK?!
AND SAILOR V-CHAN!
THEY'VE GOTTA BE ON OUR SIDE, RIGHT?!
I ALREADY HAVE MY EYE ON SOMEONE...
...WHO MIGHT BE THE SECOND GUARDIAN.

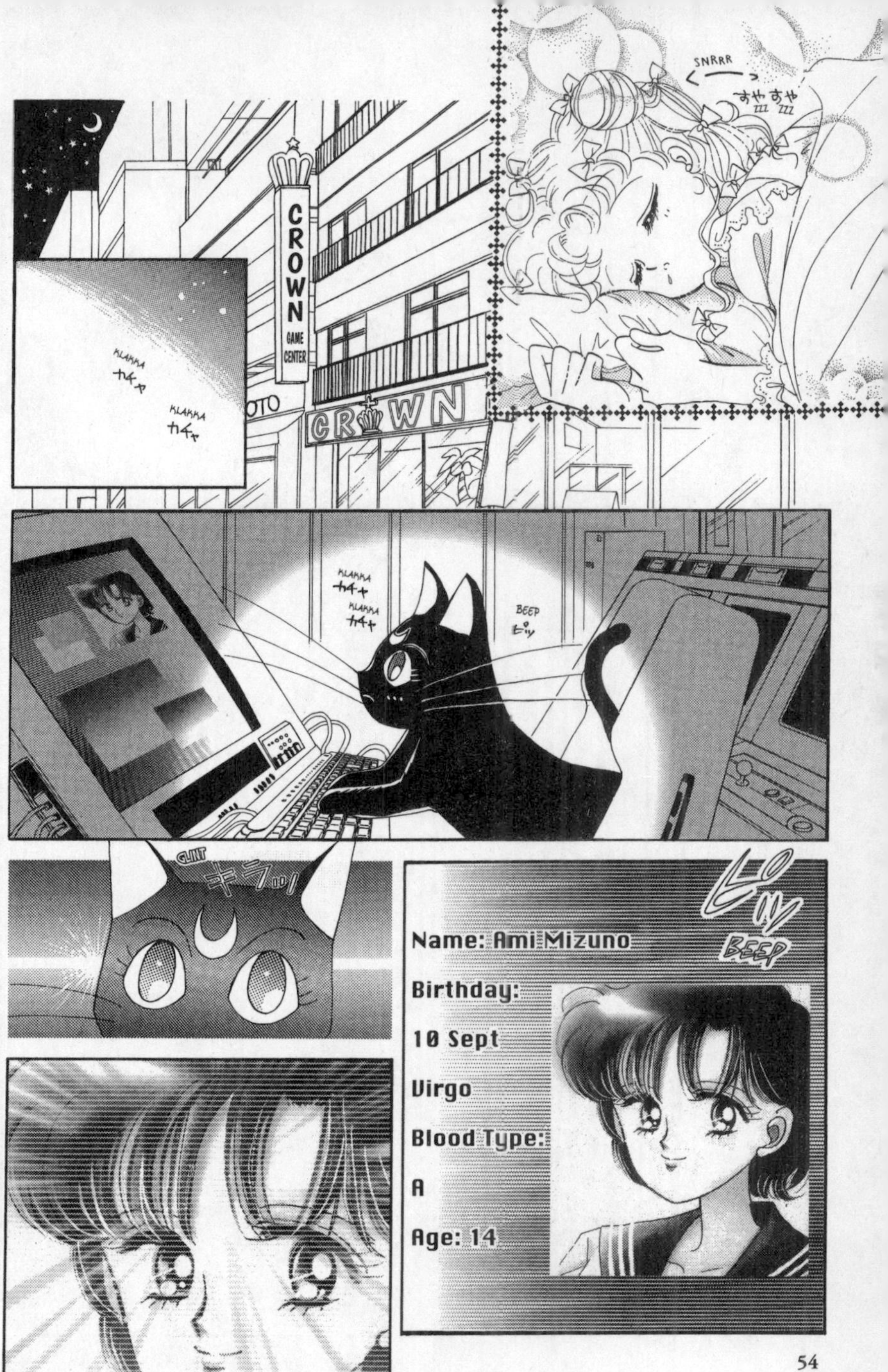
SNRRR
くー
すやすや
ZZZ ZZZ
CROWN
GAME CENTER
CROWN
KLAKKA
カチャ
KLAKKA
カチャ
KLAKKA
カチャ
KLAKKA
カチャ
BEEP
ピッ
ピッ
BEEP
Name: Ami Mizuno
Birthday:
10 Sept
Virgo
Blood Type:
A
Age: 14
GLINT
キラッ

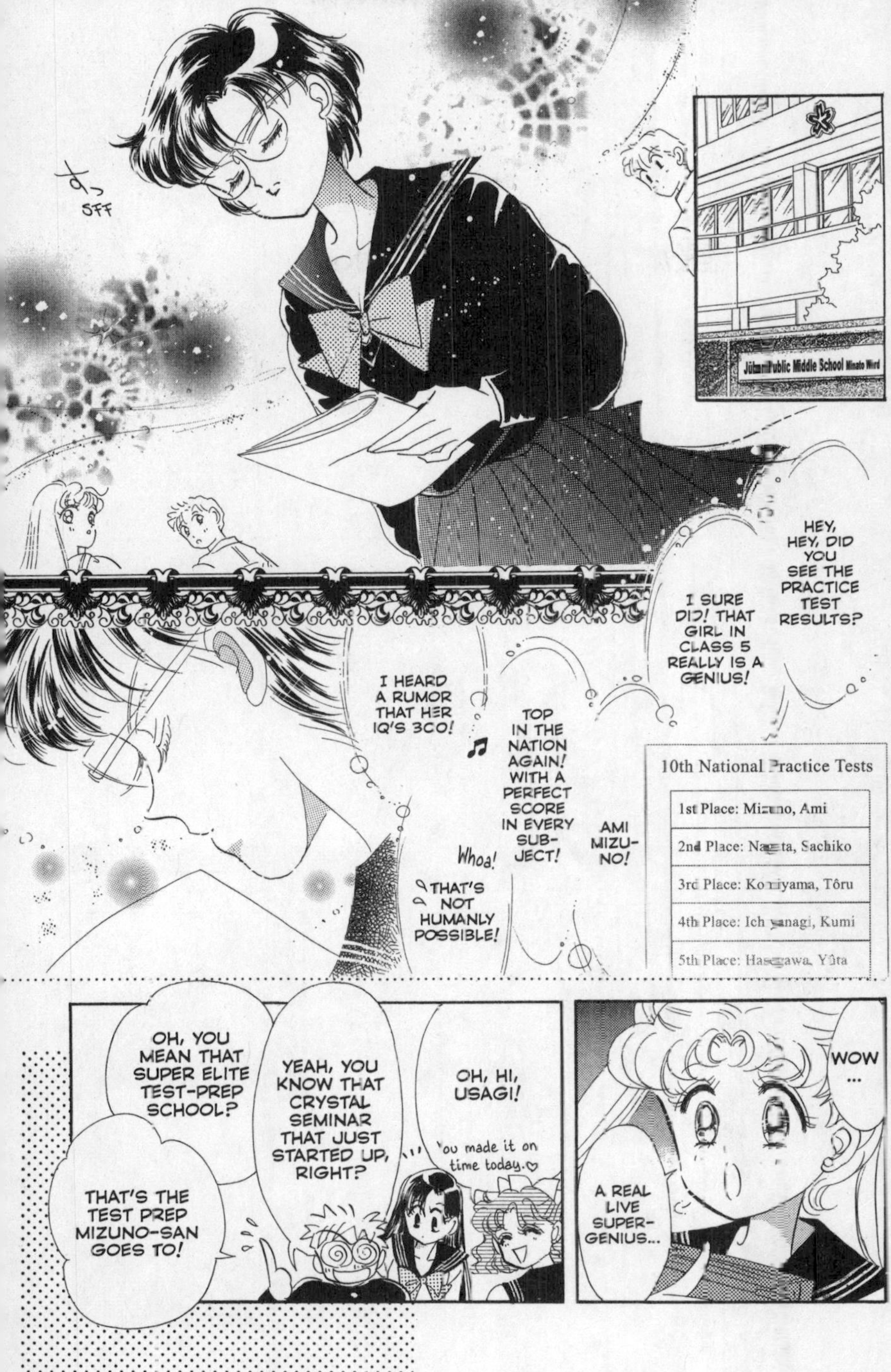
Jūban Public Middle School Minato Ward
すっ
SFF
HEY, HEY, DID YOU SEE THE PRACTICE TEST RESULTS?
I SURE DID! THAT GIRL IN CLASS 5 REALLY IS A GENIUS!
10th National Practice Tests
1st Place: Mizuno, Ami
2nd Place: Nagata, Sachiko
3rd Place: Komiyama, Tôru
4th Place: Ichiyanagi, Kumi
5th Place: Hasegawa, Yûta
TOP IN THE NATION AGAIN! WITH A PERFECT SCORE IN EVERY SUBJECT!
AMI MIZUNO!
I HEARD A RUMOR THAT HER IQ'S 300!
Whoa!
THAT'S NOT HUMANLY POSSIBLE!
WOW ...
A REAL LIVE SUPER-GENIUS...
OH, HI, USAGI!
You made it on time today.♡
YEAH, YOU KNOW THAT CRYSTAL SEMINAR THAT JUST STARTED UP, RIGHT?
OH, YOU MEAN THAT SUPER ELITE TEST-PREP SCHOOL?
THAT'S THE TEST PREP MIZUNO-SAN GOES TO!

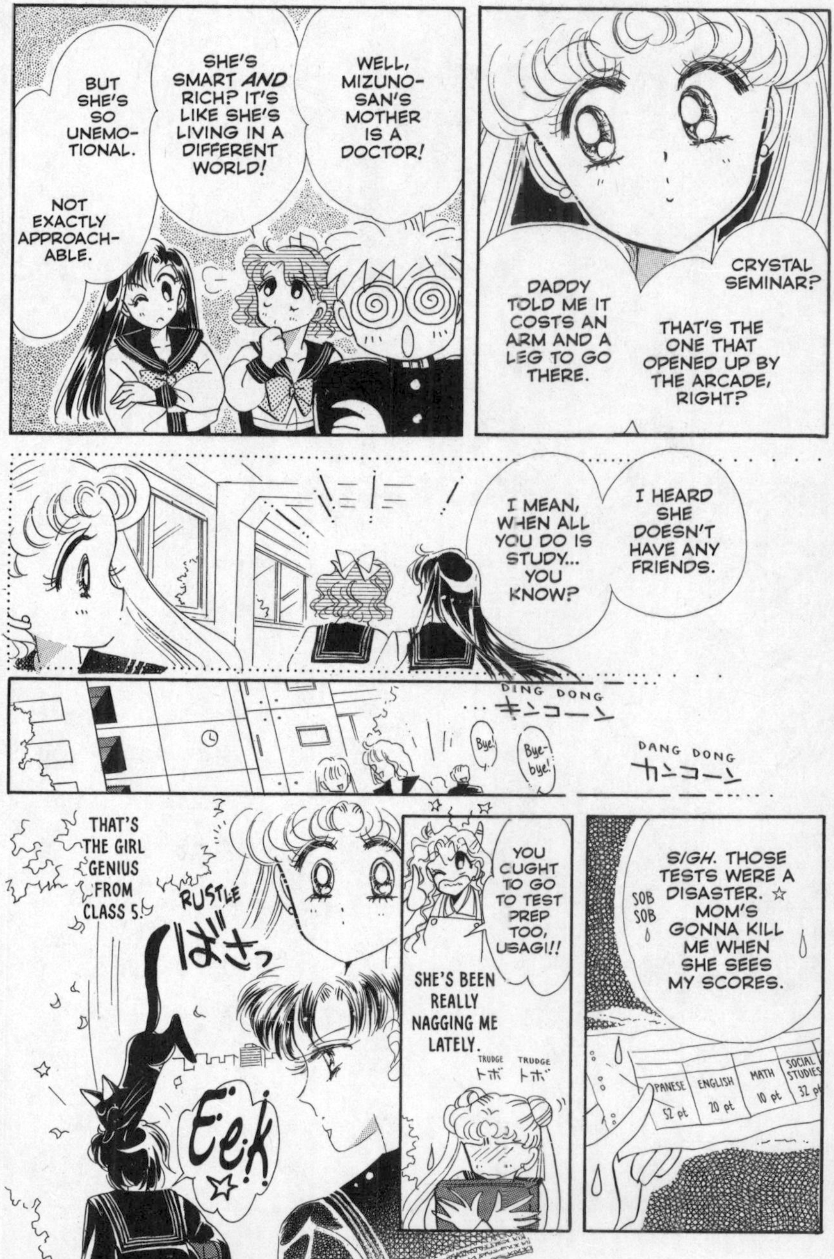
CRYSTAL SEMINAR?
THAT'S THE ONE THAT OPENED UP BY THE ARCADE, RIGHT?
DADDY TOLD ME IT COSTS AN ARM AND A LEG TO GO THERE.
WELL, MIZUNO-SAN'S MOTHER IS A DOCTOR!
SHE'S SMART *AND* RICH? IT'S LIKE SHE'S LIVING IN A DIFFERENT WORLD!
BUT SHE'S SO UNEMOTIONAL.
NOT EXACTLY APPROACHABLE.
I HEARD SHE DOESN'T HAVE ANY FRIENDS.
I MEAN, WHEN ALL YOU DO IS STUDY... YOU KNOW?
DING DONG キンコーン
DANG DONG カンコーン
Bye-bye!
Bye!
SOB SOB
SIGH. THOSE TESTS WERE A DISASTER. ☆ MOM'S GONNA KILL ME WHEN SHE SEES MY SCORES.
PANESE 52 pt
ENGLISH 20 pt
MATH 10 pt
SOCIAL STUDIES 32 pt
YOU OUGHT TO GO TO TEST PREP TOO, USAGI!!
SHE'S BEEN REALLY NAGGING ME LATELY.
TRUDGE TRUDGE トボ トボ
THAT'S THE GIRL GENIUS FROM CLASS 5.
RUSTLE ばさっ
Eek!

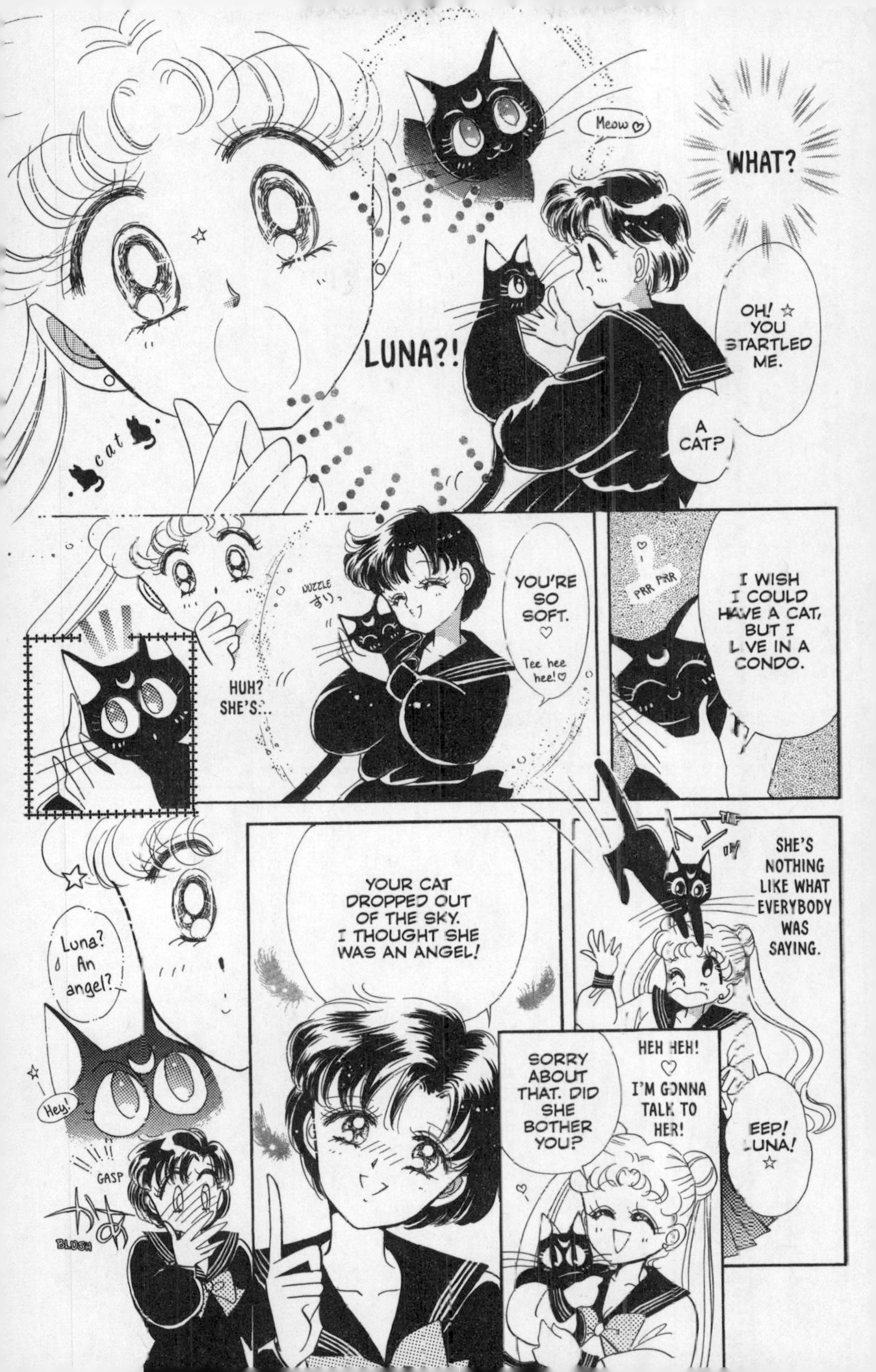

WHAT?
Meow ♡
OH! ☆ YOU STARTLED ME.
A CAT?
LUNA?!
cat
PRR PRR
I WISH I COULD HAVE A CAT, BUT I LIVE IN A CONDO.
YOU'RE SO SOFT. ♡
Tee hee hee! ♡
NUZZLE
すりっ
HUH? SHE'S...
SHE'S NOTHING LIKE WHAT EVERYBODY WAS SAYING.
EEP! LUNA! ☆
HEH HEH! ♡ I'M GONNA TALK TO HER!
SORRY ABOUT THAT. DID SHE BOTHER YOU?
YOUR CAT DROPPED OUT OF THE SKY. I THOUGHT SHE WAS AN ANGEL!
Luna? An angel?
Hey!
GASP
BLUSH

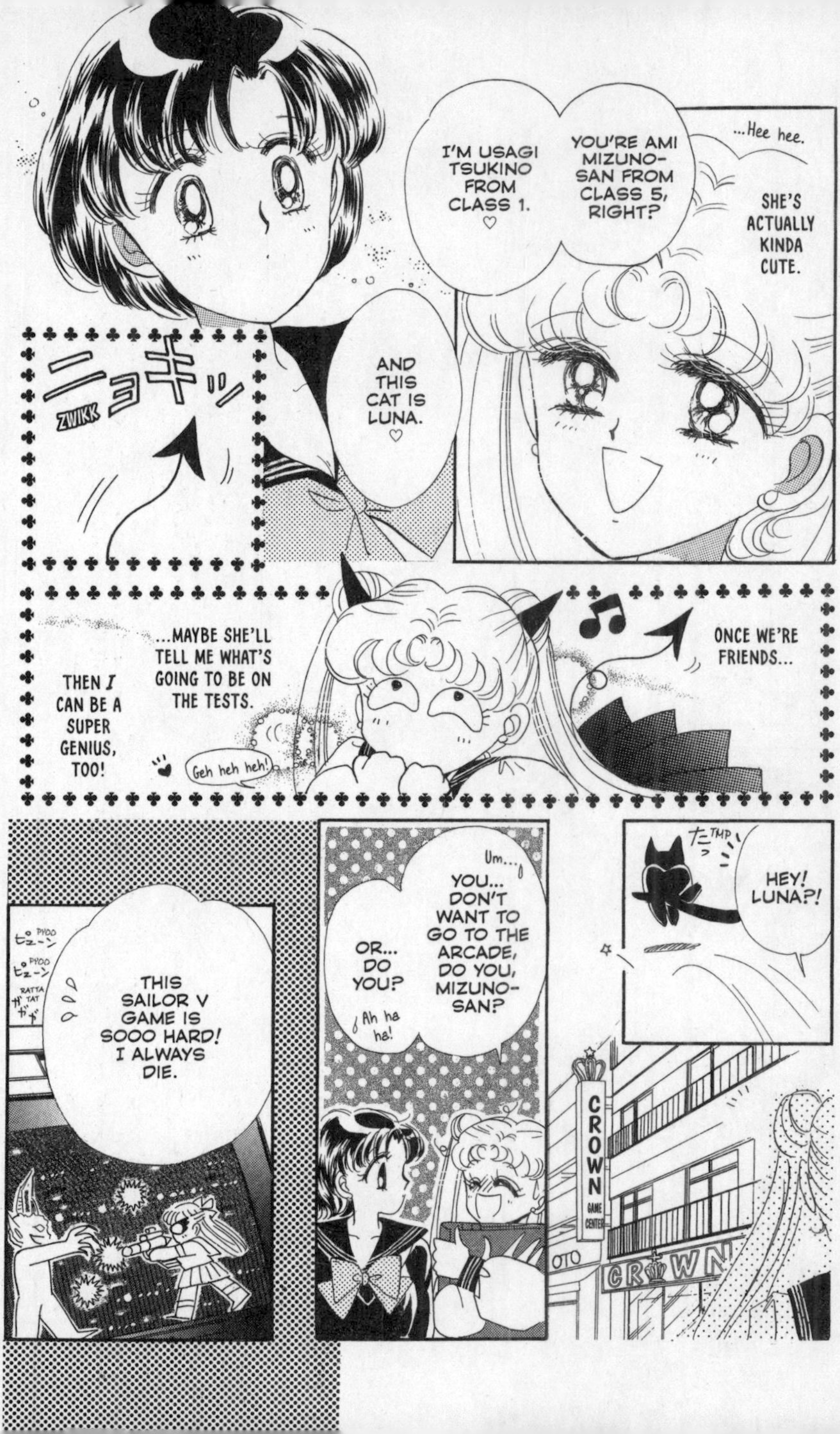
...Hee hee.
SHE'S ACTUALLY KINDA CUTE.
YOU'RE AMI MIZUNO-SAN FROM CLASS 5, RIGHT?
I'M USAGI TSUKINO FROM CLASS 1. ♡
AND THIS CAT IS LUNA. ♡
ニョキッ
ZWIKK
ONCE WE'RE FRIENDS...
...MAYBE SHE'LL TELL ME WHAT'S GOING TO BE ON THE TESTS.
THEN I CAN BE A SUPER GENIUS, TOO!
Geh heh heh!
タ TMP
HEY! LUNA?!
CROWN
GAME CENTER
CROWN
Um...
YOU... DON'T WANT TO GO TO THE ARCADE, DO YOU, MIZUNO-SAN?
OR... DO YOU?
Ah ha ha!
ピューン PYOO
ピューン PYOO
ガガ RATTA TAT
THIS SAILOR V GAME IS SOOO HARD! I ALWAYS DIE.

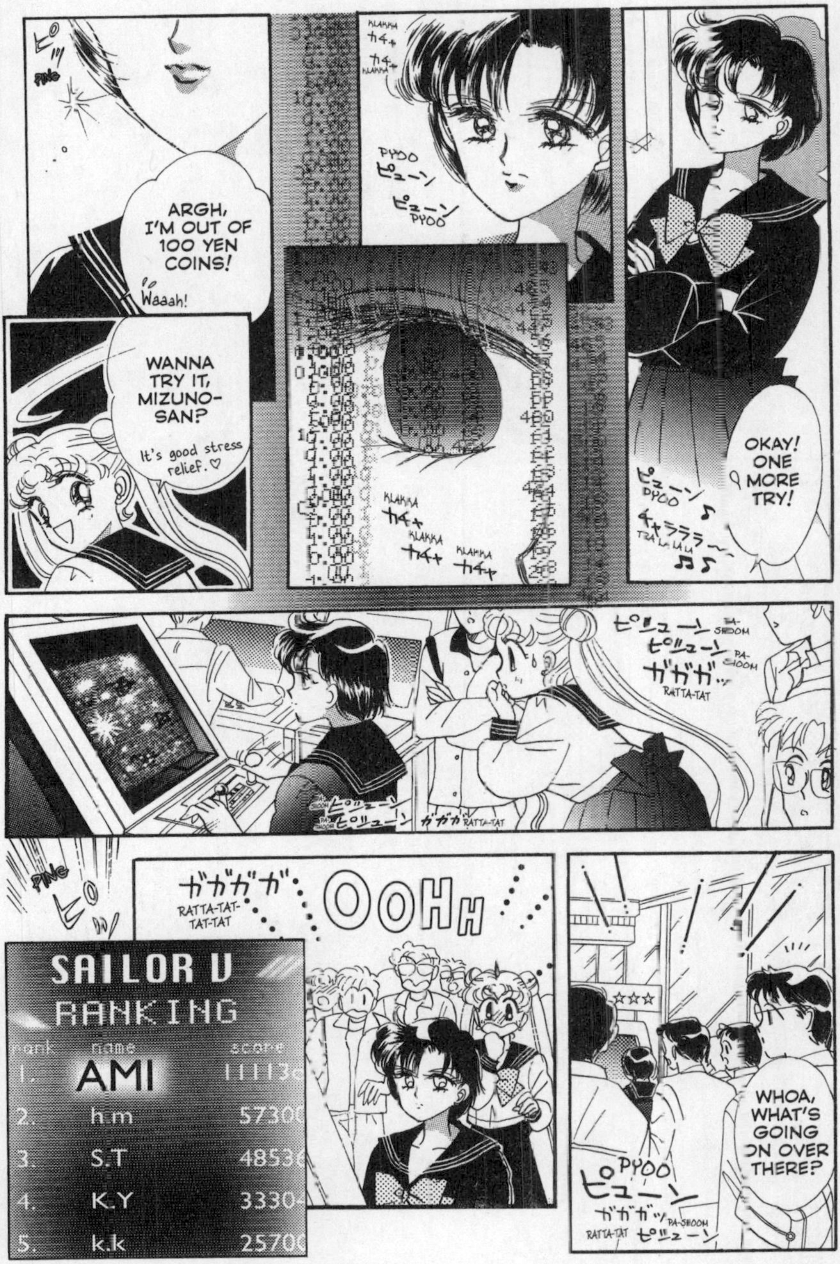

KLAKKA
カチャ
カチャ
KLAKKA
PYOO
ピューン
ピューン
PYOO
ピ
PING
ARGH, I'M OUT OF 100 YEN COINS!
Waaah!
KLAKKA
カチャ
KLAKKA
カチャ
KLAKKA
カチャ
WANNA TRY IT, MIZUNO-SAN?
It's good stress relief. ♡
OKAY! ONE MORE TRY!
ピューン
PYOO
チャラララ〜
TRA LA LA LA
ピシューン
PA-SHOOM
ピシューン
PA-SHOOM
ガガガッ
RATTA-TAT
ピシューン
ピシューン
ガガガ
RATTA-TAT
WHOA, WHAT'S GOING ON OVER THERE?
PYOO
ピューン
ガガガッ
RATTA-TAT
PA-SHOOM
ピシューン
OOHH
ガガガガ
RATTA-TAT-TAT-TAT
PING
ピ
SAILOR V
RANKING
rank name score
1. AMI 11113
2. h.m 57300
3. S.T 48536
4. K.Y 3330
5. k.k 25700

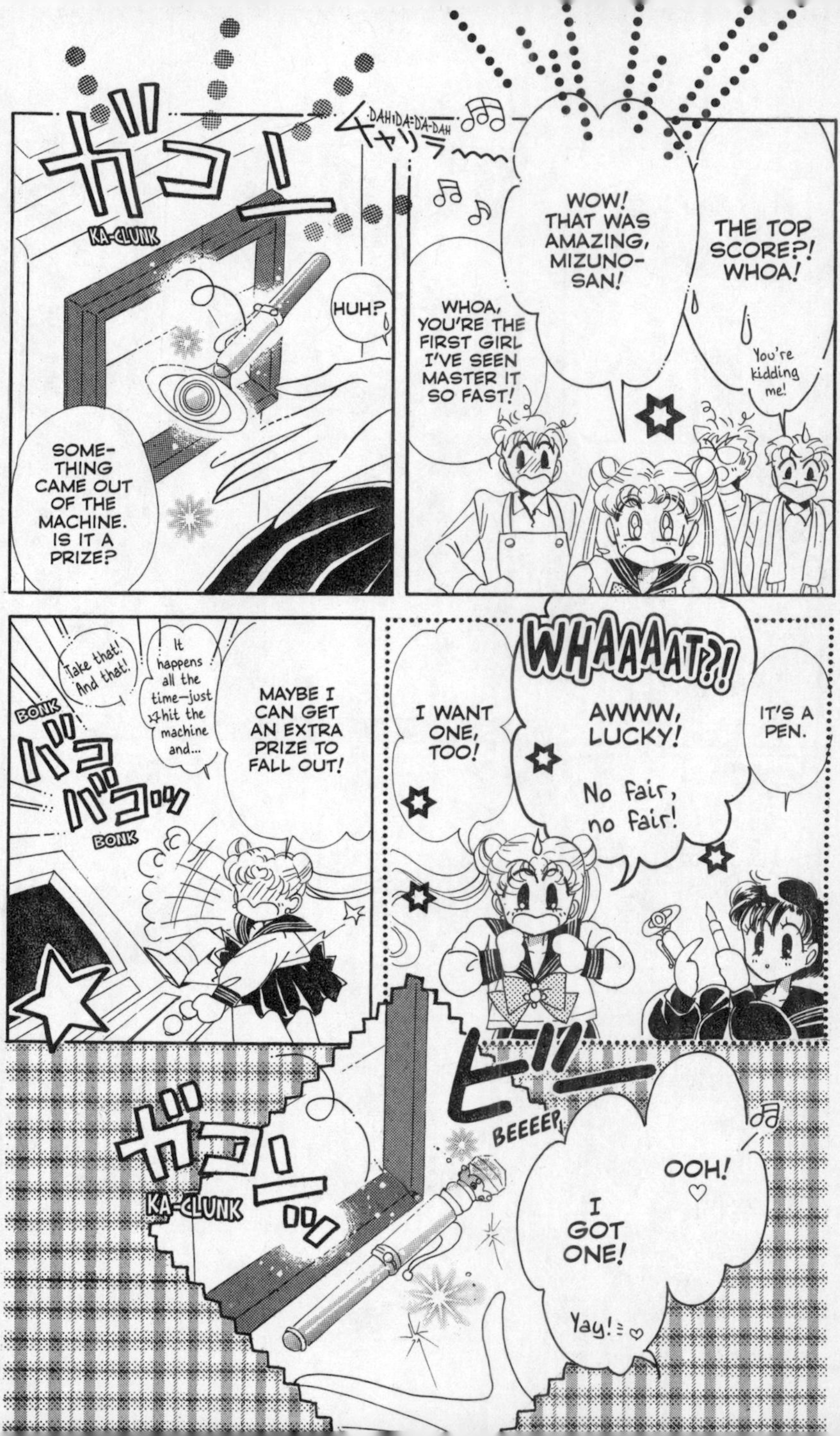
DAHIDA-DA-DAH
THE TOP SCORE?! WHOA!
You're kidding me!
WOW! THAT WAS AMAZING, MIZUNO-SAN!
WHOA, YOU'RE THE FIRST GIRL I'VE SEEN MASTER IT SO FAST!
KA-CLUNK
HUH?
SOME-THING CAME OUT OF THE MACHINE. IS IT A PRIZE?
IT'S A PEN.
WHAAAAT?!
AWWW, LUCKY!
No fair, no fair!
I WANT ONE, TOO!
MAYBE I CAN GET AN EXTRA PRIZE TO FALL OUT!
It happens all the time—just hit the machine and...
Take that! And that!
BONK
BONK
OOH!
I GOT ONE!
Yay!
BEEEEP
KA-CLUNK

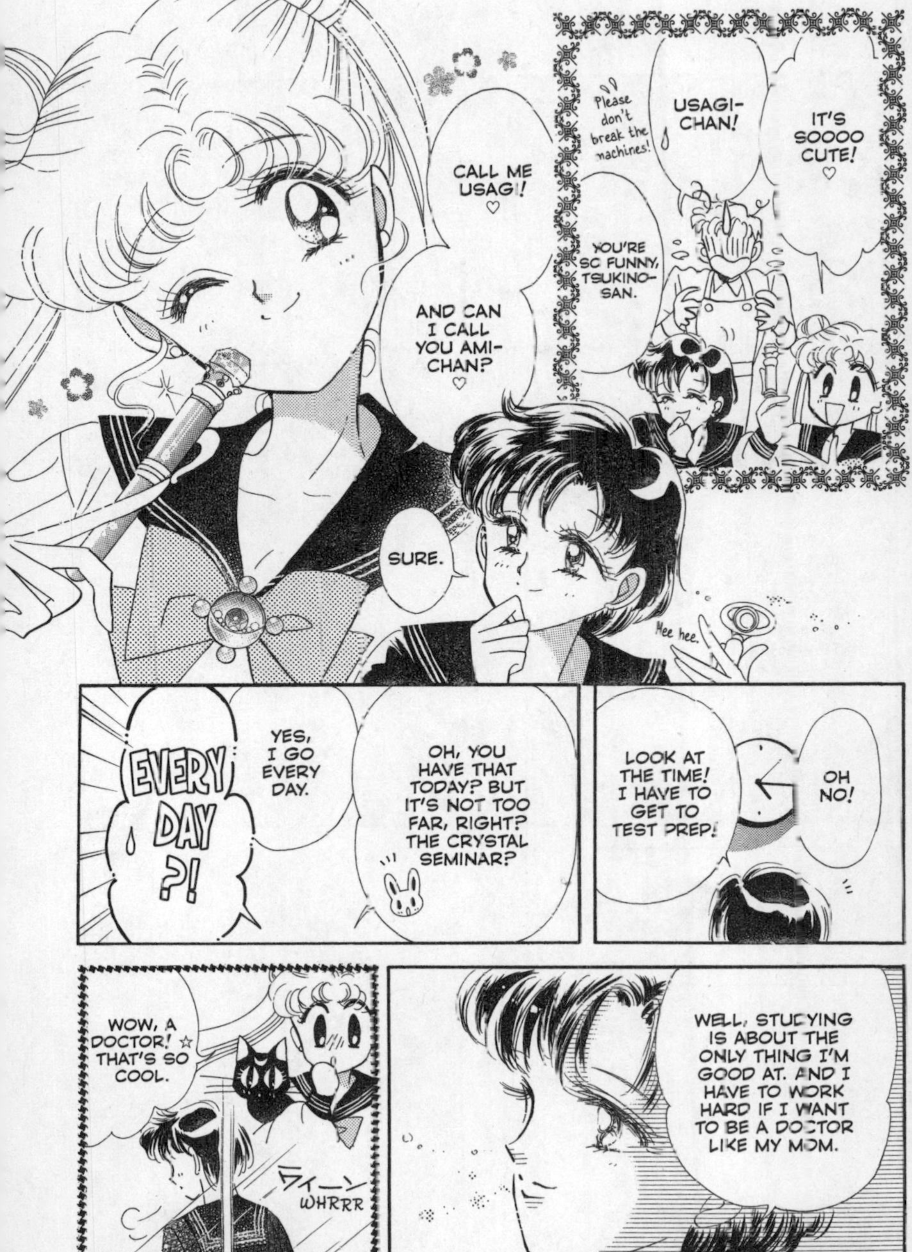
IT'S SOOOO CUTE! ♡
USAGI-CHAN!
Please don't break the machines!
YOU'RE SO FUNNY, TSUKINO-SAN.
CALL ME USAGI! ♡
AND CAN I CALL YOU AMI-CHAN? ♡
SURE.
Hee hee.
OH NO!
LOOK AT THE TIME! I HAVE TO GET TO TEST PREP!
OH, YOU HAVE THAT TODAY? BUT IT'S NOT TOO FAR, RIGHT? THE CRYSTAL SEMINAR?
YES, I GO EVERY DAY.
EVERY DAY ?!
WELL, STUDYING IS ABOUT THE ONLY THING I'M GOOD AT. AND I HAVE TO WORK HARD IF I WANT TO BE A DOCTOR LIKE MY MOM.
WOW, A DOCTOR! ☆ THAT'S SO COOL.
ウィーン
WHRRR

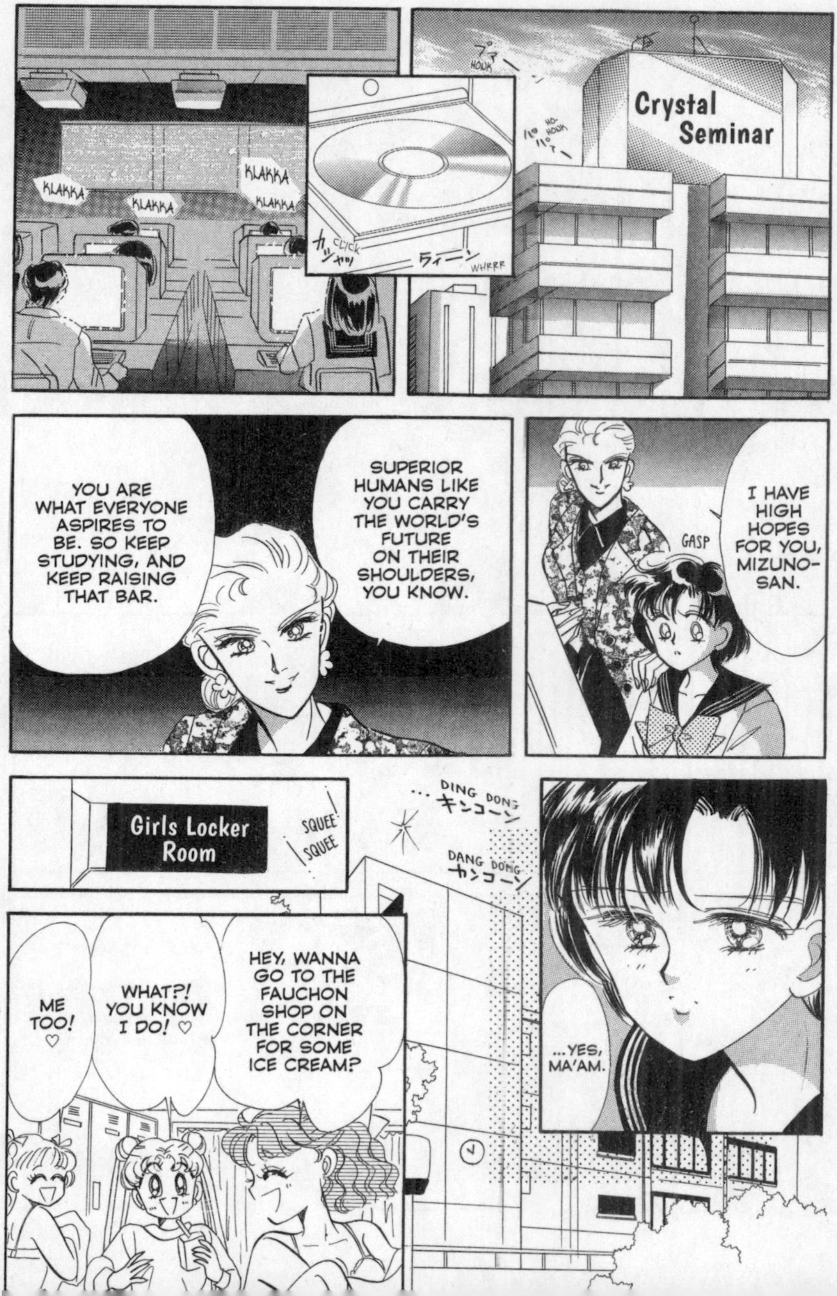
HOOK
HO-HOOK
Crystal Seminar
CLICK
WHRRR
KLAKKA
KLAKKA
KLAKKA
KLAKKA
GASP
I HAVE HIGH HOPES FOR YOU, MIZUNO-SAN.
SUPERIOR HUMANS LIKE YOU CARRY THE WORLD'S FUTURE ON THEIR SHOULDERS, YOU KNOW.
YOU ARE WHAT EVERYONE ASPIRES TO BE. SO KEEP STUDYING, AND KEEP RAISING THAT BAR.
...YES, MA'AM.
DING DONG キンコーン
DANG DONG カンコーン
Girls Locker Room
SQUEE
SQUEE
HEY, WANNA GO TO THE FAUCHON SHOP ON THE CORNER FOR SOME ICE CREAM?
WHAT?! YOU KNOW I DO! ♡
ME TOO! ♡

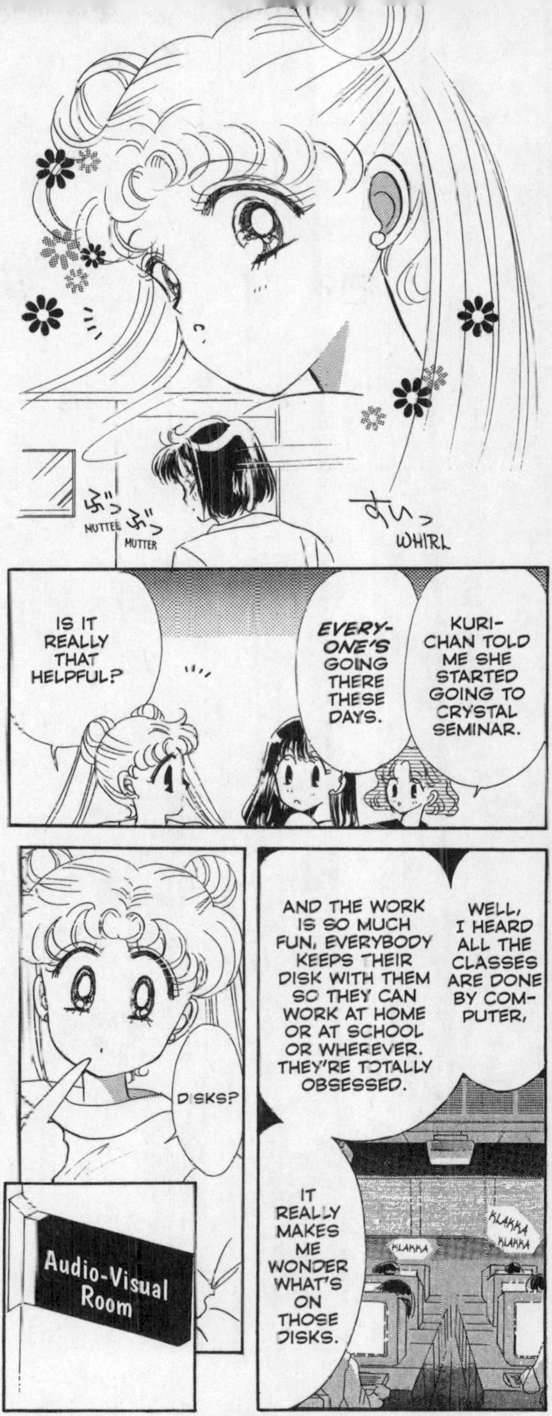

すいっ
WHIRL
ぶっ
MUTTEE
ぶっ
MUTTER
KURI-CHAN TOLD ME SHE STARTED GOING TO CRYSTAL SEMINAR.
EVERYONE'S GOING THERE THESE DAYS.
IS IT REALLY THAT HELPFUL?
WELL, I HEARD ALL THE CLASSES ARE DONE BY COMPUTER,
AND THE WORK IS SO MUCH FUN, EVERYBODY KEEPS THEIR DISK WITH THEM SO THEY CAN WORK AT HOME OR AT SCHOOL OR WHEREVER. THEY'RE TOTALLY OBSESSED.
KLAKKA KLAKKA
KLAKKA
IT REALLY MAKES ME WONDER WHAT'S ON THOSE DISKS.
DISKS?
Audio-Visual Room

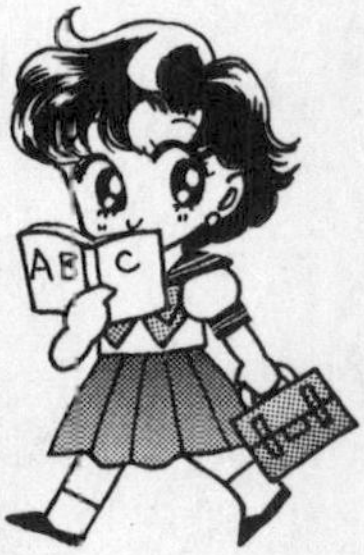

AB C

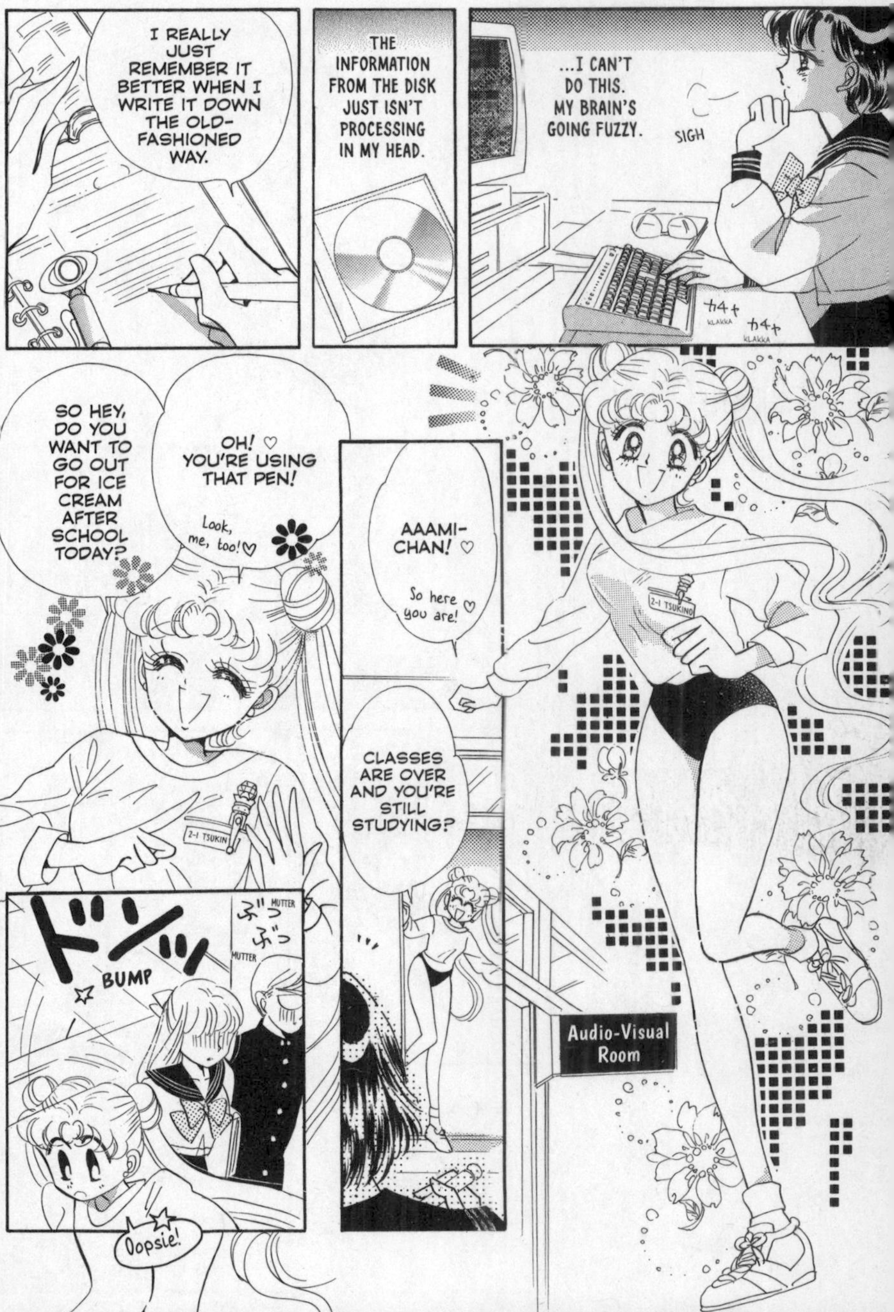
...I CAN'T DO THIS. MY BRAIN'S GOING FUZZY.
SIGH
KLAKKA
KLAKKA
THE INFORMATION FROM THE DISK JUST ISN'T PROCESSING IN MY HEAD.
I REALLY JUST REMEMBER IT BETTER WHEN I WRITE IT DOWN THE OLD-FASHIONED WAY.
2-1 TSUKINO
Audio-Visual Room
AAAMI-CHAN! ♡
So here you are! ♡
CLASSES ARE OVER AND YOU'RE STILL STUDYING?
OH! ♡ YOU'RE USING THAT PEN!
Look, me, too! ♡
SO HEY, DO YOU WANT TO GO OUT FOR ICE CREAM AFTER SCHOOL TODAY?
2-1 TSUKIN
ぶつ MUTTER
ぶつ MUTTER
BUMP
Oopsie!

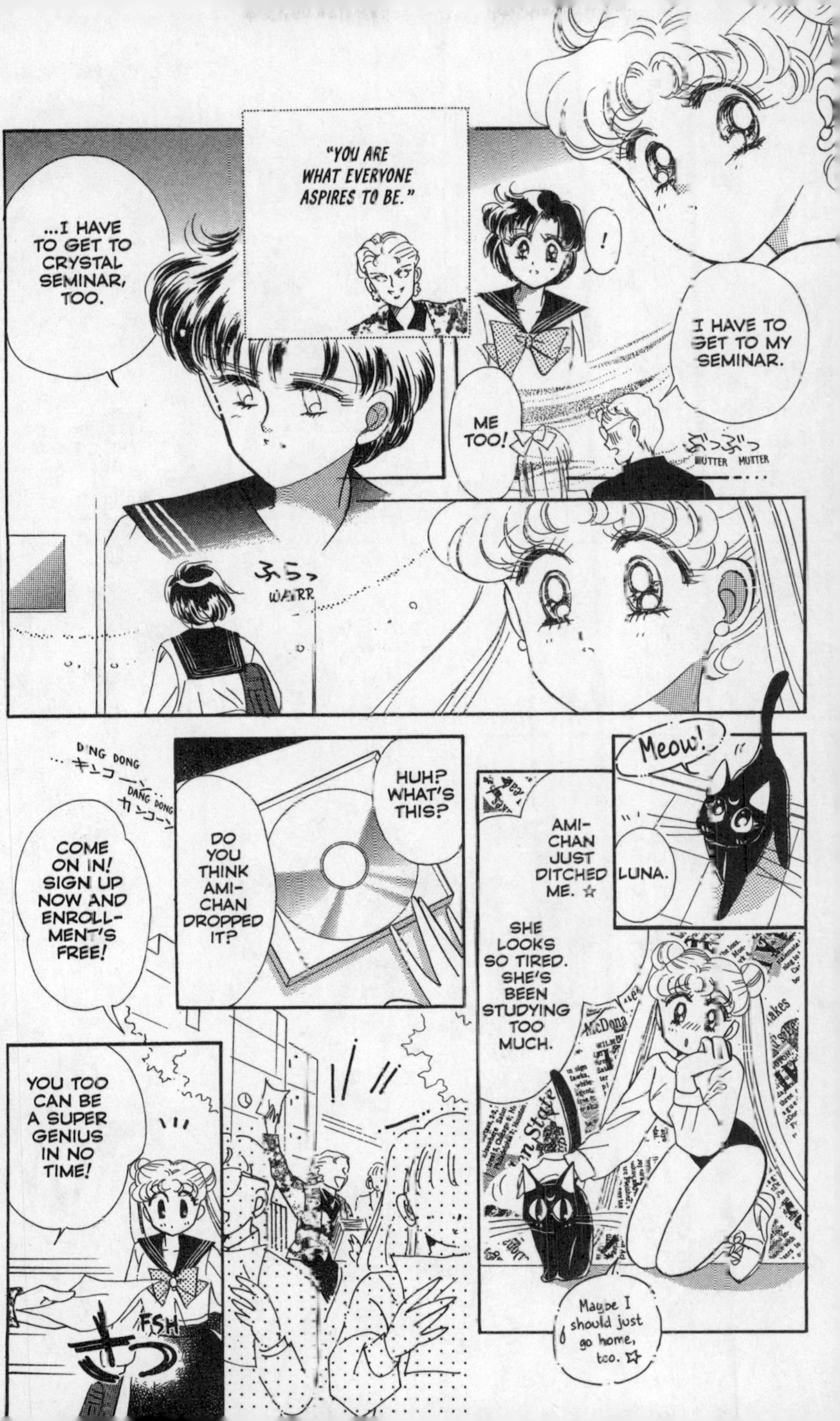

I HAVE TO GET TO MY SEMINAR.
!
ぶつぶつ
MUTTER MUTTER
ME TOO!
"YOU ARE WHAT EVERYONE ASPIRES TO BE."
...I HAVE TO GET TO CRYSTAL SEMINAR, TOO.
ふらっ
WAFRR
Meow!
LUNA.
AMI-CHAN JUST DITCHED ME. ☆
SHE LOOKS SO TIRED. SHE'S BEEN STUDYING TOO MUCH.
Maybe I should just go home, too. ☆
HUH? WHAT'S THIS?
DO YOU THINK AMI-CHAN DROPPED IT?
DING DONG
キンコーン
DANG DONG
カンコーン
COME ON IN! SIGN UP NOW AND ENROLLMENT'S FREE!
YOU TOO CAN BE A SUPER GENIUS IN NO TIME!
FSH
さっ

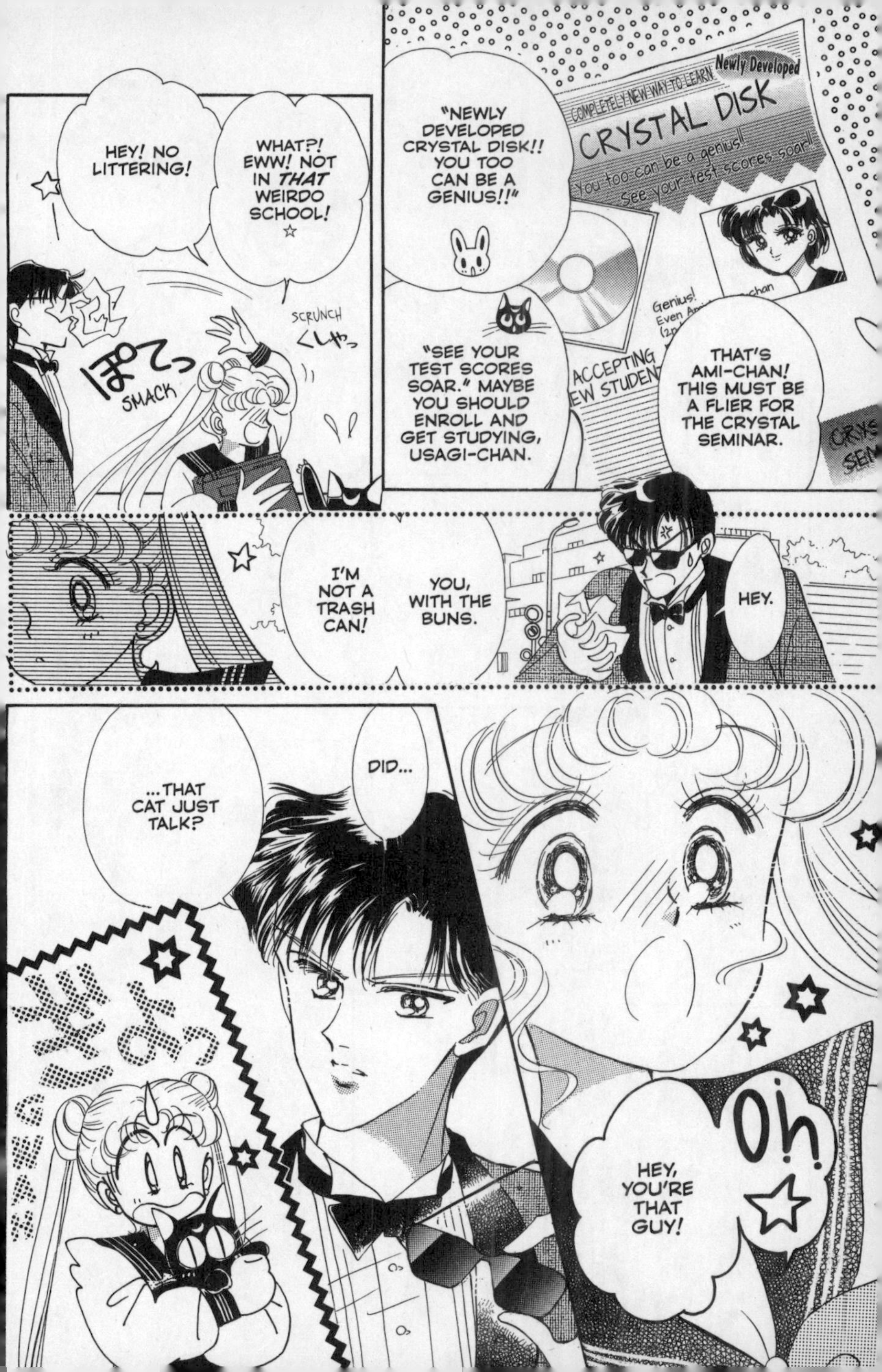
Newly Developed
COMPLETELY NEW WAY TO LEARN
CRYSTAL DISK
You too can be a genius!!
See your test scores soar!!
"NEWLY DEVELOPED CRYSTAL DISK!! YOU TOO CAN BE A GENIUS!!"
THAT'S AMI-CHAN! THIS MUST BE A FLIER FOR THE CRYSTAL SEMINAR.
"SEE YOUR TEST SCORES SOAR." MAYBE YOU SHOULD ENROLL AND GET STUDYING, USAGI-CHAN.
WHAT?! EWW! NOT IN *THAT* WEIRDO SCHOOL!
HEY! NO LITTERING!
くしゃっ
SCRUNCH
ぽてっ
SMACK
HEY.
YOU, WITH THE BUNS.
I'M NOT A TRASH CAN!
Oh!
HEY, YOU'RE THAT GUY!
DID...
...THAT CAT JUST TALK?

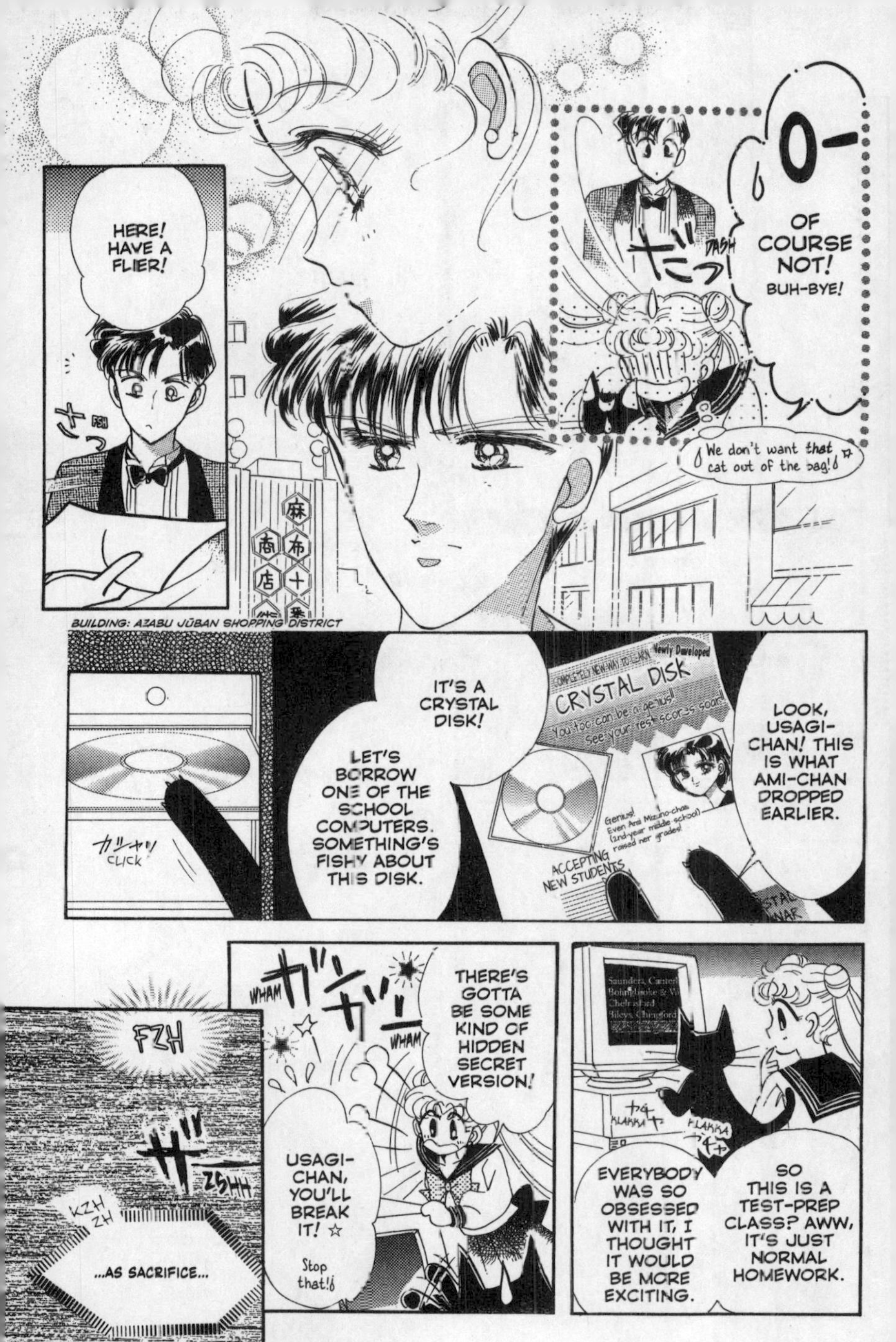
O-
OF COURSE NOT! BUH-BYE!
DASH
We don't want that cat out of the bag!
麻布十番商店街
BUILDING: AZABU JŪBAN SHOPPING DISTRICT
HERE! HAVE A FLIER!
FSH
LOOK, USAGI-CHAN! THIS IS WHAT AMI-CHAN DROPPED EARLIER.
Newly Developed
CRYSTAL DISK
You too can be a genius!! See your test scores soar!!
Genius! Even Ami Mizuno-chan (2nd-year middle school) raised her grades!
ACCEPTING NEW STUDENTS
IT'S A CRYSTAL DISK!
LET'S BORROW ONE OF THE SCHOOL COMPUTERS. SOMETHING'S FISHY ABOUT THIS DISK.
CLICK
SO THIS IS A TEST-PREP CLASS? AWW, IT'S JUST NORMAL HOMEWORK.
EVERYBODY WAS SO OBSESSED WITH IT, I THOUGHT IT WOULD BE MORE EXCITING.
KLAKKA
KLAKKA
THERE'S GOTTA BE SOME KIND OF HIDDEN SECRET VERSION!
WHAM
WHAM
USAGI-CHAN, YOU'LL BREAK IT! ☆
Stop that!
FZH
ZSHH
KZH ZH
...AS SACRIFICE...

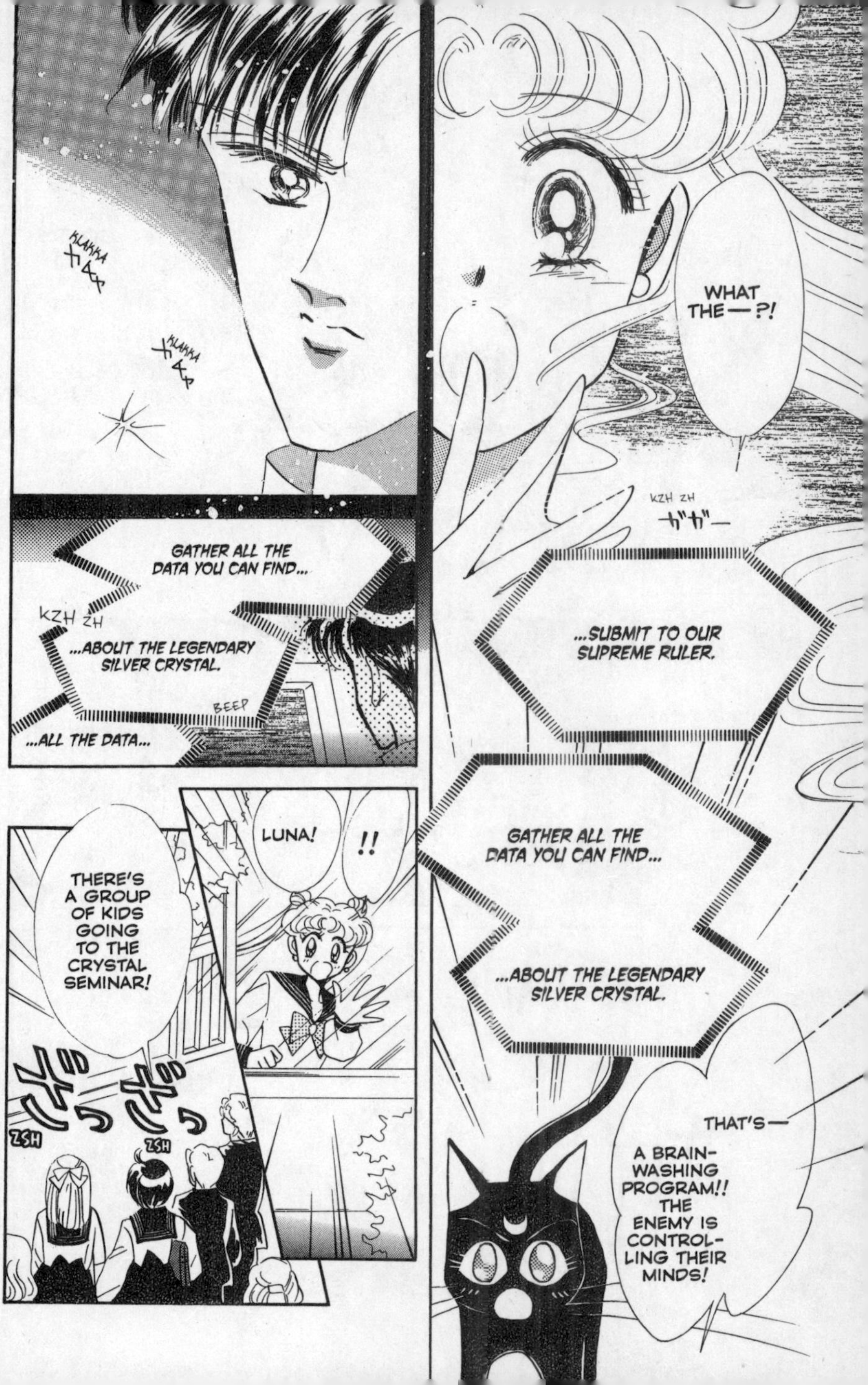
WHAT THE—?!
KZH ZH
...SUBMIT TO OUR SUPREME RULER.
GATHER ALL THE DATA YOU CAN FIND...
...ABOUT THE LEGENDARY SILVER CRYSTAL.
THAT'S—
A BRAIN-WASHING PROGRAM!! THE ENEMY IS CONTROL-LING THEIR MINDS!
KLAKKA
KLAKKA
GATHER ALL THE DATA YOU CAN FIND...
KZH ZH
...ABOUT THE LEGENDARY SILVER CRYSTAL.
BEEP
...ALL THE DATA...
!!
LUNA!
THERE'S A GROUP OF KIDS GOING TO THE CRYSTAL SEMINAR!
ZSH
ZSH

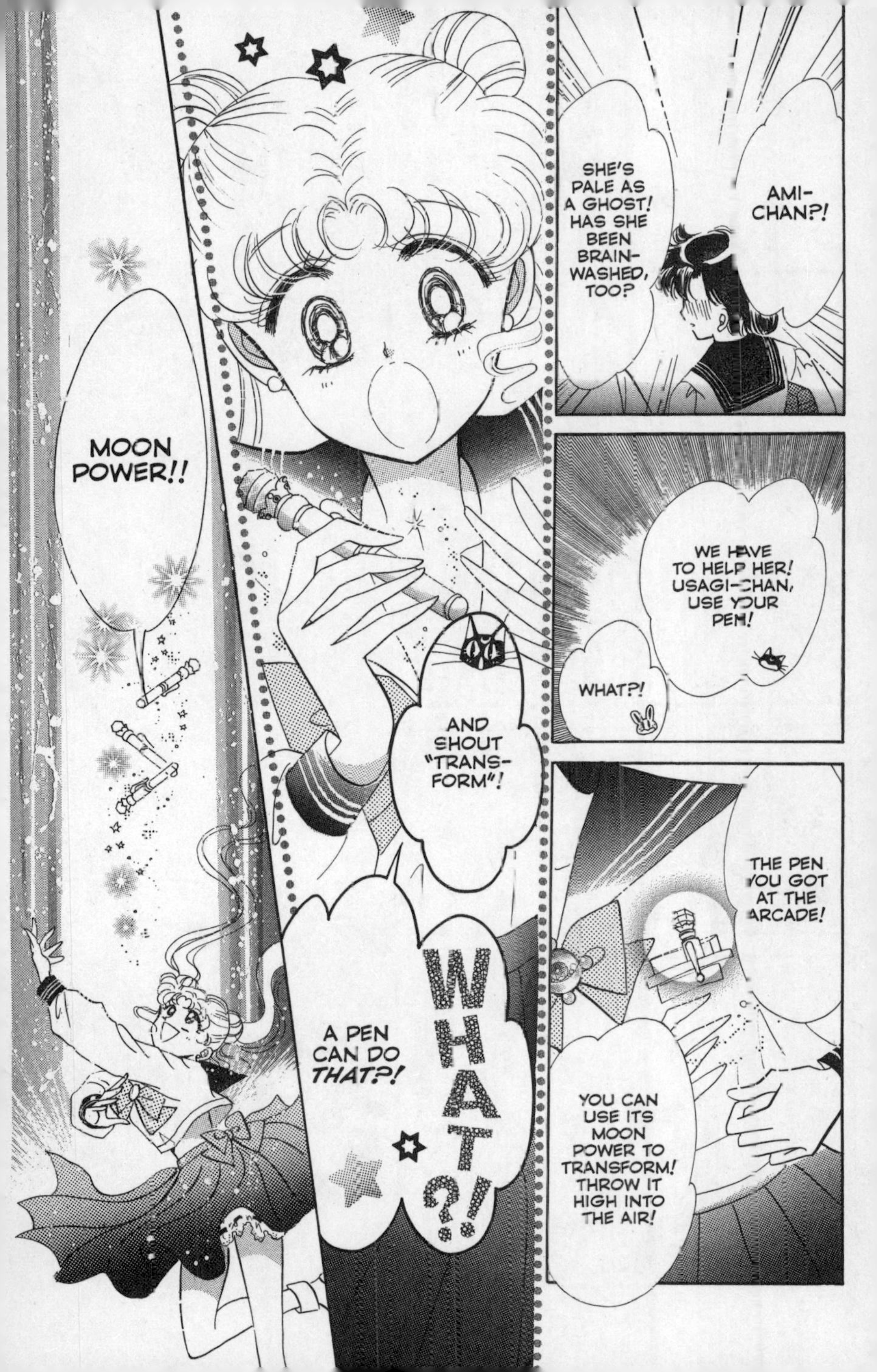
AMI-CHAN?!
SHE'S PALE AS A GHOST! HAS SHE BEEN BRAIN-WASHED, TOO?
WE HAVE TO HELP HER! USAGI-CHAN, USE YOUR PEN!
WHAT?!
THE PEN YOU GOT AT THE ARCADE!
YOU CAN USE ITS MOON POWER TO TRANSFORM! THROW IT HIGH INTO THE AIR!
AND SHOUT "TRANSFORM"!
WHAT?!
A PEN CAN DO *THAT*?!
MOON POWER!!

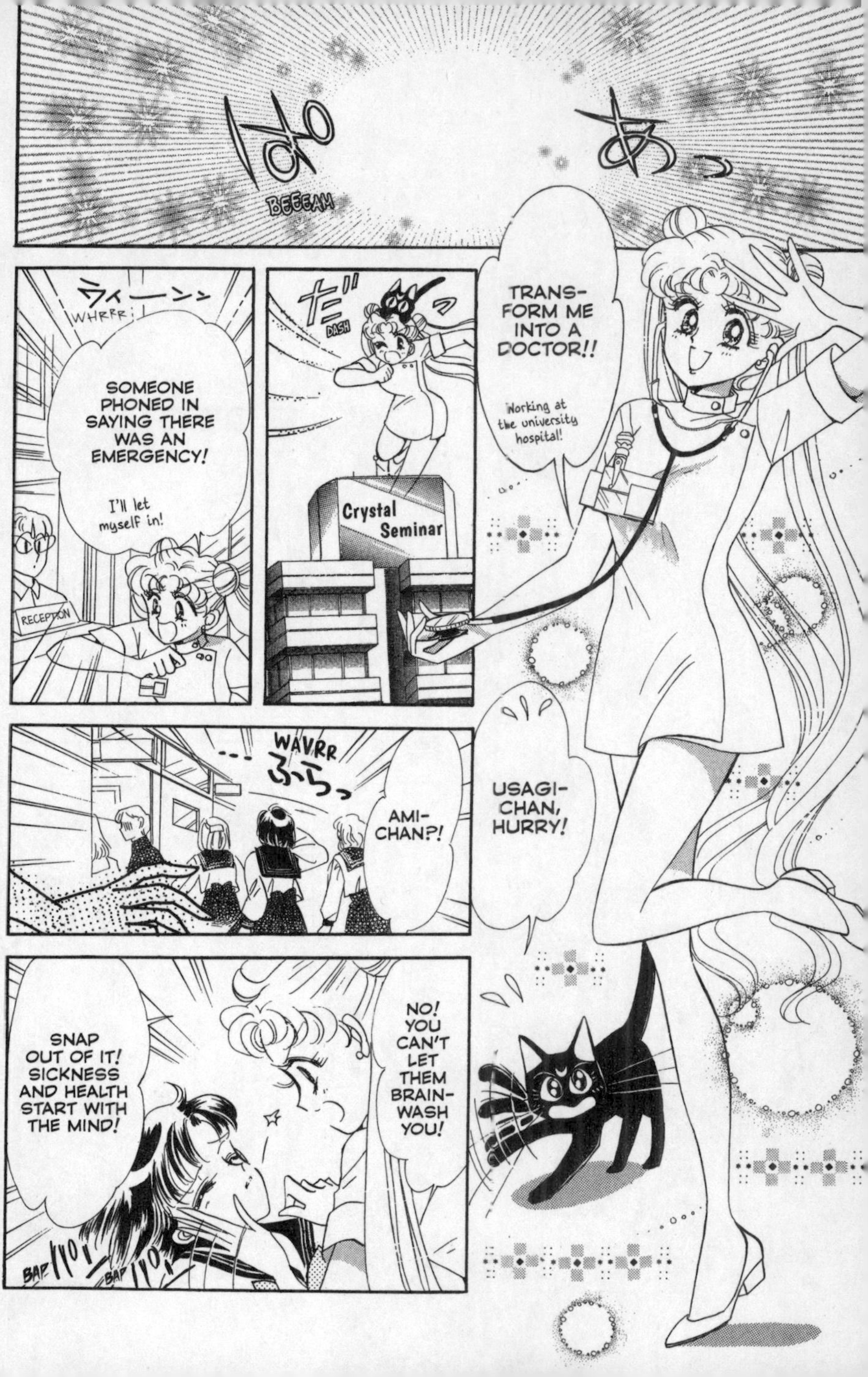
ぱあっ
BEEEAM
TRANS-FORM ME INTO A DOCTOR!!
Working at the university hospital!
USAGI-CHAN, HURRY!
だっ
DASH
Crystal Seminar
ウィーンン
WHRRR
SOMEONE PHONED IN SAYING THERE WAS AN EMERGENCY!
I'll let myself in!
RECEPTION
...
WAVRR
ふらっ
AMI-CHAN?!
NO! YOU CAN'T LET THEM BRAIN-WASH YOU!
SNAP OUT OF IT! SICKNESS AND HEALTH START WITH THE MIND!
パン
BAP
パン
BAP

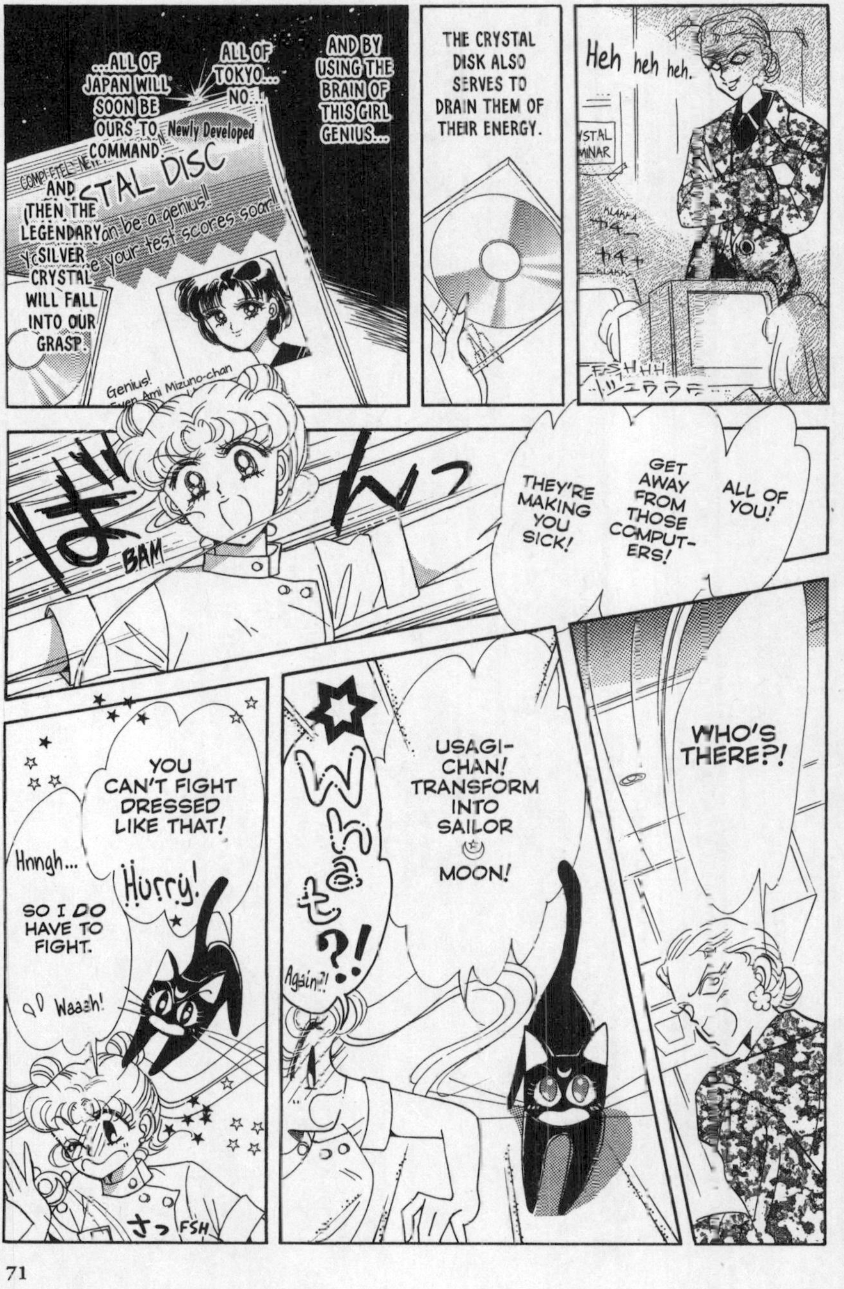
Heh heh heh.
KLAKKA
KLAKKA
FSHHH
THE CRYSTAL DISK ALSO SERVES TO DRAIN THEM OF THEIR ENERGY.
AND BY USING THE BRAIN OF THIS GIRL GENIUS...
ALL OF TOKYO... NO...
...ALL OF JAPAN WILL SOON BE OURS TO COMMAND
Newly Developed
AND THEN THE LEGENDARY SILVER CRYSTAL WILL FALL INTO OUR GRASP.
Genius! Even Ami Mizuno-chan
ALL OF YOU!
GET AWAY FROM THOSE COMPUTERS!
THEY'RE MAKING YOU SICK!
BAM
WHO'S THERE?!
USAGI-CHAN! TRANSFORM INTO SAILOR MOON!
What?!
Again?!
YOU CAN'T FIGHT DRESSED LIKE THAT!
Hurry!
Hnngh...
SO I DO HAVE TO FIGHT.
Waaah!
FSH

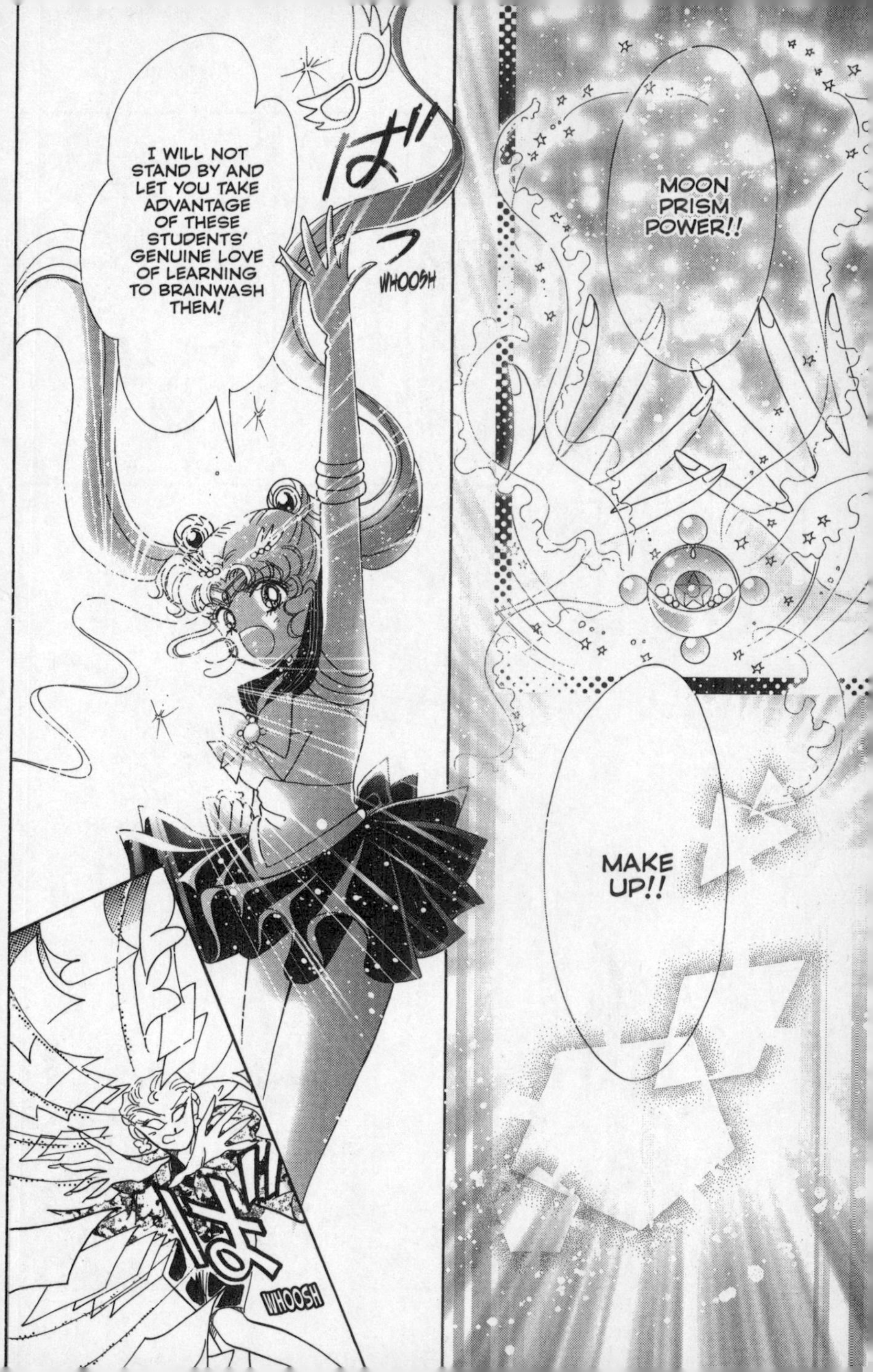
MOON PRISM POWER!!
MAKE UP!!
I WILL NOT STAND BY AND LET YOU TAKE ADVANTAGE OF THESE STUDENTS' GENUINE LOVE OF LEARNING TO BRAINWASH THEM!
ばっ
WHOOSH
WHOOSH

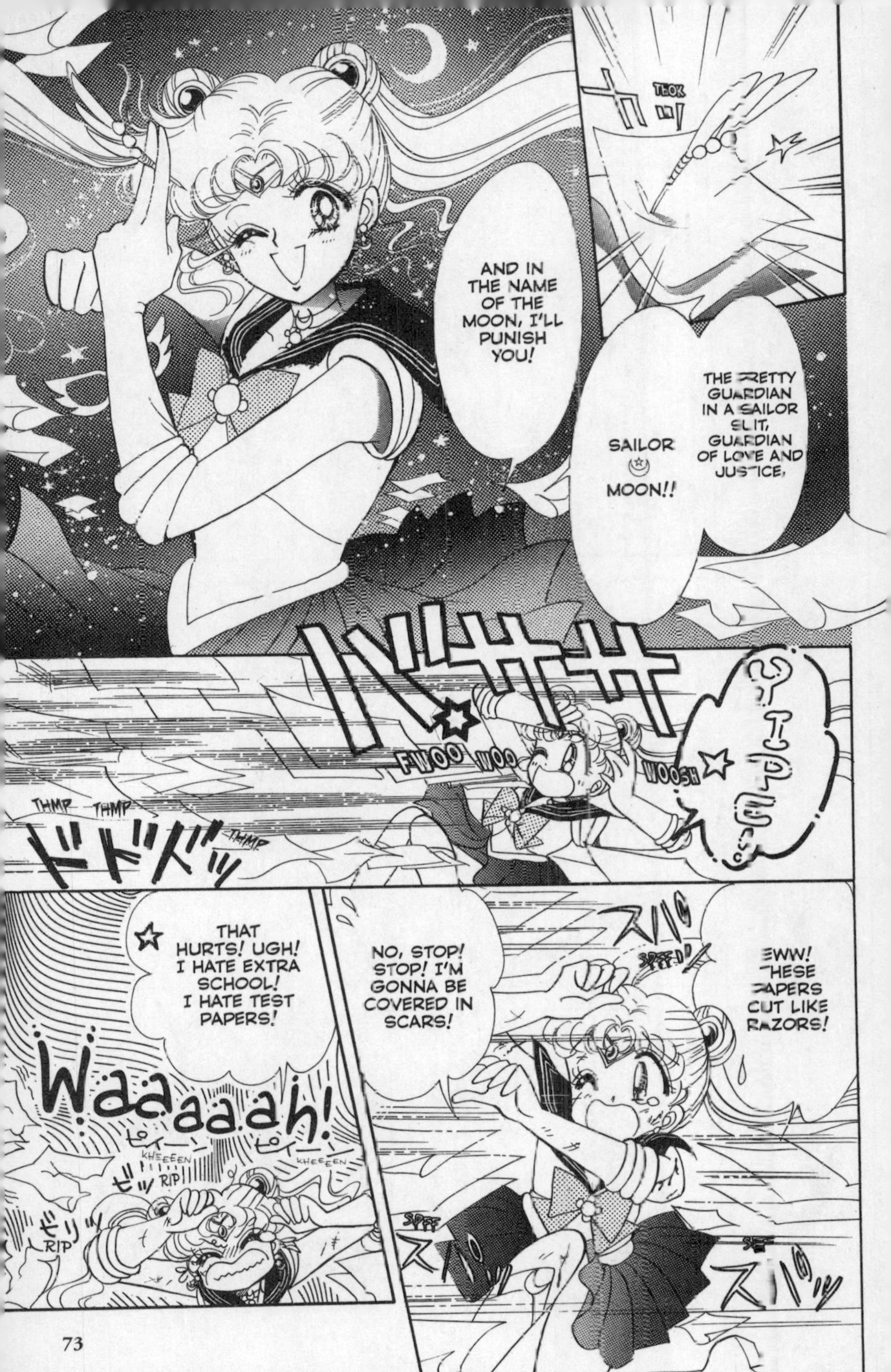
THOK
THE PRETTY GUARDIAN IN A SAILOR SUIT, GUARDIAN OF LOVE AND JUSTICE,
SAILOR MOON!!
AND IN THE NAME OF THE MOON, I'LL PUNISH YOU!
WOOSH
FWOO WOO
THMP THMP THMP
EWW! THESE PAPERS CUT LIKE RAZORS!
SPFFD
NO, STOP! STOP! I'M GONNA BE COVERED IN SCARS!
SPFF
SFF
THAT HURTS! UGH! I HATE EXTRA SCHOOL! I HATE TEST PAPERS!
Waaaaaah!
KHEEEEN
KHEEEEN
RIP
RIP

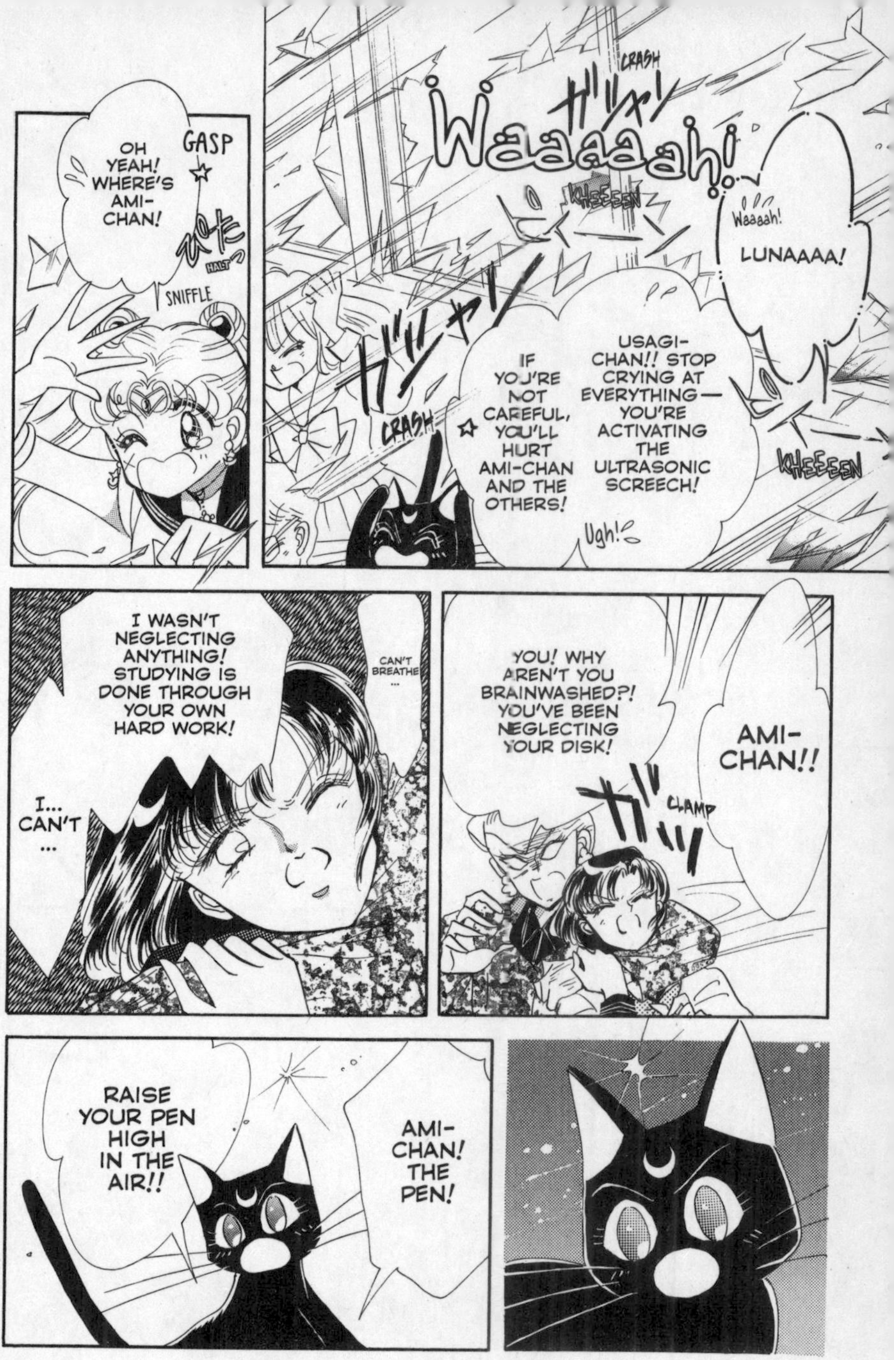
Waaaah!
LUNAAAA!
CRASH
Waaaaaah!
KHEEEEN
USAGI-CHAN!! STOP CRYING AT EVERYTHING—YOU'RE ACTIVATING THE ULTRASONIC SCREECH!
IF YOU'RE NOT CAREFUL, YOU'LL HURT AMI-CHAN AND THE OTHERS!
KHEEEEN
CRASH
Ugh!
GASP
OH YEAH! WHERE'S AMI-CHAN!
HALT
SNIFFLE
AMI-CHAN!!
YOU! WHY AREN'T YOU BRAINWASHED?! YOU'VE BEEN NEGLECTING YOUR DISK!
CLAMP
CAN'T BREATHE ...
I WASN'T NEGLECTING ANYTHING! STUDYING IS DONE THROUGH YOUR OWN HARD WORK!
I... CAN'T ...
AMI-CHAN! THE PEN!
RAISE YOUR PEN HIGH IN THE AIR!!

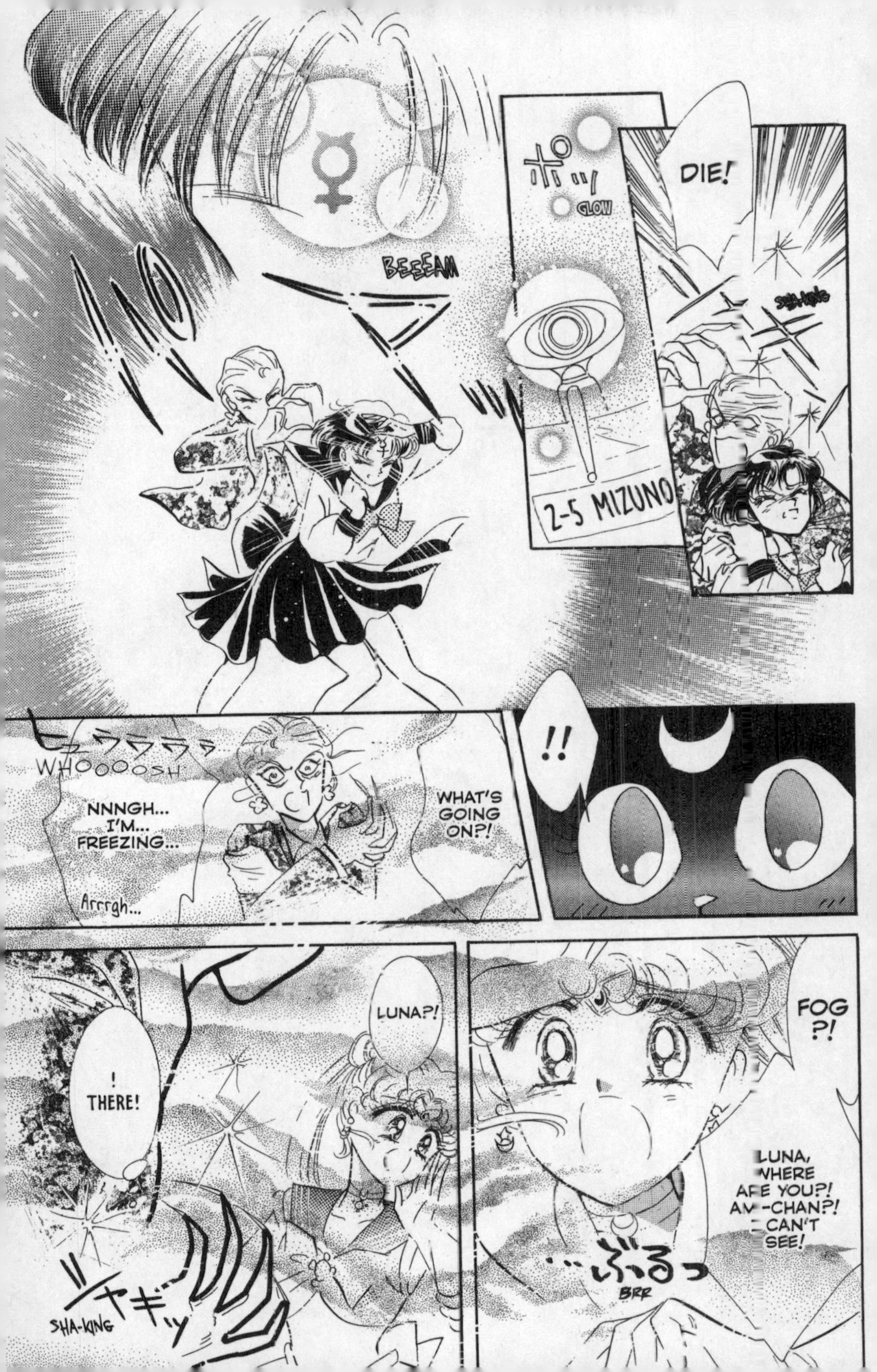
DIE!
SHA-KING
ポッ
GLOW
2-5 MIZUNO
BEEEAM
!!
ヒュウウウウ
WHOOOOOSH
WHAT'S GOING ON?!
NNNGH... I'M... FREEZING...
Arrrgh...
FOG ?!
LUNA, WHERE ARE YOU?! AMI-CHAN?! I CAN'T SEE!
...ぶるっ
BRR
LUNA?!
! THERE!
シャギッ
SHA-KING

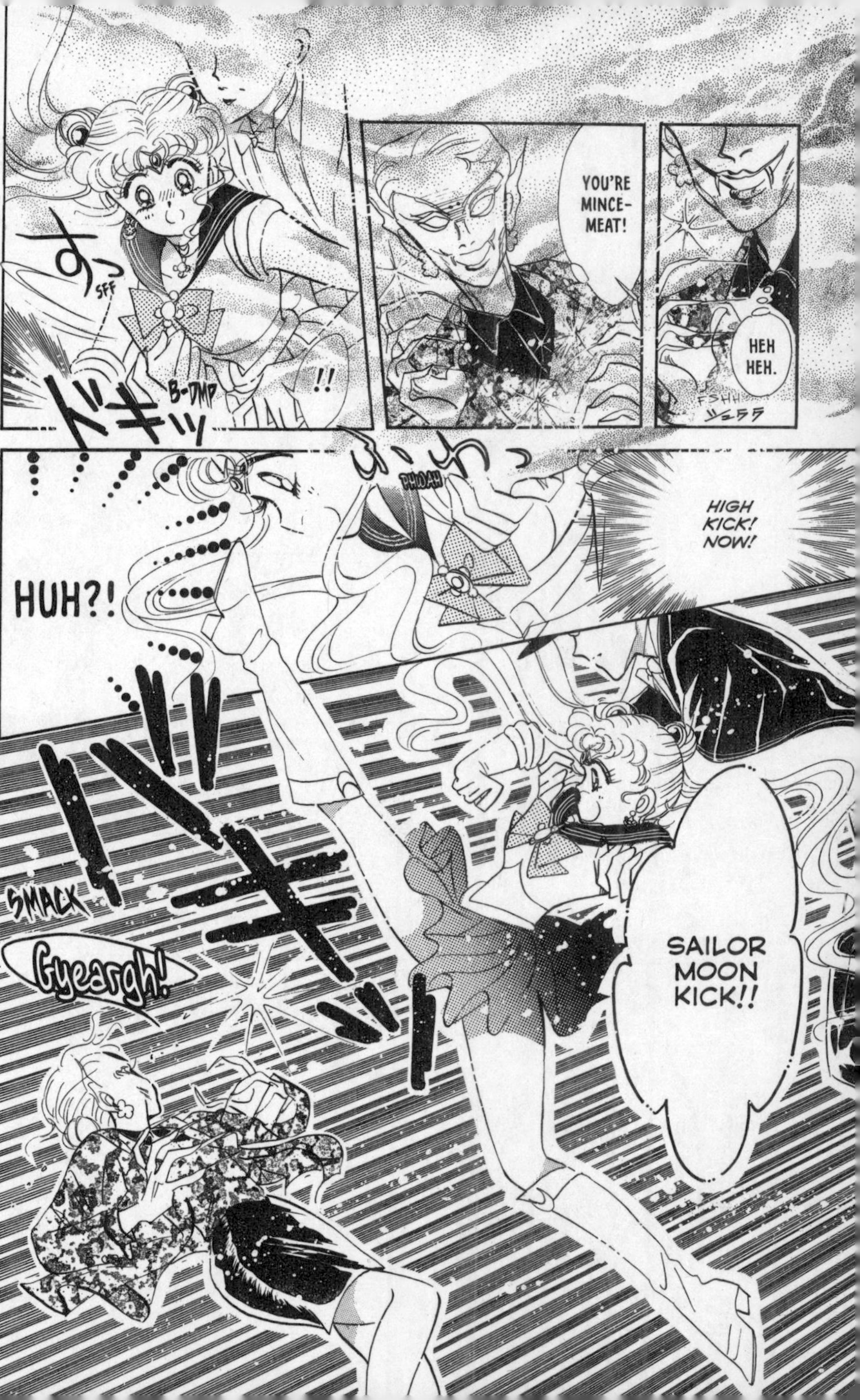
HEH HEH.
FSHH
YOU'RE MINCE-MEAT!
SFF
B-DMP
!!
HIGH KICK! NOW!
PHOAH
HUH?!
SAILOR MOON KICK!!
SMACK
Gyeargh!

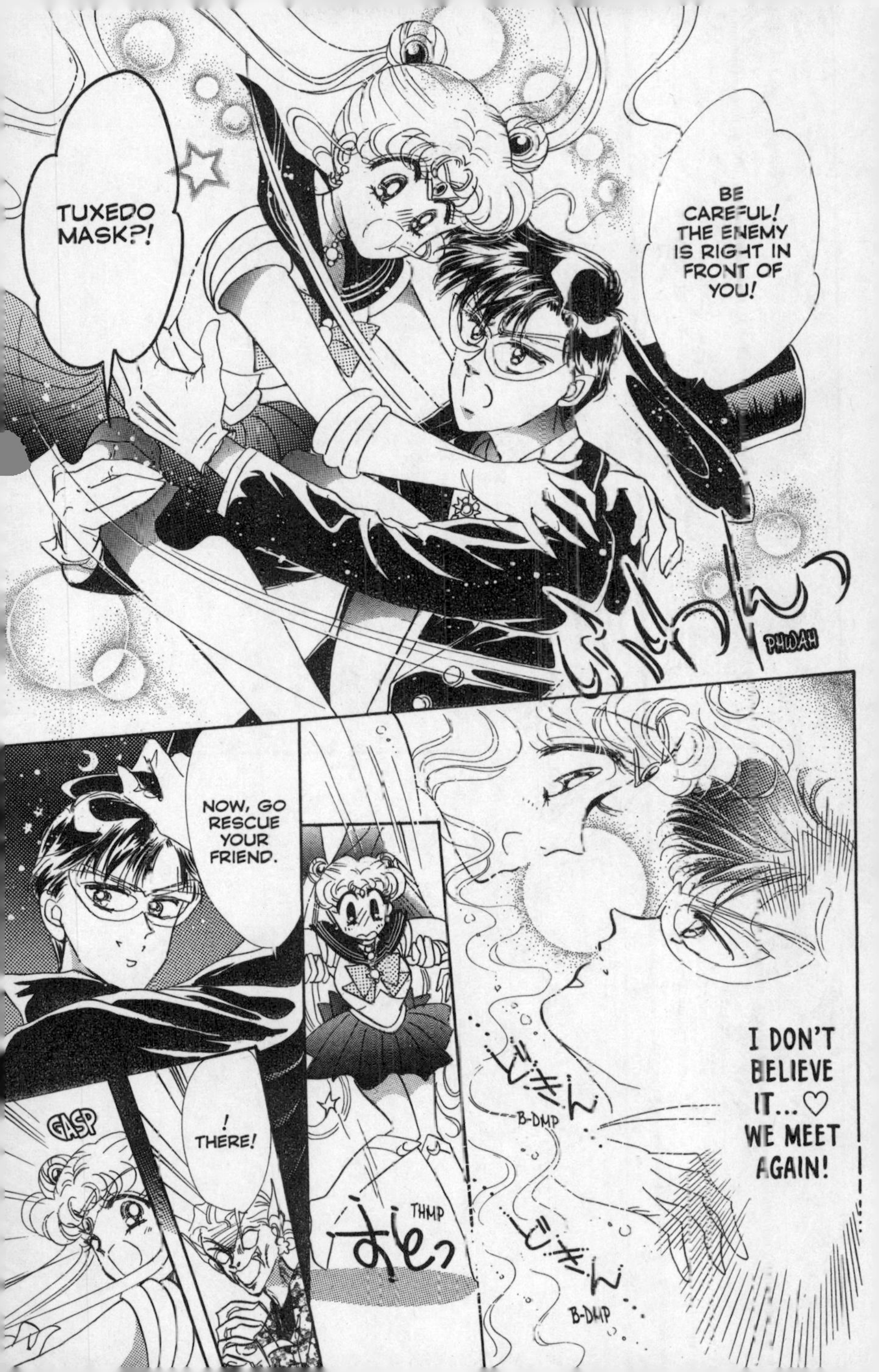
BE CAREFUL! THE ENEMY IS RIGHT IN FRONT OF YOU!
TUXEDO MASK?!
PHWAH
I DON'T BELIEVE IT... ♡ WE MEET AGAIN!
B-DMP
B-DMP
THMP
NOW, GO RESCUE YOUR FRIEND.
GASP
! THERE!

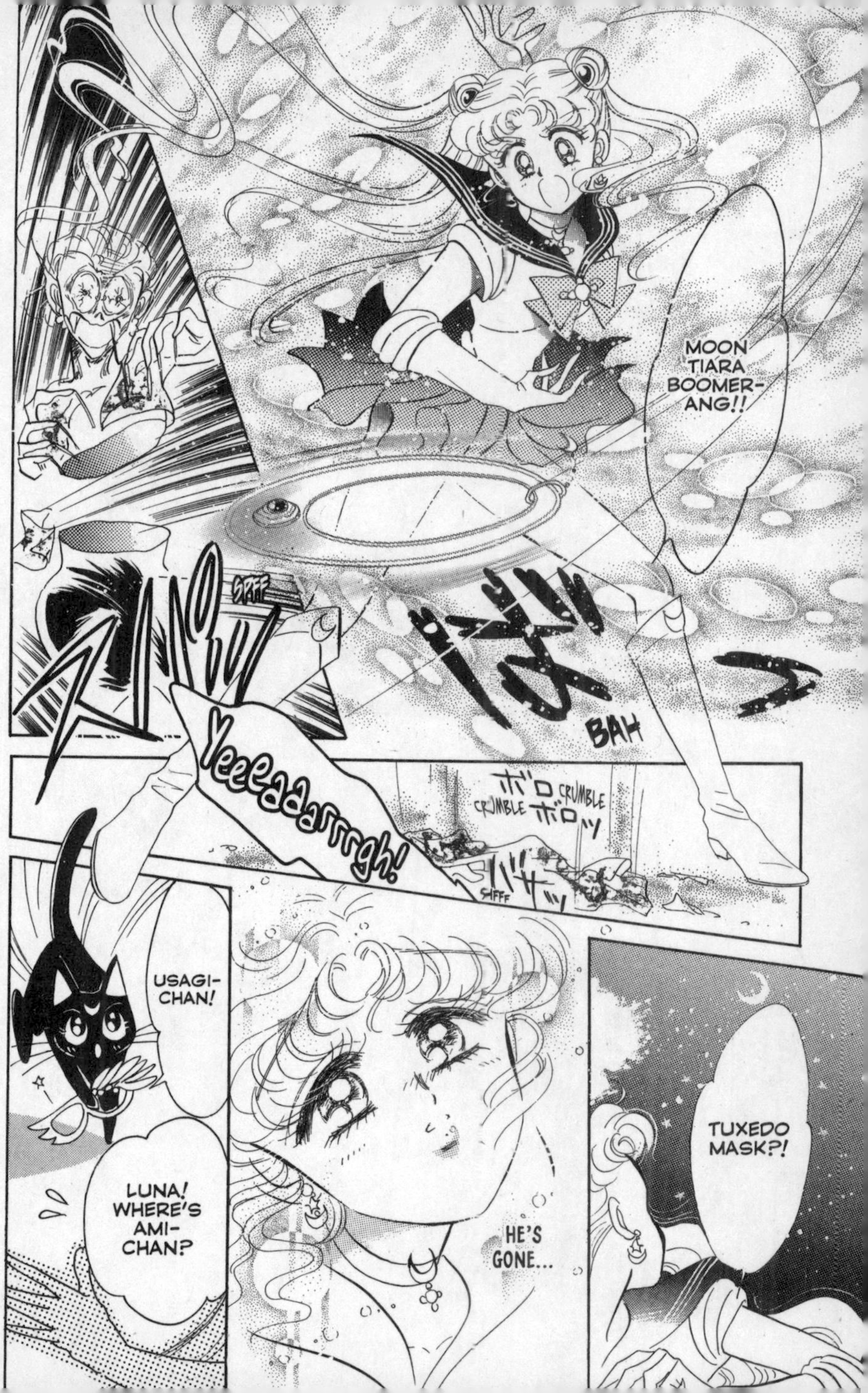
MOON TIARA BOOMER-ANG!!
SPFF
BAH
Yeeeaaarrrgh!
CRUMBLE CRUMBLE
SHFFF
TUXEDO MASK?!
HE'S GONE...
USAGI-CHAN!
LUNA! WHERE'S AMI-CHAN?

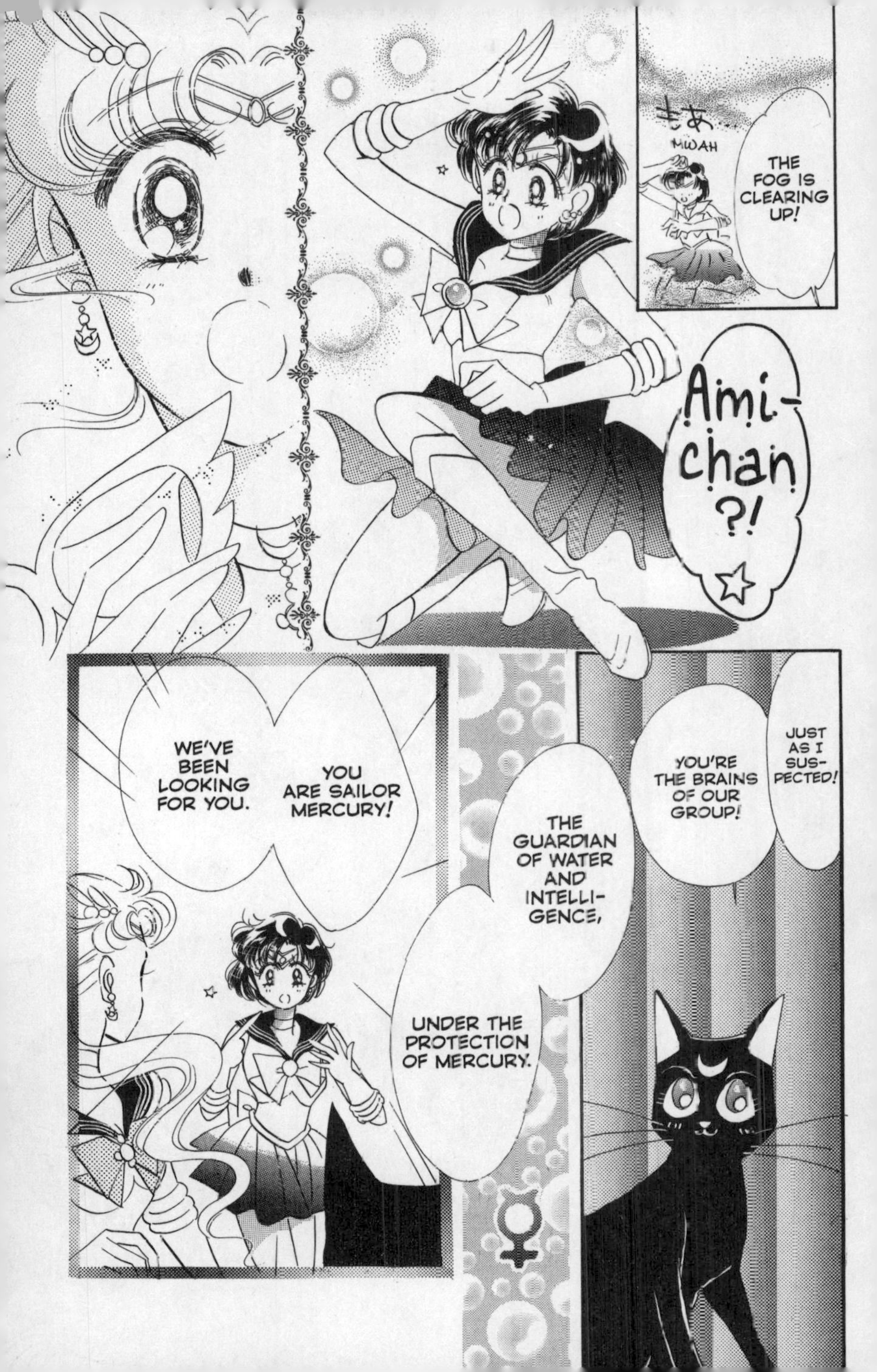
もあ…
MWAH
THE FOG IS CLEARING UP!
Ami-chan?!
JUST AS I SUSPECTED!
YOU'RE THE BRAINS OF OUR GROUP!
THE GUARDIAN OF WATER AND INTELLIGENCE,
UNDER THE PROTECTION OF MERCURY.
YOU ARE SAILOR MERCURY!
WE'VE BEEN LOOKING FOR YOU.

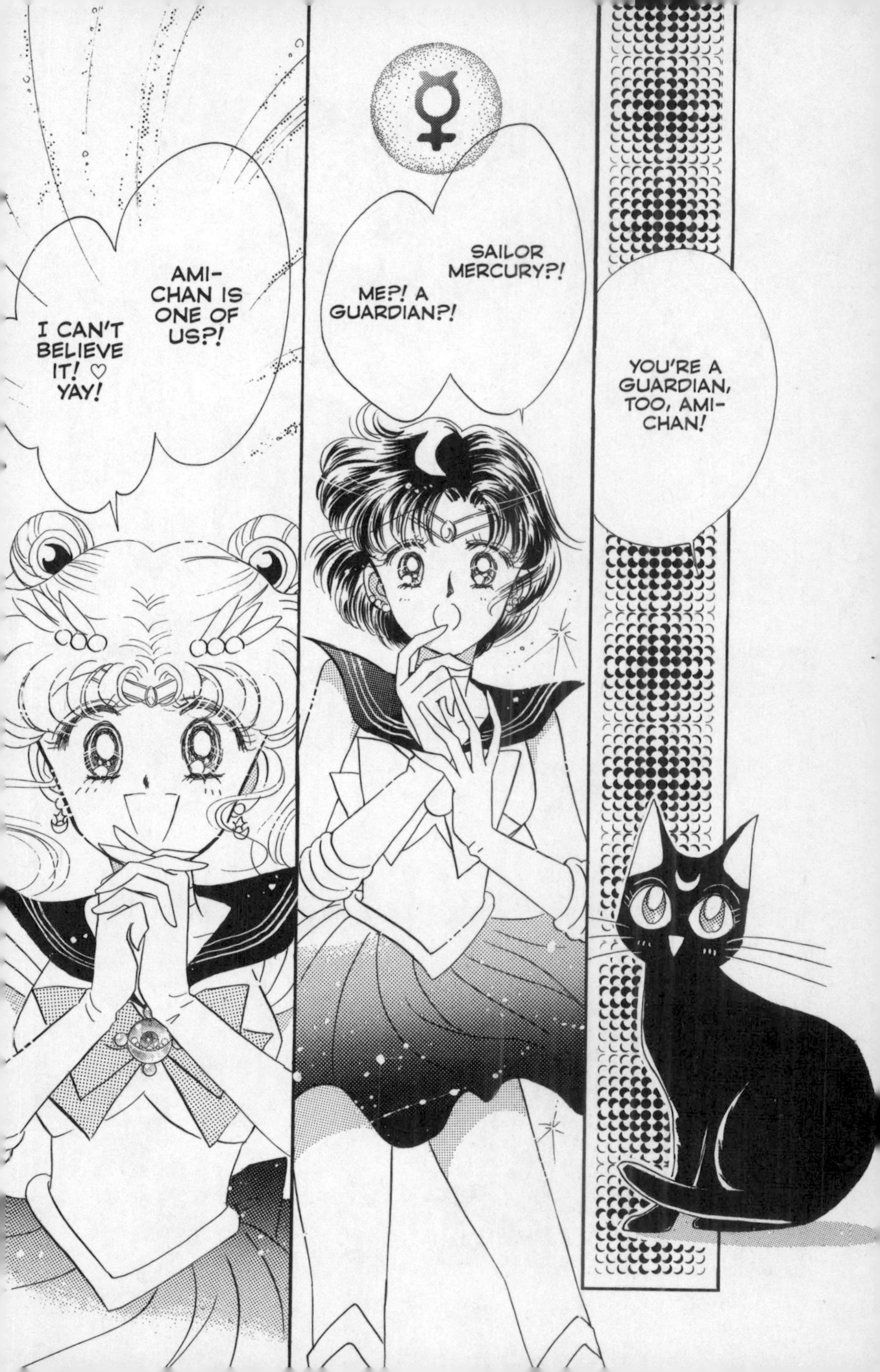
YOU'RE A GUARDIAN, TOO, AMI-CHAN!
SAILOR MERCURY?!
ME?! A GUARDIAN?!
AMI-CHAN IS ONE OF US?!
I CAN'T BELIEVE IT! ♡ YAY!

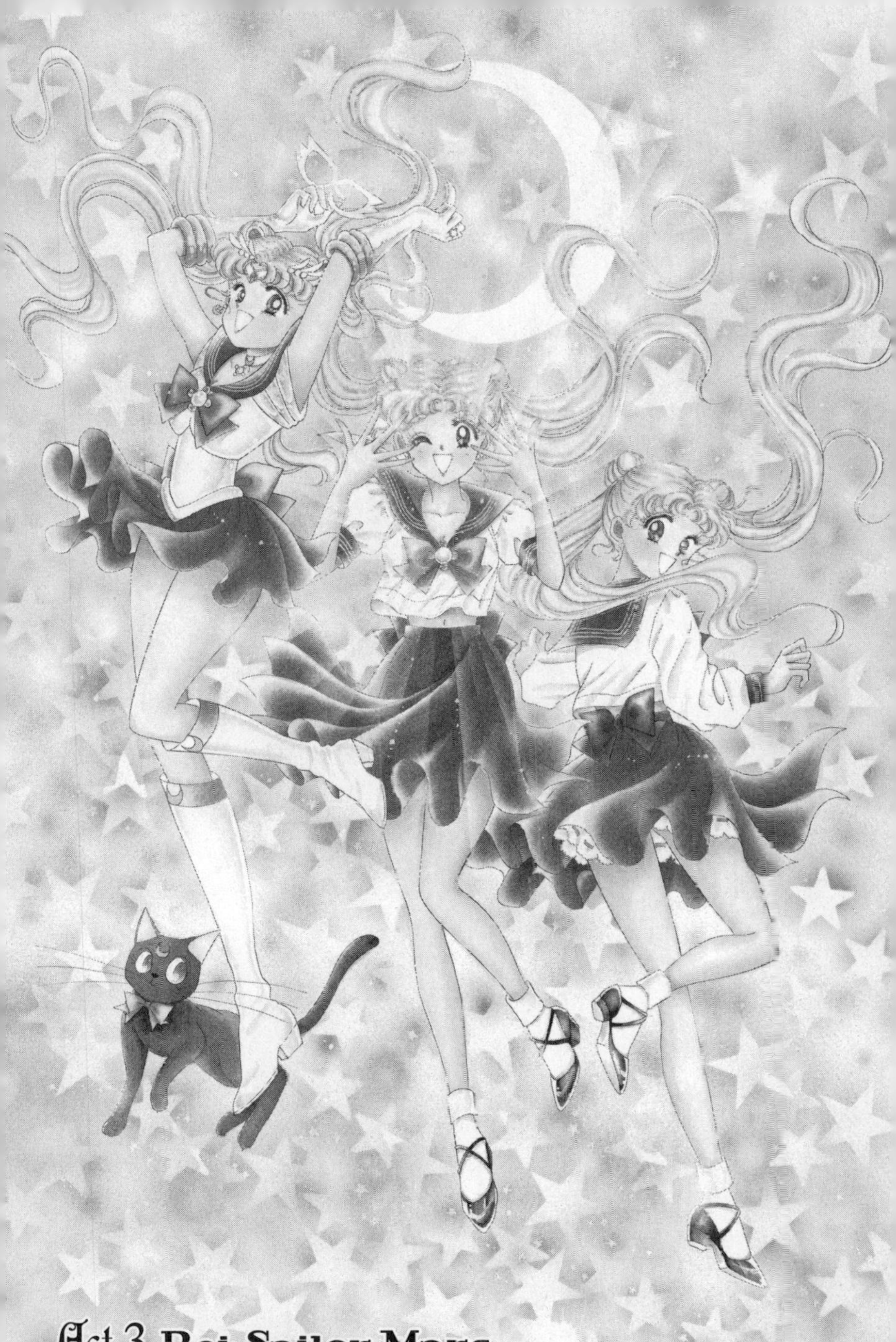

Act.3 Rei: Sailor Mars

Pretty Guardian

Sailor Moon

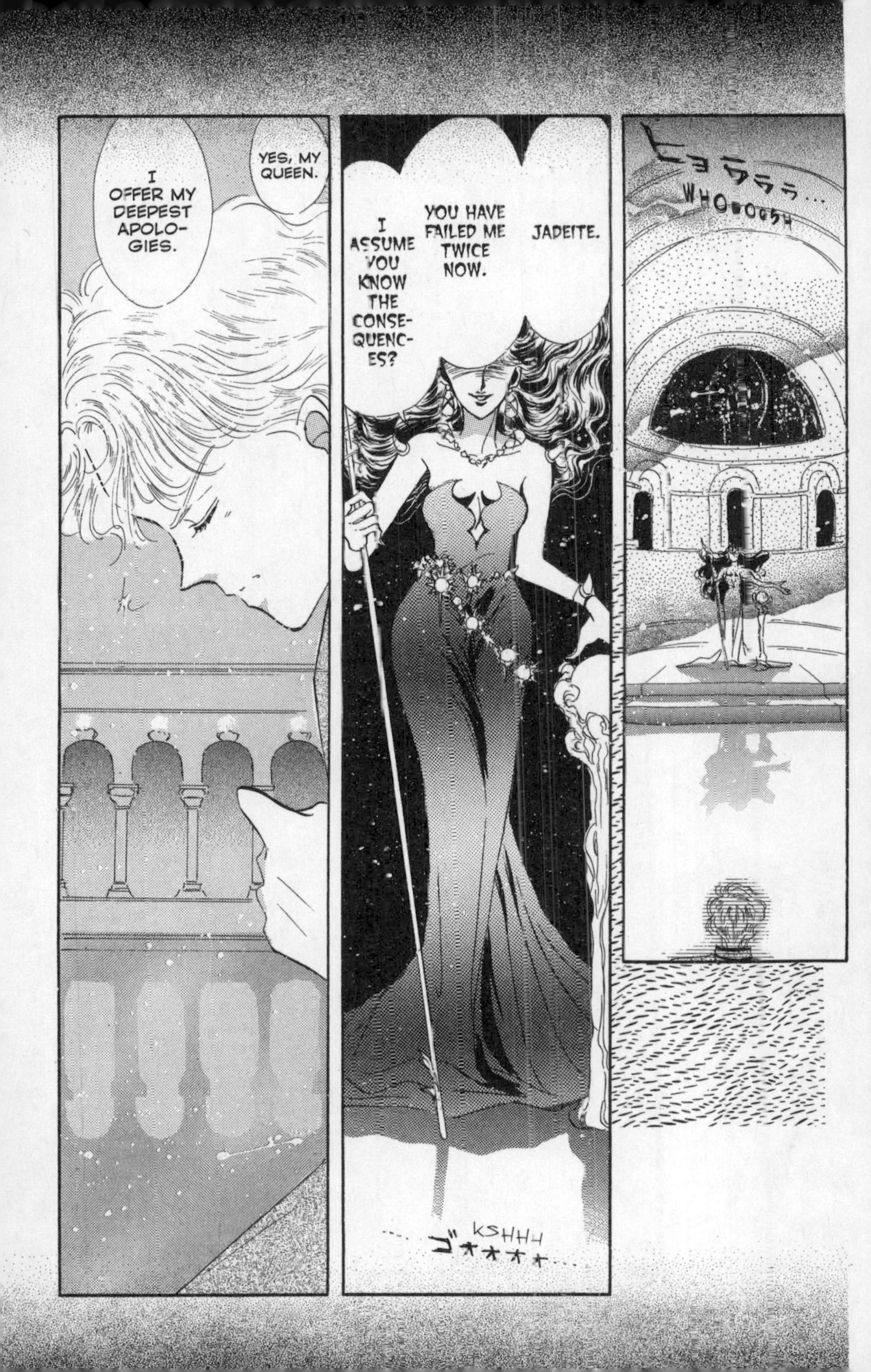
WHOOOOSH
JADEITE.
YOU HAVE FAILED ME TWICE NOW.
I ASSUME YOU KNOW THE CONSE-QUENC-ES?
KSHHH
ゴオオオオ
YES, MY QUEEN.
I OFFER MY DEEPEST APOLO-GIES.

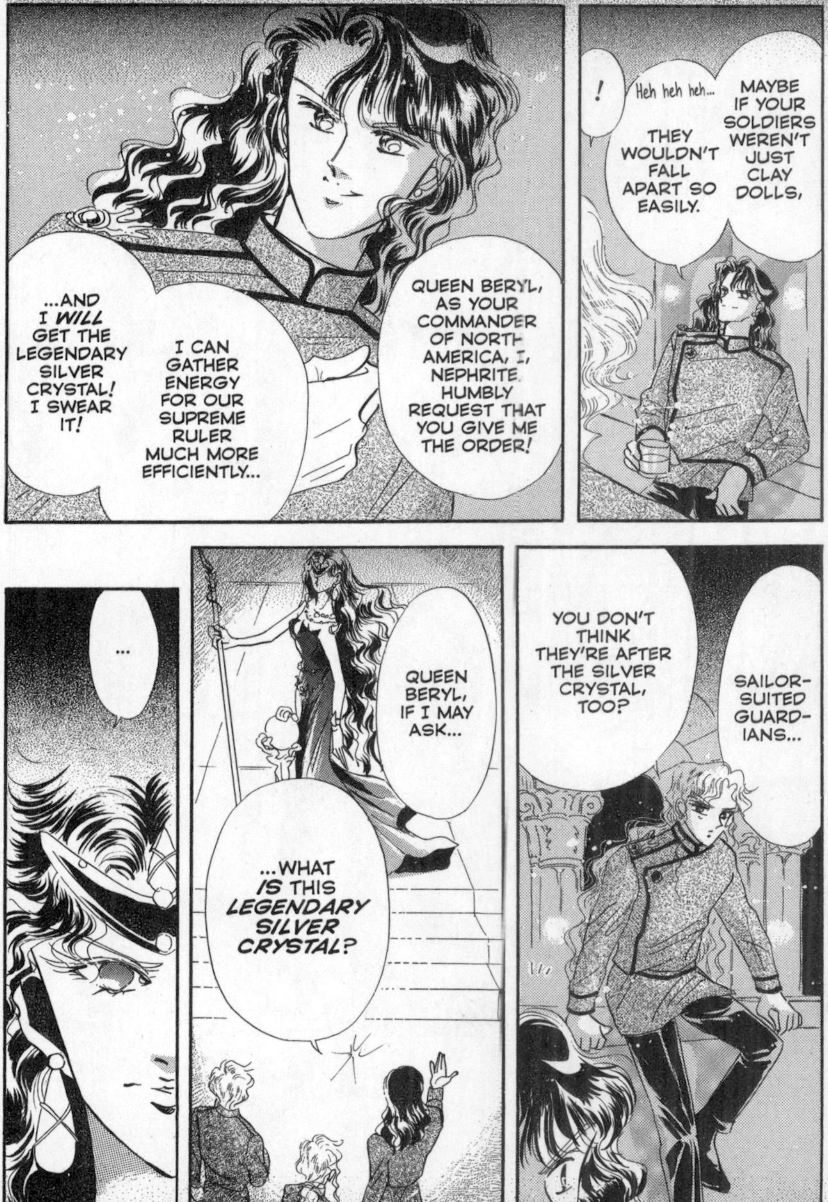
MAYBE IF YOUR SOLDIERS WEREN'T JUST CLAY DOLLS,
Heh heh heh...
THEY WOULDN'T FALL APART SO EASILY.
!
QUEEN BERYL, AS YOUR COMMANDER OF NORTH AMERICA, I, NEPHRITE, HUMBLY REQUEST THAT YOU GIVE ME THE ORDER!
I CAN GATHER ENERGY FOR OUR SUPREME RULER MUCH MORE EFFICIENTLY...
...AND I *WILL* GET THE LEGENDARY SILVER CRYSTAL! I SWEAR IT!
SAILOR-SUITED GUARD-IANS...
YOU DON'T THINK THEY'RE AFTER THE SILVER CRYSTAL, TOO?
QUEEN BERYL, IF I MAY ASK...
...WHAT *IS* THIS *LEGENDARY SILVER CRYSTAL*?
...

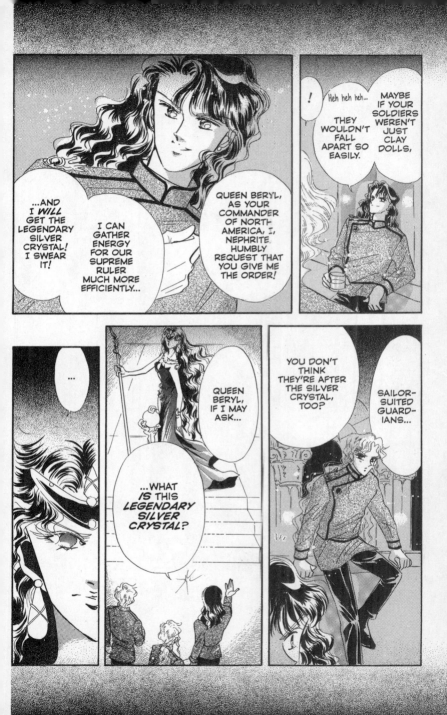

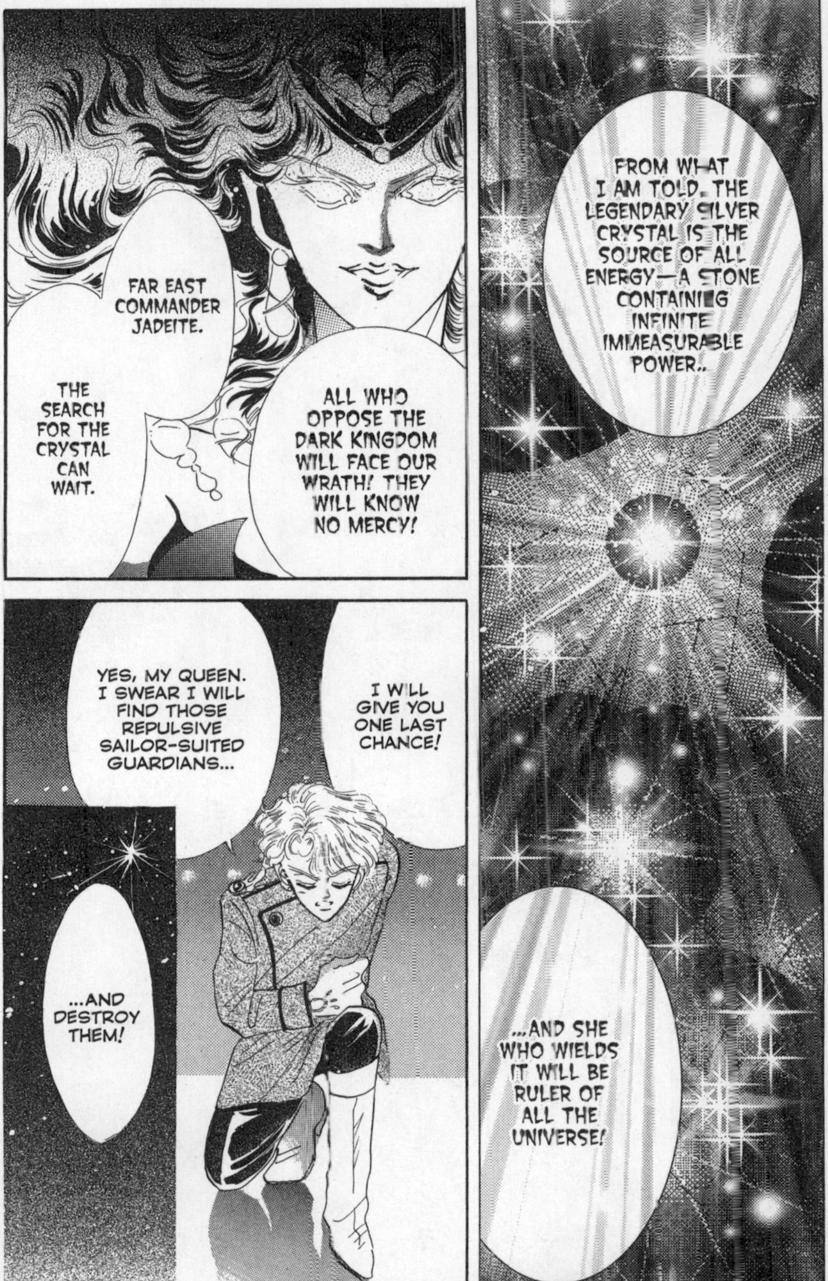
FROM WHAT I AM TOLD, THE LEGENDARY SILVER CRYSTAL IS THE SOURCE OF ALL ENERGY—A STONE CONTAINING INFINITE IMMEASURABLE POWER..
...AND SHE WHO WIELDS IT WILL BE RULER OF ALL THE UNIVERSE!
FAR EAST COMMANDER JADEITE.
THE SEARCH FOR THE CRYSTAL CAN WAIT.
ALL WHO OPPOSE THE DARK KINGDOM WILL FACE OUR WRATH! THEY WILL KNOW NO MERCY!
I WILL GIVE YOU ONE LAST CHANCE!
YES, MY QUEEN. I SWEAR I WILL FIND THOSE REPULSIVE SAILOR-SUITED GUARDIANS...
...AND DESTROY THEM!

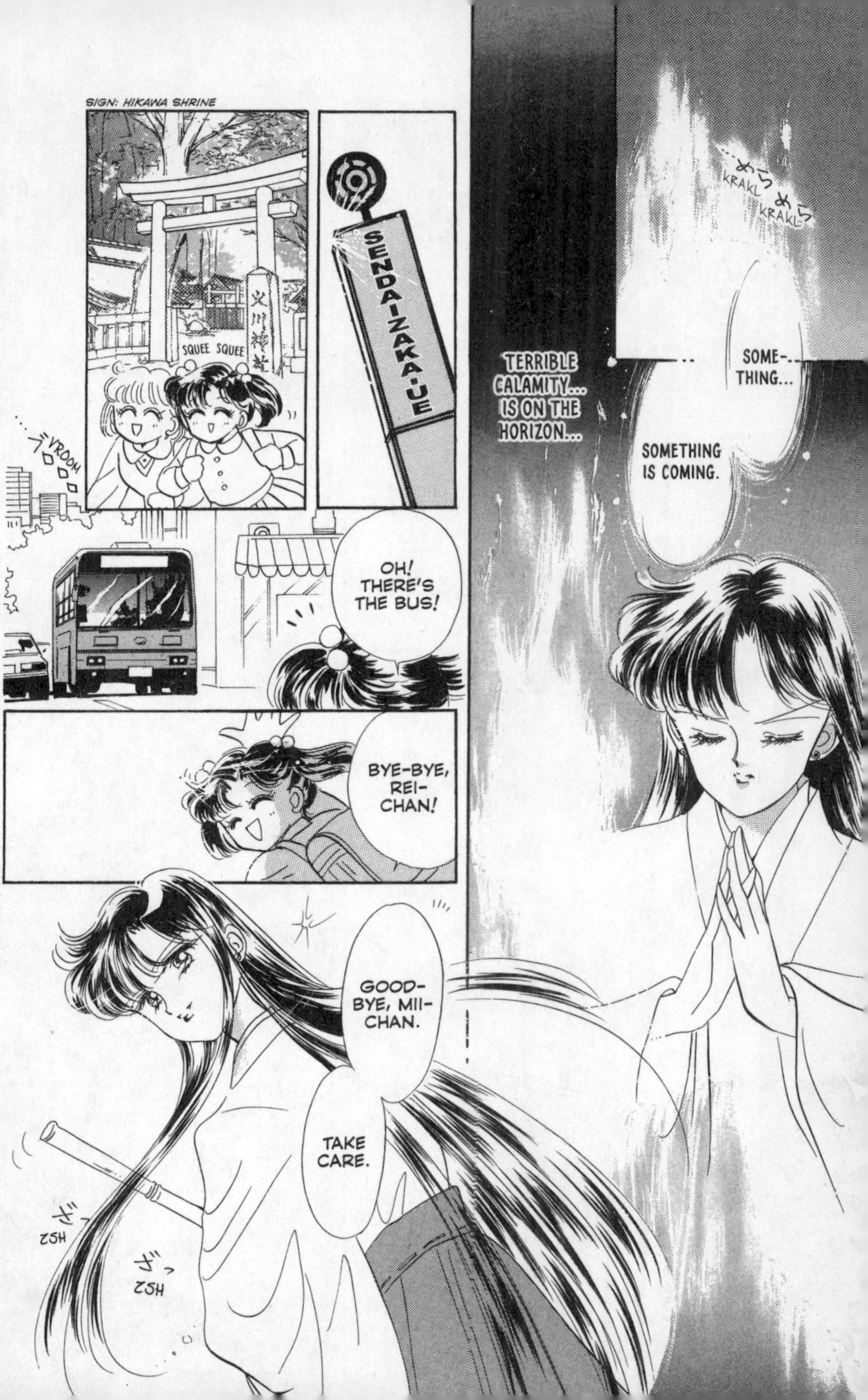
KRAKL
KRAKL
SOME-THING...
SOMETHING IS COMING.
TERRIBLE CALAMITY... IS ON THE HORIZON...
SENDAIZAKA-UE
SIGN: HIKAWA SHRINE
SQUEE SQUEE
VROOM
OH! THERE'S THE BUS!
BYE-BYE, REI-CHAN!
GOOD-BYE, MII-CHAN.
TAKE CARE.

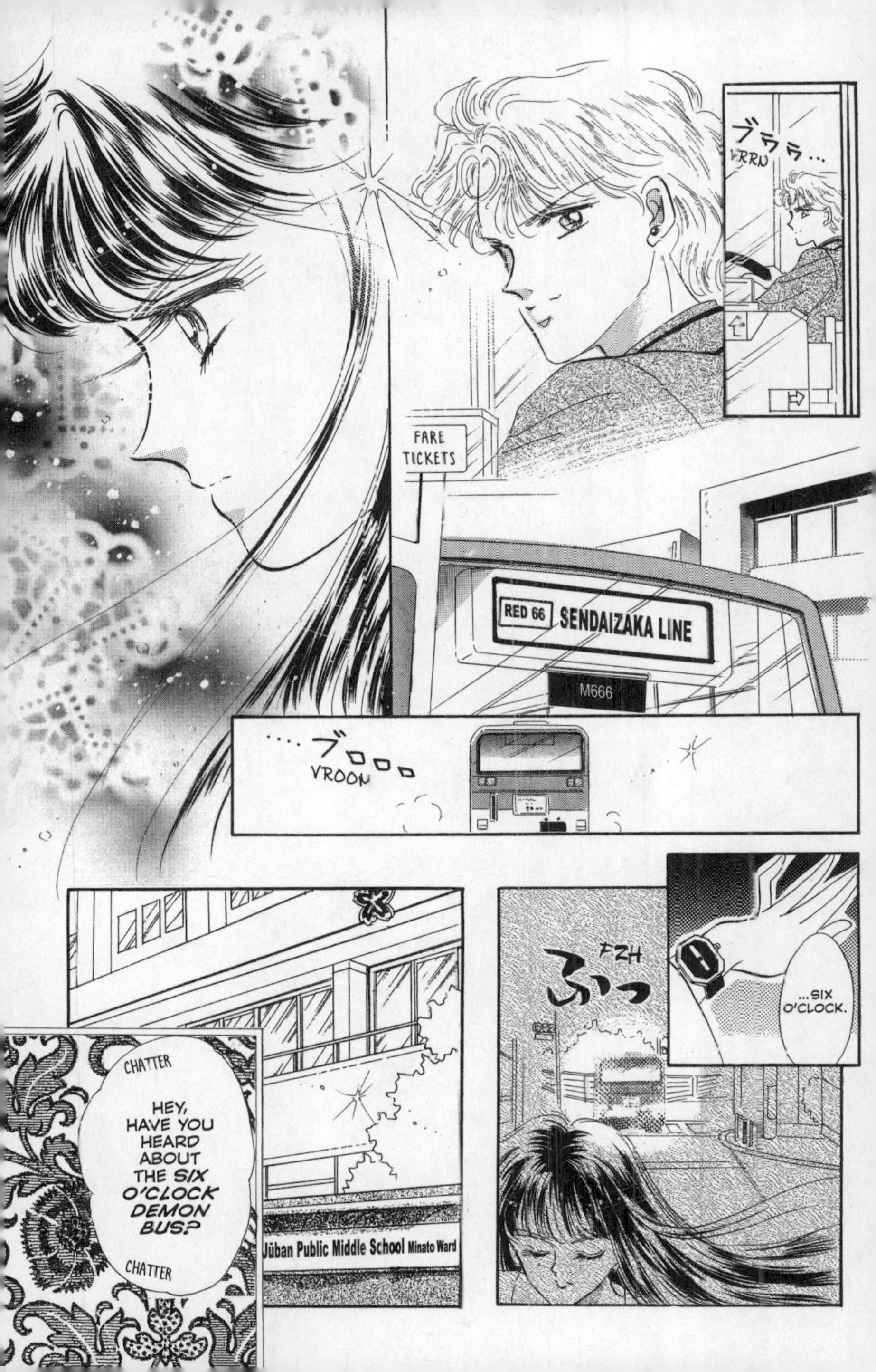
ブララ…
VRRN
FARE TICKETS
RED 66 SENDAIZAKA LINE
M666
…ブロロロ
VROOM
…SIX O'CLOCK.
ふっ
FZH
Jūban Public Middle School Minato Ward
CHATTER
HEY, HAVE YOU HEARD ABOUT THE SIX O'CLOCK DEMON BUS?
CHATTER

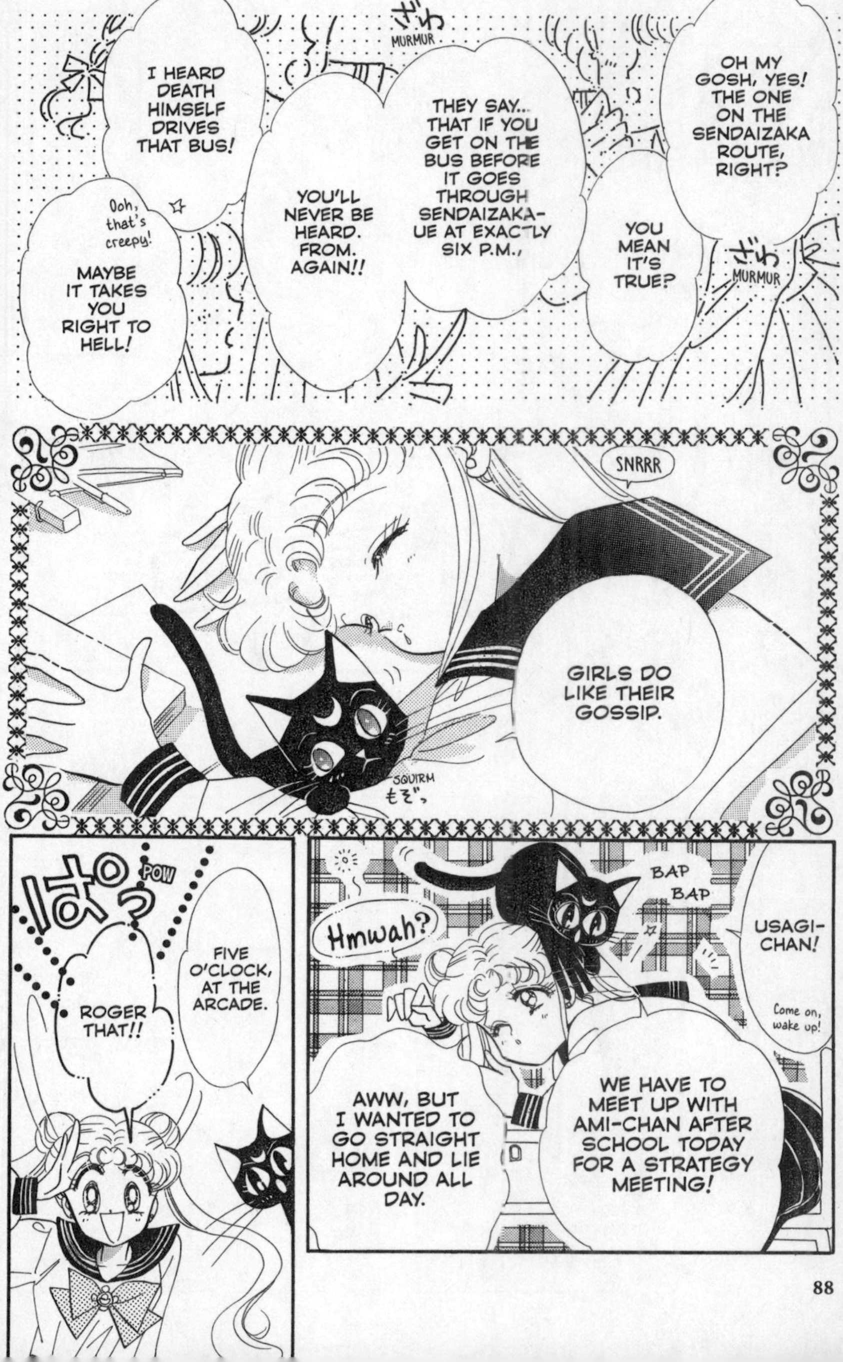
ざわ
MURMUR
OH MY GOSH, YES! THE ONE ON THE SENDAIZAKA ROUTE, RIGHT?
ざわ
MURMUR
YOU MEAN IT'S TRUE?
THEY SAY... THAT IF YOU GET ON THE BUS BEFORE IT GOES THROUGH SENDAIZAKA-UE AT EXACTLY SIX P.M.,
YOU'LL NEVER BE HEARD. FROM. AGAIN!!
I HEARD DEATH HIMSELF DRIVES THAT BUS!
Ooh, that's creepy!
MAYBE IT TAKES YOU RIGHT TO HELL!
SNRRR
GIRLS DO LIKE THEIR GOSSIP.
SQUIRM
もぞっ
USAGI-CHAN!
Come on, wake up!
BAP
BAP
Hmwah?
WE HAVE TO MEET UP WITH AMI-CHAN AFTER SCHOOL TODAY FOR A STRATEGY MEETING!
AWW, BUT I WANTED TO GO STRAIGHT HOME AND LIE AROUND ALL DAY.
はっ
POW
FIVE O'CLOCK, AT THE ARCADE.
ROGER THAT!!

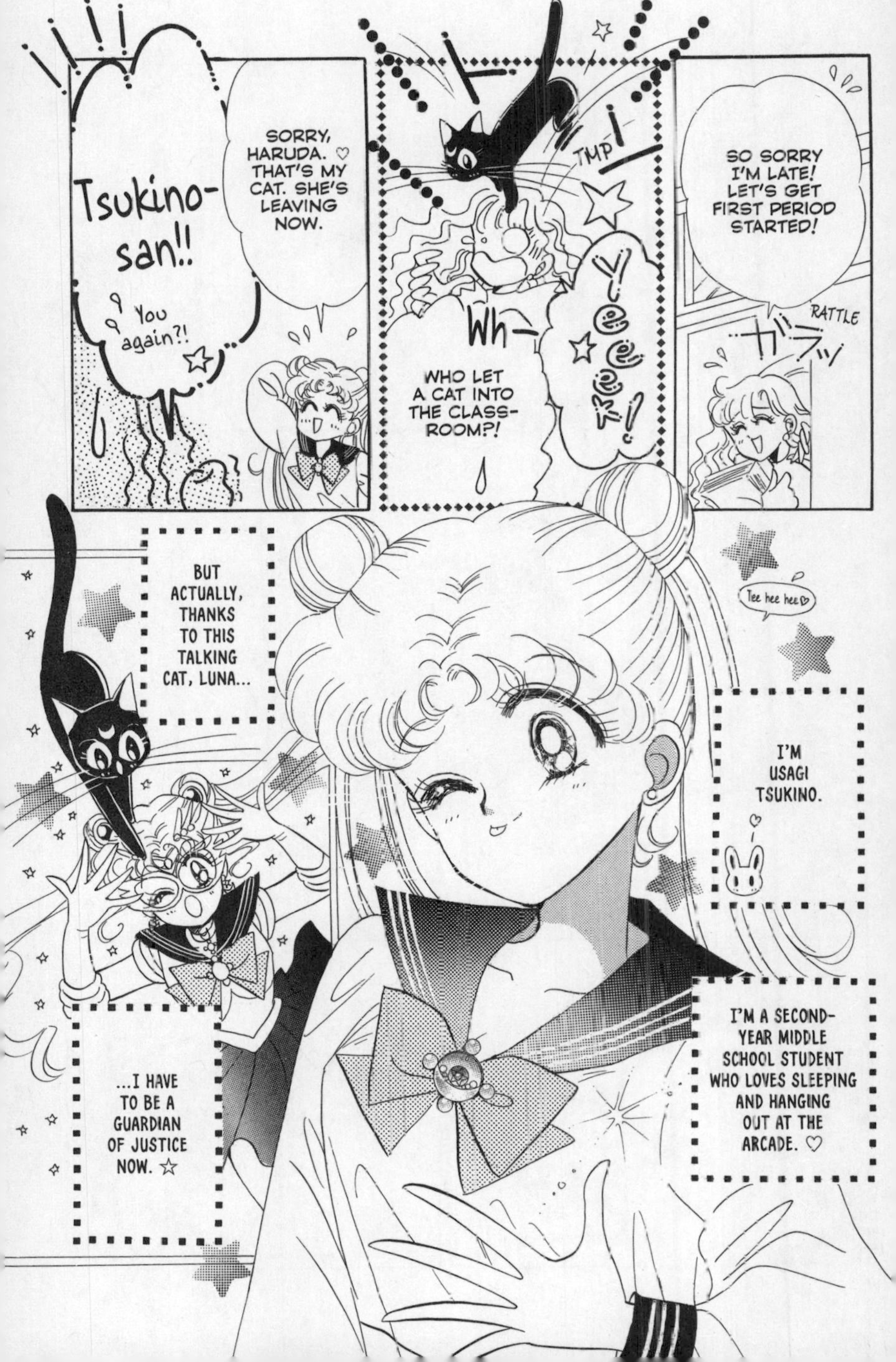
SO SORRY I'M LATE! LET'S GET FIRST PERIOD STARTED!
RATTLE
ガラッ
TMP
Yeeek!
Wh-
WHO LET A CAT INTO THE CLASSROOM?!
SORRY, HARUDA. ♡ THAT'S MY CAT. SHE'S LEAVING NOW.
Tsukino-san!!
You again?!
Tee hee hee♡
I'M USAGI TSUKINO.
I'M A SECOND-YEAR MIDDLE SCHOOL STUDENT WHO LOVES SLEEPING AND HANGING OUT AT THE ARCADE. ♡
BUT ACTUALLY, THANKS TO THIS TALKING CAT, LUNA...
...I HAVE TO BE A GUARDIAN OF JUSTICE NOW. ☆

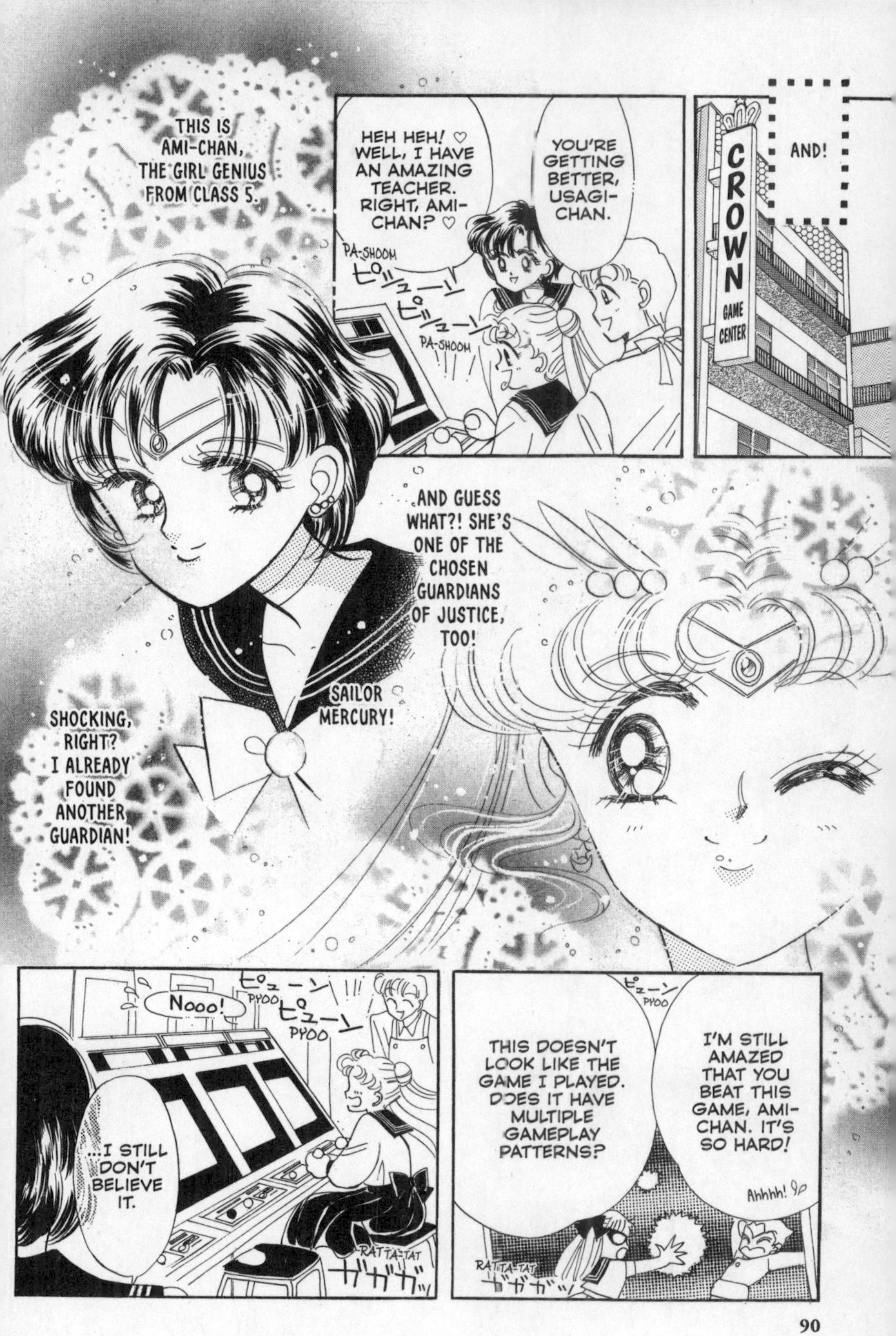
AND!
YOU'RE GETTING BETTER, USAGI-CHAN.
HEH HEH! ♡ WELL, I HAVE AN AMAZING TEACHER. RIGHT, AMI-CHAN? ♡
PA-SHOOM
PA-SHOOM
THIS IS AMI-CHAN, THE GIRL GENIUS FROM CLASS 5.
AND GUESS WHAT?! SHE'S ONE OF THE CHOSEN GUARDIANS OF JUSTICE, TOO!
SAILOR MERCURY!
SHOCKING, RIGHT? I ALREADY FOUND ANOTHER GUARDIAN!
PYOO
I'M STILL AMAZED THAT YOU BEAT THIS GAME, AMI-CHAN. IT'S SO HARD!
THIS DOESN'T LOOK LIKE THE GAME I PLAYED. DOES IT HAVE MULTIPLE GAMEPLAY PATTERNS?
Ahhhh!
RAT-TA-TAT
PYOO
Nooo!
PYOO
...I STILL DON'T BELIEVE IT.
RAT-TA-TAT

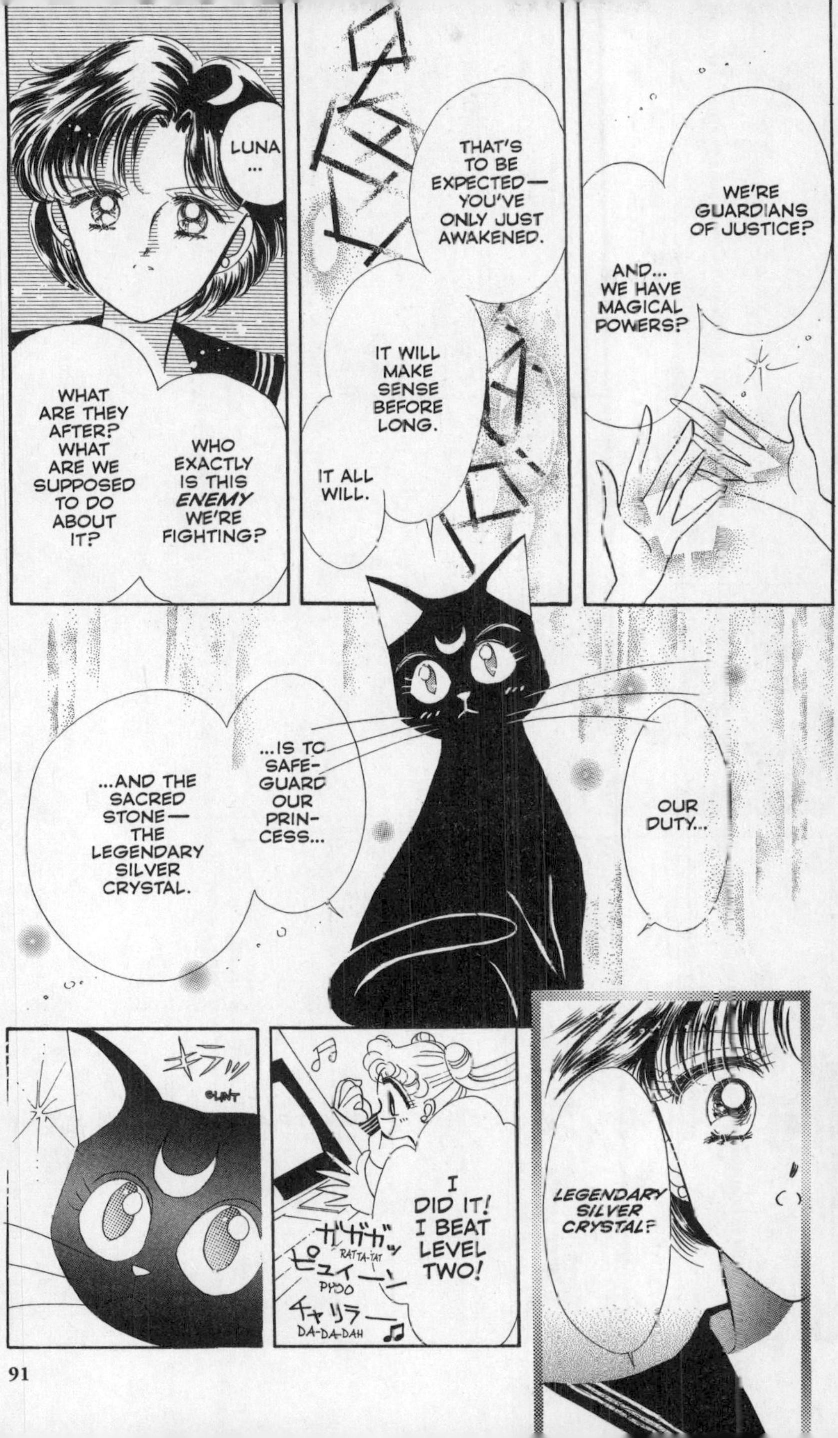
WE'RE GUARDIANS OF JUSTICE?
AND... WE HAVE MAGICAL POWERS?
THAT'S TO BE EXPECTED— YOU'VE ONLY JUST AWAKENED.
IT WILL MAKE SENSE BEFORE LONG.
IT ALL WILL.
LUNA ...
WHO EXACTLY IS THIS *ENEMY* WE'RE FIGHTING?
WHAT ARE THEY AFTER? WHAT ARE WE SUPPOSED TO DO ABOUT IT?
OUR DUTY...
...IS TO SAFE-GUARD OUR PRIN-CESS...
...AND THE SACRED STONE— THE LEGENDARY SILVER CRYSTAL.
LEGENDARY SILVER CRYSTAL?
I DID IT! I BEAT LEVEL TWO!
ガガガッ
RATTA-TAT
ピュイーン
PYOO
チャリラー
DA-DA-DAH
キラッ
GLINT

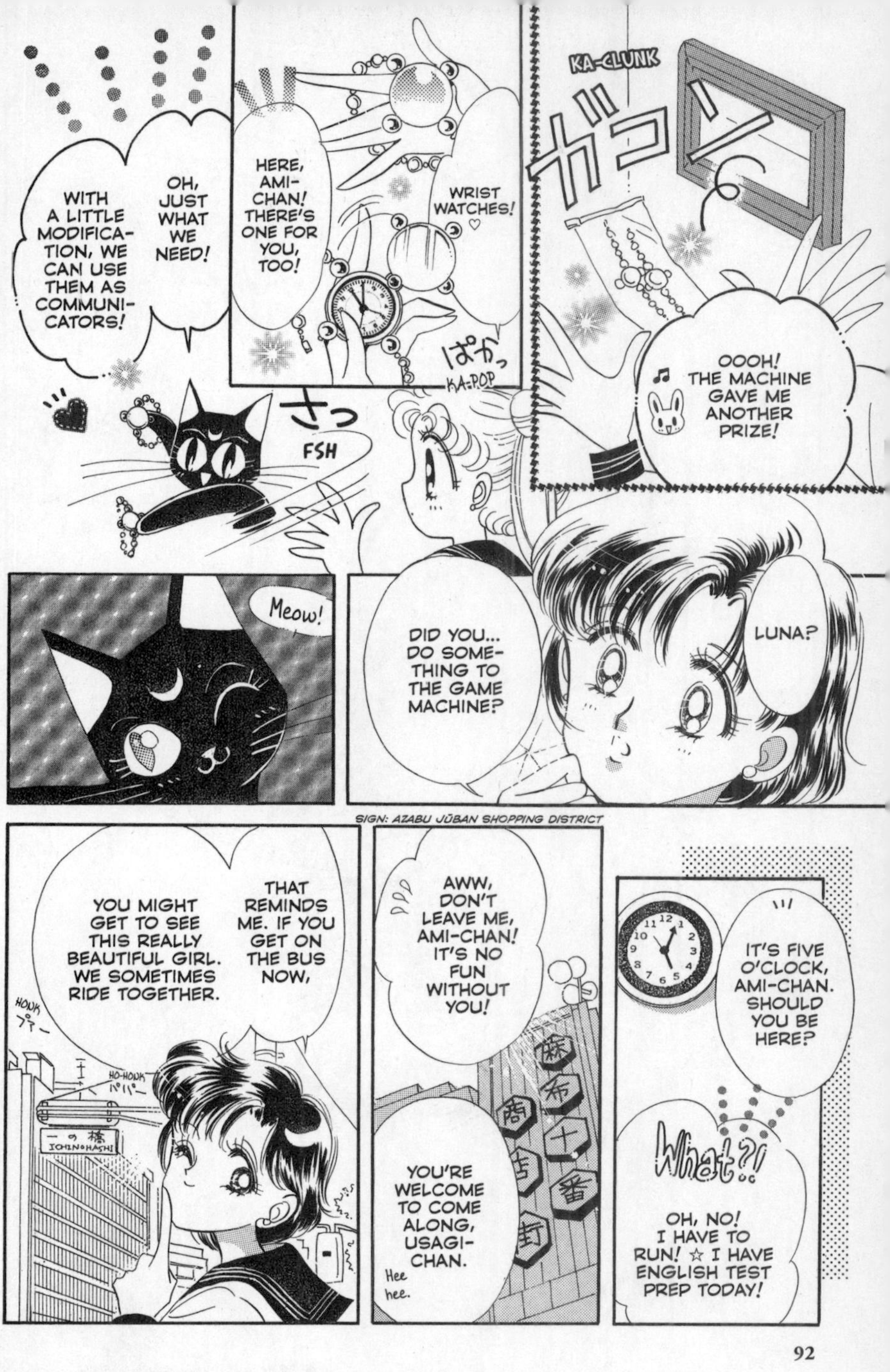
KA-CLUNK
ガコン
OOOH! ♫ THE MACHINE GAVE ME ANOTHER PRIZE!
WRIST WATCHES! ♡
HERE, AMI-CHAN! THERE'S ONE FOR YOU, TOO!
ぱかっ
KA-POP
OH, JUST WHAT WE NEED!
WITH A LITTLE MODIFICATION, WE CAN USE THEM AS COMMUNICATORS!
さっ
FSH
LUNA?
DID YOU... DO SOMETHING TO THE GAME MACHINE?
Meow!
IT'S FIVE O'CLOCK, AMI-CHAN. SHOULD YOU BE HERE?
What?!
OH, NO! I HAVE TO RUN! ☆ I HAVE ENGLISH TEST PREP TODAY!
SIGN: AZABU JŪBAN SHOPPING DISTRICT
AWW, DON'T LEAVE ME, AMI-CHAN! IT'S NO FUN WITHOUT YOU!
YOU'RE WELCOME TO COME ALONG, USAGI-CHAN.
Hee hee.
THAT REMINDS ME. IF YOU GET ON THE BUS NOW,
YOU MIGHT GET TO SEE THIS REALLY BEAUTIFUL GIRL. WE SOMETIMES RIDE TOGETHER.
HONK
プァー
HO-HONK
パパー
一の橋
ICHINOHASHI

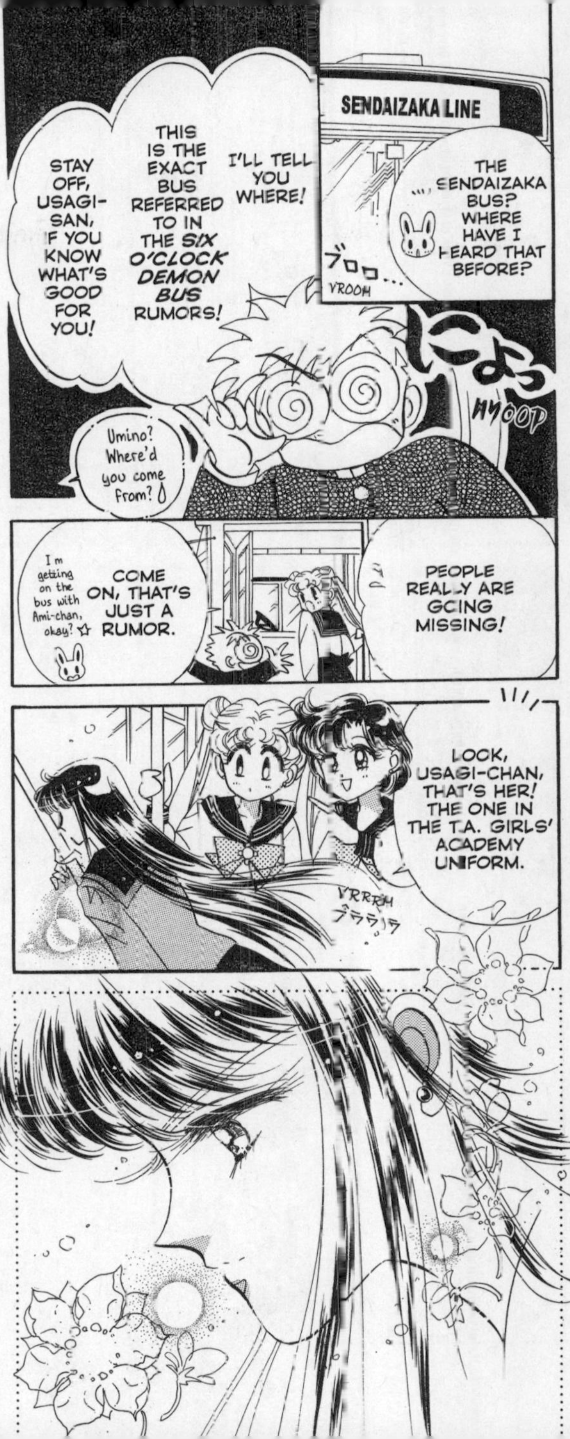
SENDAIZAKA LINE
...THE SENDAIZAKA BUS? WHERE HAVE I HEARD THAT BEFORE?
ブロロ... VROOM
I'LL TELL YOU WHERE!
THIS IS THE EXACT BUS REFERRED TO IN THE *SIX O'CLOCK DEMON BUS* RUMORS!
STAY OFF, USAGI-SAN, IF YOU KNOW WHAT'S GOOD FOR YOU!
にょっ NYOOP
Umino? Where'd you come from?
PEOPLE REALLY ARE GOING MISSING!
COME ON, THAT'S JUST A RUMOR.
I'm getting on the bus with Ami-chan, okay? ☆
LOOK, USAGI-CHAN, THAT'S HER! THE ONE IN THE T.A. GIRLS' ACADEMY UNIFORM.
VRRRM ブラララ

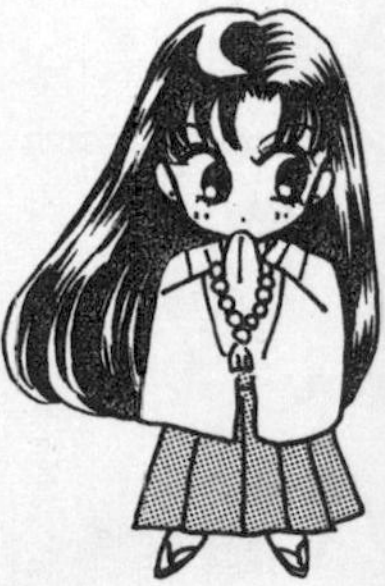

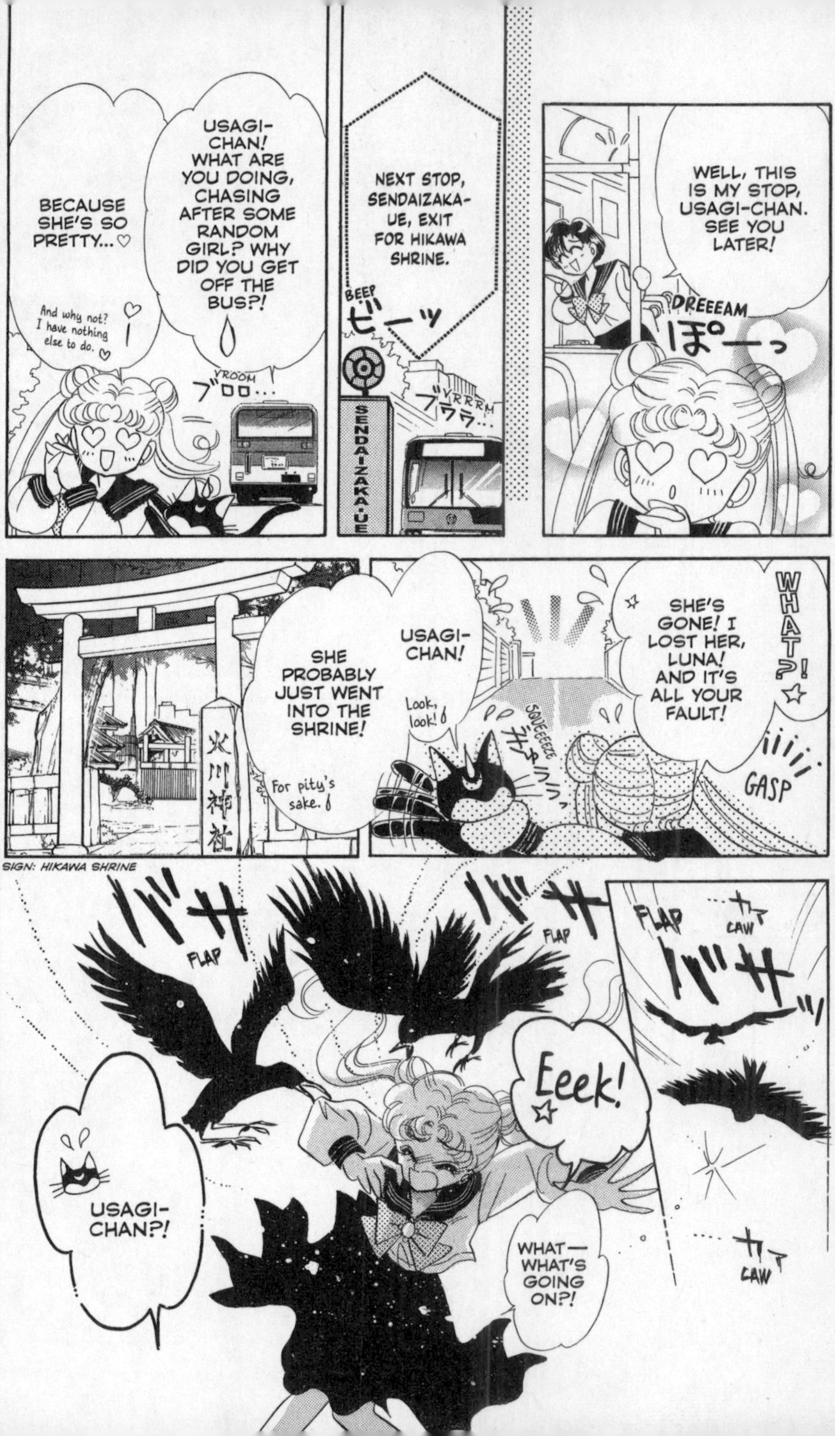
WELL, THIS IS MY STOP, USAGI-CHAN. SEE YOU LATER!
DREEEAM
ぽーっ
NEXT STOP, SENDAIZAKA-UE, EXIT FOR HIKAWA SHRINE.
BEEP
ビーッ
SENDAIZAKA-UE
VRRRM
ブララ...
USAGI-CHAN! WHAT ARE YOU DOING, CHASING AFTER SOME RANDOM GIRL? WHY DID YOU GET OFF THE BUS?!
BECAUSE SHE'S SO PRETTY...♡
And why not? I have nothing else to do. ♡
VROOM
ブロロ...
WHAT?!
SHE'S GONE! I LOST HER, LUNA! AND IT'S ALL YOUR FAULT!
GASP
SQUEEEEZE
USAGI-CHAN!
Look, look!
SHE PROBABLY JUST WENT INTO THE SHRINE!
For pity's sake.
火川神社
FLAP
CAW
バサッ
バサ
FLAP
バサ
FLAP
Eeek!
WHAT—WHAT'S GOING ON?!
USAGI-CHAN?!
CAW

SIGN: HIKAWA SHRINE

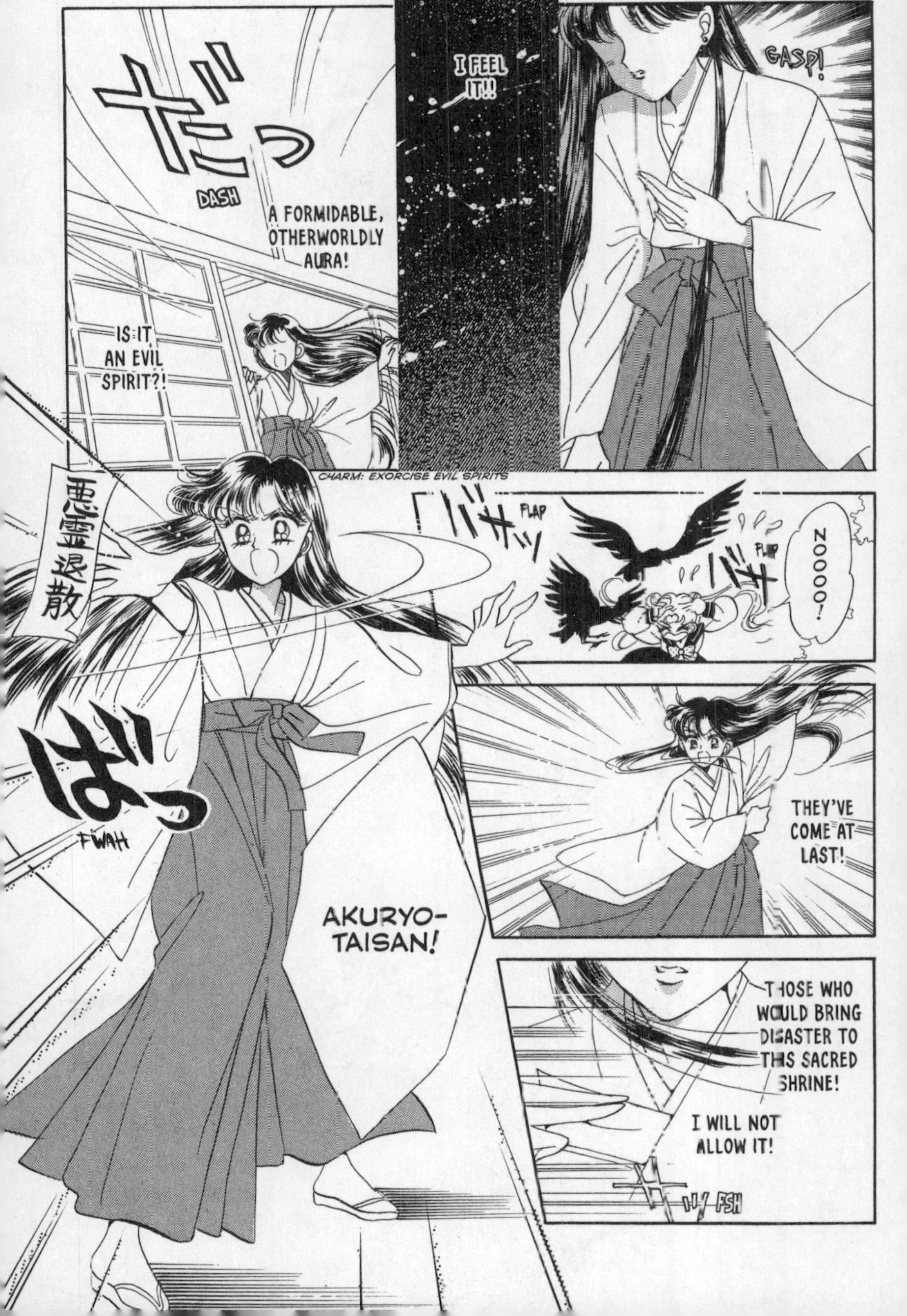
GASP!
I FEEL IT!!
だっ
DASH
A FORMIDABLE, OTHERWORLDLY AURA!
IS IT AN EVIL SPIRIT?!
バサッ
FLAP
バサ
FLAP
NOOOO!
THEY'VE COME AT LAST!
THOSE WHO WOULD BRING DISASTER TO THIS SACRED SHRINE!
I WILL NOT ALLOW IT!
FSH
悪霊退散
CHARM: EXORCISE EVIL SPIRITS
ばっ
FWAH
AKURYO-TAISAN!

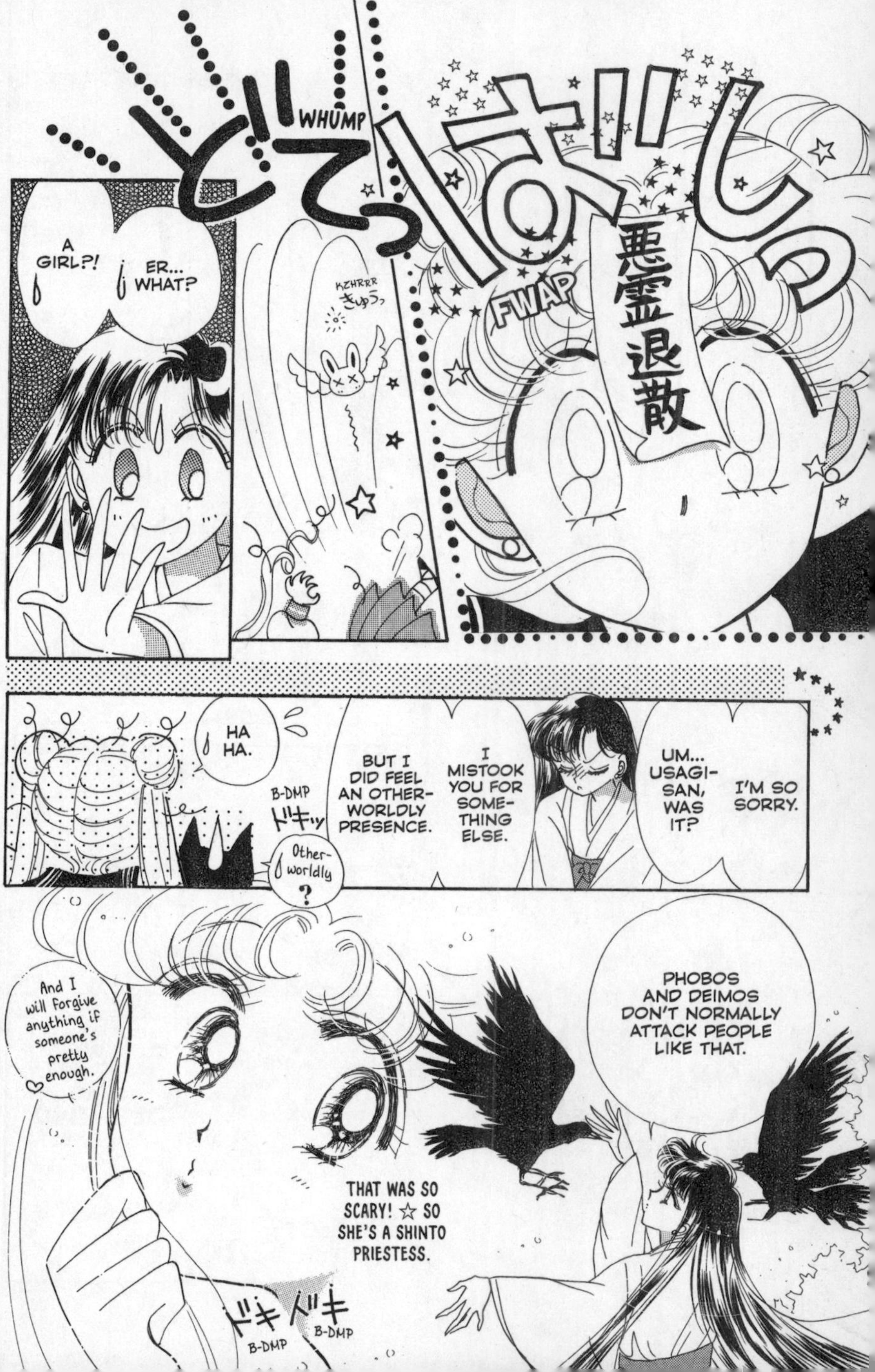
はしっ
FWAP
悪霊退散
どてっ
WHUMP
きゅうっ
KZHRRR
ER... WHAT?
A GIRL?!
I'M SO SORRY.
UM... USAGI-SAN, WAS IT?
I MISTOOK YOU FOR SOMETHING ELSE.
BUT I DID FEEL AN OTHER-WORLDLY PRESENCE.
ドキッ
B-DMP
HA HA.
Other-worldly?
PHOBOS AND DEIMOS DON'T NORMALLY ATTACK PEOPLE LIKE THAT.
THAT WAS SO SCARY! ☆ SO SHE'S A SHINTO PRIESTESS.
And I will forgive anything if someone's pretty enough. ♡
ドキドキ
B-DMP B-DMP

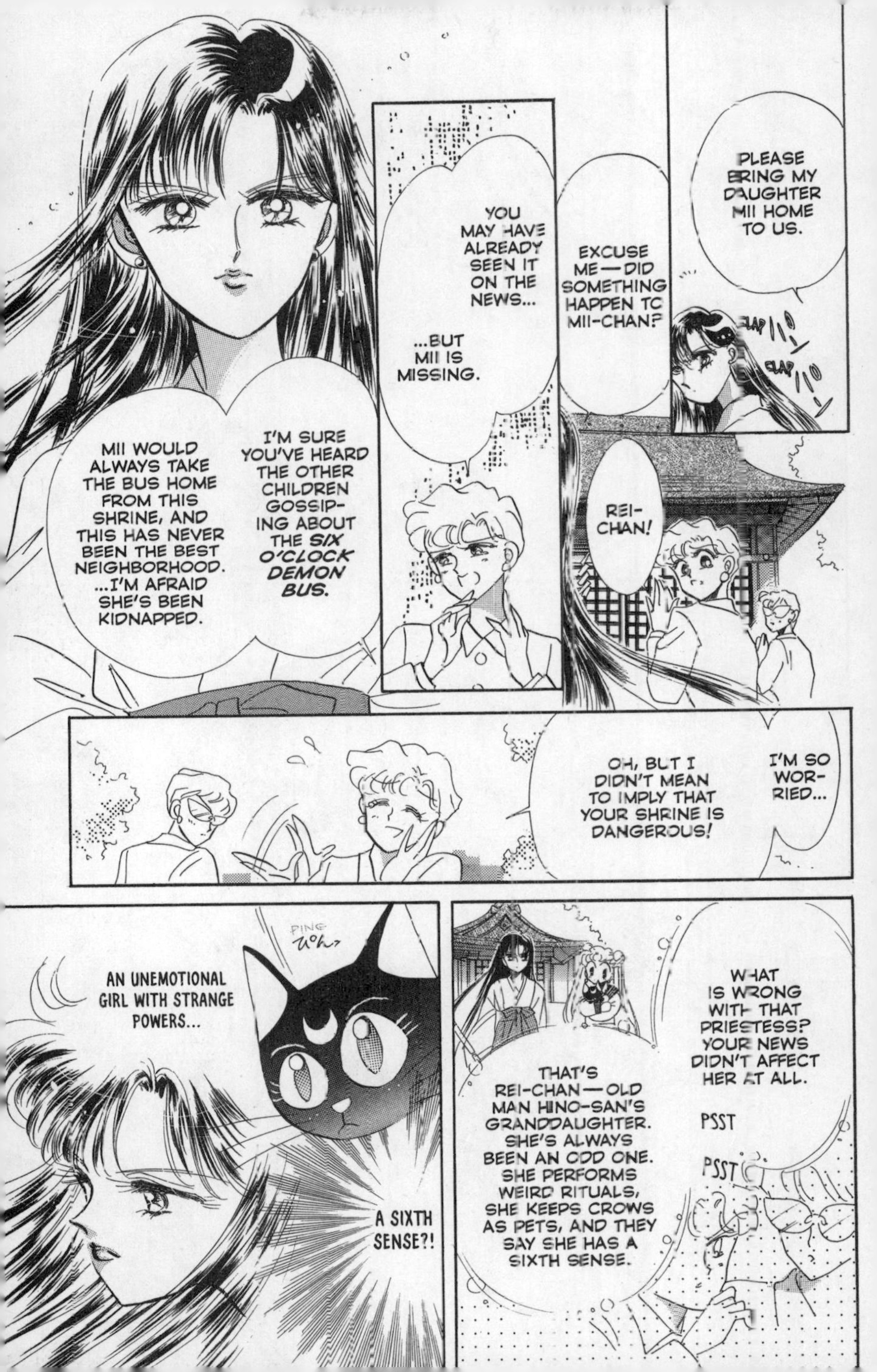
PLEASE BRING MY DAUGHTER MII HOME TO US.
SLAP
SLAP
EXCUSE ME—DID SOMETHING HAPPEN TO MII-CHAN?
REI-CHAN!
YOU MAY HAVE ALREADY SEEN IT ON THE NEWS...
...BUT MII IS MISSING.
I'M SURE YOU'VE HEARD THE OTHER CHILDREN GOSSIP-ING ABOUT THE *SIX O'CLOCK DEMON BUS.*
MII WOULD ALWAYS TAKE THE BUS HOME FROM THIS SHRINE, AND THIS HAS NEVER BEEN THE BEST NEIGHBORHOOD. ...I'M AFRAID SHE'S BEEN KIDNAPPED.
I'M SO WOR-RIED...
OH, BUT I DIDN'T MEAN TO IMPLY THAT YOUR SHRINE IS DANGEROUS!
WHAT IS WRONG WITH THAT PRIESTESS? YOUR NEWS DIDN'T AFFECT HER AT ALL.
PSST
PSST
THAT'S REI-CHAN—OLD MAN HINO-SAN'S GRANDDAUGHTER. SHE'S ALWAYS BEEN AN ODD ONE. SHE PERFORMS WEIRD RITUALS, SHE KEEPS CROWS AS PETS, AND THEY SAY SHE HAS A SIXTH SENSE.
PING
AN UNEMOTIONAL GIRL WITH STRANGE POWERS...
A SIXTH SENSE?!

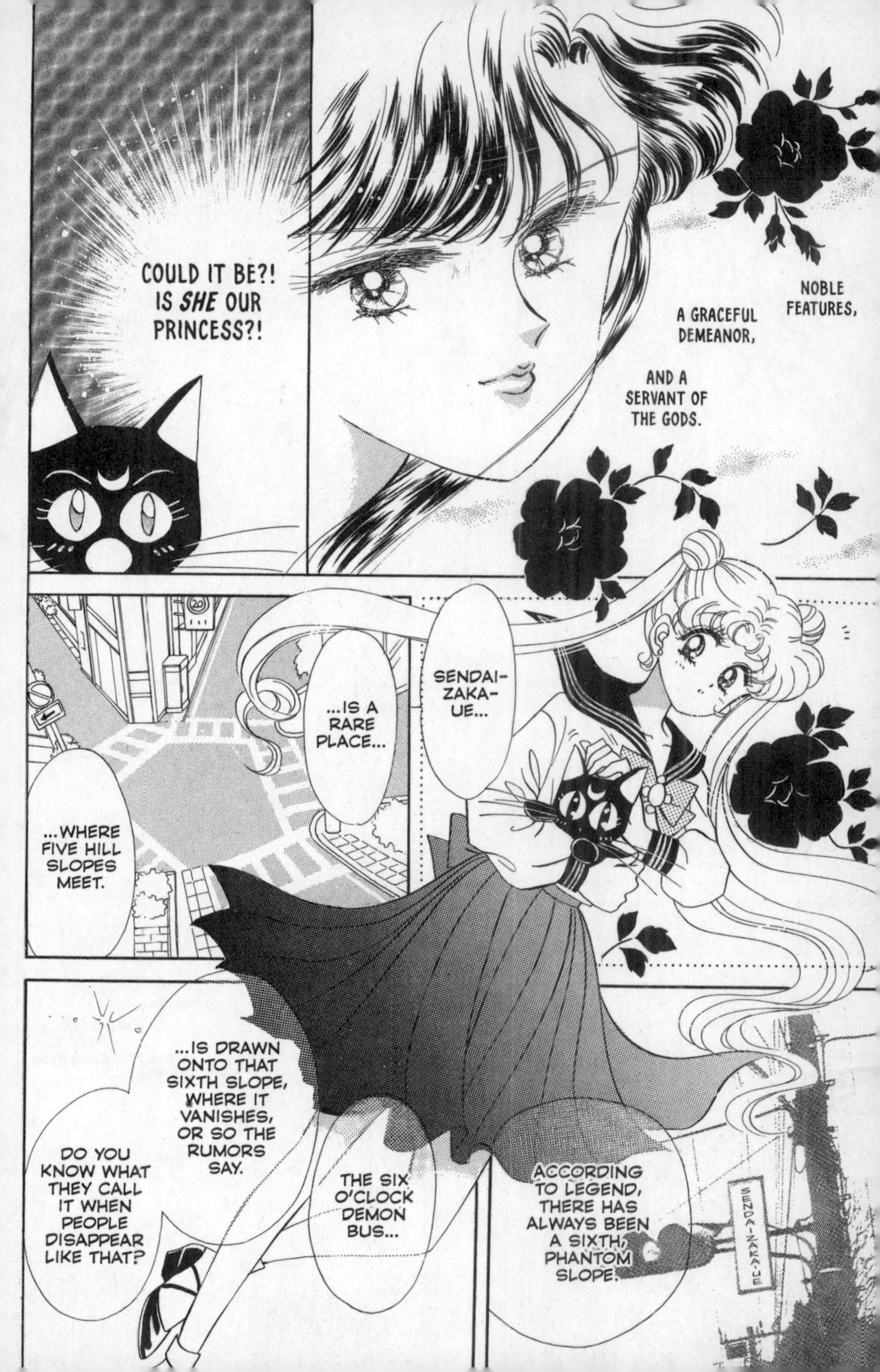
NOBLE FEATURES,
A GRACEFUL DEMEANOR,
AND A SERVANT OF THE GODS.
COULD IT BE?! IS *SHE* OUR PRINCESS?!
SENDAI-ZAKA-UE...
...IS A RARE PLACE...
...WHERE FIVE HILL SLOPES MEET.
ACCORDING TO LEGEND, THERE HAS ALWAYS BEEN A SIXTH, PHANTOM SLOPE.
SENDAI-ZAKA-UE
THE SIX O'CLOCK DEMON BUS...
...IS DRAWN ONTO THAT SIXTH SLOPE, WHERE IT VANISHES, OR SO THE RUMORS SAY.
DO YOU KNOW WHAT THEY CALL IT WHEN PEOPLE DISAPPEAR LIKE THAT?

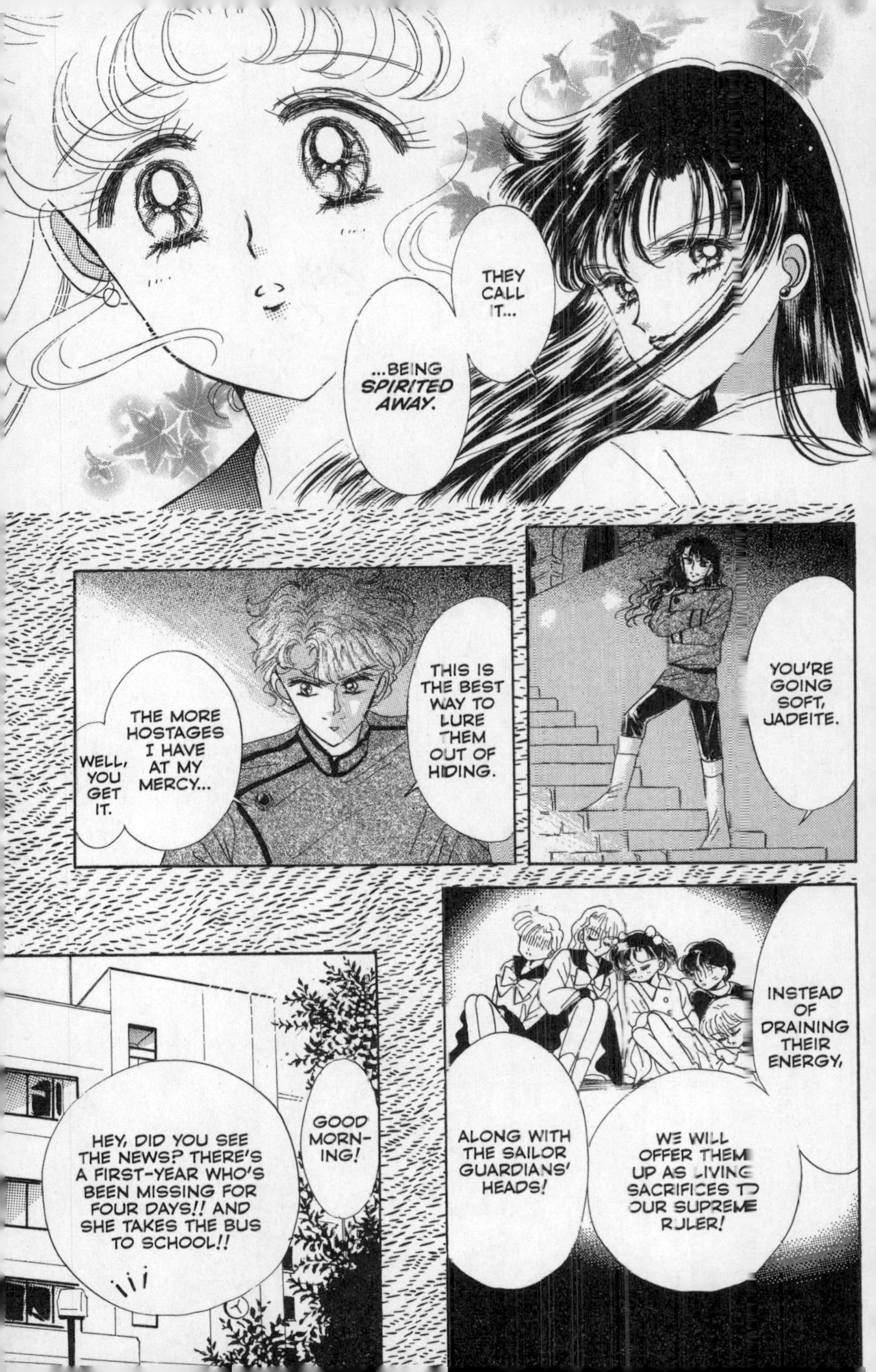
THEY CALL IT...
...BEING SPIRITED AWAY.
YOU'RE GOING SOFT, JADEITE.
THIS IS THE BEST WAY TO LURE THEM OUT OF HIDING.
THE MORE HOSTAGES I HAVE AT MY MERCY...
WELL, YOU GET IT.
INSTEAD OF DRAINING THEIR ENERGY,
WE WILL OFFER THEM UP AS LIVING SACRIFICES TO OUR SUPREME RULER!
ALONG WITH THE SAILOR GUARDIANS' HEADS!
GOOD MORNING!
HEY, DID YOU SEE THE NEWS? THERE'S A FIRST-YEAR WHO'S BEEN MISSING FOR FOUR DAYS!! AND SHE TAKES THE BUS TO SCHOOL!!

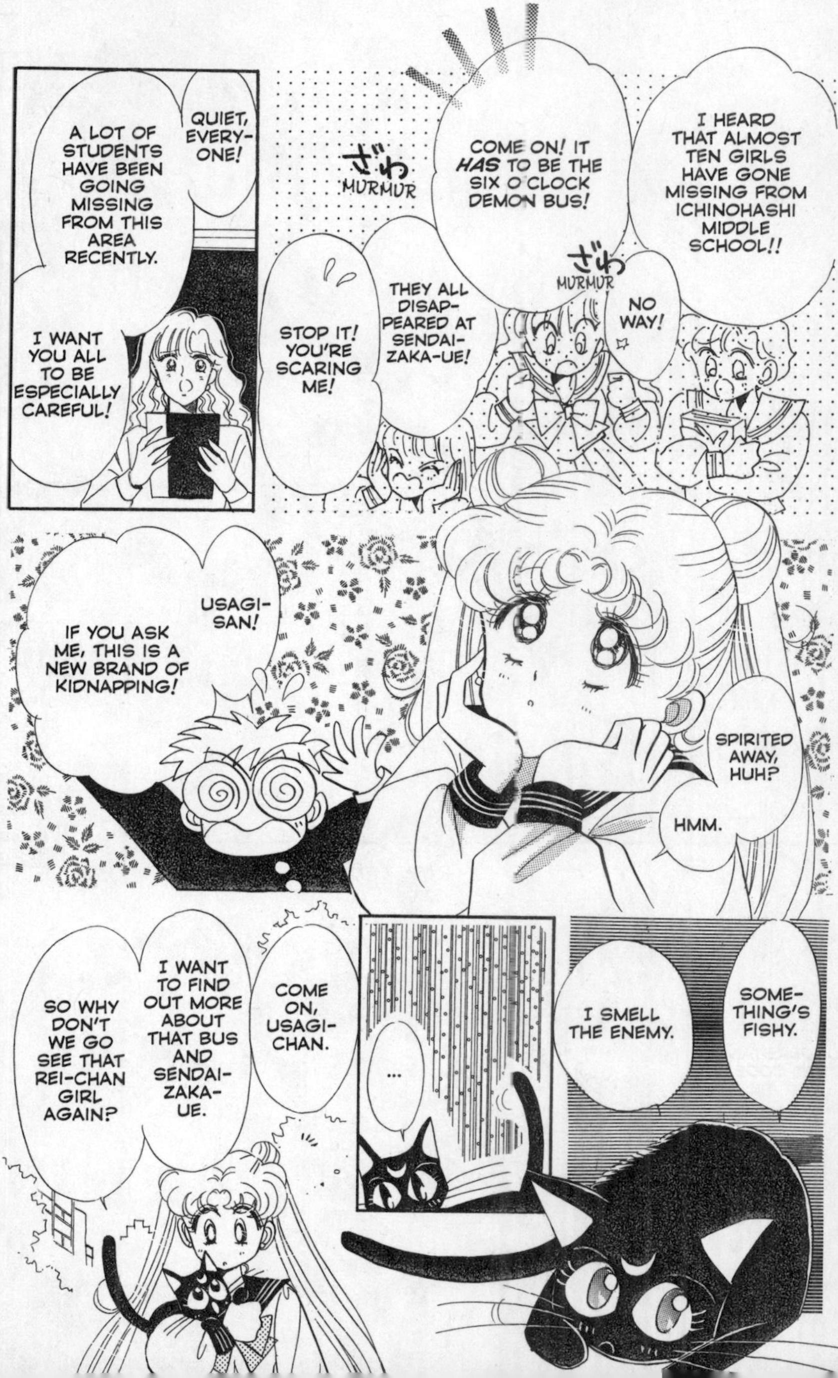
I HEARD THAT ALMOST TEN GIRLS HAVE GONE MISSING FROM ICHINOHASHI MIDDLE SCHOOL!!
COME ON! IT *HAS* TO BE THE SIX O'CLOCK DEMON BUS!
ざわ MURMUR
NO WAY!
ざわ MURMUR
THEY ALL DISAPPEARED AT SENDAI-ZAKA-UE!
STOP IT! YOU'RE SCARING ME!
QUIET, EVERYONE!
A LOT OF STUDENTS HAVE BEEN GOING MISSING FROM THIS AREA RECENTLY.
I WANT YOU ALL TO BE ESPECIALLY CAREFUL!
SPIRITED AWAY, HUH?
HMM.
USAGI-SAN!
IF YOU ASK ME, THIS IS A NEW BRAND OF KIDNAPPING!
SOMETHING'S FISHY.
I SMELL THE ENEMY.
...
COME ON, USAGI-CHAN.
I WANT TO FIND OUT MORE ABOUT THAT BUS AND SENDAI-ZAKA-UE.
SO WHY DON'T WE GO SEE THAT REI-CHAN GIRL AGAIN?

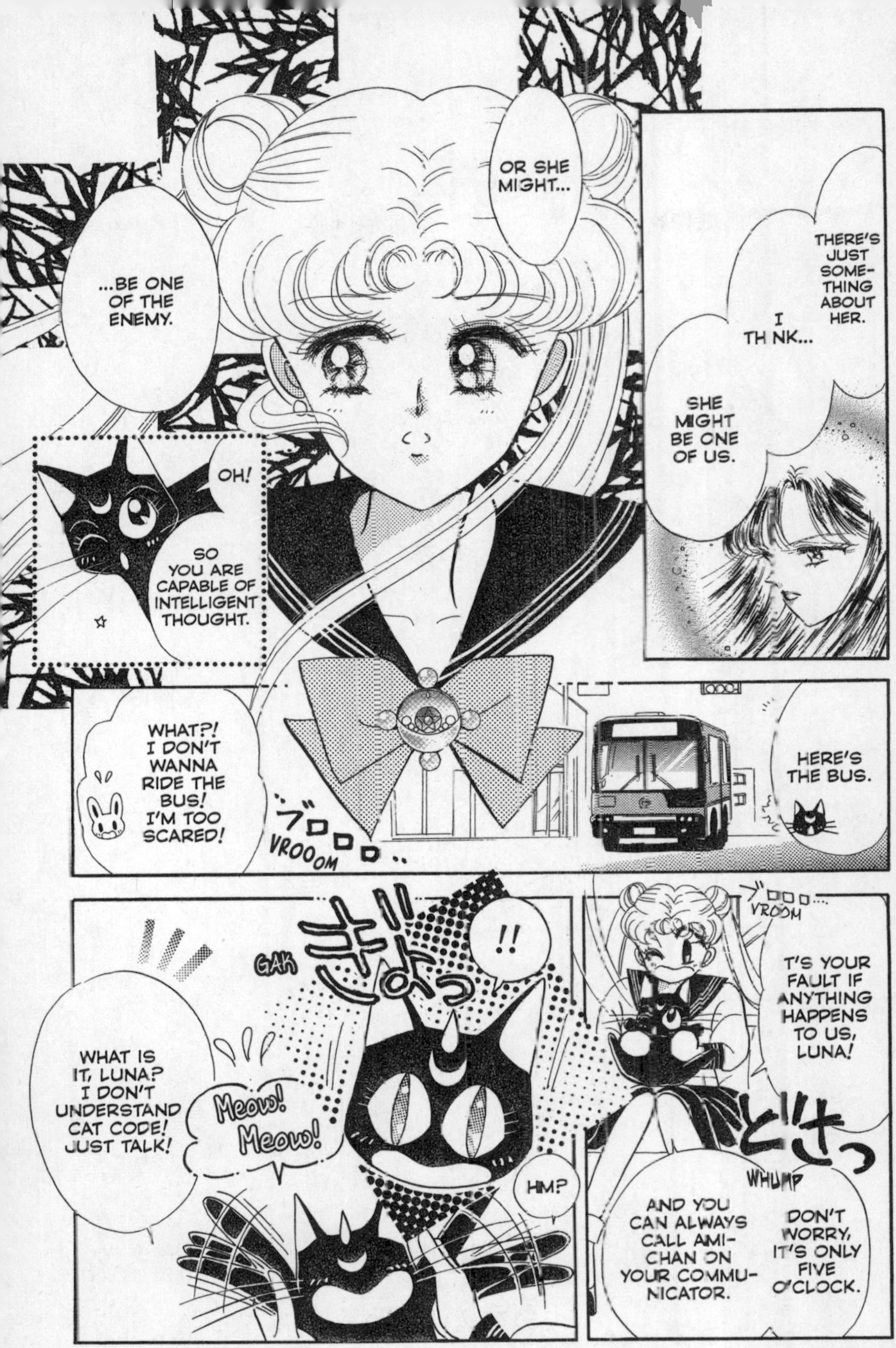
THERE'S JUST SOMETHING ABOUT HER.
I TH NK...
SHE MIGHT BE ONE OF US.
OR SHE MIGHT...
...BE ONE OF THE ENEMY.
OH!
SO YOU ARE CAPABLE OF INTELLIGENT THOUGHT.
HERE'S THE BUS.
ブロロロ
VROOOM
WHAT?! I DON'T WANNA RIDE THE BUS! I'M TOO SCARED!
ブロロロ
VROOM
T'S YOUR FAULT IF ANYTHING HAPPENS TO US, LUNA!
どさっ
WHUMP
DON'T WORRY, IT'S ONLY FIVE O'CLOCK.
AND YOU CAN ALWAYS CALL AMI-CHAN ON YOUR COMMUNICATOR.
!!
ぎょっ
GAK
HM?
Meow! Meow!
WHAT IS IT, LUNA? I DON'T UNDERSTAND CAT CODE! JUST TALK!

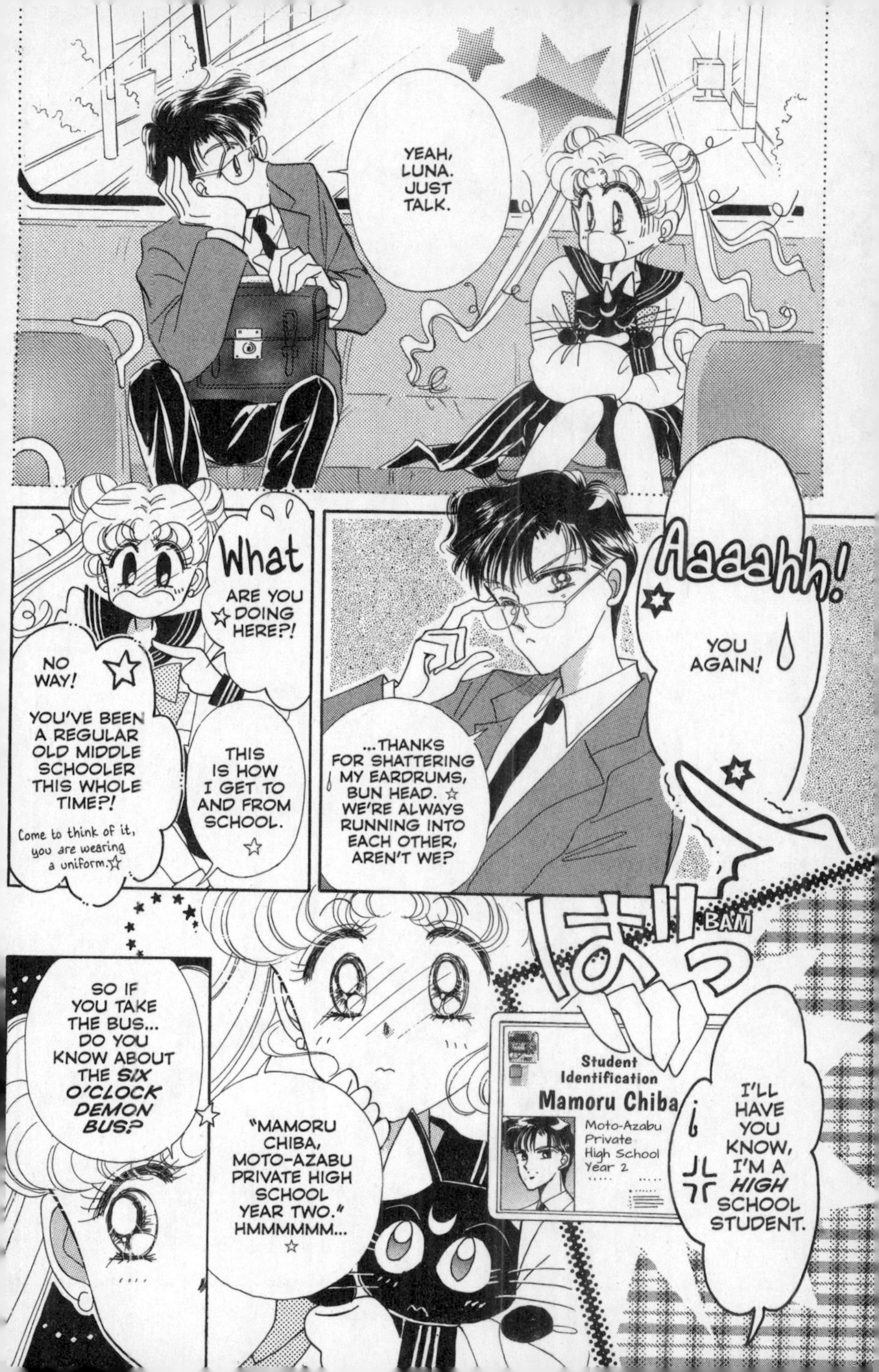
YEAH, LUNA. JUST TALK.
Aaaahh!
YOU AGAIN!
...THANKS FOR SHATTERING MY EARDRUMS, BUN HEAD. ☆ WE'RE ALWAYS RUNNING INTO EACH OTHER, AREN'T WE?
What ARE YOU ☆ DOING HERE?!
THIS IS HOW I GET TO AND FROM SCHOOL. ☆
NO WAY! ☆ YOU'VE BEEN A REGULAR OLD MIDDLE SCHOOLER THIS WHOLE TIME?!
Come to think of it, you are wearing a uniform.☆
はっ
BAM
I'LL HAVE YOU KNOW, I'M A *HIGH* SCHOOL STUDENT.
Student Identification
Mamoru Chiba
Moto-Azabu Private High School Year 2
"MAMORU CHIBA, MOTO-AZABU PRIVATE HIGH SCHOOL YEAR TWO." HMMMMMM... ☆
SO IF YOU TAKE THE BUS... DO YOU KNOW ABOUT THE *SIX O'CLOCK DEMON BUS?*

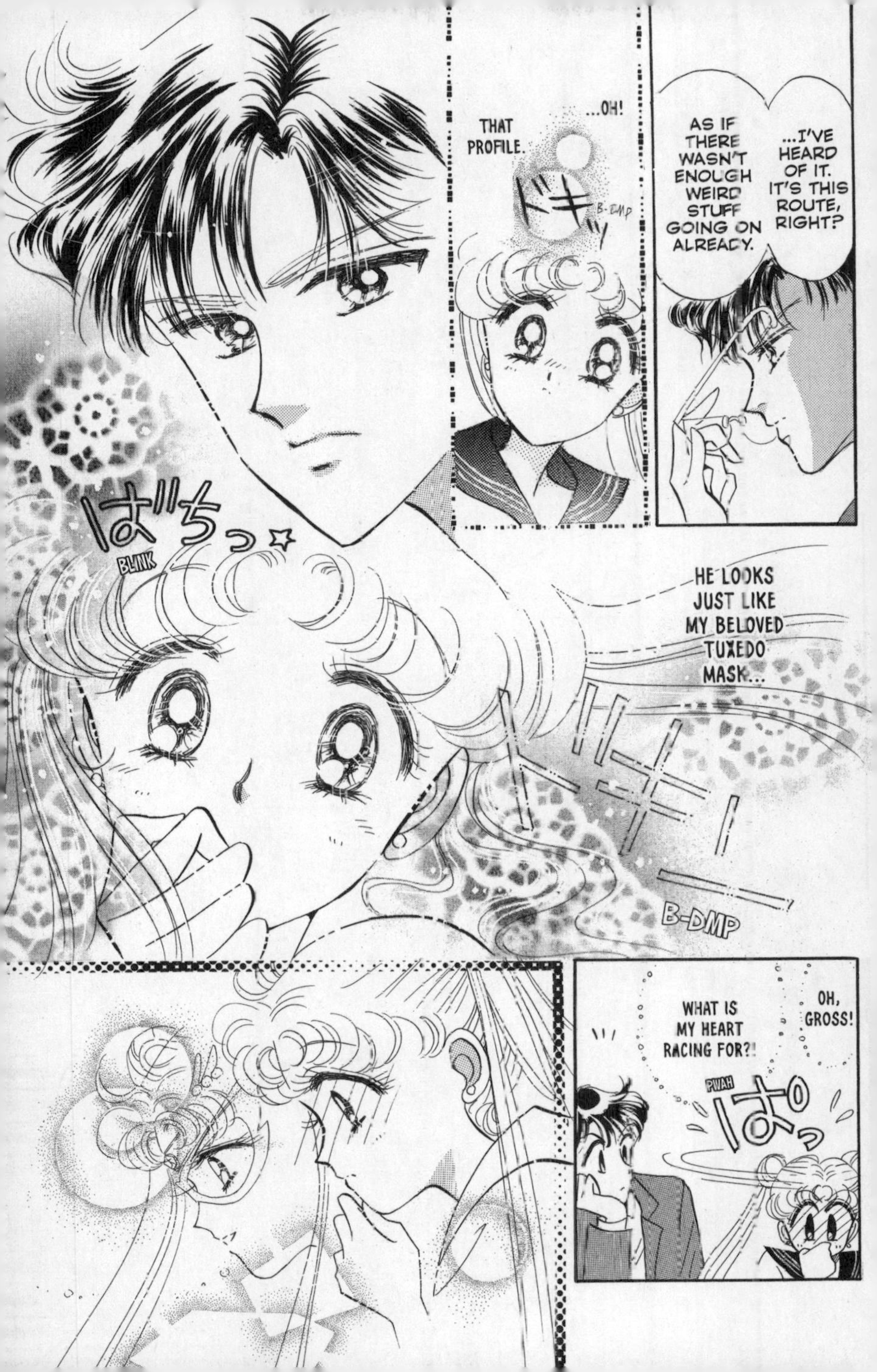
...I'VE HEARD OF IT. IT'S THIS ROUTE, RIGHT?
AS IF THERE WASN'T ENOUGH WEIRD STUFF GOING ON ALREADY.
...OH!
B-DMP
THAT PROFILE.
ばちっ
BLINK
HE LOOKS JUST LIKE MY BELOVED TUXEDO MASK...
B-DMP
OH, GROSS!
WHAT IS MY HEART RACING FOR?!
ぱっ
PWAH

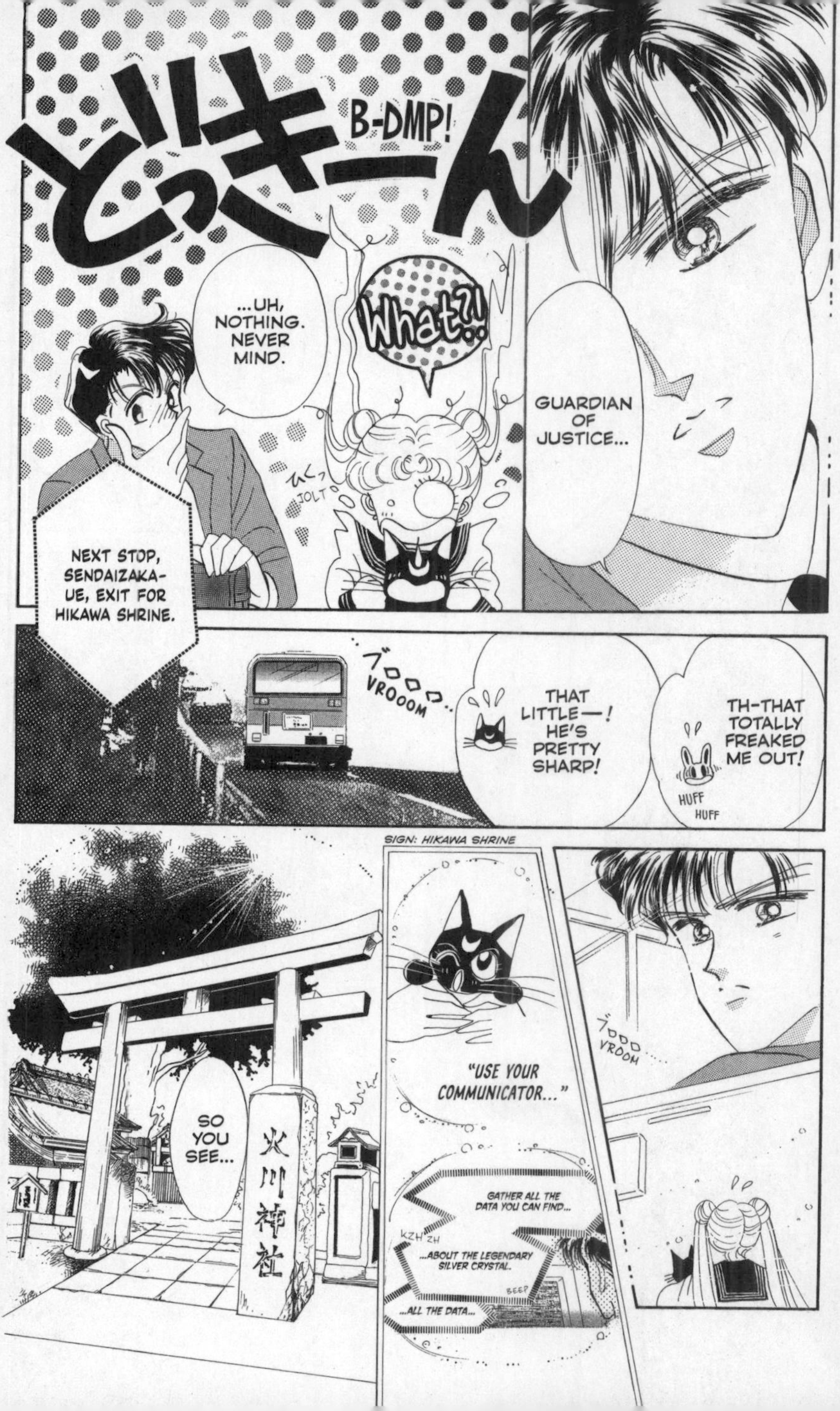
GUARDIAN OF JUSTICE...
どっきーん
B-DMP!
...UH, NOTHING. NEVER MIND.
What?!
ひくっ
JOLT
NEXT STOP, SENDAIZAKA-UE, EXIT FOR HIKAWA SHRINE.
TH-THAT TOTALLY FREAKED ME OUT!
HUFF HUFF
THAT LITTLE—! HE'S PRETTY SHARP!
ブロロロ
VROOOM
ブロロロ
VROOM
"USE YOUR COMMUNICATOR..."
GATHER ALL THE DATA YOU CAN FIND...
KZH ZH
...ABOUT THE LEGENDARY SILVER CRYSTAL.
BEEP
...ALL THE DATA...
SIGN: HIKAWA SHRINE
火川神社
SO YOU SEE...

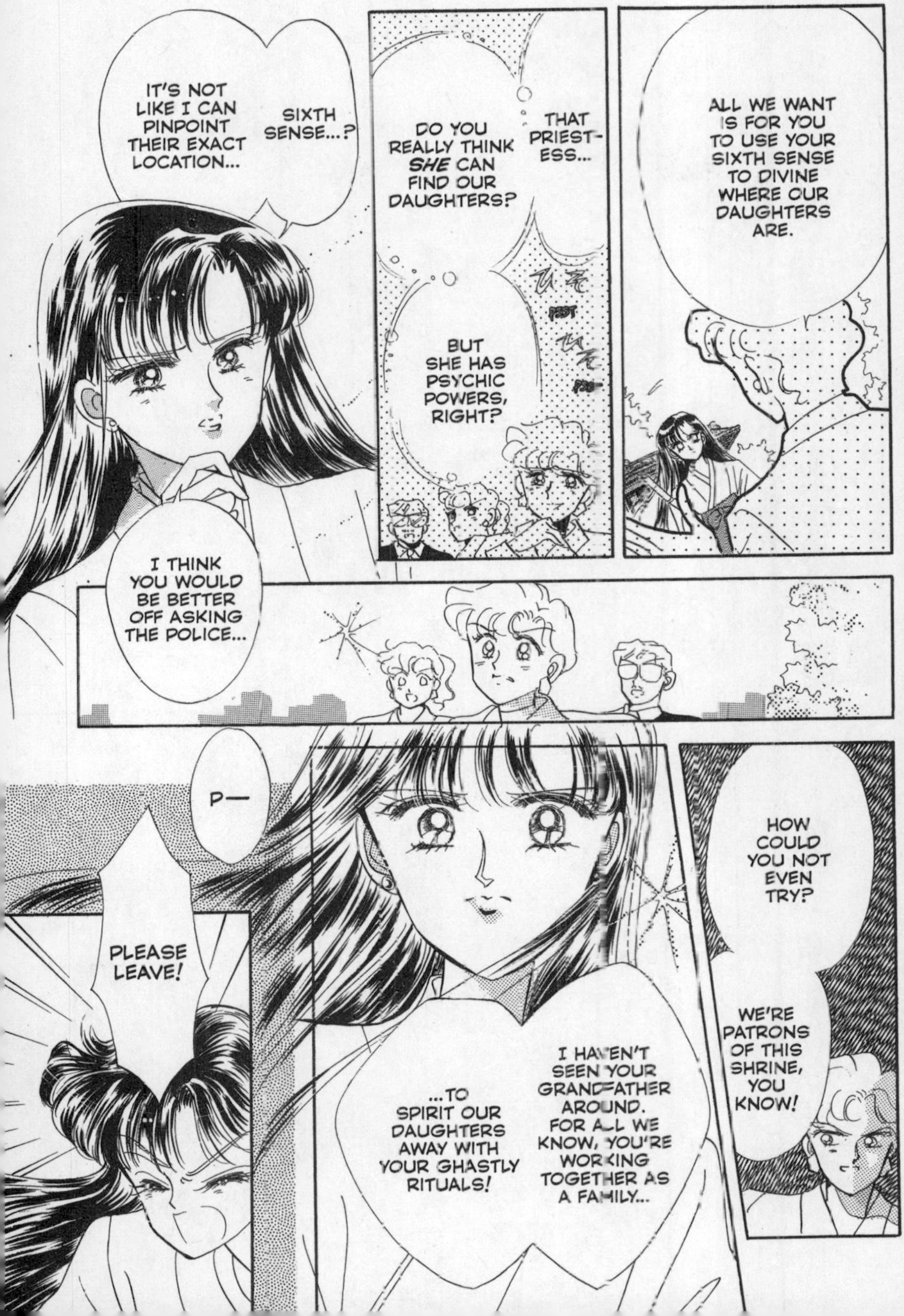
ALL WE WANT IS FOR YOU TO USE YOUR SIXTH SENSE TO DIVINE WHERE OUR DAUGHTERS ARE.
THAT PRIEST-ESS...
DO YOU REALLY THINK *SHE* CAN FIND OUR DAUGHTERS?
BUT SHE HAS PSYCHIC POWERS, RIGHT?
PSST
SIXTH SENSE...?
IT'S NOT LIKE I CAN PINPOINT THEIR EXACT LOCATION...
I THINK YOU WOULD BE BETTER OFF ASKING THE POLICE...
HOW COULD YOU NOT EVEN TRY?
WE'RE PATRONS OF THIS SHRINE, YOU KNOW!
I HAVEN'T SEEN YOUR GRANDFATHER AROUND. FOR ALL WE KNOW, YOU'RE WORKING TOGETHER AS A FAMILY...
...TO SPIRIT OUR DAUGHTERS AWAY WITH YOUR GHASTLY RITUALS!
P—
PLEASE LEAVE!

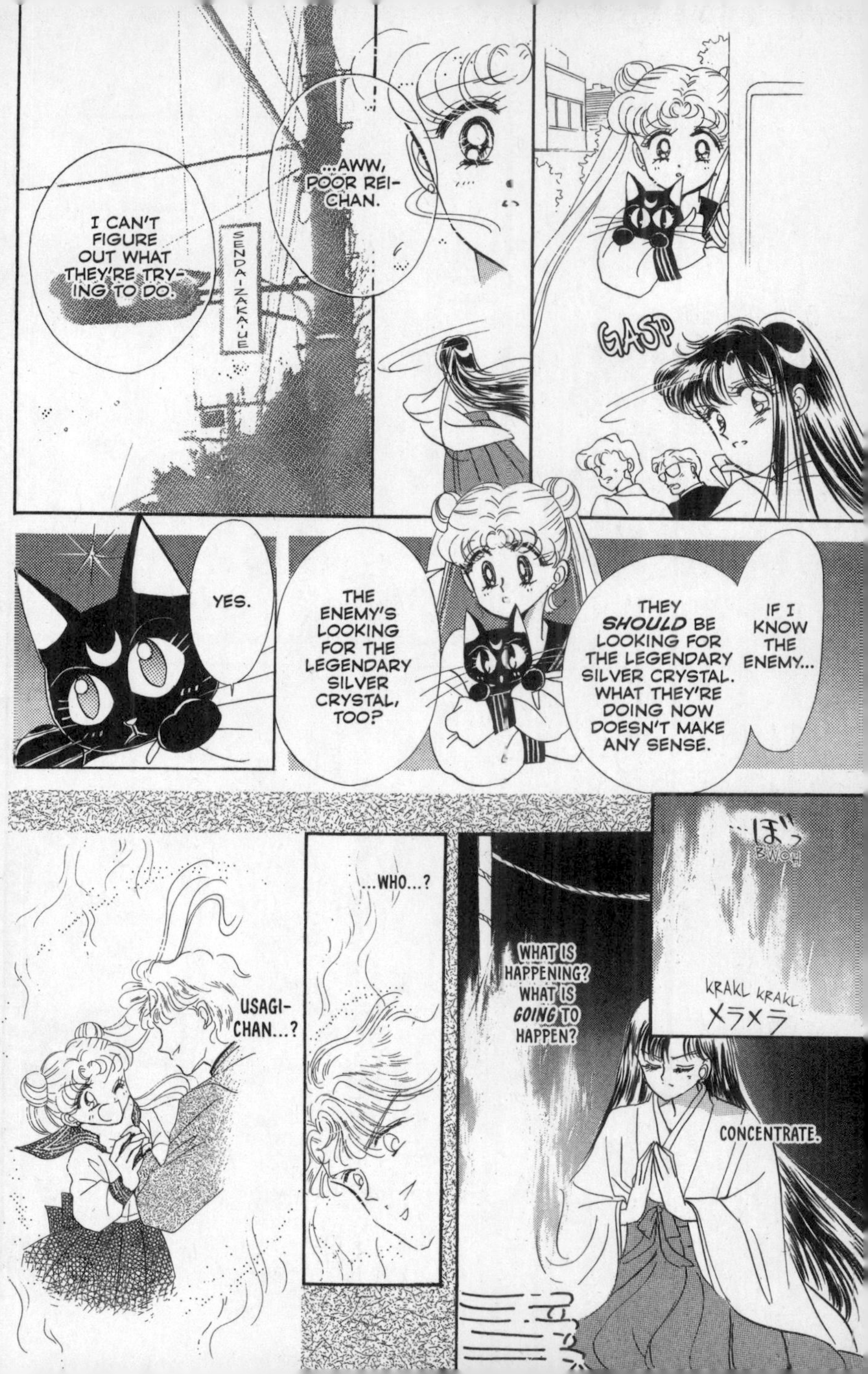
GASP
...AWW, POOR REI-CHAN.
I CAN'T FIGURE OUT WHAT THEY'RE TRYING TO DO.
SENDAI-ZAKA-UE
IF I KNOW THE ENEMY...
THEY SHOULD BE LOOKING FOR THE LEGENDARY SILVER CRYSTAL. WHAT THEY'RE DOING NOW DOESN'T MAKE ANY SENSE.
THE ENEMY'S LOOKING FOR THE LEGENDARY SILVER CRYSTAL, TOO?
YES.
ぼっ
BWOH
KRAKL KRAKL
メラメラ
CONCENTRATE.
WHAT IS HAPPENING? WHAT IS GOING TO HAPPEN?
...WHO...?
USAGI-CHAN...?

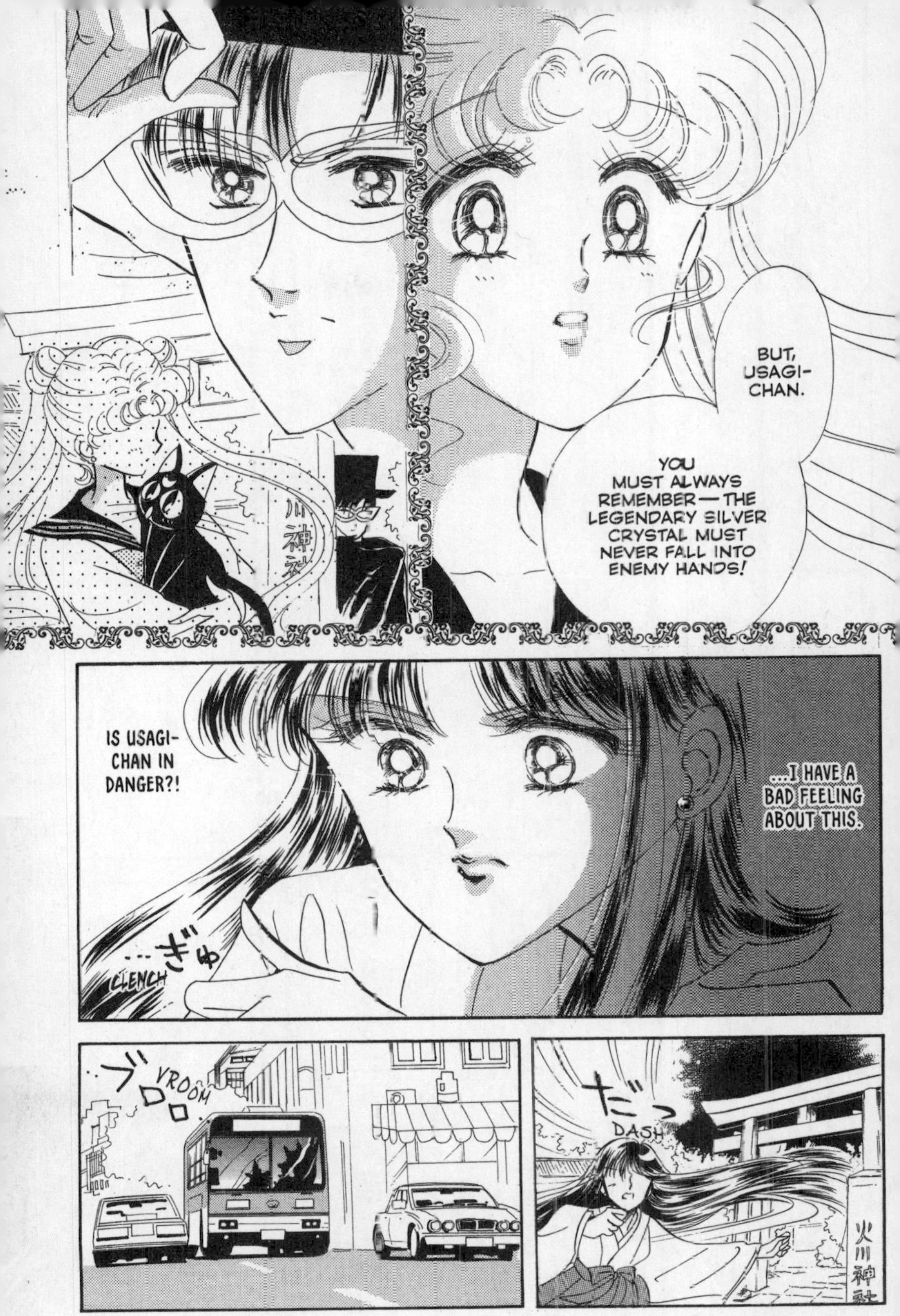
BUT, USAGI-CHAN.
YOU MUST ALWAYS REMEMBER—THE LEGENDARY SILVER CRYSTAL MUST NEVER FALL INTO ENEMY HANDS!
...I HAVE A BAD FEELING ABOUT THIS.
IS USAGI-CHAN IN DANGER?!
ぎゅ
CLENCH
だっ
DASH
火川神社
ブロロ
VROOM

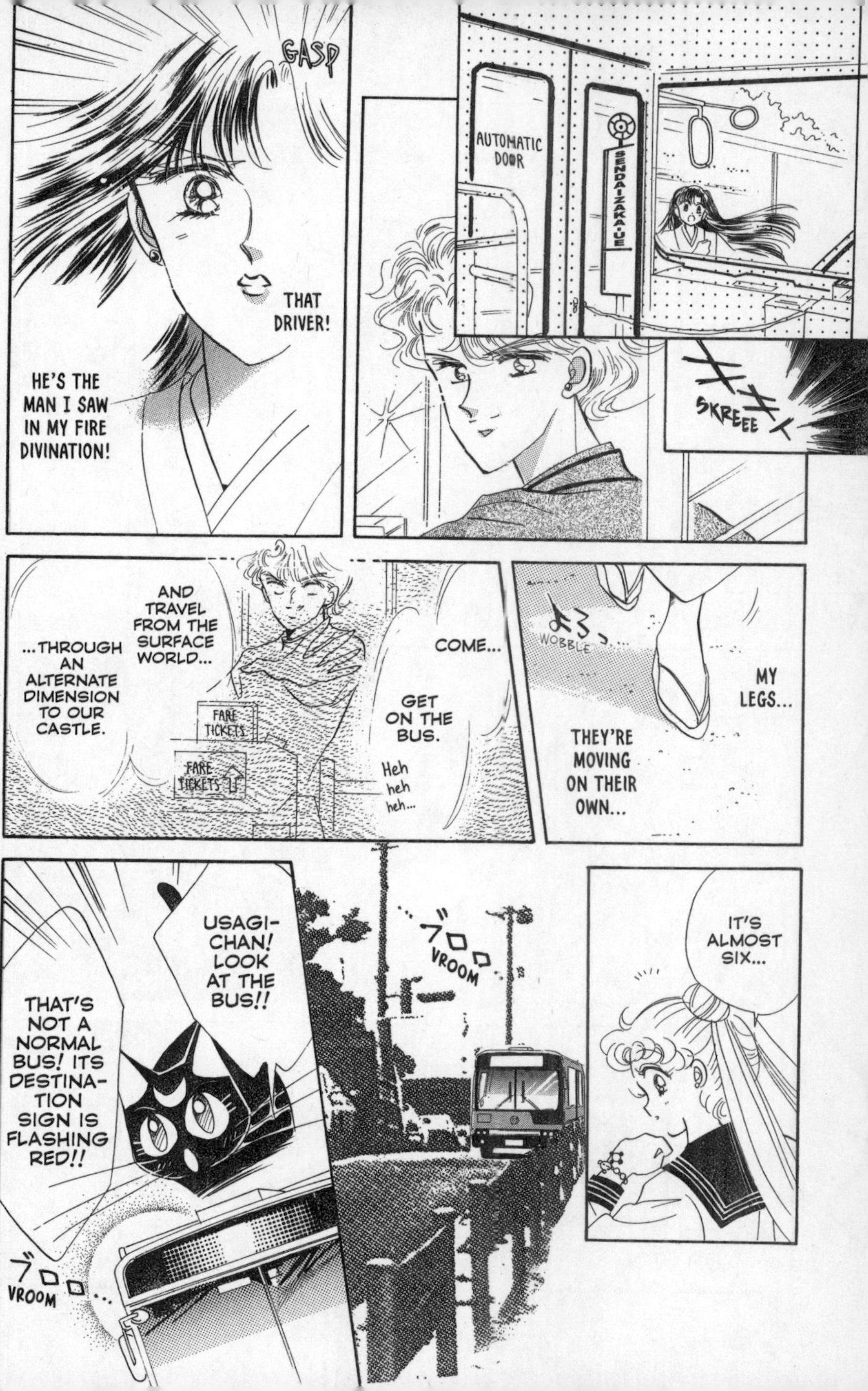
AUTOMATIC DOOR
SENDAIZAKA-UE
SKREEE
GASP
THAT DRIVER!
HE'S THE MAN I SAW IN MY FIRE DIVINATION!
WOBBLE
MY LEGS...
THEY'RE MOVING ON THEIR OWN...
COME...
GET ON THE BUS.
Heh heh heh...
FARE TICKETS
FARE TICKETS
AND TRAVEL FROM THE SURFACE WORLD...
...THROUGH AN ALTERNATE DIMENSION TO OUR CASTLE.
IT'S ALMOST SIX...
VROOM
USAGI-CHAN! LOOK AT THE BUS!!
THAT'S NOT A NORMAL BUS! ITS DESTINATION SIGN IS FLASHING RED!!
VROOM

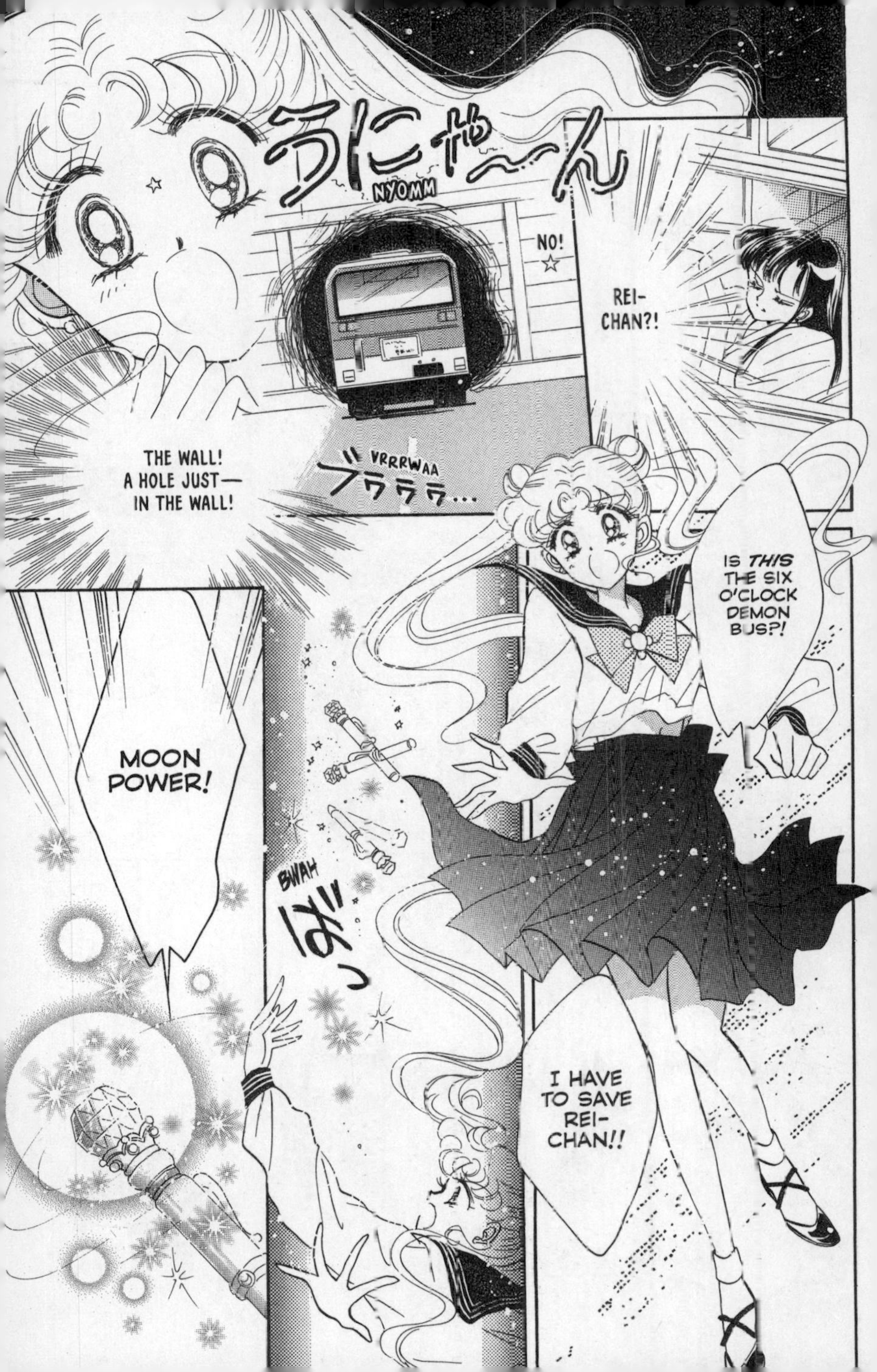

うにゃ〜ん
NYOMM
REI-CHAN?!
NO!
THE WALL! A HOLE JUST— IN THE WALL!
VRRRWAA
IS THIS THE SIX O'CLOCK DEMON BUS?!
I HAVE TO SAVE REI-CHAN!!
BWAH
MOON POWER!

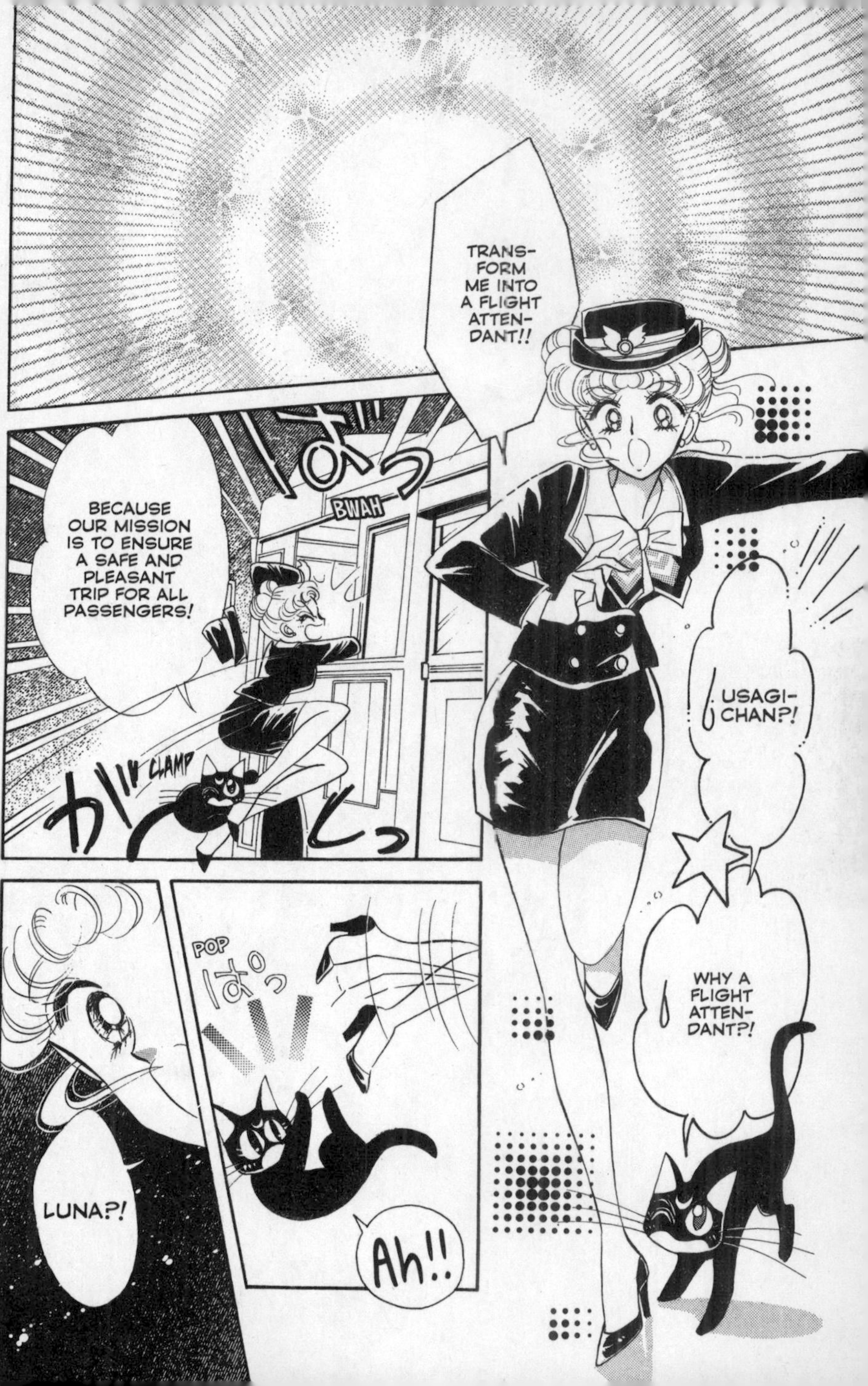
TRANS-FORM ME INTO A FLIGHT ATTEN-DANT!!
USAGI-CHAN?!
WHY A FLIGHT ATTEN-DANT?!
BWAH
BECAUSE OUR MISSION IS TO ENSURE A SAFE AND PLEASANT TRIP FOR ALL PASSENGERS!
CLAMP
POP
Ah!!
LUNA?!

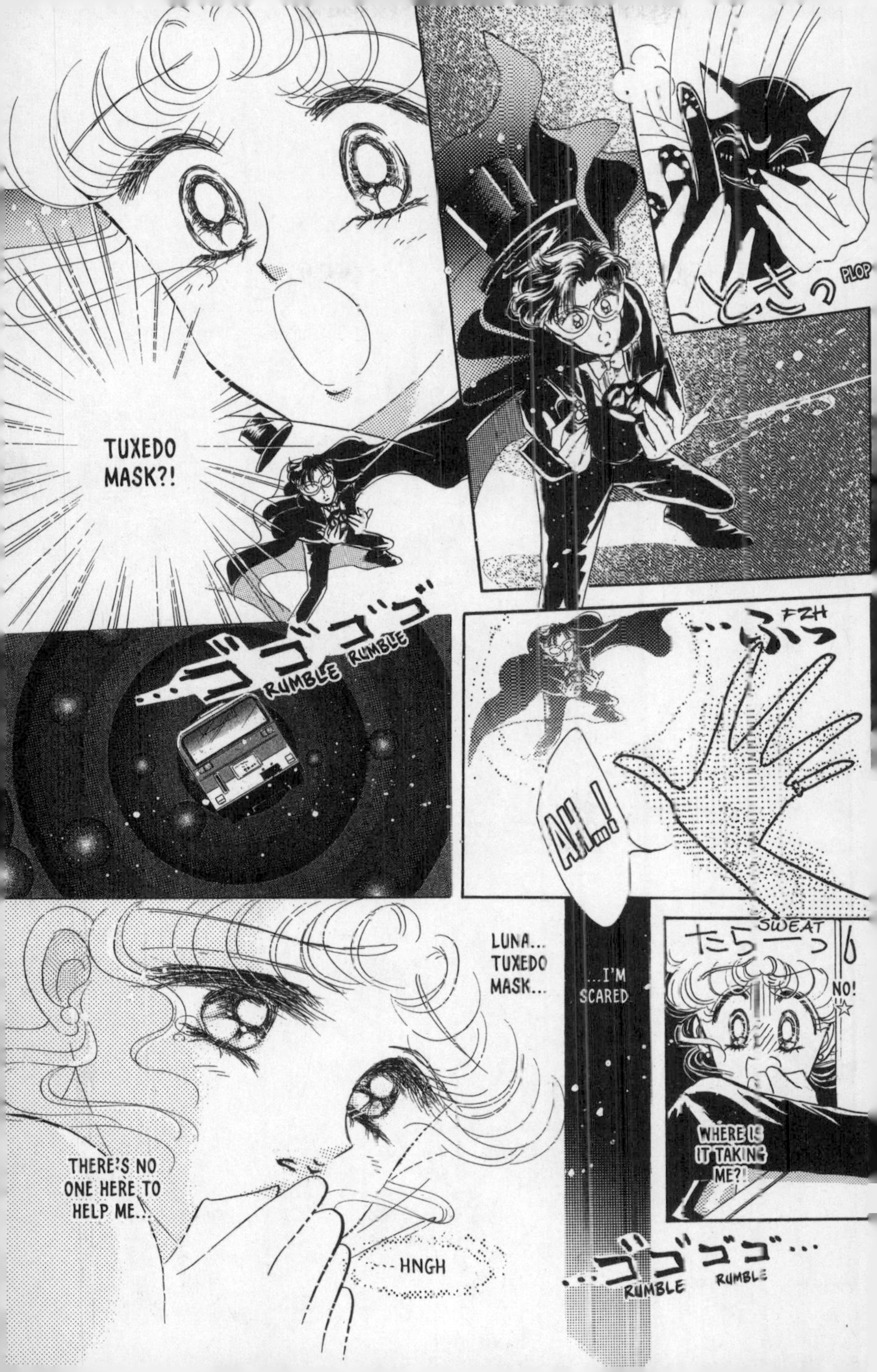

とさっ
PLOP
TUXEDO MASK?!
…ふっ
FZH
AH…!
…ゴゴゴ
RUMBLE RUMBLE
たらーっ
SWEAT
NO!☆
WHERE IS IT TAKING ME?!
…I'M SCARED
LUNA… TUXEDO MASK…
THERE'S NO ONE HERE TO HELP ME…
---HNGH
…ゴゴゴゴ…
RUMBLE RUMBLE

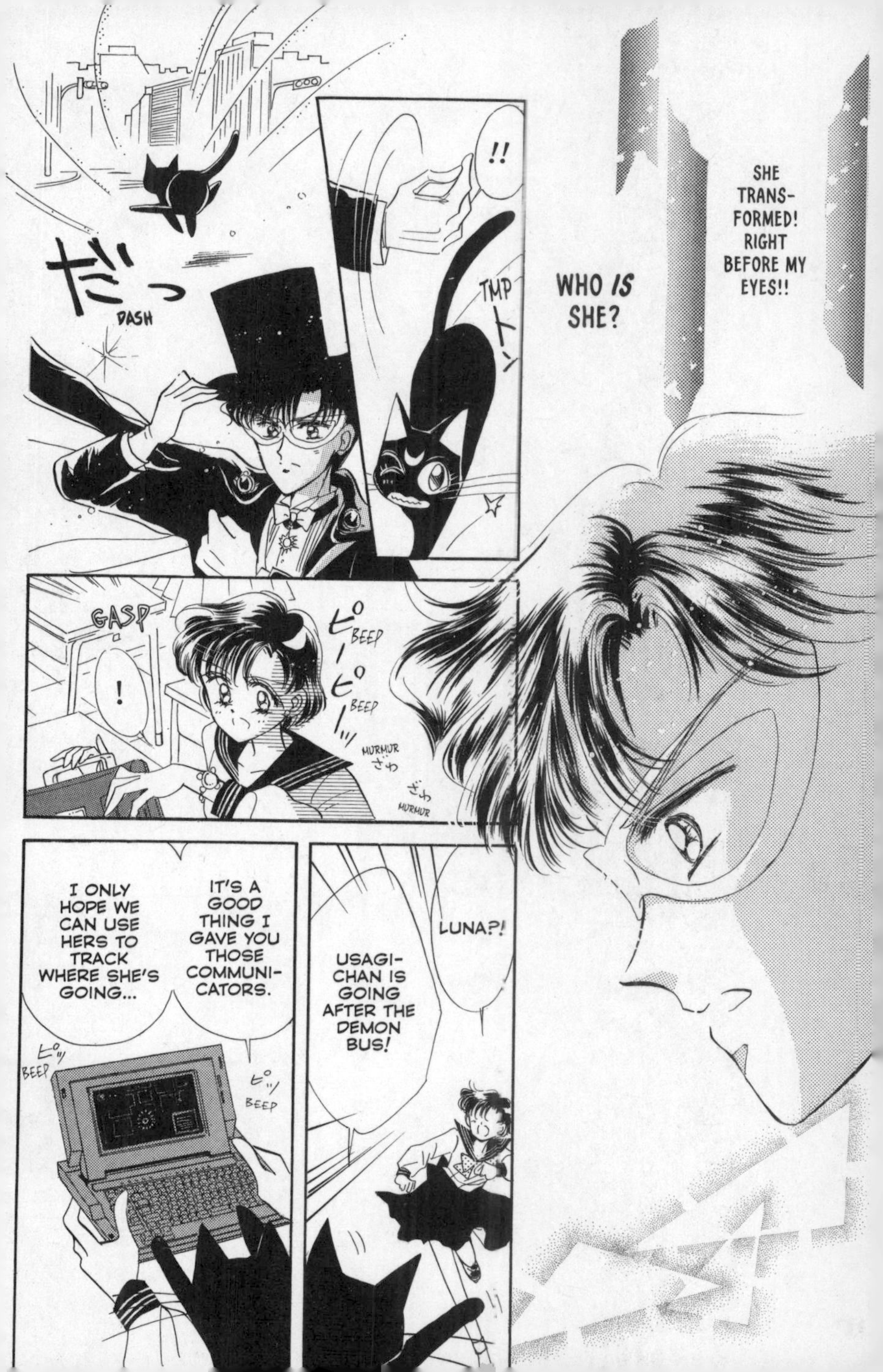
SHE TRANSFORMED! RIGHT BEFORE MY EYES!!
WHO *IS* SHE?
!!
TMP
だっ
DASH
ピーピッ
BEEP
BEEP
GASP
!
ざわ
MURMUR
ざわ
MURMUR
LUNA?!
USAGI-CHAN IS GOING AFTER THE DEMON BUS!
IT'S A GOOD THING I GAVE YOU THOSE COMMUNICATORS.
I ONLY HOPE WE CAN USE HERS TO TRACK WHERE SHE'S GOING...
ピッ
BEEP
ピッ
BEEP

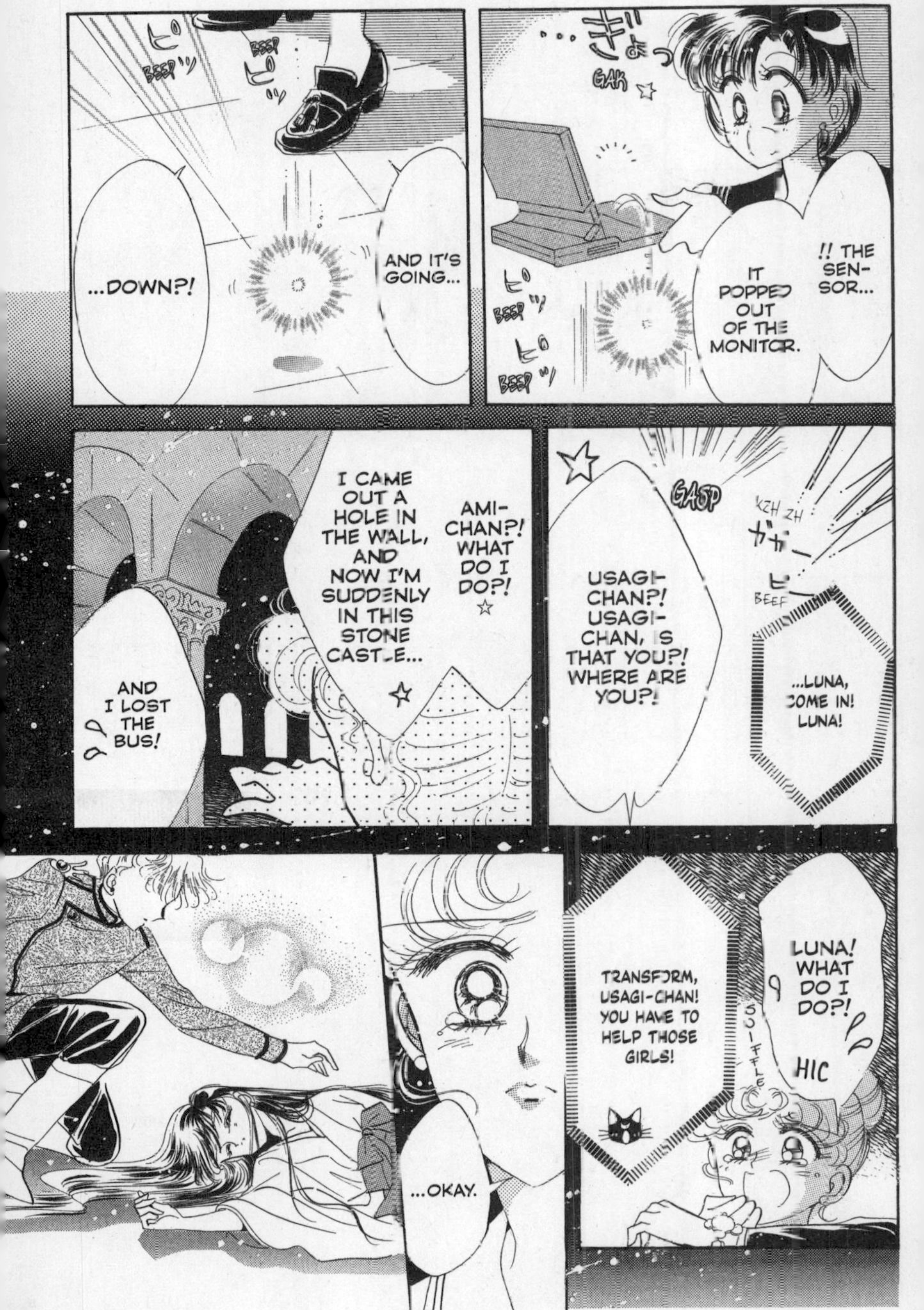
...ぎょっ
GAK
!! THE SEN-SOR...
IT POPPED OUT OF THE MONITOR.
ピッ BEEP
ピッ BEEP
ピッ BEEP
ピッ BEEP
AND IT'S GOING...
...DOWN?!
GASP
KZH ZH
ガガー
ピ BEEP
...LUNA, COME IN! LUNA!
USAGI-CHAN?! USAGI-CHAN, IS THAT YOU?! WHERE ARE YOU?!
AMI-CHAN?! WHAT DO I DO?!
I CAME OUT A HOLE IN THE WALL, AND NOW I'M SUDDENLY IN THIS STONE CASTLE...
AND I LOST THE BUS!
LUNA! WHAT DO I DO?!
HIC
SNIFFLE
TRANSFORM, USAGI-CHAN! YOU HAVE TO HELP THOSE GIRLS!
...OKAY.

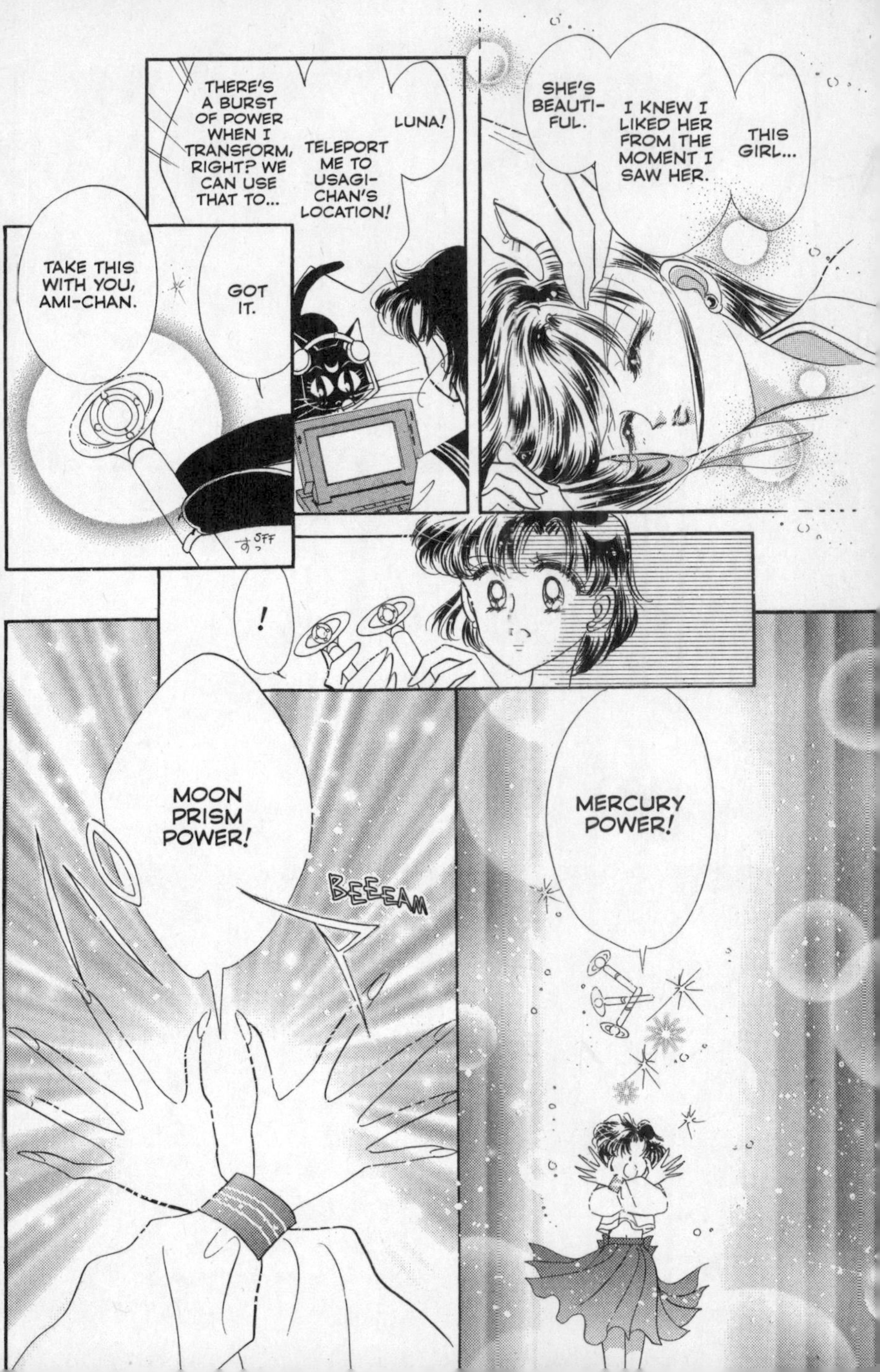
THIS GIRL...
I KNEW I LIKED HER FROM THE MOMENT I SAW HER.
SHE'S BEAUTI-FUL.
LUNA!
TELEPORT ME TO USAGI-CHAN'S LOCATION!
THERE'S A BURST OF POWER WHEN I TRANSFORM, RIGHT? WE CAN USE THAT TO...
GOT IT.
TAKE THIS WITH YOU, AMI-CHAN.
すっ SFF
!
MERCURY POWER!
MOON PRISM POWER!
BEEEAM

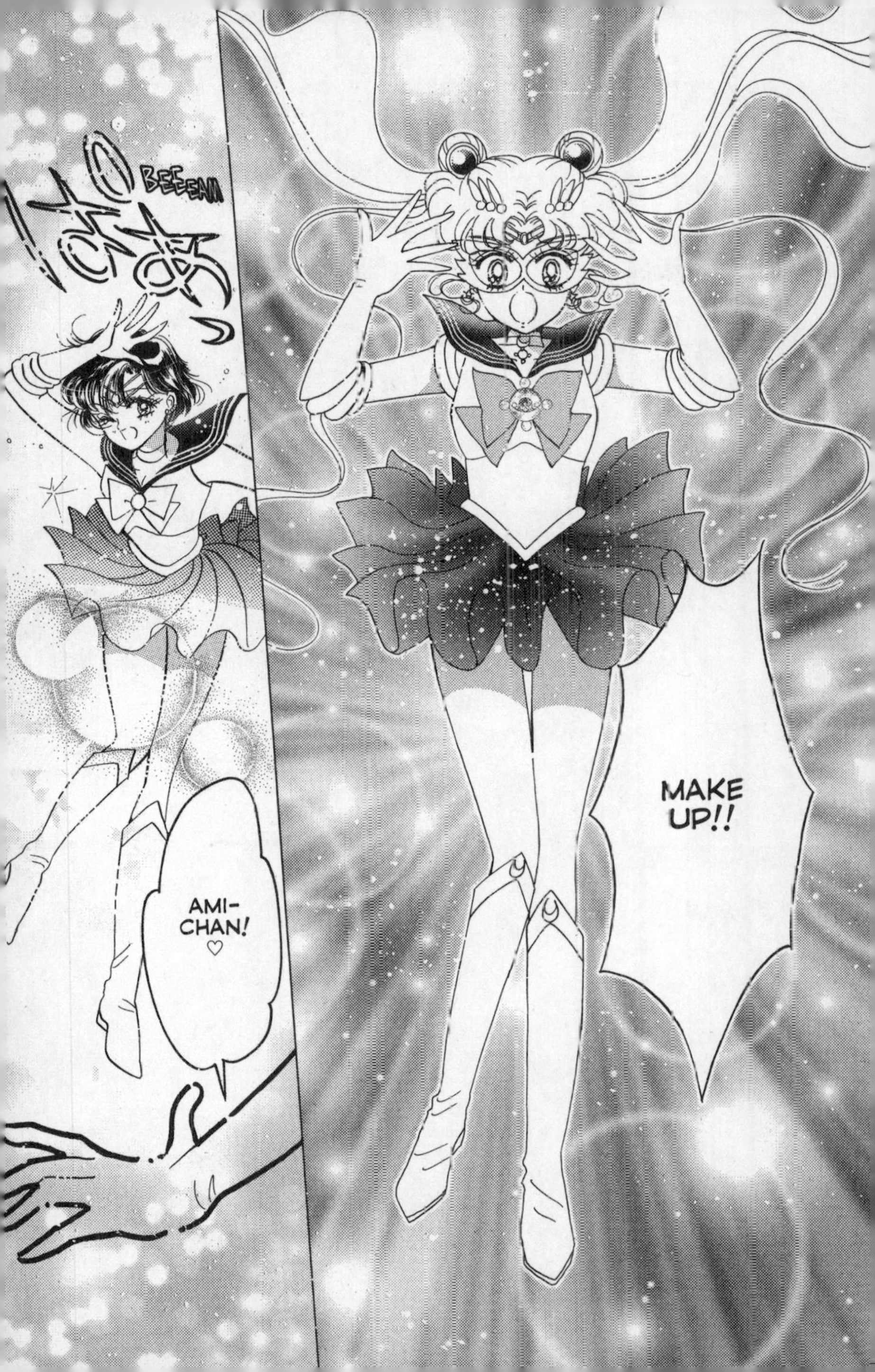
MAKE UP!!
BEEEAM
AMI-CHAN! ♡

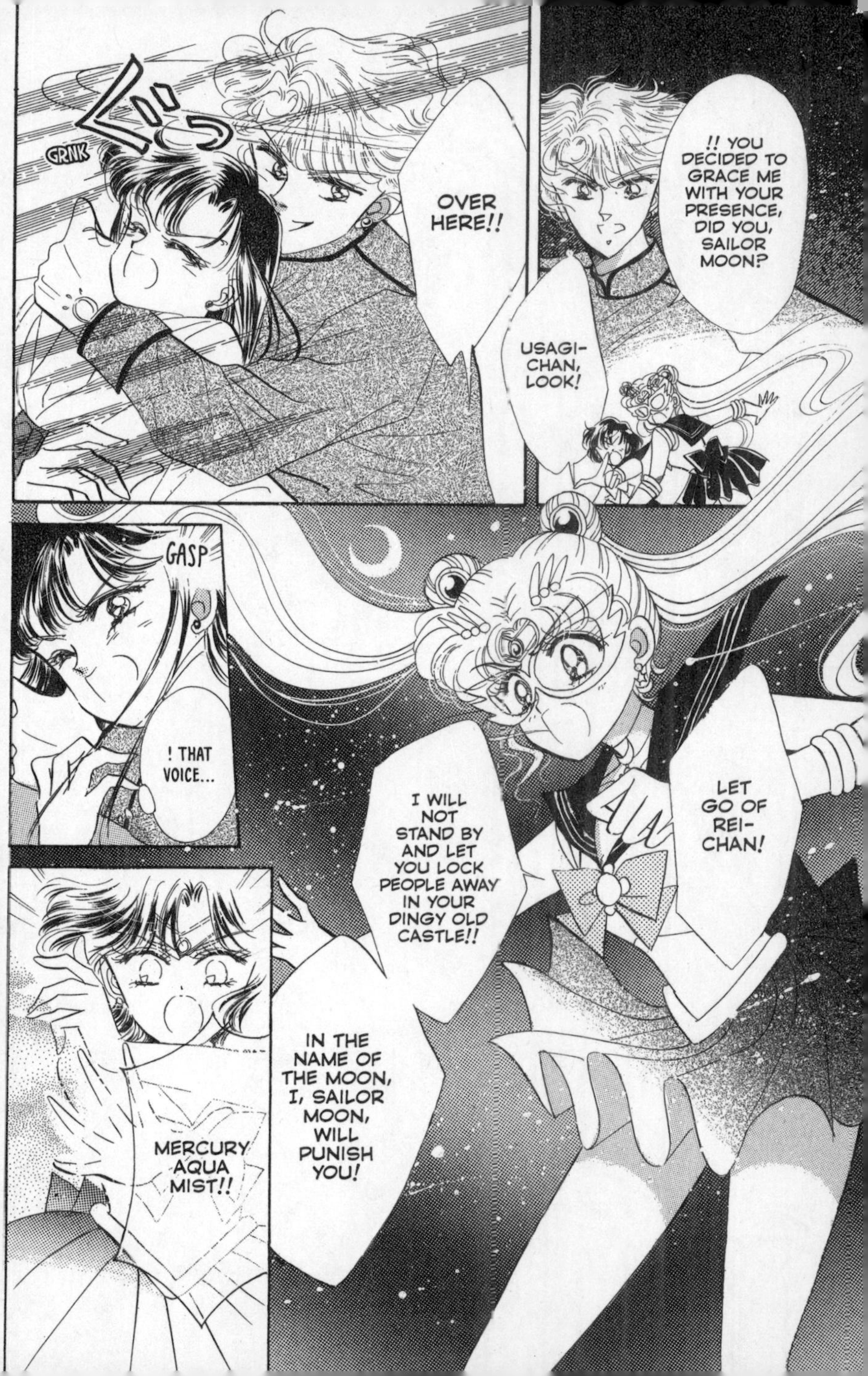
!! YOU DECIDED TO GRACE ME WITH YOUR PRESENCE, DID YOU, SAILOR MOON?
USAGI-CHAN, LOOK!
OVER HERE!!
GRNK
LET GO OF REI-CHAN!
I WILL NOT STAND BY AND LET YOU LOCK PEOPLE AWAY IN YOUR DINGY OLD CASTLE!!
IN THE NAME OF THE MOON, I, SAILOR MOON, WILL PUNISH YOU!
GASP
! THAT VOICE...
MERCURY AQUA MIST!!

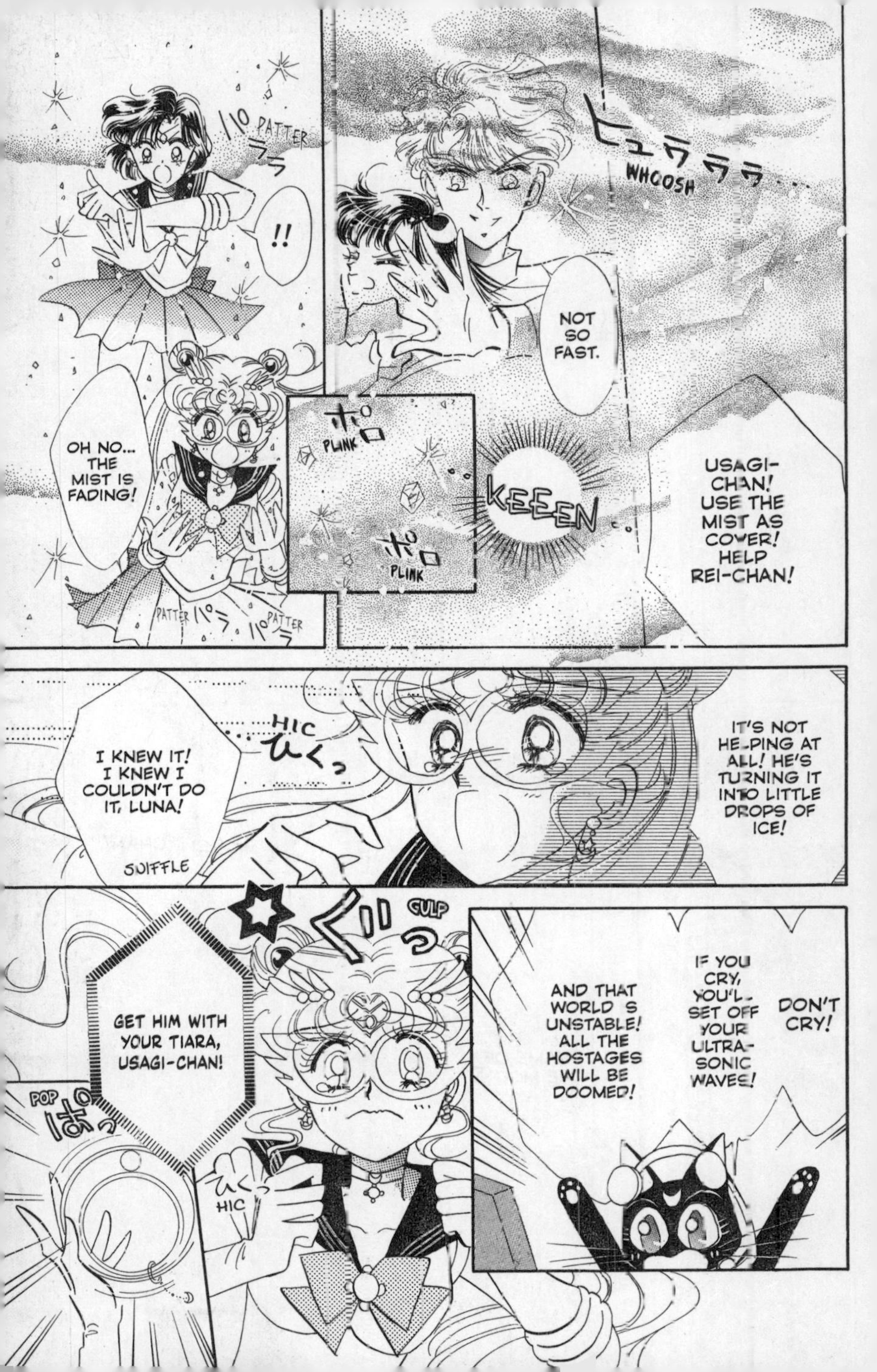
WHOOSH
USAGI-CHAN! USE THE MIST AS COVER! HELP REI-CHAN!
NOT SO FAST.
PLINK
KEEEN
PLINK
PATTER
!!
OH NO... THE MIST IS FADING!
PATTER
PATTER
IT'S NOT HELPING AT ALL! HE'S TURNING IT INTO LITTLE DROPS OF ICE!
HIC
I KNEW IT! I KNEW I COULDN'T DO IT, LUNA!
SNIFFLE
DON'T CRY!
IF YOU CRY, YOU'LL SET OFF YOUR ULTRA-SONIC WAVES!
AND THAT WORLD IS UNSTABLE! ALL THE HOSTAGES WILL BE DOOMED!
GULP
GET HIM WITH YOUR TIARA, USAGI-CHAN!
POP
HIC

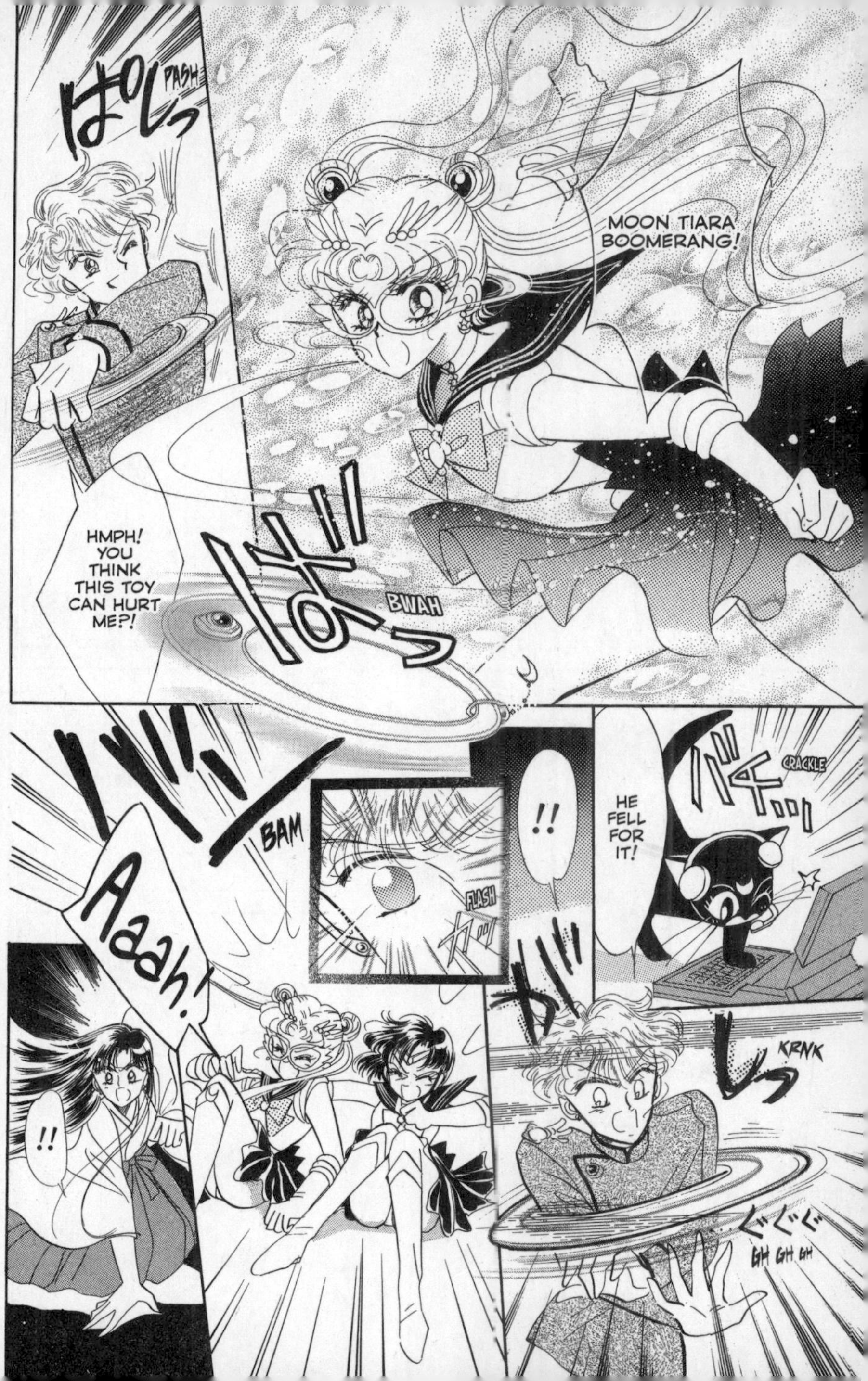
MOON TIARA BOOMERANG!
PASH
HMPH! YOU THINK THIS TOY CAN HURT ME?!
BWAH
CRACKLE
!!
HE FELL FOR IT!
FLASH
BAM
KRNK
GH GH GH
Aaaah!
!!

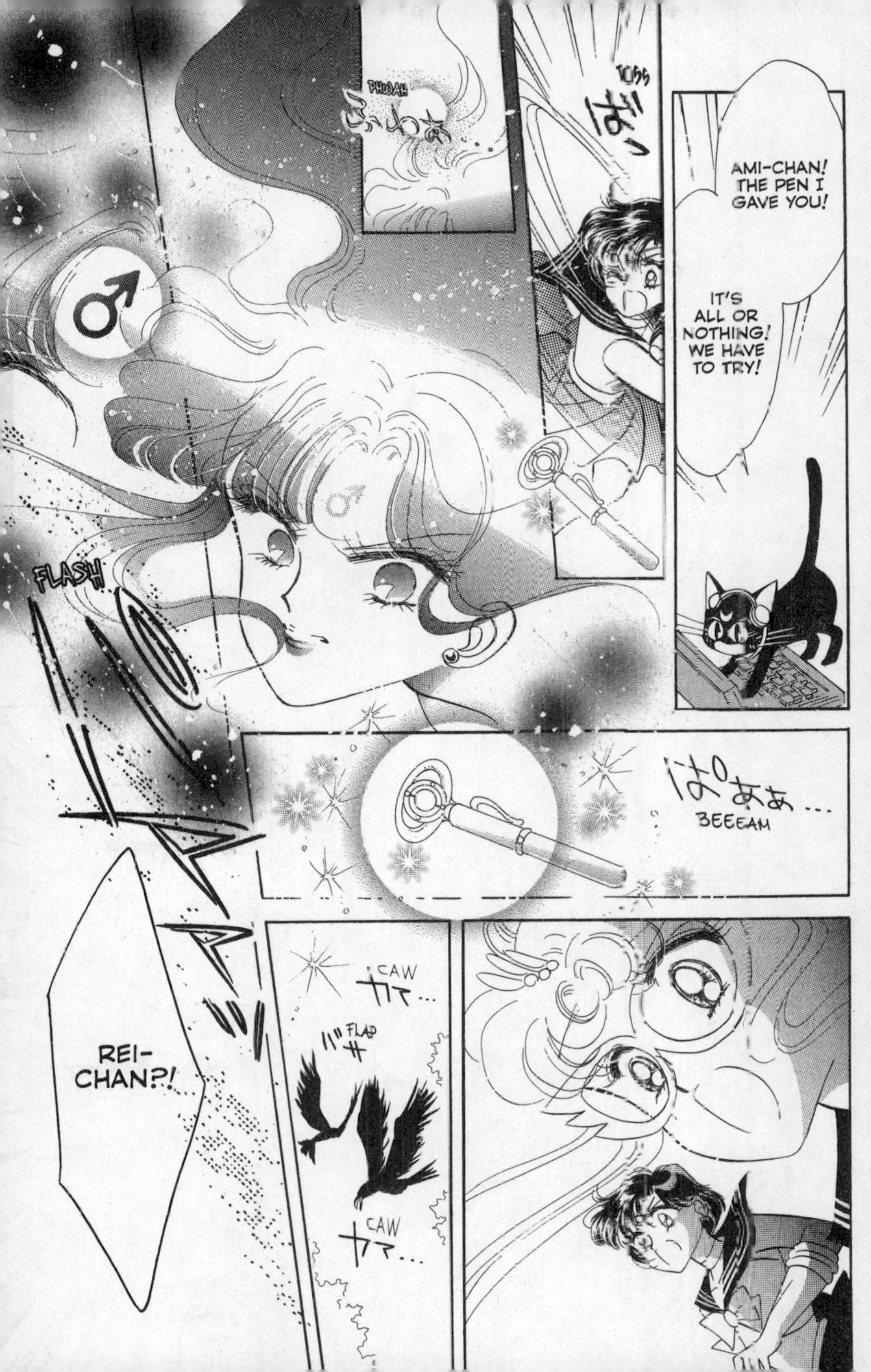
AMI-CHAN! THE PEN I GAVE YOU!
IT'S ALL OR NOTHING! WE HAVE TO TRY!
TOSS
PHWOAH
FLASH
ぱぁぁ…
BEEEAM
CAW
FLAP
CAW
REI-CHAN?!

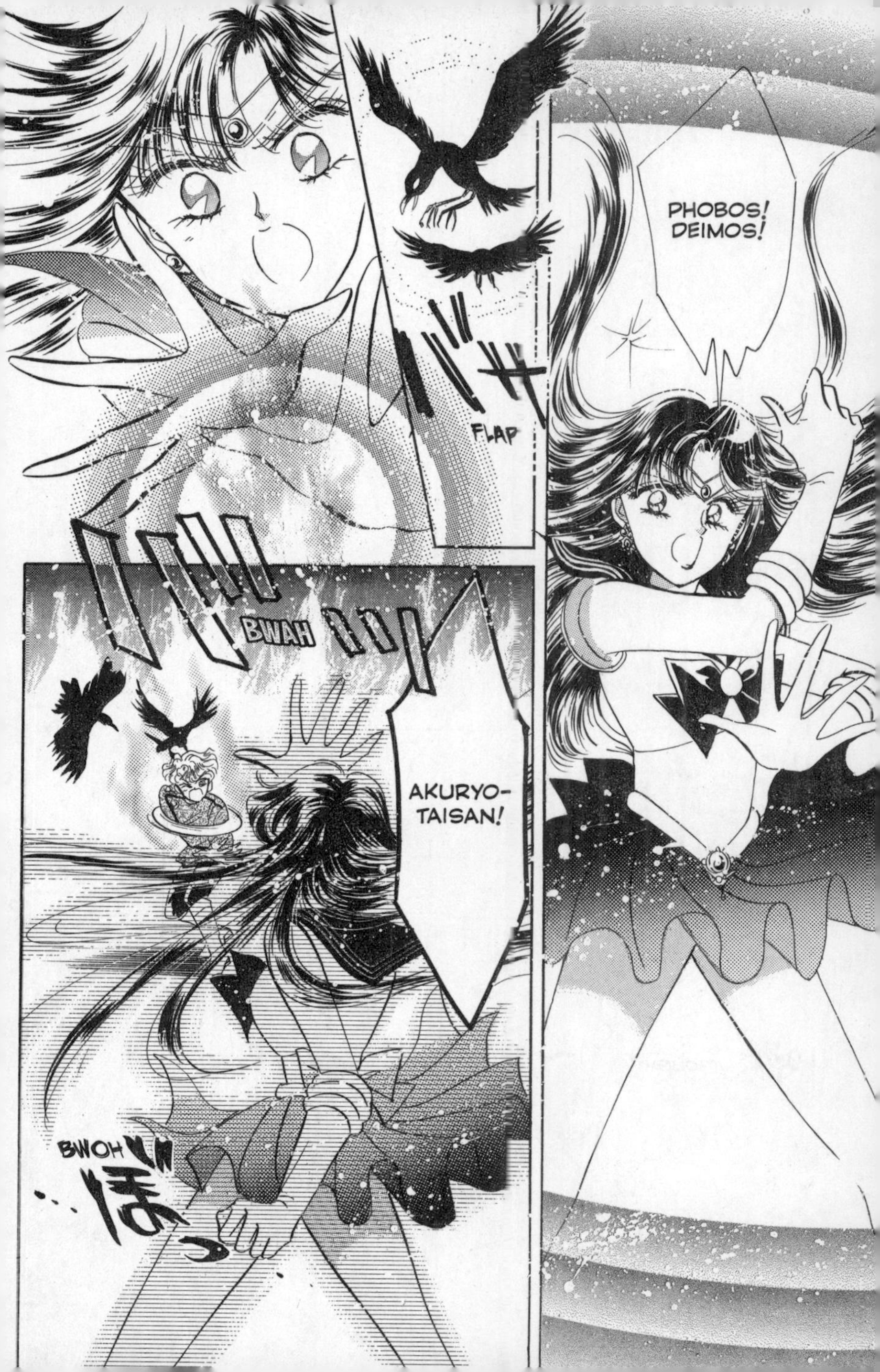
PHOBOS!
DEIMOS!
FLAP
BWAH
AKURYO-
TAISAN!
BWOH

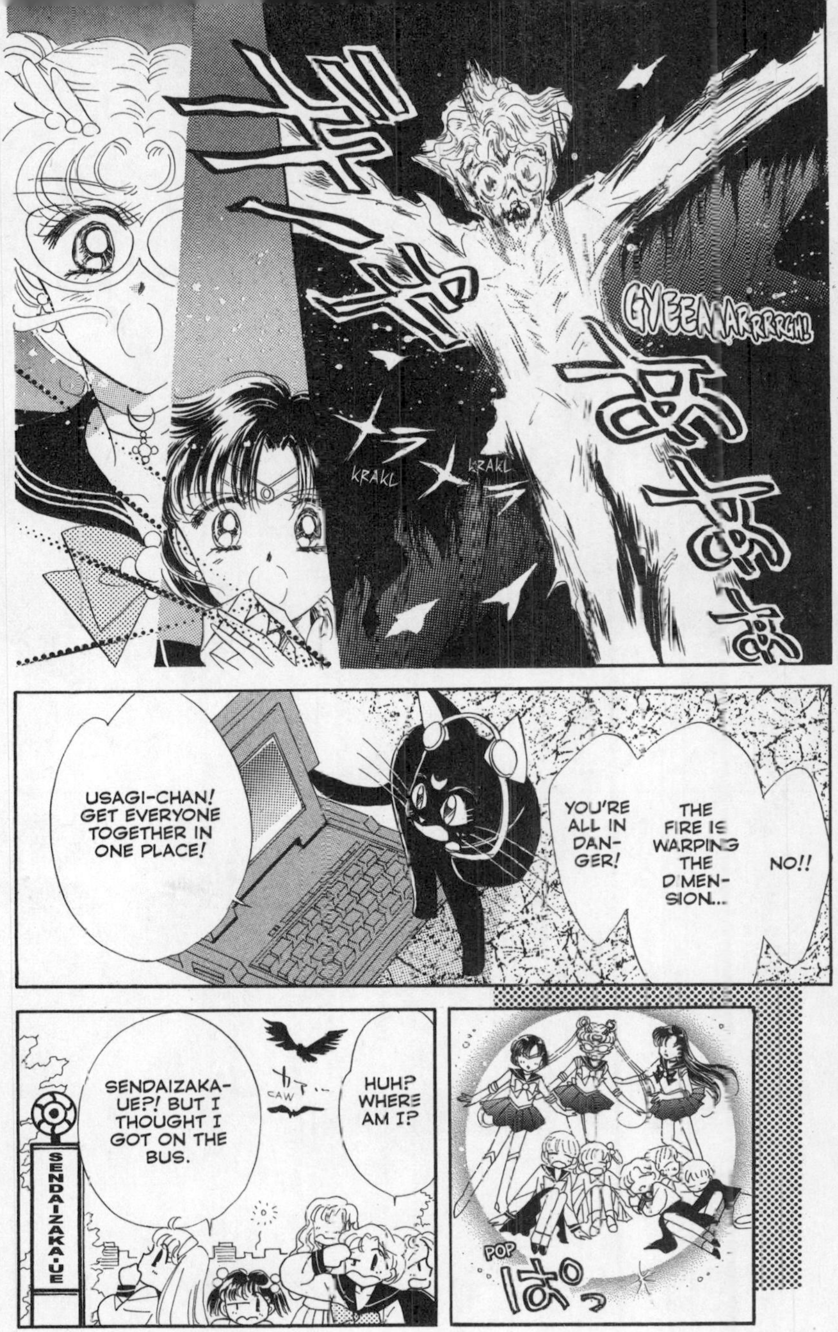
GYEEAARRRGH!!
KRAKL
KRAKL
NO!!
THE FIRE IS WARPING THE DIMENSION...
YOU'RE ALL IN DANGER!
USAGI-CHAN! GET EVERYONE TOGETHER IN ONE PLACE!
POP
ぱっ
HUH? WHERE AM I?
CAW
SENDAIZAKA-UE?! BUT I THOUGHT I GOT ON THE BUS.
SENDAIZAKA-UE

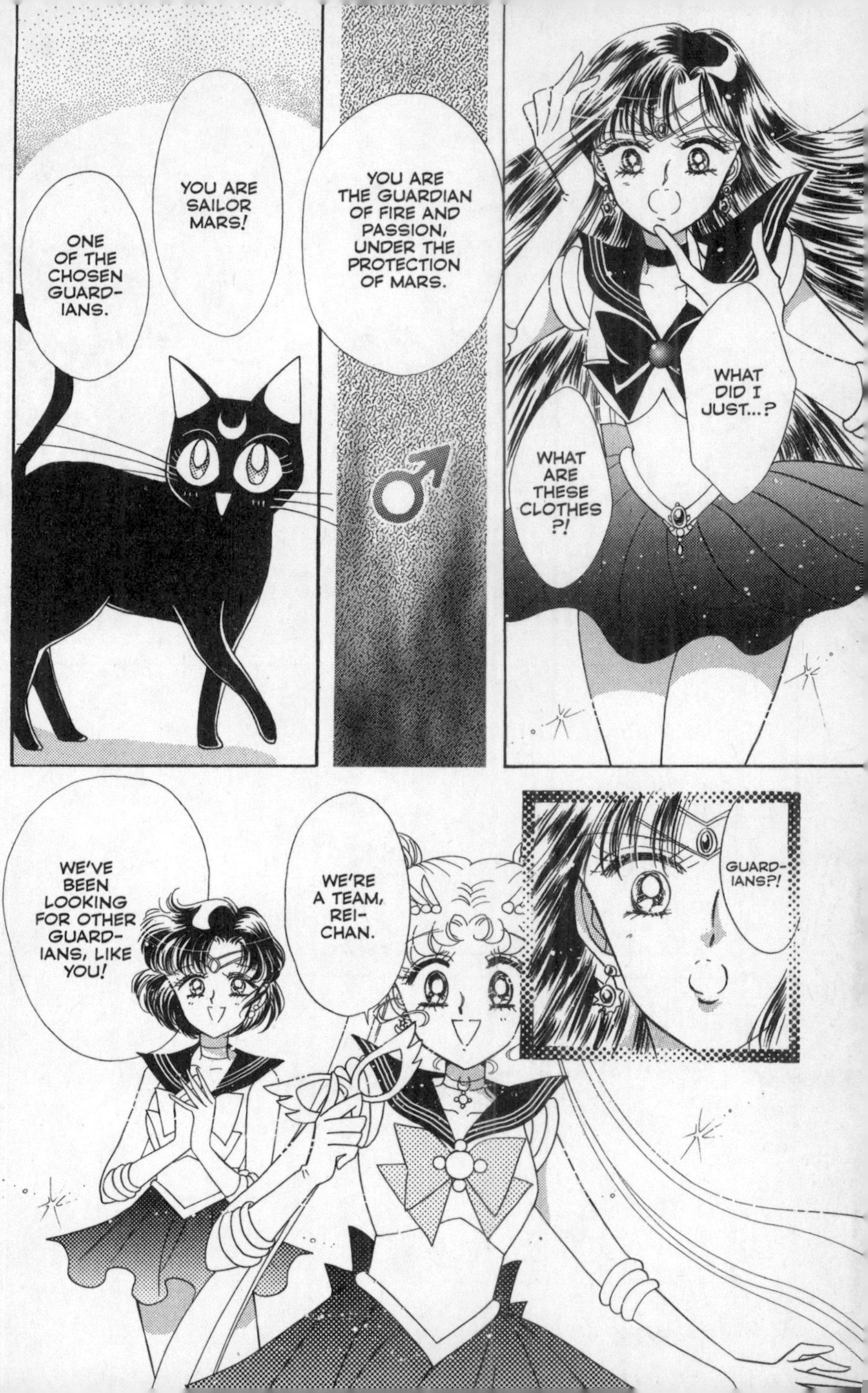
WHAT DID I JUST...?
WHAT ARE THESE CLOTHES?!
YOU ARE THE GUARDIAN OF FIRE AND PASSION, UNDER THE PROTECTION OF MARS.
YOU ARE SAILOR MARS!
ONE OF THE CHOSEN GUARD-IANS.
GUARD-IANS?!
WE'RE A TEAM, REI-CHAN.
WE'VE BEEN LOOKING FOR OTHER GUARD-IANS, LIKE YOU!

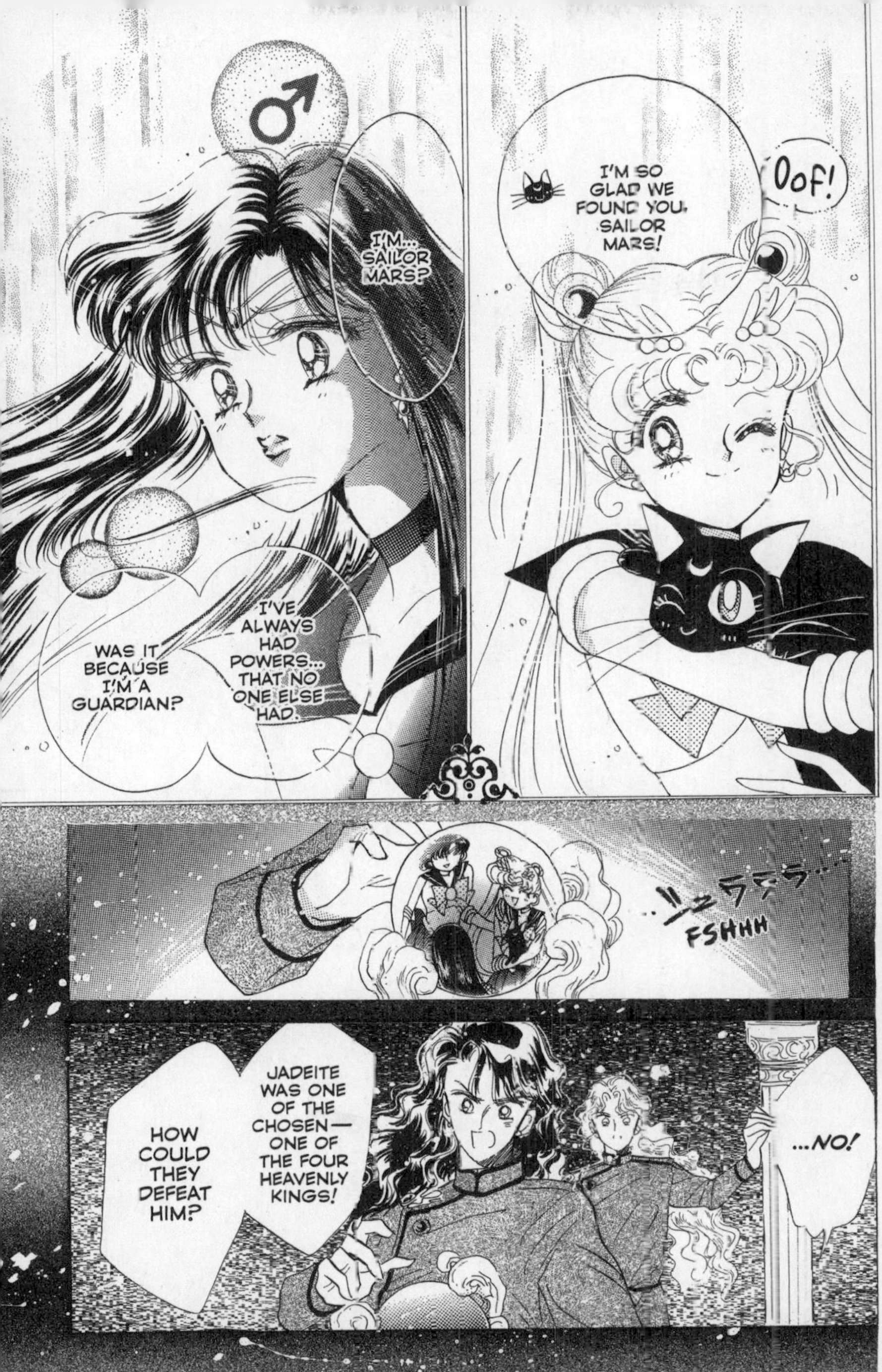
Oof!
I'M SO GLAD WE FOUND YOU, SAILOR MARS!
I'M... SAILOR MARS?
I'VE ALWAYS HAD POWERS... THAT NO ONE ELSE HAD.
WAS IT BECAUSE I'M A GUARDIAN?
FSHHH
...NO!
JADEITE WAS ONE OF THE CHOSEN— ONE OF THE FOUR HEAVENLY KINGS!
HOW COULD THEY DEFEAT HIM?

Pretty Guardian Sailor Moon

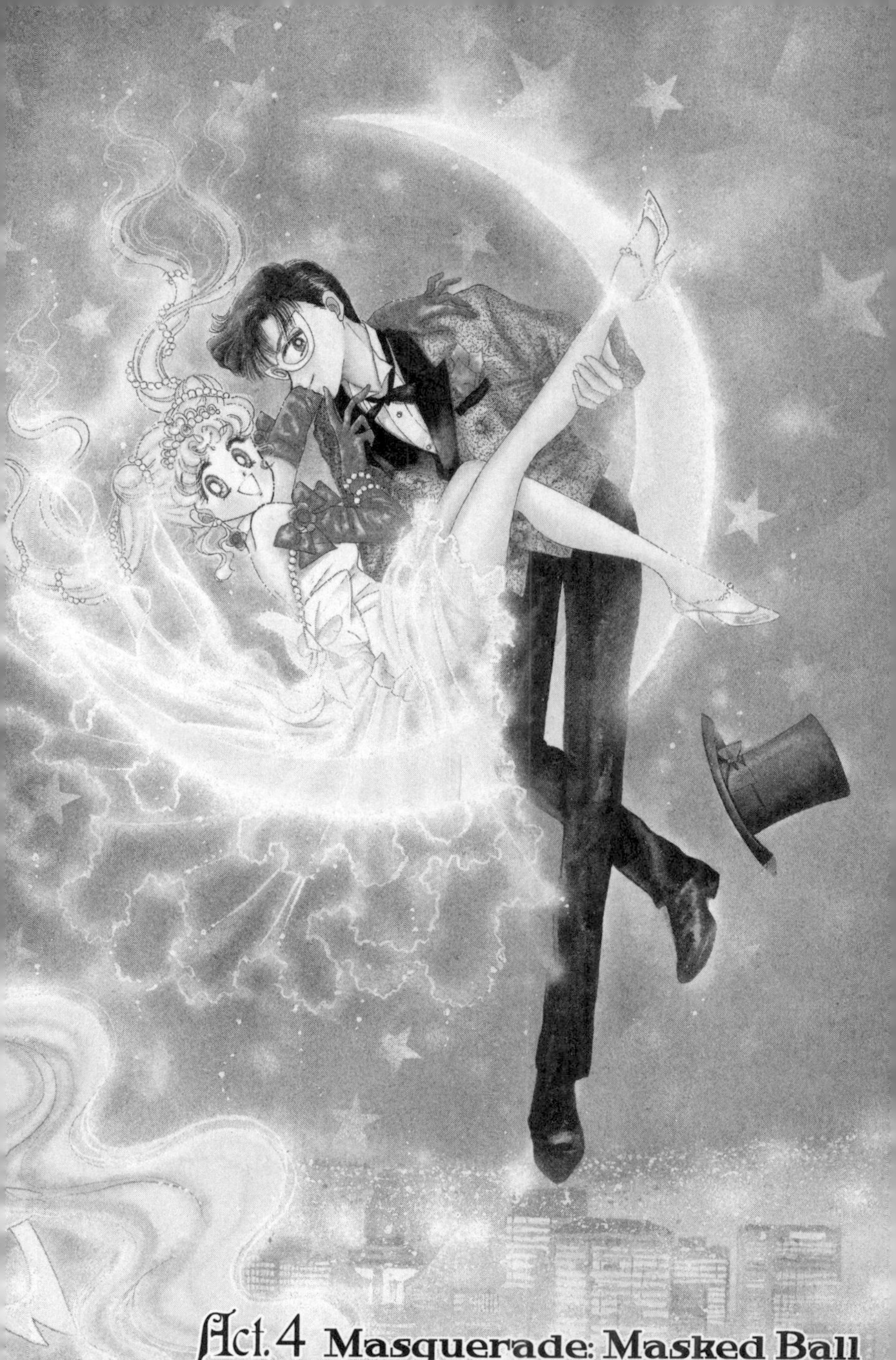

Act. 4 Masquerade: Masked Ball

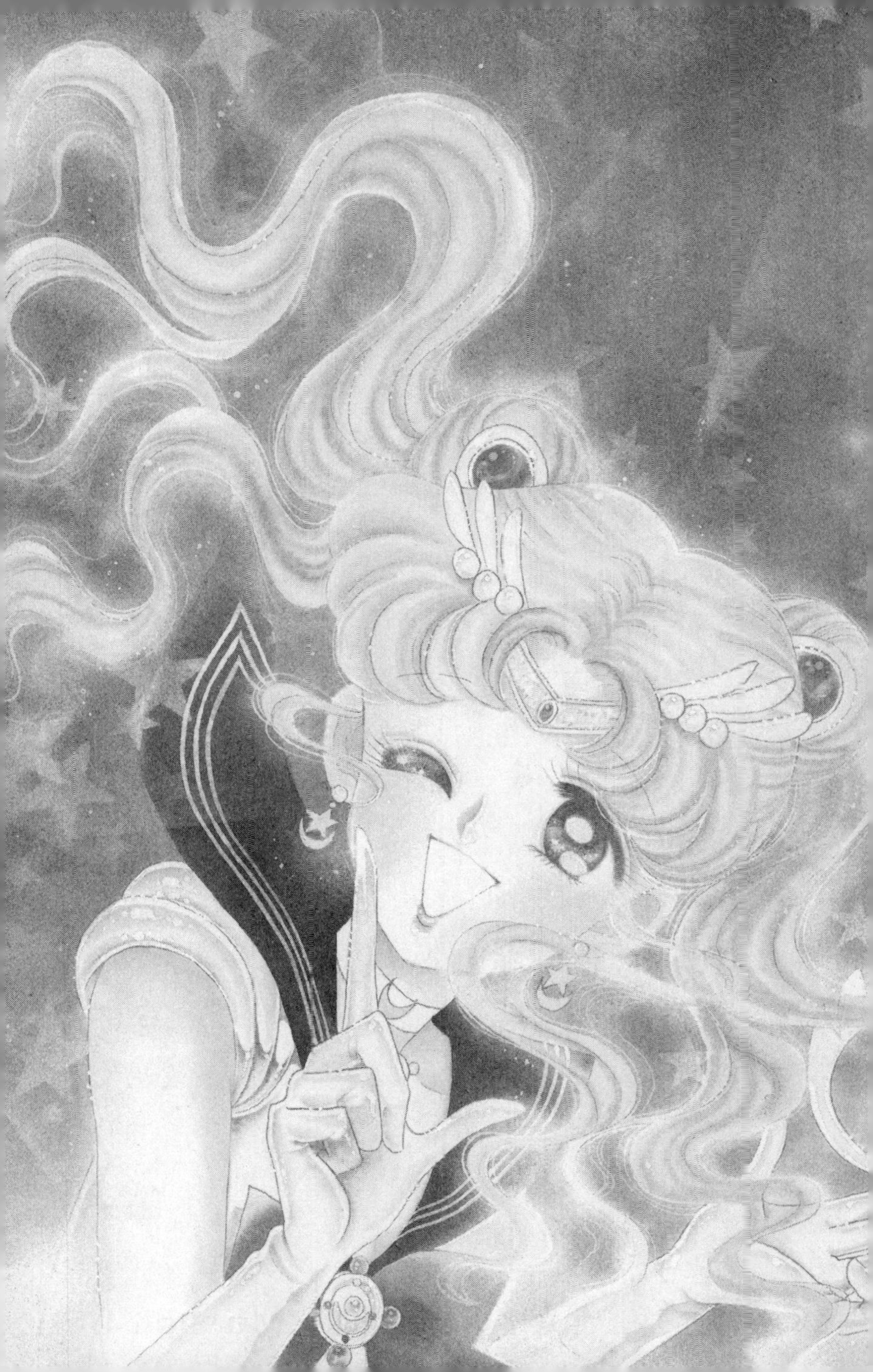

Pretty Guardian Sailor Moon

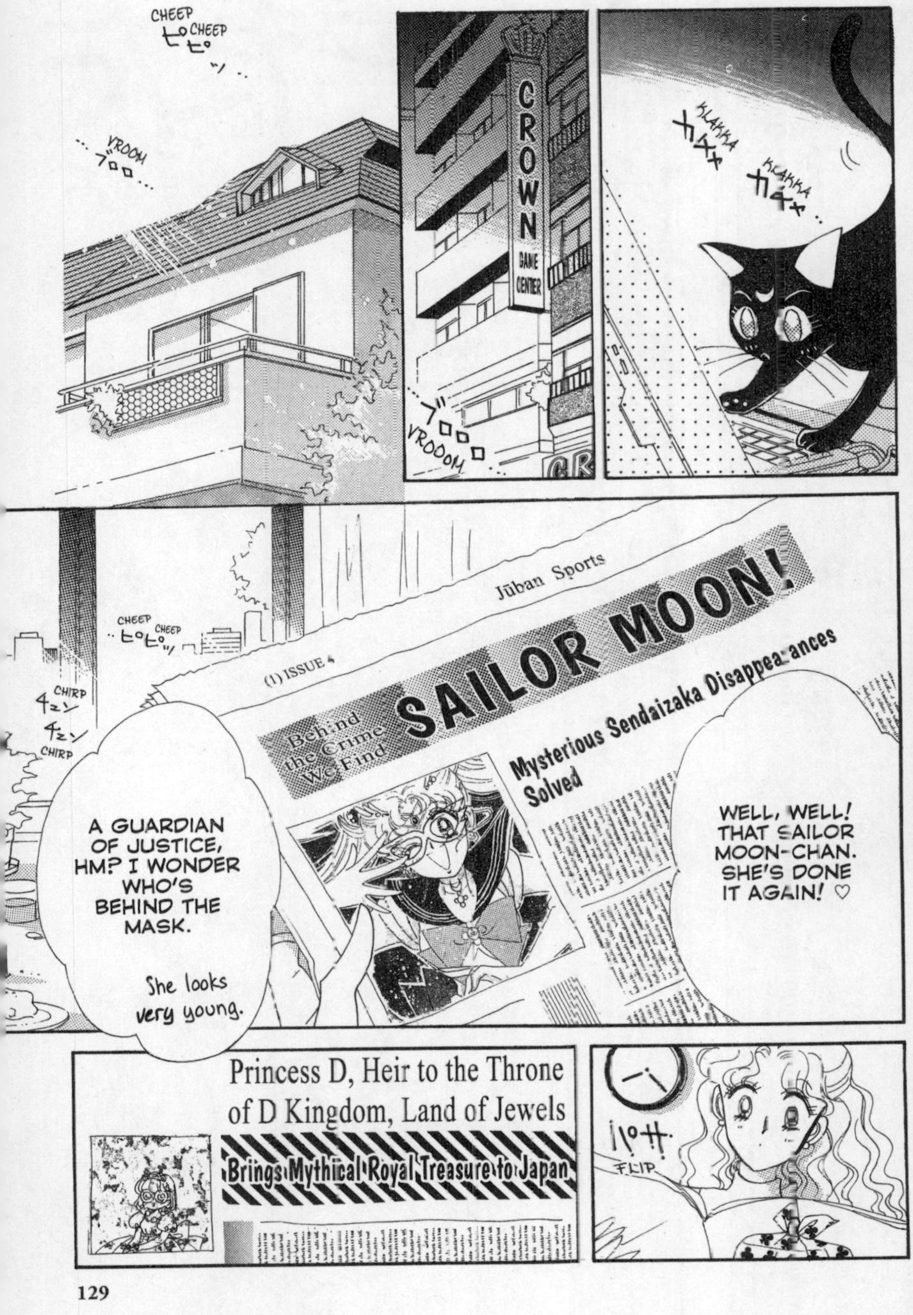
KLAKKA
KLAKKA
CROWN
GAME CENTER
VROOOM
CHEEP
CHEEP
VROOM
Jūban Sports
SAILOR MOON!
(1) ISSUE
Behind the Crime We Find
Mysterious Sendaizaka Disappearances Solved
WELL, WELL! THAT SAILOR MOON-CHAN. SHE'S DONE IT AGAIN! ♡
CHEEP
CHEEP
CHIRP
CHIRP
A GUARDIAN OF JUSTICE, HM? I WONDER WHO'S BEHIND THE MASK.
She looks very young.
FLIP
Princess D, Heir to the Throne of D Kingdom, Land of Jewels
Brings Mythical Royal Treasure to Japan

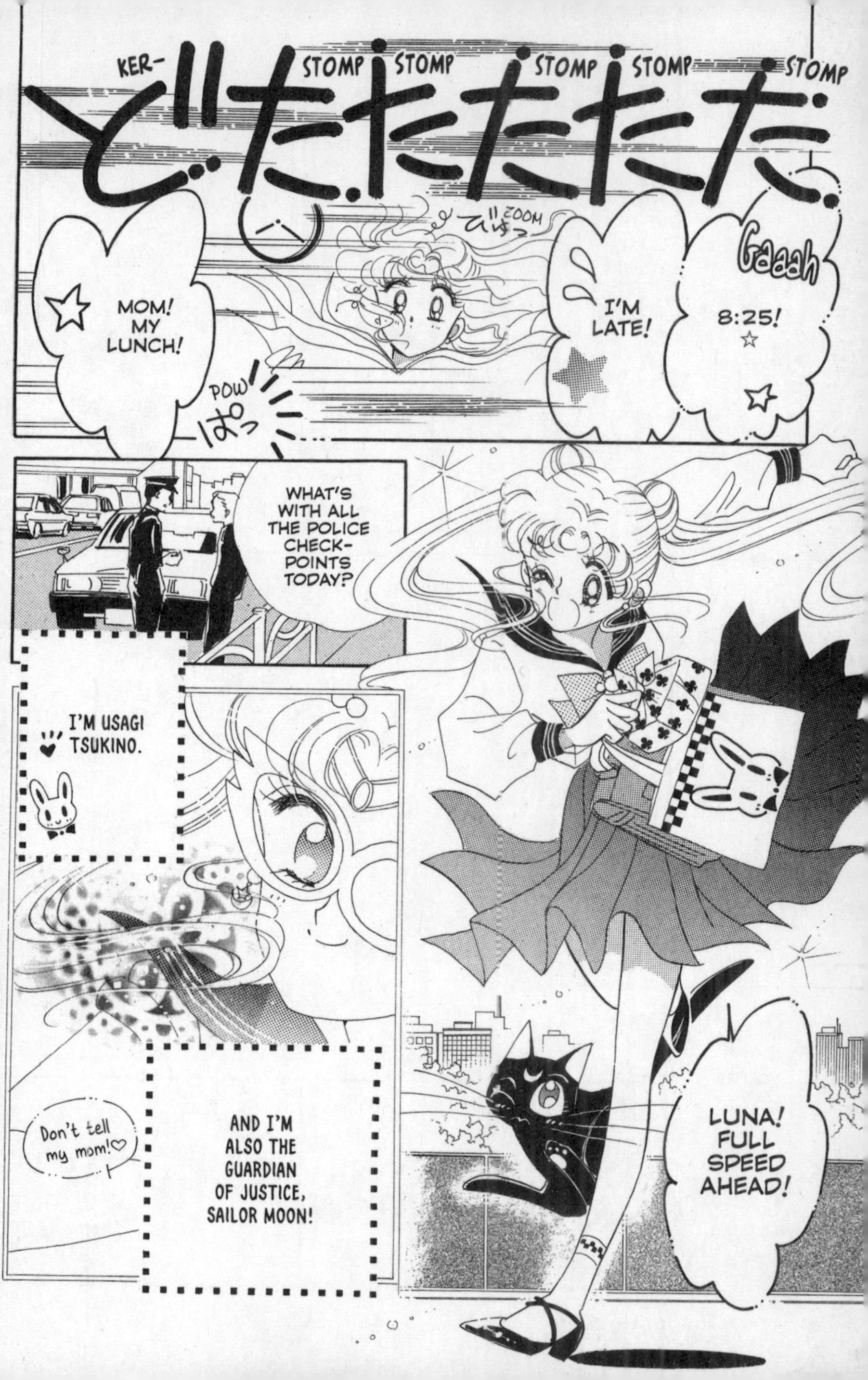
KER- STOMP STOMP STOMP STOMP STOMP
どたたたたた
Gaaah
8:25!
I'M LATE!
ZOOM
びゅっ
MOM! MY LUNCH!
POW
ぱっ
LUNA! FULL SPEED AHEAD!
WHAT'S WITH ALL THE POLICE CHECKPOINTS TODAY?
I'M USAGI TSUKINO.
AND I'M ALSO THE GUARDIAN OF JUSTICE, SAILOR MOON!
Don't tell my mom!♡

PRINCESS D IS HERE IN JAPAN! SHE'S THE CROWN PRINCESS OF D KINGDOM...

...THE WORLD'S BIGGEST PRODUCER OF JEWELS!

SO HEY, YOU KNOW ALL THE POLICE CHECKS THEY WERE DOING TODAY?

YEAH. IS SOMETHING GOING ON?

THEY'RE HAVING A BANQUET FOR HER AT THE EMBASSY TONIGHT!

OOOOH, A PRINCESS!

YOU KNOW THE D KINGDOM EMBASSY, RIGHT? THE ONE AT SENDAIZAKA-SHITA! IT'S PRACTICALLY NEXT DOOR!

ばさっ
RUSTLE

AND THEY'RE GOING TO REVEAL IT TO THE WORLD FOR THE FIRST TIME EVER AT THE PARTY TONIGHT!

SO I GUESS...

...PRINCESS D IS SET TO INHERIT SOME SECRET HIDDEN TREASURE THAT'S BEEN IN THE ROYAL FAMILY FOR GENERATIONS.

IT'S A WHOLE KINGDOM OF JEWELS, AND THIS IS THEIR SPECIAL SECRET TREASURE! CAN YOU EVEN IMAGINE IT?!

♡ I know I can't!

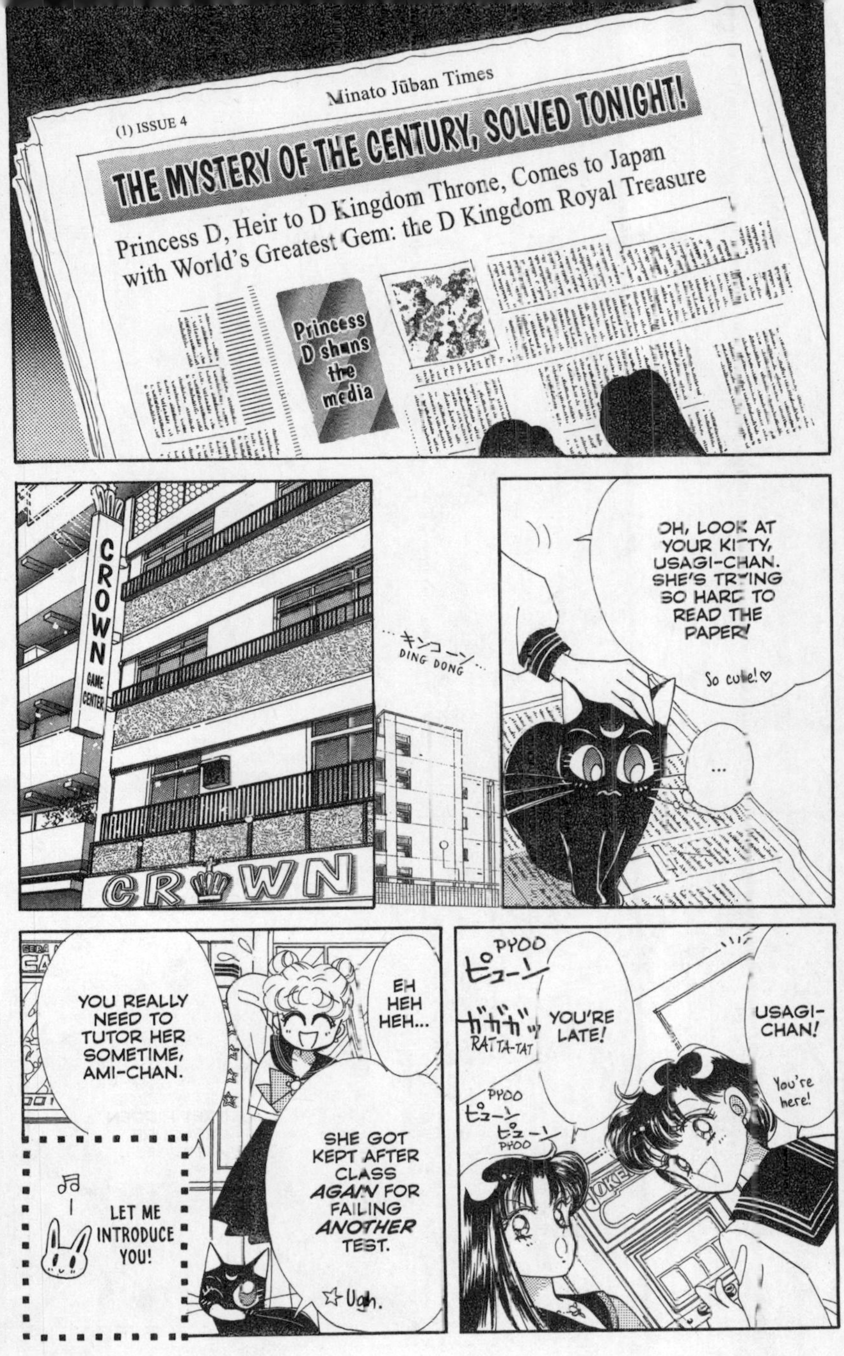

Minato Jūban Times
(1) ISSUE 4
THE MYSTERY OF THE CENTURY, SOLVED TONIGHT!
Princess D, Heir to D Kingdom Throne, Comes to Japan with World's Greatest Gem: the D Kingdom Royal Treasure
Princess D shuns the media
OH, LOOK AT YOUR KITTY, USAGI-CHAN. SHE'S TRYING SO HARD TO READ THE PAPER!
So cute!♡
...
キンコーン
DING DONG
CROWN GAME CENTER
CROWN
USAGI-CHAN!
You're here!
YOU'RE LATE!
ピュー
PYOO
ガガガッ
RATTA-TAT
ピュー
PYOO
ピュー
PYOO
EH HEH HEH...
YOU REALLY NEED TO TUTOR HER SOMETIME, AMI-CHAN.
SHE GOT KEPT AFTER CLASS AGAIN FOR FAILING ANOTHER TEST.
☆Ugh.
LET ME INTRODUCE YOU!

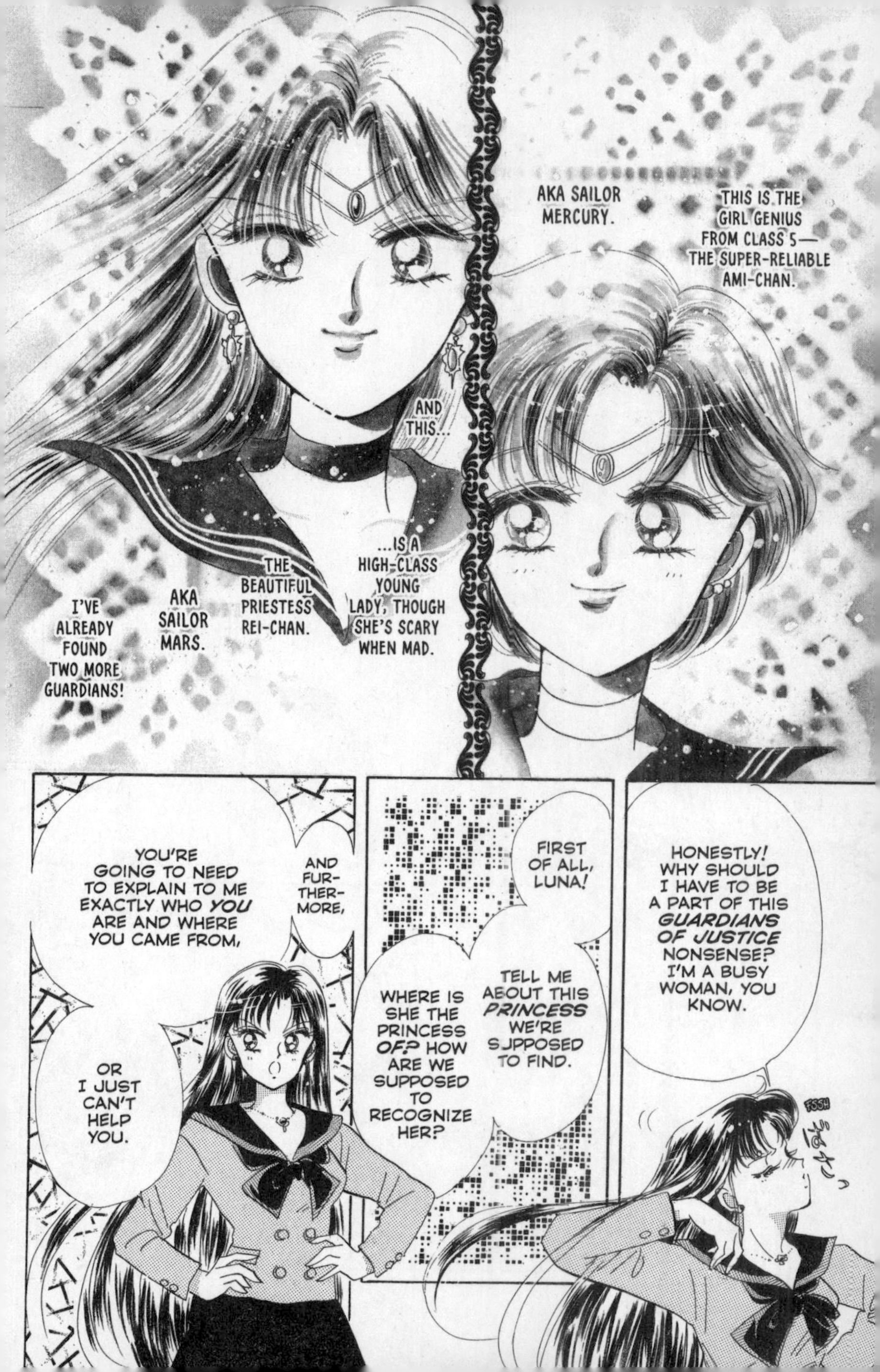
THIS IS THE GIRL GENIUS FROM CLASS 5—THE SUPER-RELIABLE AMI-CHAN.
AKA SAILOR MERCURY.
AND THIS...
...IS A HIGH-CLASS YOUNG LADY, THOUGH SHE'S SCARY WHEN MAD.
THE BEAUTIFUL PRIESTESS REI-CHAN.
AKA SAILOR MARS.
I'VE ALREADY FOUND TWO MORE GUARDIANS!
HONESTLY! WHY SHOULD I HAVE TO BE A PART OF THIS *GUARDIANS OF JUSTICE* NONSENSE? I'M A BUSY WOMAN, YOU KNOW.
FSSH
FIRST OF ALL, LUNA!
TELL ME ABOUT THIS *PRINCESS* WE'RE SUPPOSED TO FIND.
WHERE IS SHE THE PRINCESS *OF?* HOW ARE WE SUPPOSED TO RECOGNIZE HER?
AND FURTHERMORE,
YOU'RE GOING TO NEED TO EXPLAIN TO ME EXACTLY WHO *YOU* ARE AND WHERE YOU CAME FROM,
OR I JUST CAN'T HELP YOU.

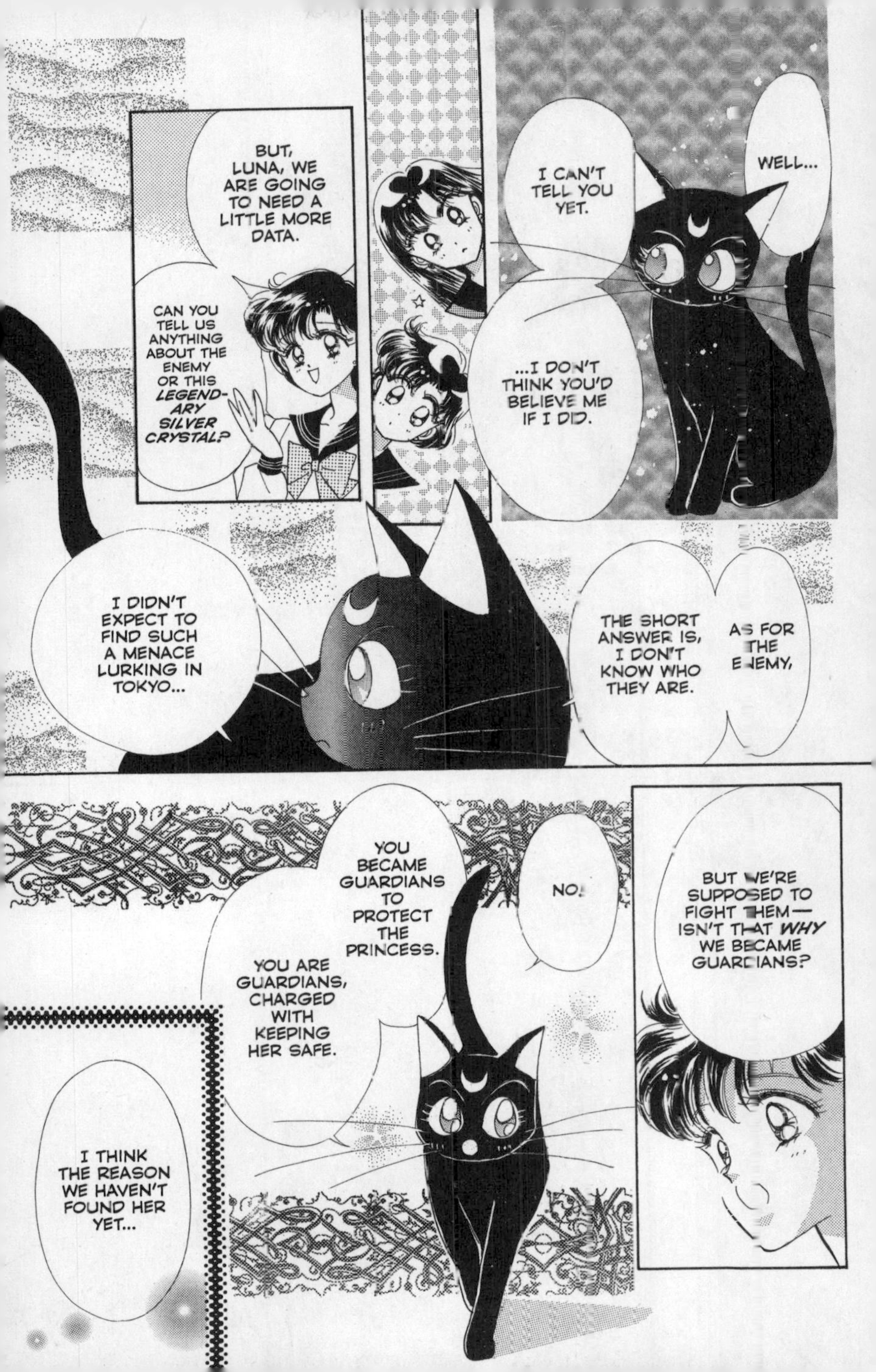
WELL...
I CAN'T TELL YOU YET.
...I DON'T THINK YOU'D BELIEVE ME IF I DID.
BUT, LUNA, WE ARE GOING TO NEED A LITTLE MORE DATA.
CAN YOU TELL US ANYTHING ABOUT THE ENEMY OR THIS *LEGENDARY SILVER CRYSTAL?*
AS FOR THE ENEMY,
THE SHORT ANSWER IS, I DON'T KNOW WHO THEY ARE.
I DIDN'T EXPECT TO FIND SUCH A MENACE LURKING IN TOKYO...
BUT WE'RE SUPPOSED TO FIGHT THEM—ISN'T THAT *WHY* WE BECAME GUARDIANS?
NO!
YOU BECAME GUARDIANS TO PROTECT THE PRINCESS.
YOU ARE GUARDIANS, CHARGED WITH KEEPING HER SAFE.
I THINK THE REASON WE HAVEN'T FOUND HER YET...

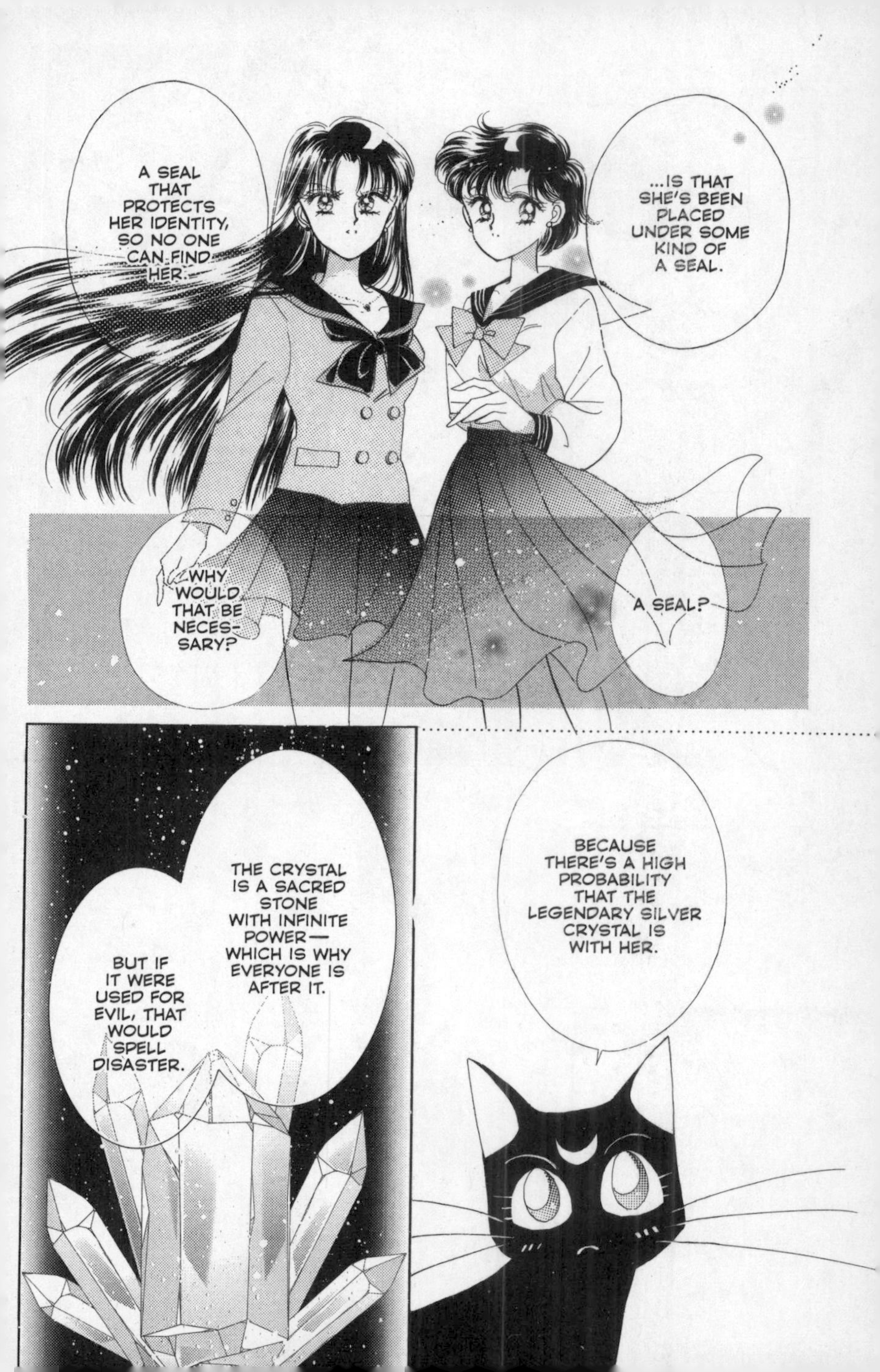
...IS THAT SHE'S BEEN PLACED UNDER SOME KIND OF A SEAL.
A SEAL?
A SEAL THAT PROTECTS HER IDENTITY, SO NO ONE CAN FIND HER.
WHY WOULD THAT BE NECES-SARY?
BECAUSE THERE'S A HIGH PROBABILITY THAT THE LEGENDARY SILVER CRYSTAL IS WITH HER.
THE CRYSTAL IS A SACRED STONE WITH INFINITE POWER—WHICH IS WHY EVERYONE IS AFTER IT.
BUT IF IT WERE USED FOR EVIL, THAT WOULD SPELL DISASTER.

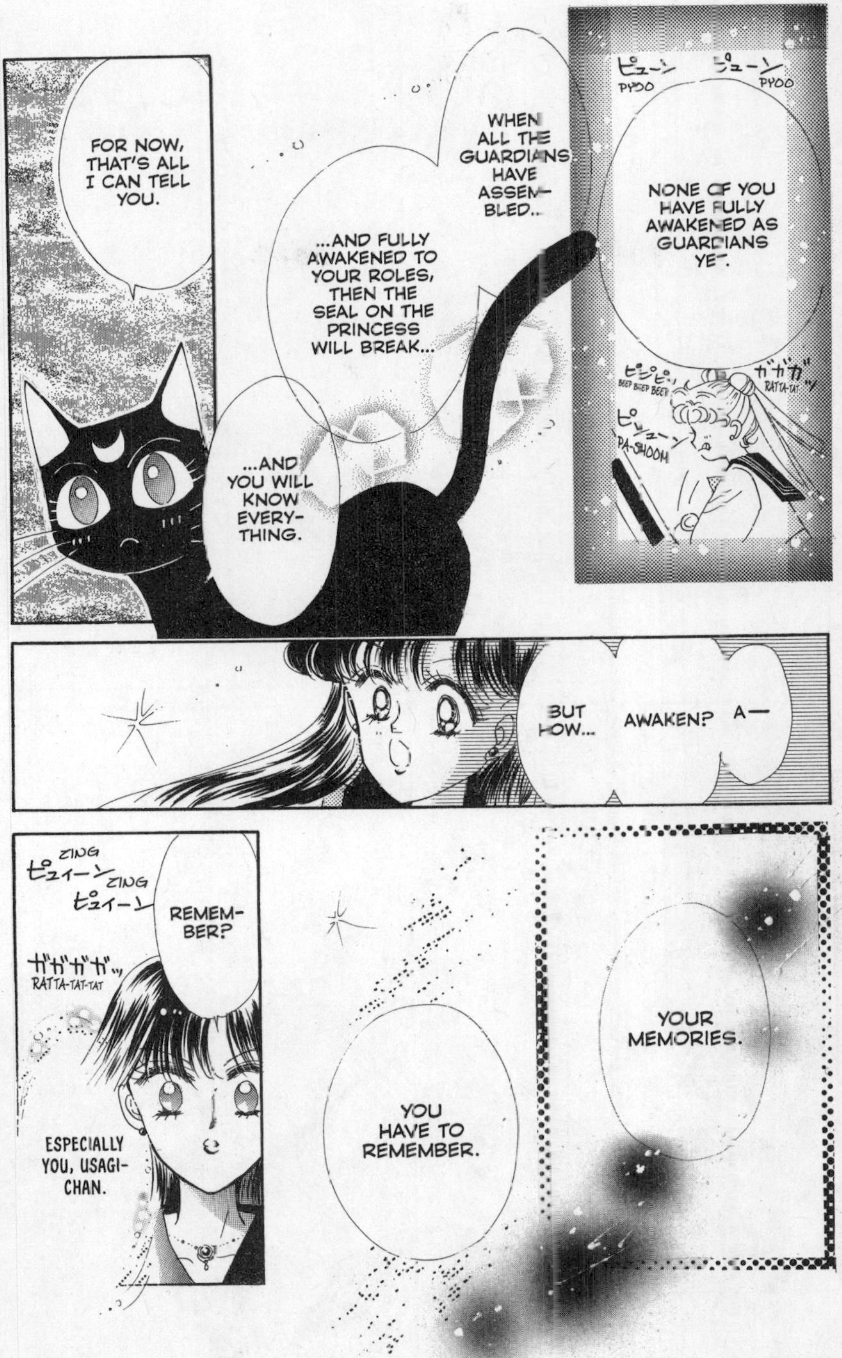
ピューン
PYOO
ピューン
PYOO
NONE OF YOU HAVE FULLY AWAKENED AS GUARDIANS YET.
ピピピッ
BEEP BEEP BEEP
ガガガッ
RATTA-TAT
ピシューン
PA-SHOOM
WHEN ALL THE GUARDIANS HAVE ASSEMBLED...
...AND FULLY AWAKENED TO YOUR ROLES, THEN THE SEAL ON THE PRINCESS WILL BREAK...
...AND YOU WILL KNOW EVERYTHING.
FOR NOW, THAT'S ALL I CAN TELL YOU.
A—
AWAKEN?
BUT HOW...
YOUR MEMORIES.
YOU HAVE TO REMEMBER.
REMEMBER?
ZING
ピュイーン
ZING
ピュイーン
ガガガガッ
RATTA-TAT-TAT
ESPECIALLY YOU, USAGI-CHAN.

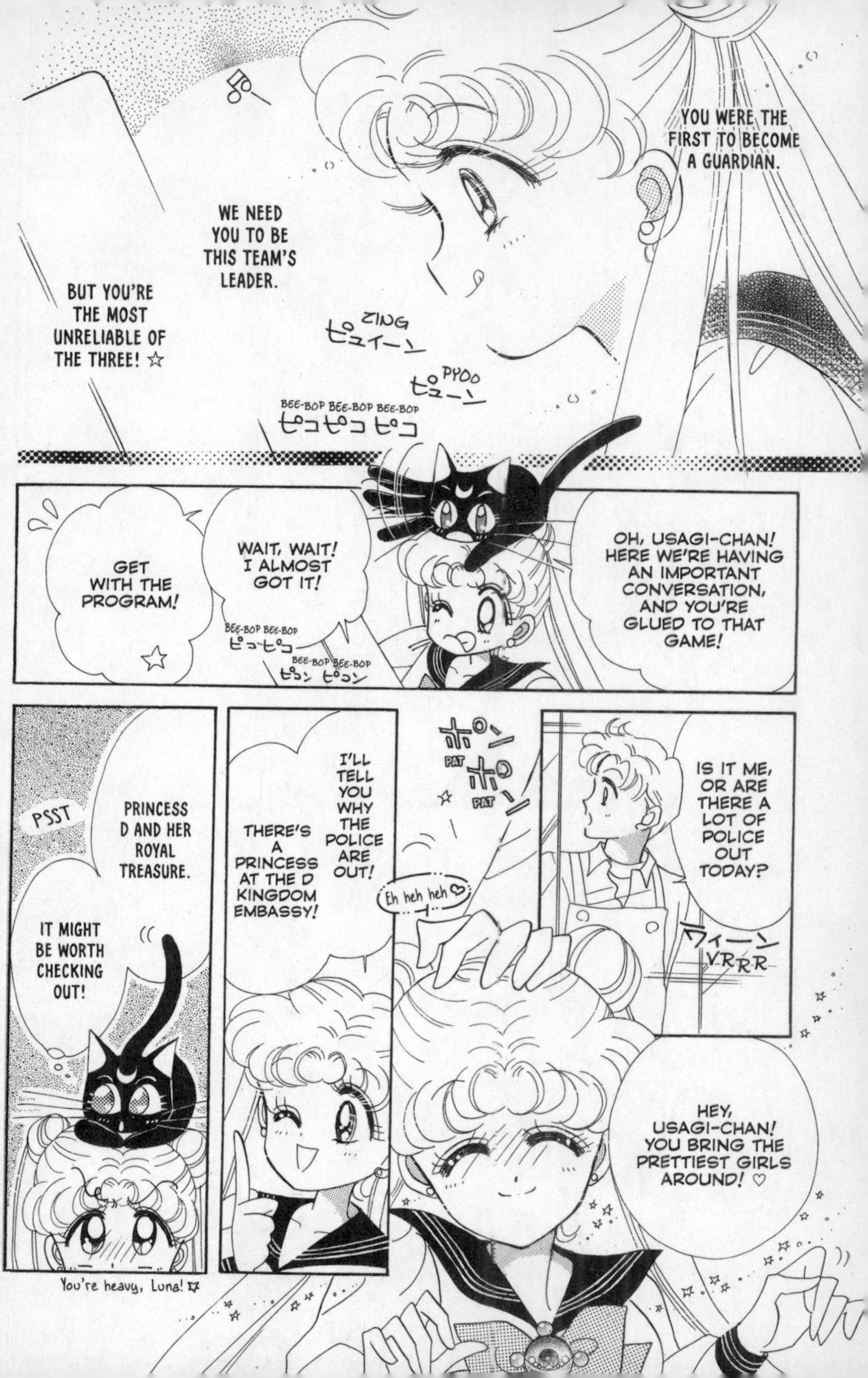
YOU WERE THE FIRST TO BECOME A GUARDIAN.
WE NEED YOU TO BE THIS TEAM'S LEADER.
BUT YOU'RE THE MOST UNRELIABLE OF THE THREE! ☆
ZING ピュイーン
PYOO ピューン
BEE-BOP BEE-BOP BEE-BOP ピコピコピコ
OH, USAGI-CHAN! HERE WE'RE HAVING AN IMPORTANT CONVERSATION, AND YOU'RE GLUED TO THAT GAME!
WAIT, WAIT! I ALMOST GOT IT!
BEE-BOP BEE-BOP ピコピコ
BEE-BOP BEE-BOP ピコンピコン
GET WITH THE PROGRAM!
IS IT ME, OR ARE THERE A LOT OF POLICE OUT TODAY?
ヴィーン VRRR
PAT ポン PAT ポン
Eh heh heh ♡
HEY, USAGI-CHAN! YOU BRING THE PRETTIEST GIRLS AROUND! ♡
I'LL TELL YOU WHY THE POLICE ARE OUT!
THERE'S A PRINCESS AT THE D KINGDOM EMBASSY!
PSST
PRINCESS D AND HER ROYAL TREASURE.
IT MIGHT BE WORTH CHECKING OUT!
You're heavy, Luna! ☆

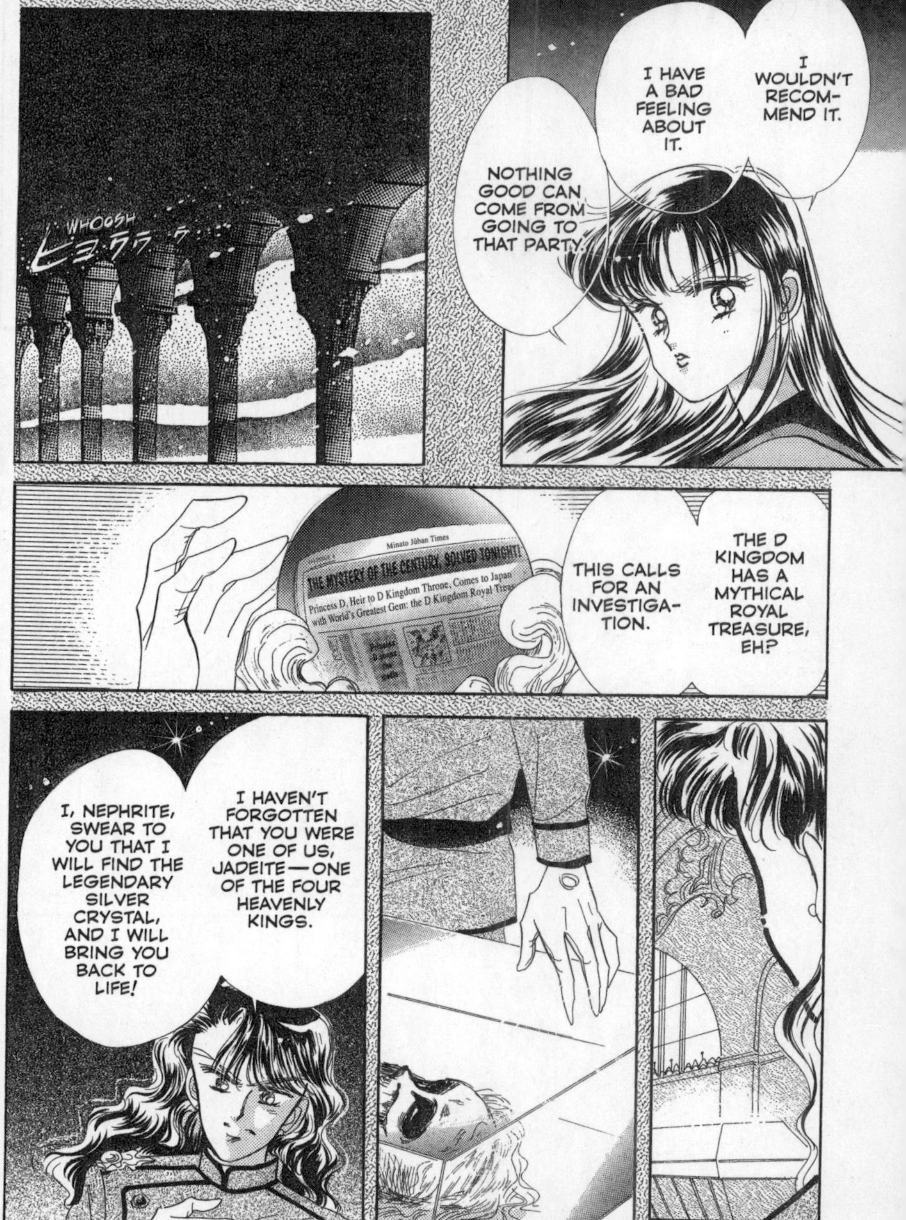
I WOULDN'T RECOMMEND IT.
I HAVE A BAD FEELING ABOUT IT.
NOTHING GOOD CAN COME FROM GOING TO THAT PARTY.
WHOOSH
THE D KINGDOM HAS A MYTHICAL ROYAL TREASURE, EH?
THIS CALLS FOR AN INVESTIGATION.
Minato Jūban Times
THE MYSTERY OF THE CENTURY, SOLVED TONIGHT!
Princess D, Heir to D Kingdom Throne, Comes to Japan with World's Greatest Gem: the D Kingdom Royal Trea
I HAVEN'T FORGOTTEN THAT YOU WERE ONE OF US, JADEITE—ONE OF THE FOUR HEAVENLY KINGS.
I, NEPHRITE, SWEAR TO YOU THAT I WILL FIND THE LEGENDARY SILVER CRYSTAL, AND I WILL BRING YOU BACK TO LIFE!

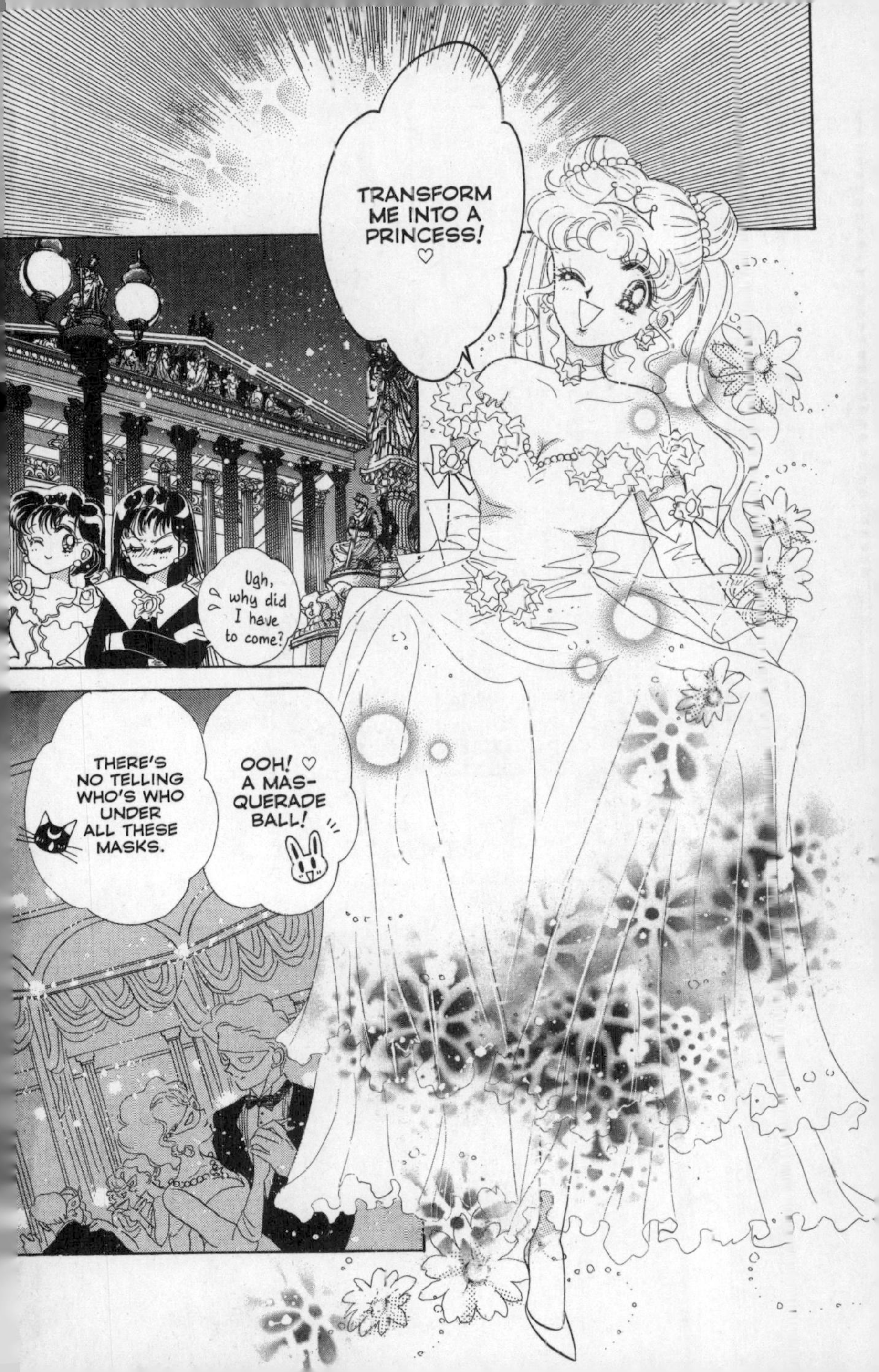
TRANSFORM ME INTO A PRINCESS! ♡
Ugh, why did I have to come?
OOH! ♡ A MAS-QUERADE BALL!
THERE'S NO TELLING WHO'S WHO UNDER ALL THESE MASKS.

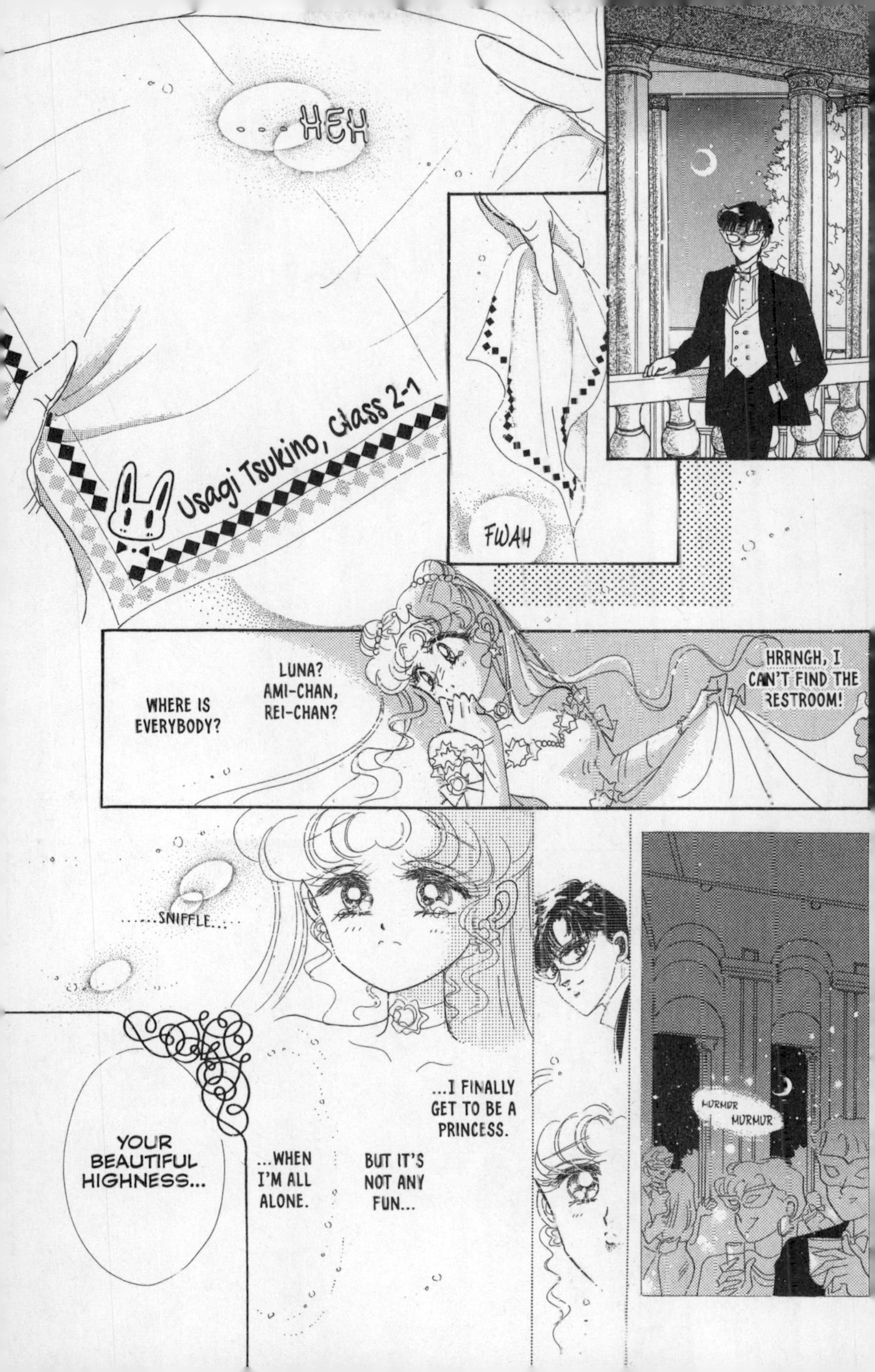
FWAH
...HEH
Usagi Tsukino, Class 2-1
HRRNGH, I CAN'T FIND THE RESTROOM!
LUNA? AMI-CHAN, REI-CHAN?
WHERE IS EVERYBODY?
MURMUR MURMUR
...I FINALLY GET TO BE A PRINCESS.
BUT IT'S NOT ANY FUN...
...WHEN I'M ALL ALONE.
......SNIFFLE...
YOUR BEAUTIFUL HIGHNESS...

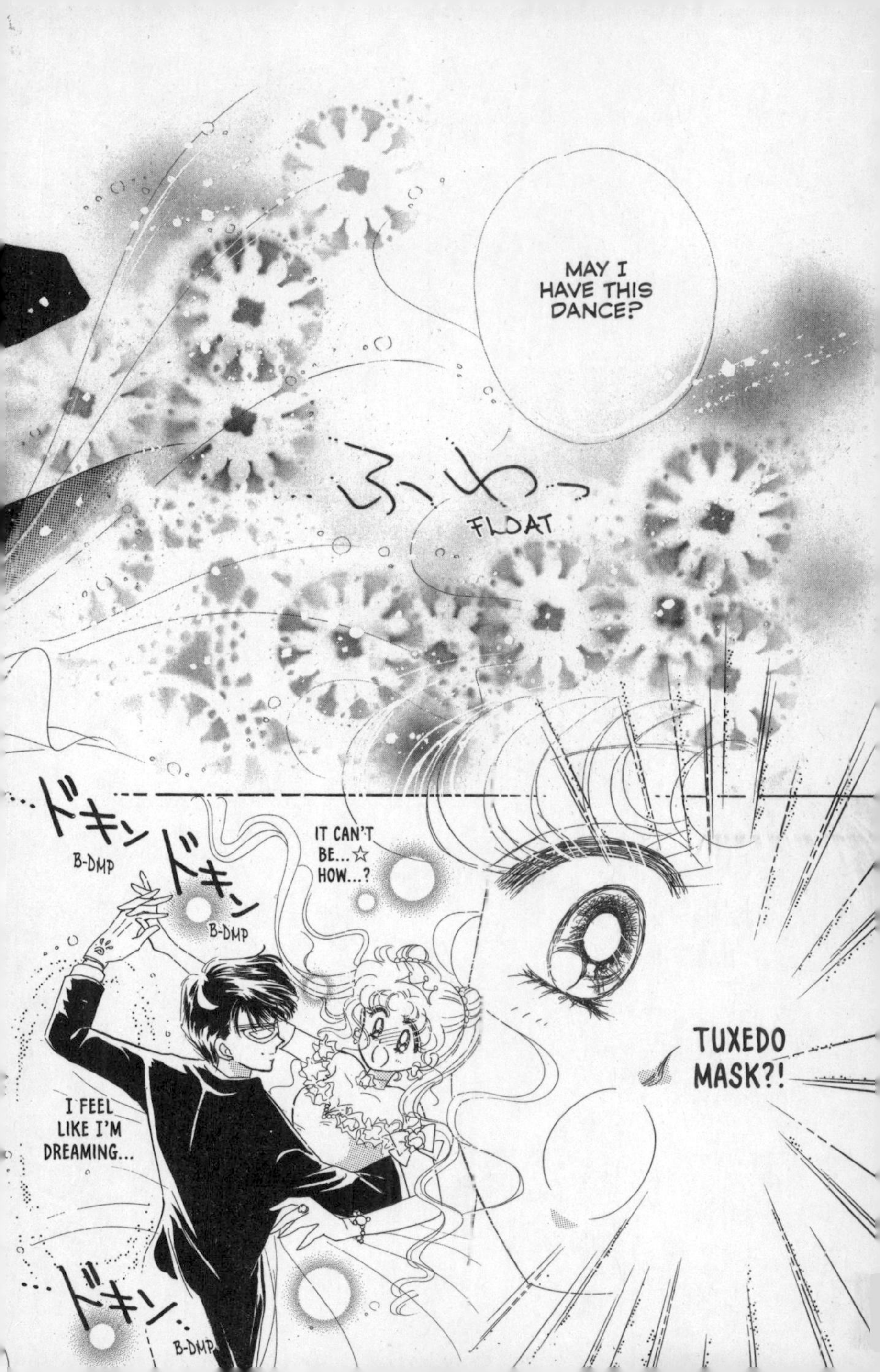
MAY I HAVE THIS DANCE?
ふわっ
FLOAT
TUXEDO MASK?!
IT CAN'T BE...☆ HOW...?
ドキン
B-DMP
ドキン
B-DMP
I FEEL LIKE I'M DREAMING...
ドキン
B-DMP

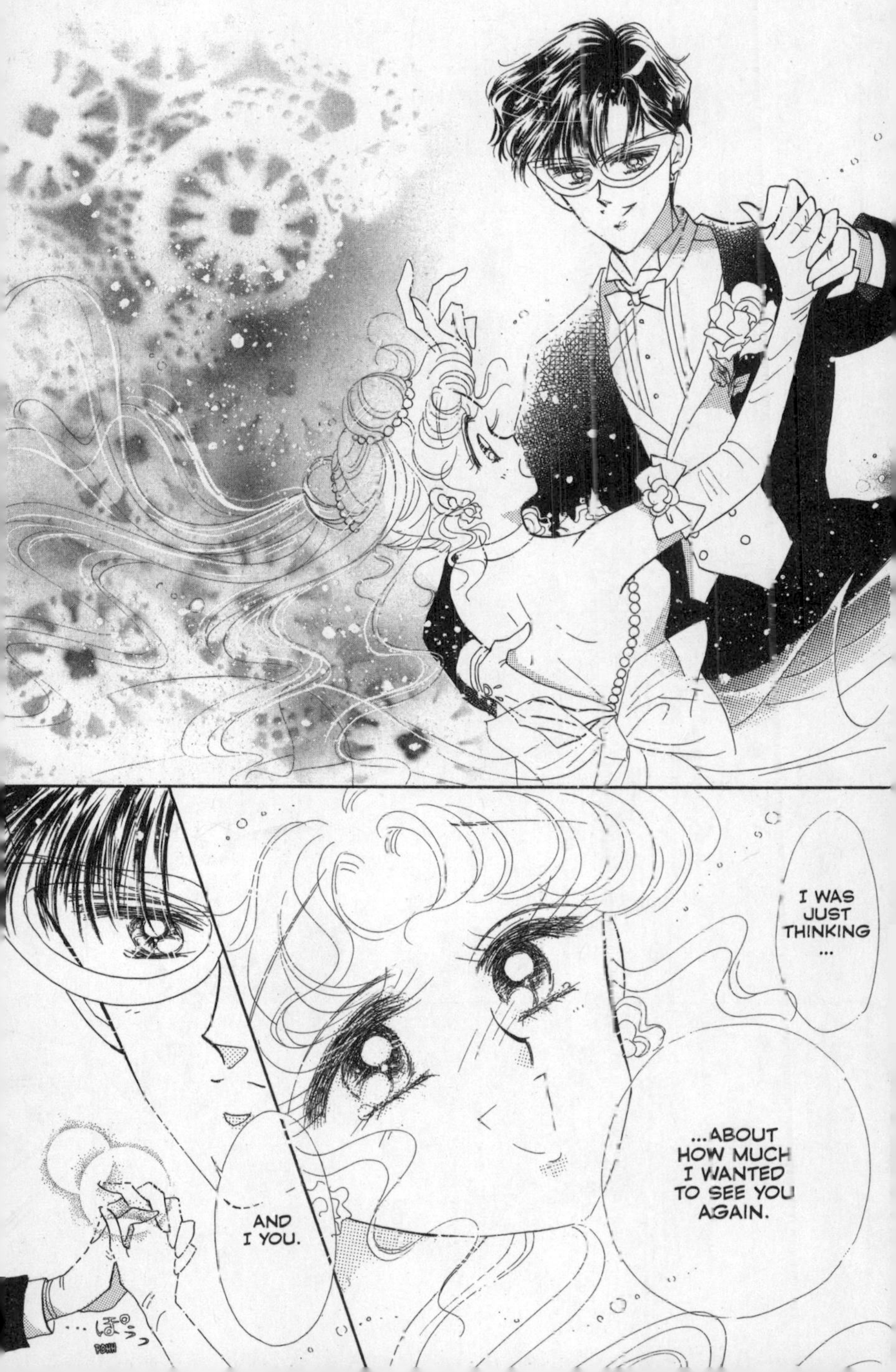
I WAS JUST THINKING ...
...ABOUT HOW MUCH I WANTED TO SEE YOU AGAIN.
AND I YOU.
...ぽうっ
POHH

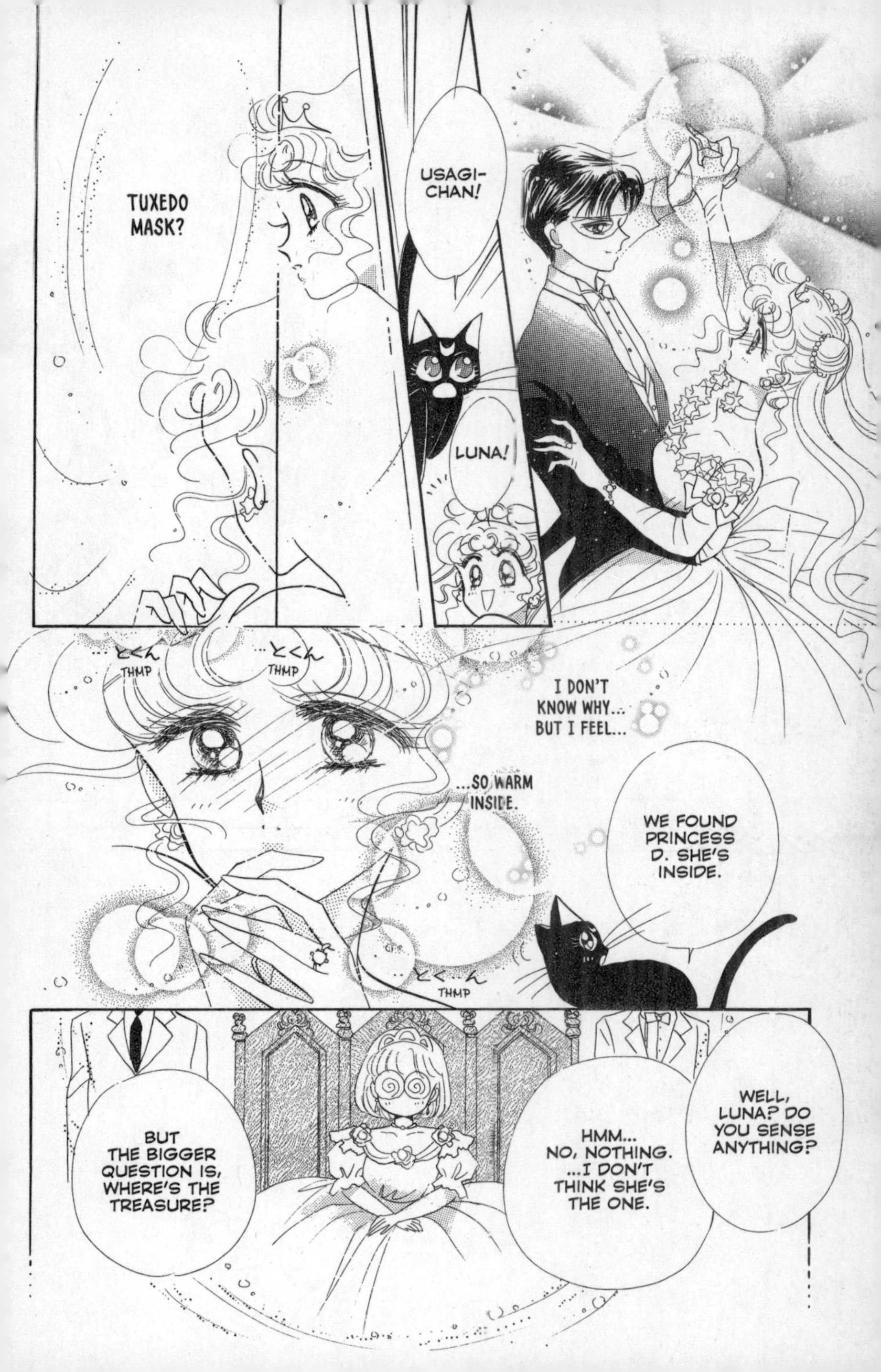
USAGI-CHAN!
LUNA!
TUXEDO MASK?
…とくん THMP
…とくん THMP
I DON'T KNOW WHY... BUT I FEEL...
...SO WARM INSIDE.
WE FOUND PRINCESS D. SHE'S INSIDE.
…とくん THMP
WELL, LUNA? DO YOU SENSE ANYTHING?
HMM... NO, NOTHING. ...I DON'T THINK SHE'S THE ONE.
BUT THE BIGGER QUESTION IS, WHERE'S THE TREASURE?

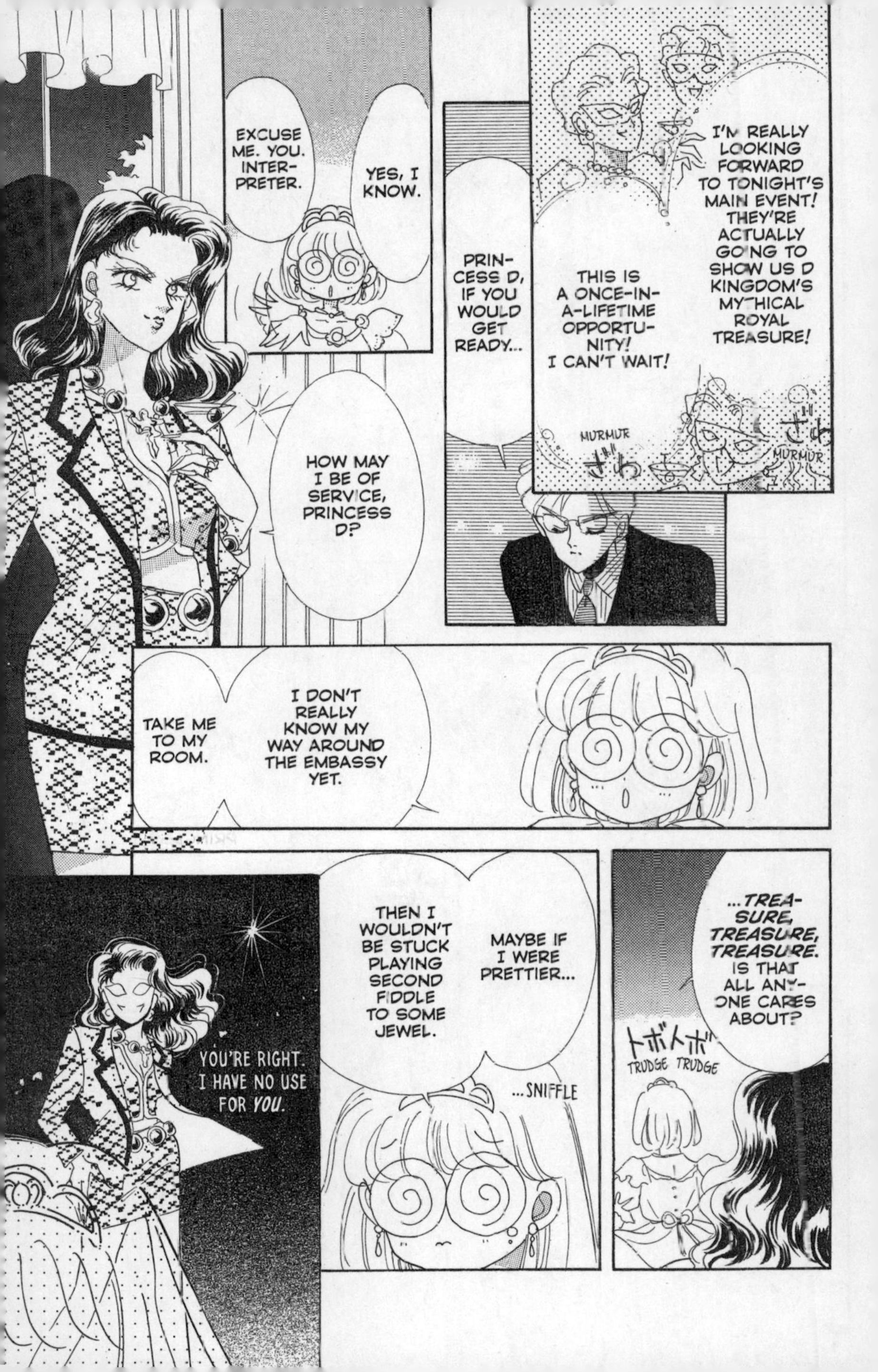

I'M REALLY LOOKING FORWARD TO TONIGHT'S MAIN EVENT! THEY'RE ACTUALLY GOING TO SHOW US D KINGDOM'S MYTHICAL ROYAL TREASURE!
THIS IS A ONCE-IN-A-LIFETIME OPPORTUNITY! I CAN'T WAIT!
ざわ
MURMUR
ざわ
MURMUR
PRINCESS D, IF YOU WOULD GET READY...
YES, I KNOW.
EXCUSE ME. YOU. INTERPRETER.
HOW MAY I BE OF SERVICE, PRINCESS D?
I DON'T REALLY KNOW MY WAY AROUND THE EMBASSY YET.
TAKE ME TO MY ROOM.
...TREASURE, TREASURE, TREASURE. IS THAT ALL ANYONE CARES ABOUT?
トボトボ
TRUDGE TRUDGE
MAYBE IF I WERE PRETTIER...
THEN I WOULDN'T BE STUCK PLAYING SECOND FIDDLE TO SOME JEWEL.
...SNIFFLE
YOU'RE RIGHT. I HAVE NO USE FOR YOU.

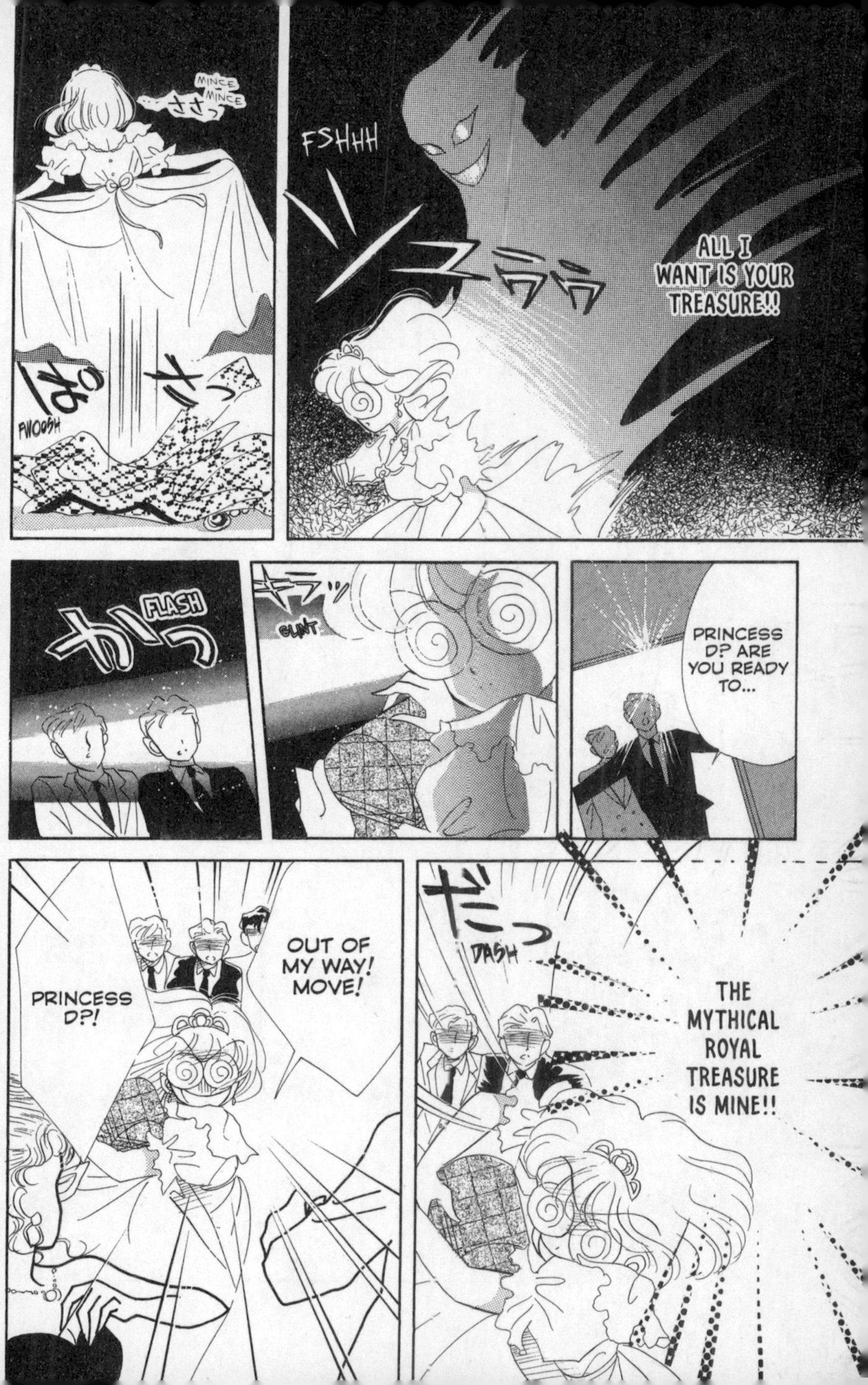
FSHHH
ALL I WANT IS YOUR TREASURE!!
MINCE MINCE
FWOOSH
PRINCESS D? ARE YOU READY TO...
GLINT
FLASH
DASH
THE MYTHICAL ROYAL TREASURE IS MINE!!
OUT OF MY WAY! MOVE!
PRINCESS D?!

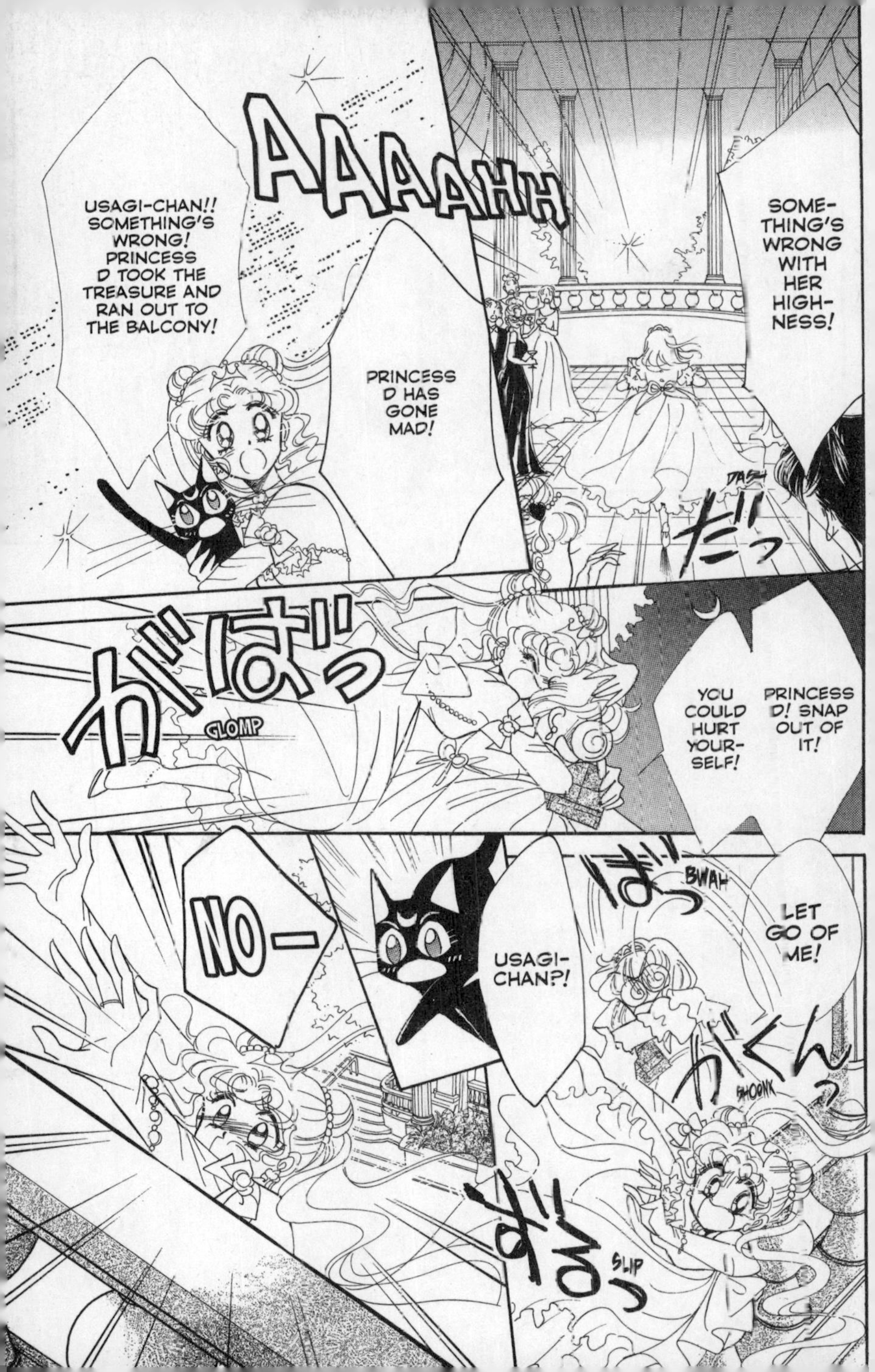
SOME-THING'S WRONG WITH HER HIGH-NESS!
だっ
DASH
AAAAHH
PRINCESS D HAS GONE MAD!
USAGI-CHAN!! SOMETHING'S WRONG! PRINCESS D TOOK THE TREASURE AND RAN OUT TO THE BALCONY!
PRINCESS D! SNAP OUT OF IT!
YOU COULD HURT YOUR-SELF!
がばっ
GLOMP
ばっ
BWAH
LET GO OF ME!
がくんっ
SHOONK
ずるっ
SLIP
USAGI-CHAN?!
NO—

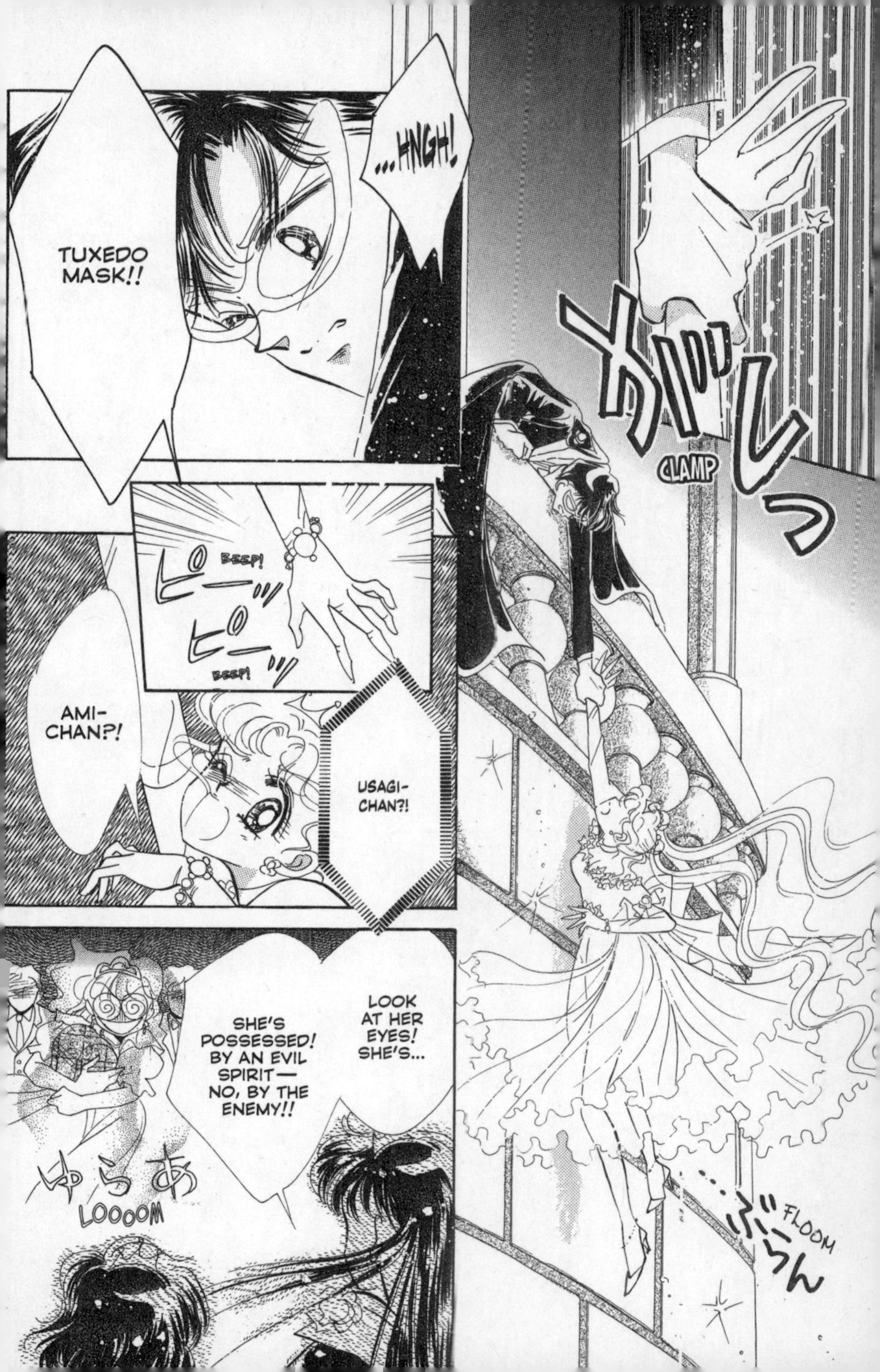
CLAMP
ぶらん
FLOOM
...HNGH!
TUXEDO MASK!!
ピーッ
BEEP!
ピーッ
BEEP!
AMI-CHAN?!
USAGI-CHAN?!
LOOK AT HER EYES! SHE'S...
SHE'S POSSESSED! BY AN EVIL SPIRIT— NO, BY THE ENEMY!!
ゆらあ
LOOOOM

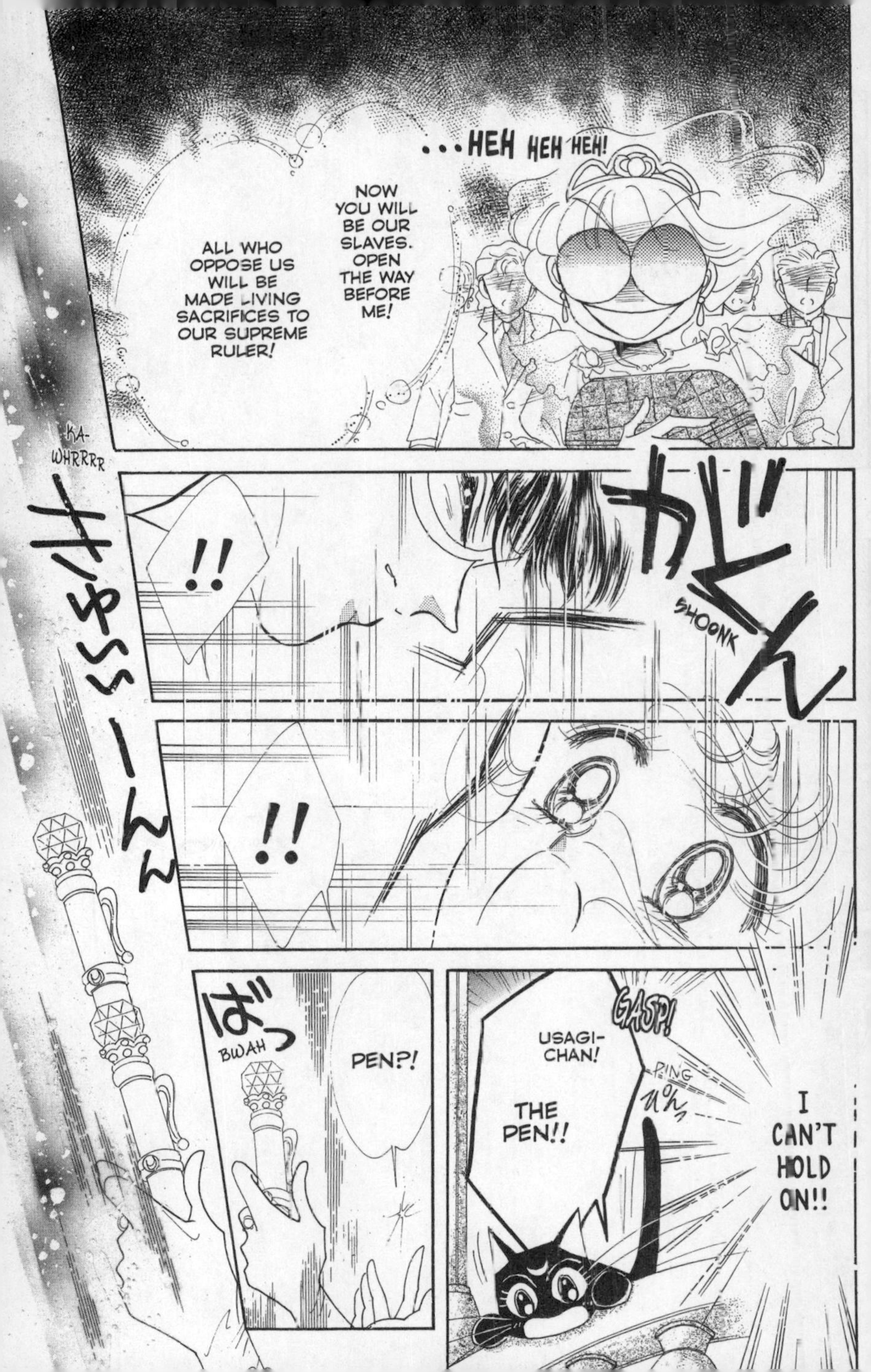
...HEH HEH HEH!
NOW YOU WILL BE OUR SLAVES. OPEN THE WAY BEFORE ME!
ALL WHO OPPOSE US WILL BE MADE LIVING SACRIFICES TO OUR SUPREME RULER!
きゅいいーんん
KA-WHRRRR
かどん
SHOONK
!!
!!
I CAN'T HOLD ON!!
GASP!
USAGI-CHAN!
PING
THE PEN!!
ばっ
BWAH
PEN?!

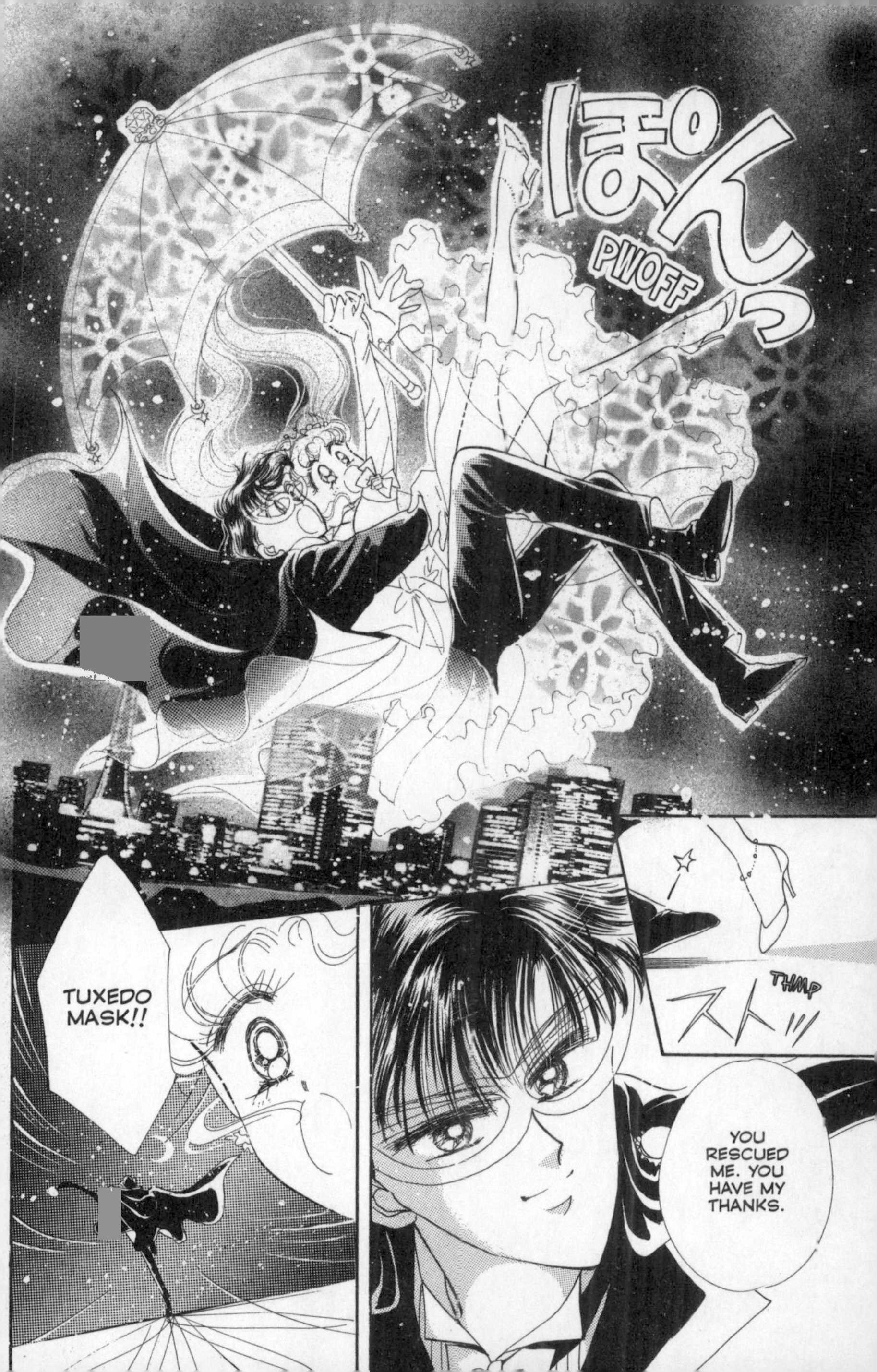
ぽんっ
PWOFF
THMP
スト
YOU RESCUED ME. YOU HAVE MY THANKS.
TUXEDO MASK!!

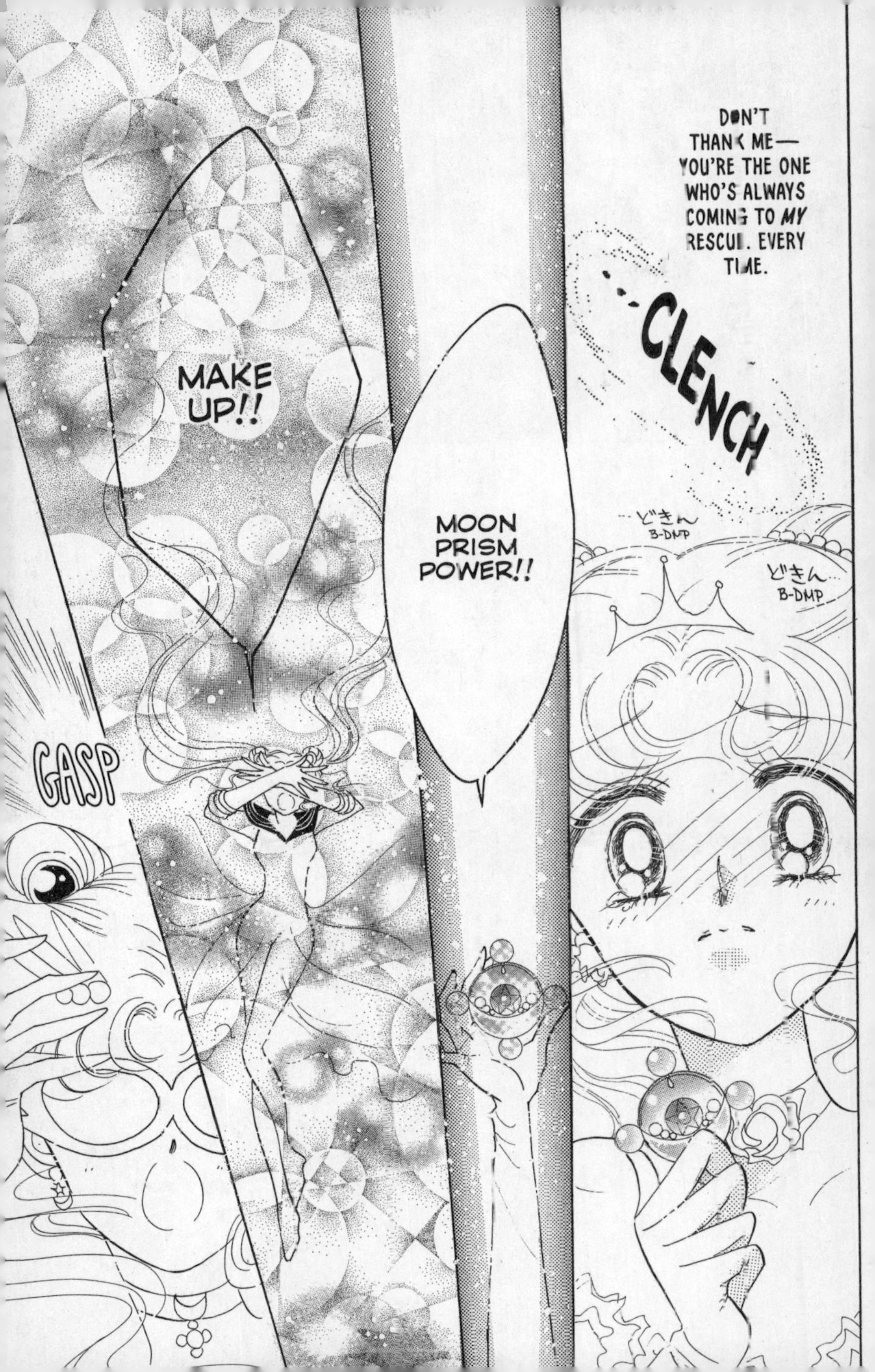
DON'T THANK ME— YOU'RE THE ONE WHO'S ALWAYS COMING TO *MY* RESCUE. EVERY TIME.
CLENCH
どきん B-DMP
どきん B-DMP
MOON PRISM POWER!!
MAKE UP!!
GASP

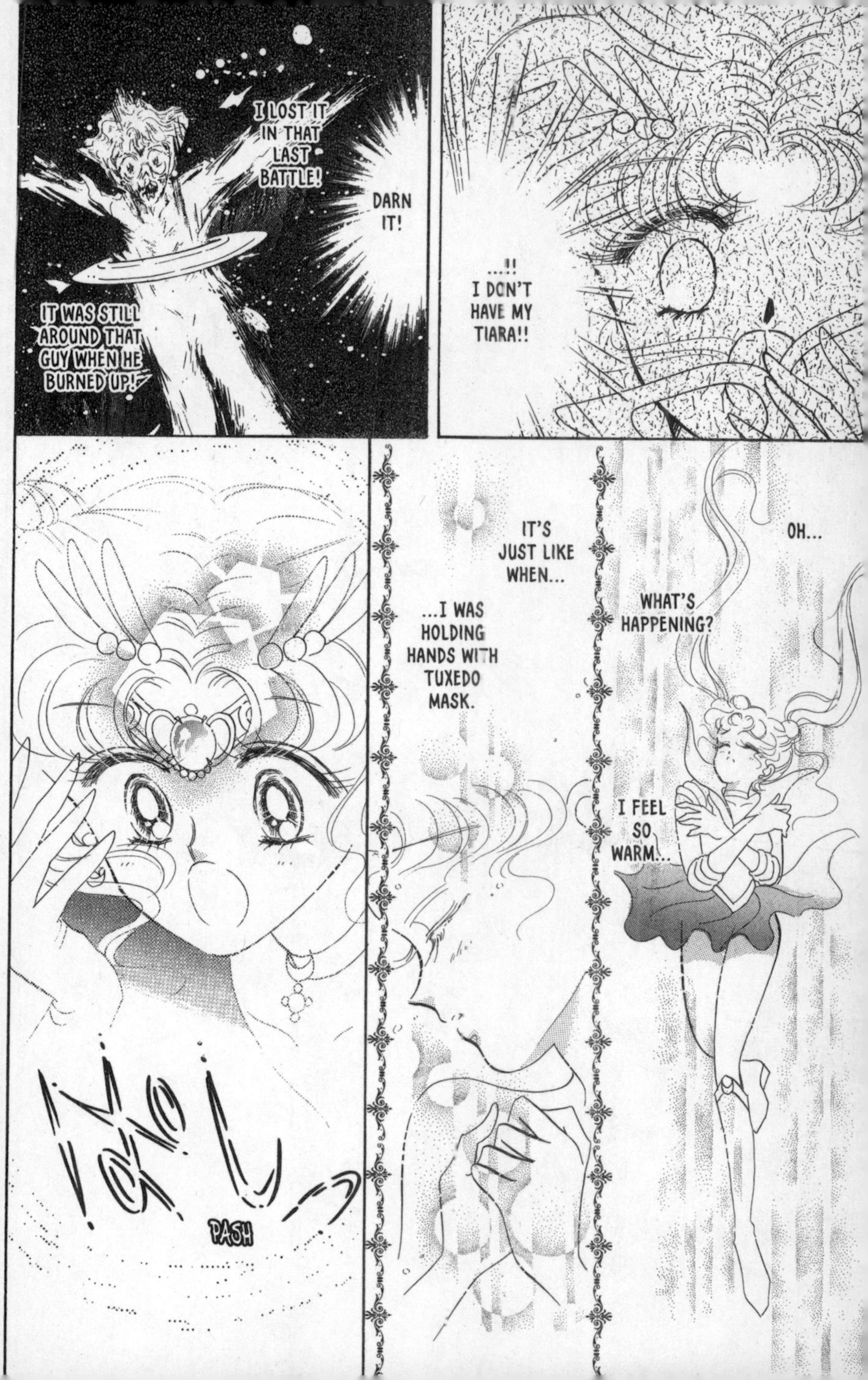
...!!
I DON'T HAVE MY TIARA!!
DARN IT!
I LOST IT IN THAT LAST BATTLE!
IT WAS STILL AROUND THAT GUY WHEN HE BURNED UP!
OH...
WHAT'S HAPPENING?
I FEEL SO WARM...
IT'S JUST LIKE WHEN...
...I WAS HOLDING HANDS WITH TUXEDO MASK.
PASH

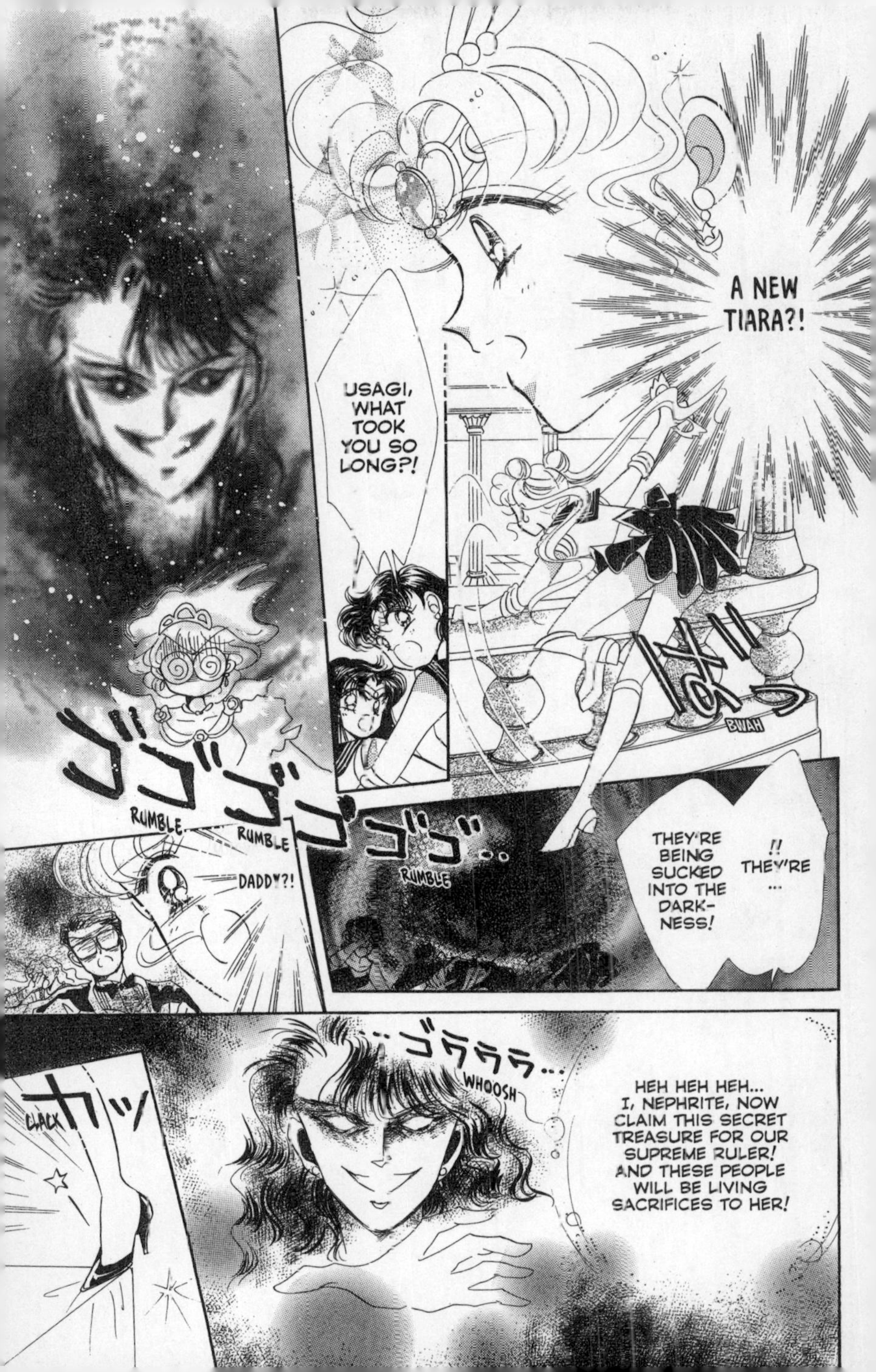
A NEW TIARA?!
BWAH
USAGI, WHAT TOOK YOU SO LONG?!
RUMBLE... RUMBLE
RUMBLE
!! THEY'RE ...
THEY'RE BEING SUCKED INTO THE DARK- NESS!
DADDY?!
WHOOSH
HEH HEH HEH... I, NEPHRITE, NOW CLAIM THIS SECRET TREASURE FOR OUR SUPREME RULER! AND THESE PEOPLE WILL BE LIVING SACRIFICES TO HER!
CLACK

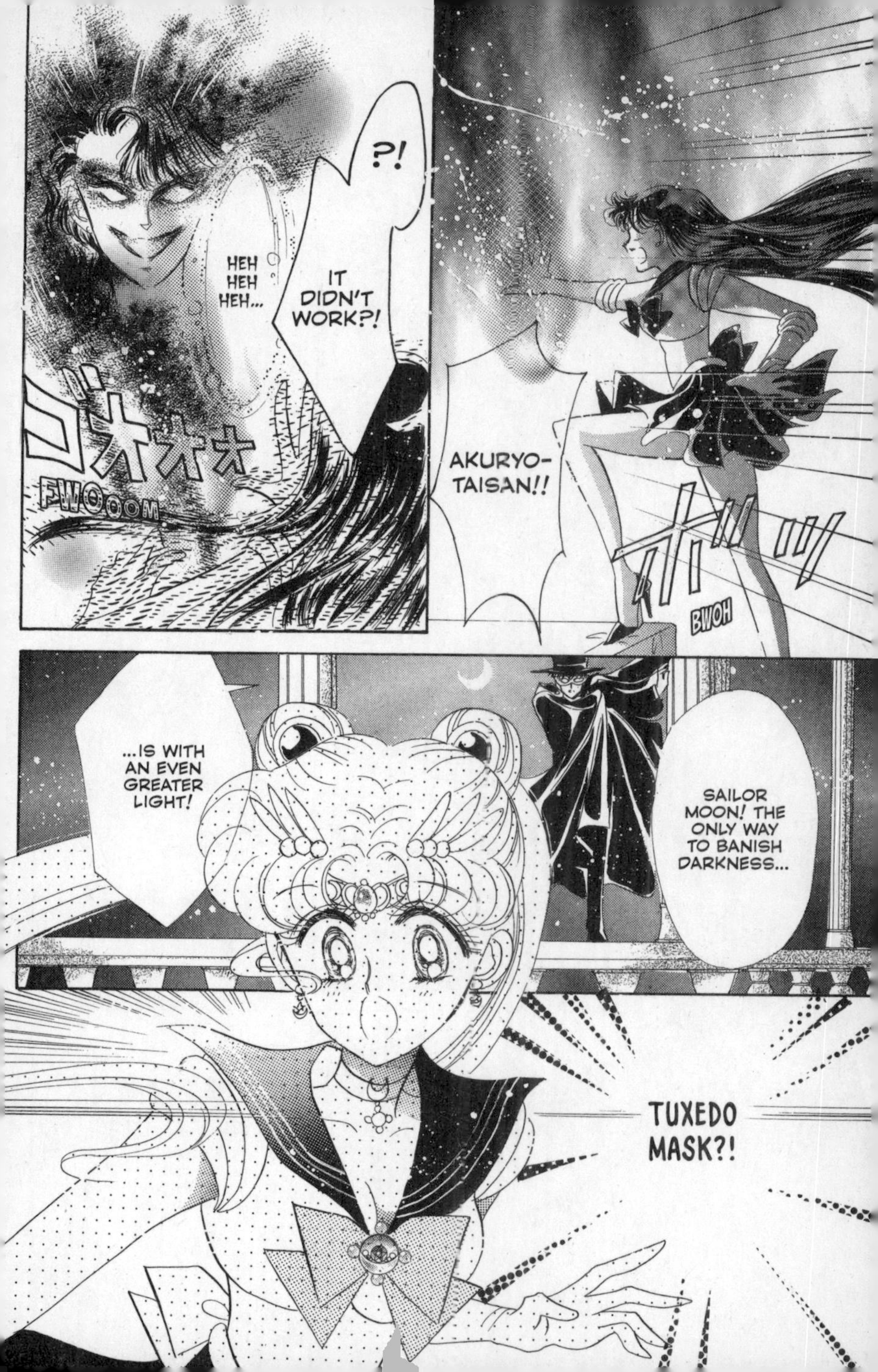
AKURYO-TAISAN!!
BWOH
?!
IT DIDN'T WORK?!
HEH HEH HEH...
ゴオオオ
FWOOOOM
SAILOR MOON! THE ONLY WAY TO BANISH DARKNESS...
...IS WITH AN EVEN GREATER LIGHT!
TUXEDO MASK?!

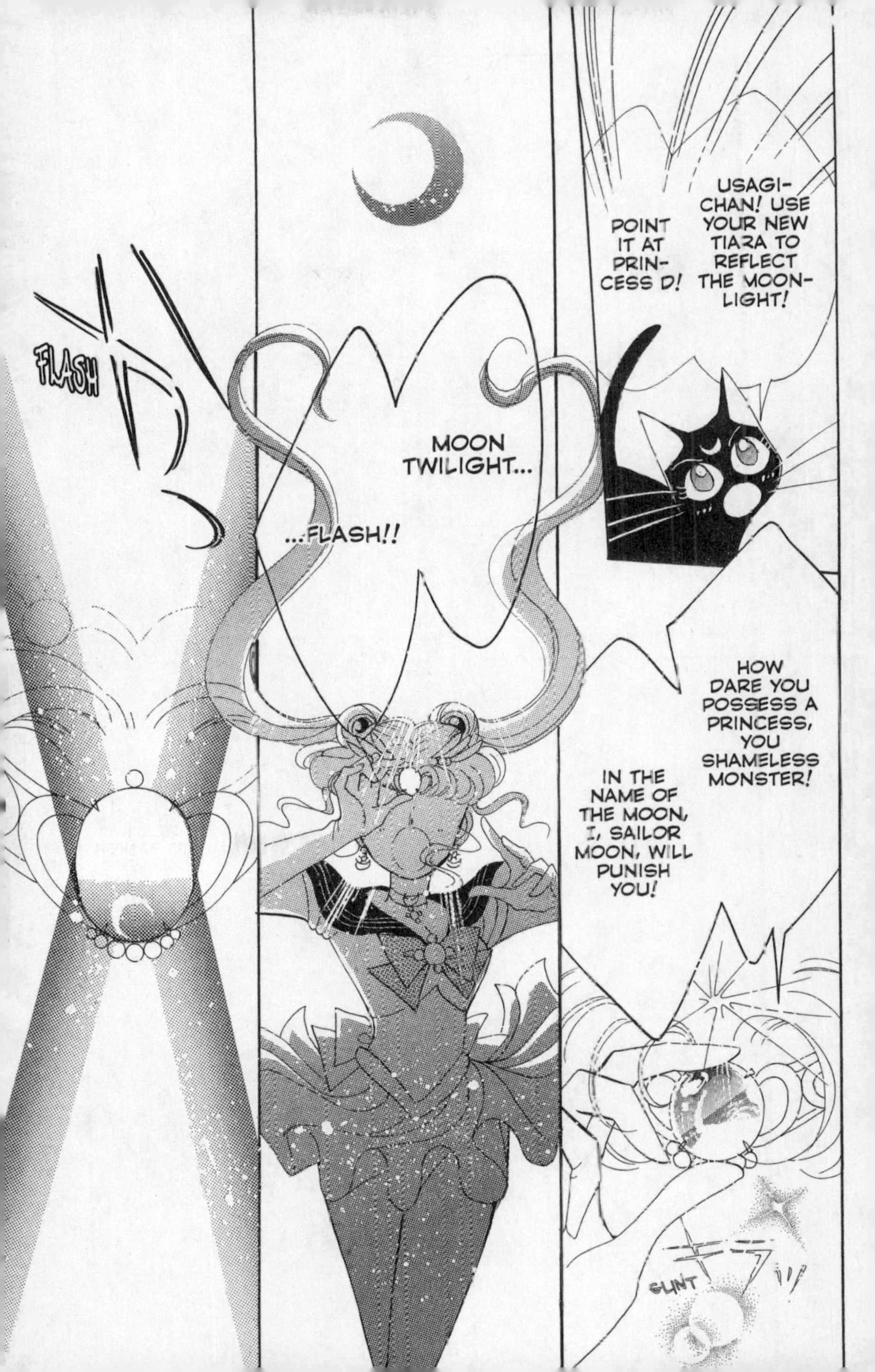
USAGI-CHAN! USE YOUR NEW TIARA TO REFLECT THE MOONLIGHT!
POINT IT AT PRINCESS D!
HOW DARE YOU POSSESS A PRINCESS, YOU SHAMELESS MONSTER!
IN THE NAME OF THE MOON, I, SAILOR MOON, WILL PUNISH YOU!
GLINT
MOON TWILIGHT...
...FLASH!!
FLASH

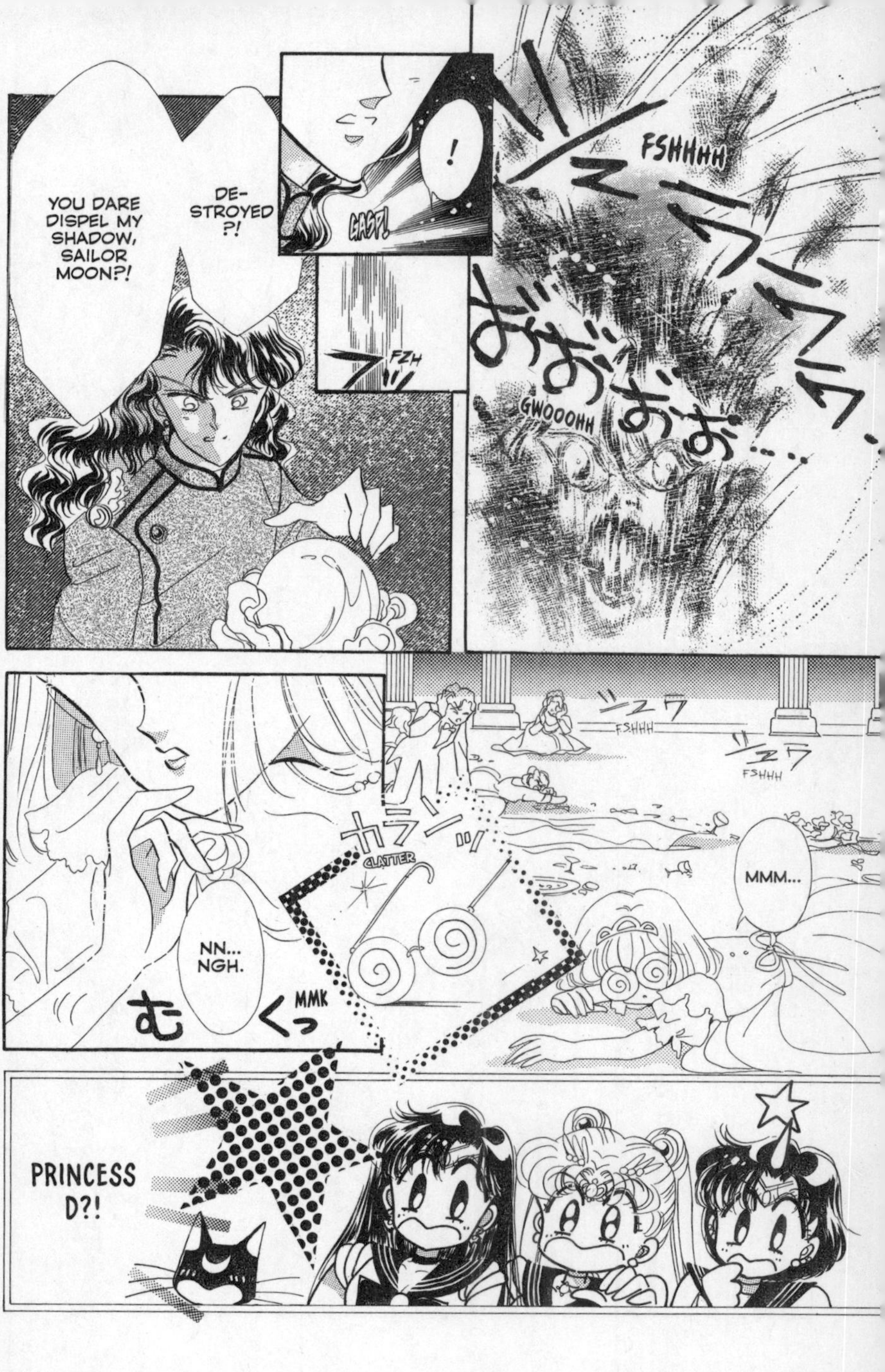
FSHHHH
GWOOOHH
!
GASP!
FZH
DE-STROYED?!
YOU DARE DISPEL MY SHADOW, SAILOR MOON?!
FSHHH
FSHHH
CLATTER
MMM...
NN... NGH.
MMK
PRINCESS D?!

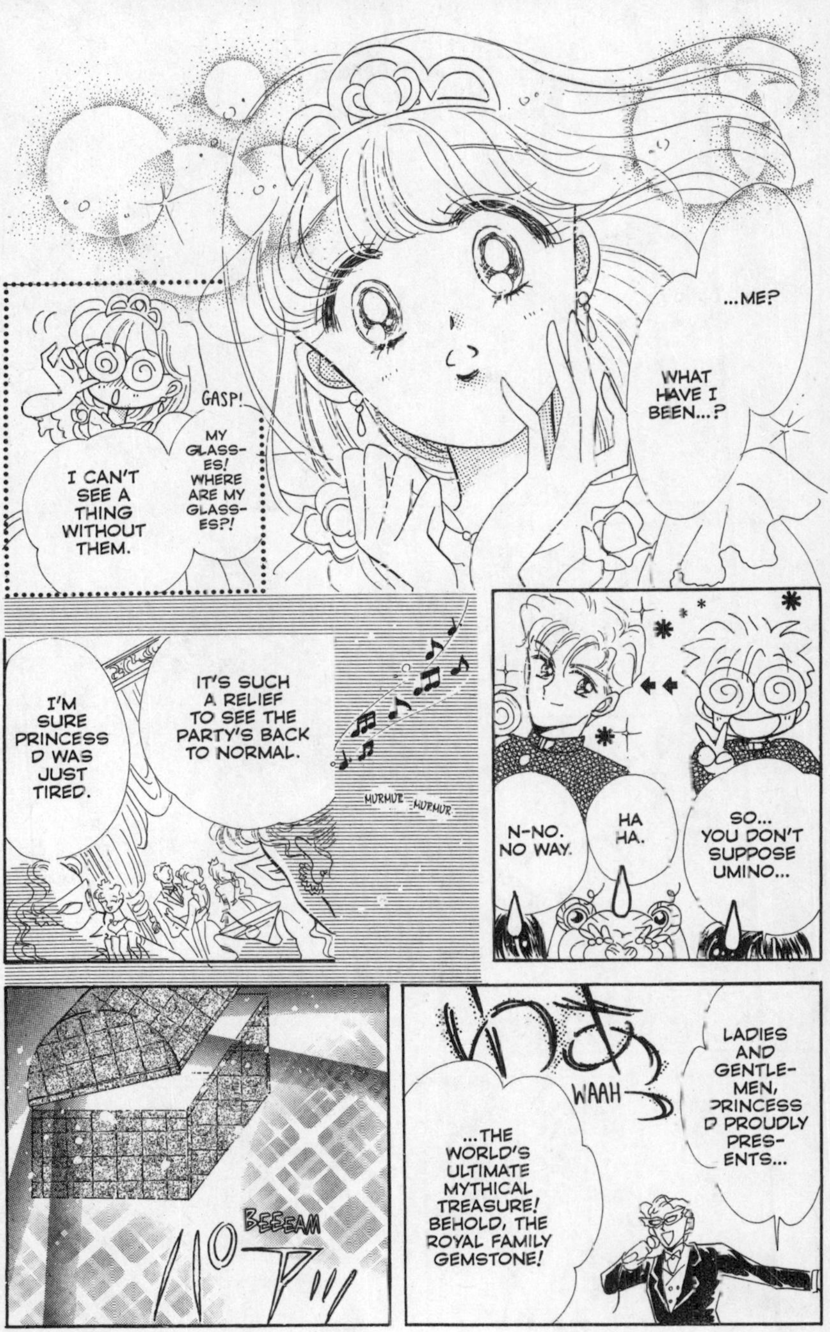
...ME?
WHAT HAVE I BEEN...?
GASP!
MY GLASS-ES! WHERE ARE MY GLASS-ES?!
I CAN'T SEE A THING WITHOUT THEM.
SO... YOU DON'T SUPPOSE UMINO...
HA HA.
N-NO. NO WAY.
MURMUR MURMUR
IT'S SUCH A RELIEF TO SEE THE PARTY'S BACK TO NORMAL.
I'M SURE PRINCESS D WAS JUST TIRED.
LADIES AND GENTLE-MEN, PRINCESS D PROUDLY PRES-ENTS...
WAAH
...THE WORLD'S ULTIMATE MYTHICAL TREASURE! BEHOLD, THE ROYAL FAMILY GEMSTONE!
BEEEAM

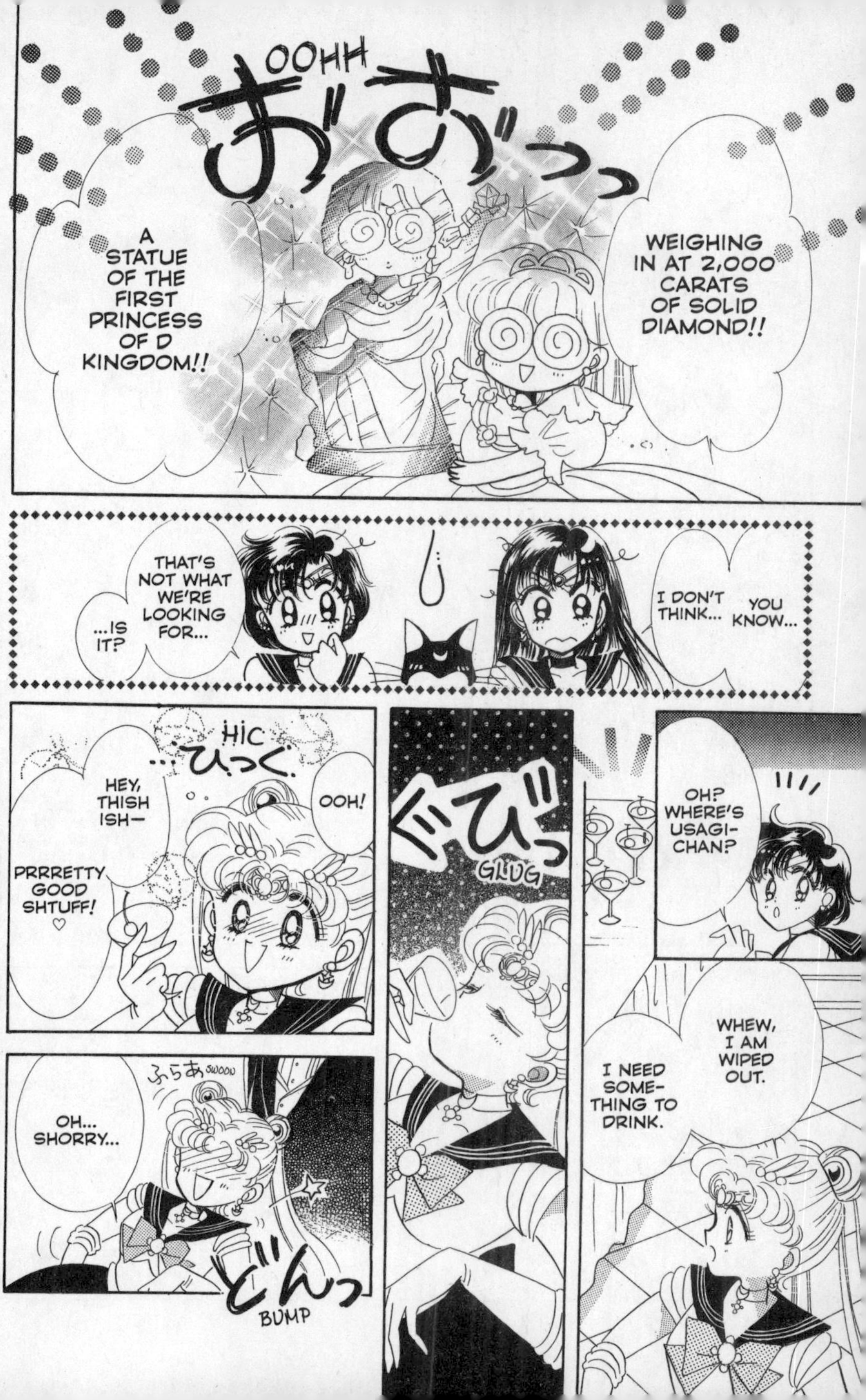
OOHH
おおっっ
WEIGHING IN AT 2,000 CARATS OF SOLID DIAMOND!!
A STATUE OF THE FIRST PRINCESS OF D KINGDOM!!
I DON'T THINK... YOU KNOW...
THAT'S NOT WHAT WE'RE LOOKING FOR...
...IS IT?
OH? WHERE'S USAGI-CHAN?
WHEW, I AM WIPED OUT.
I NEED SOME-THING TO DRINK.
ぐびっ
GLUG
HIC
…ひっく
OOH!
HEY, THISH ISH—
PRRRETTY GOOD SHTUFF! ♡
ふらあ SWOON
OH... SHORRY...
どんっ
BUMP

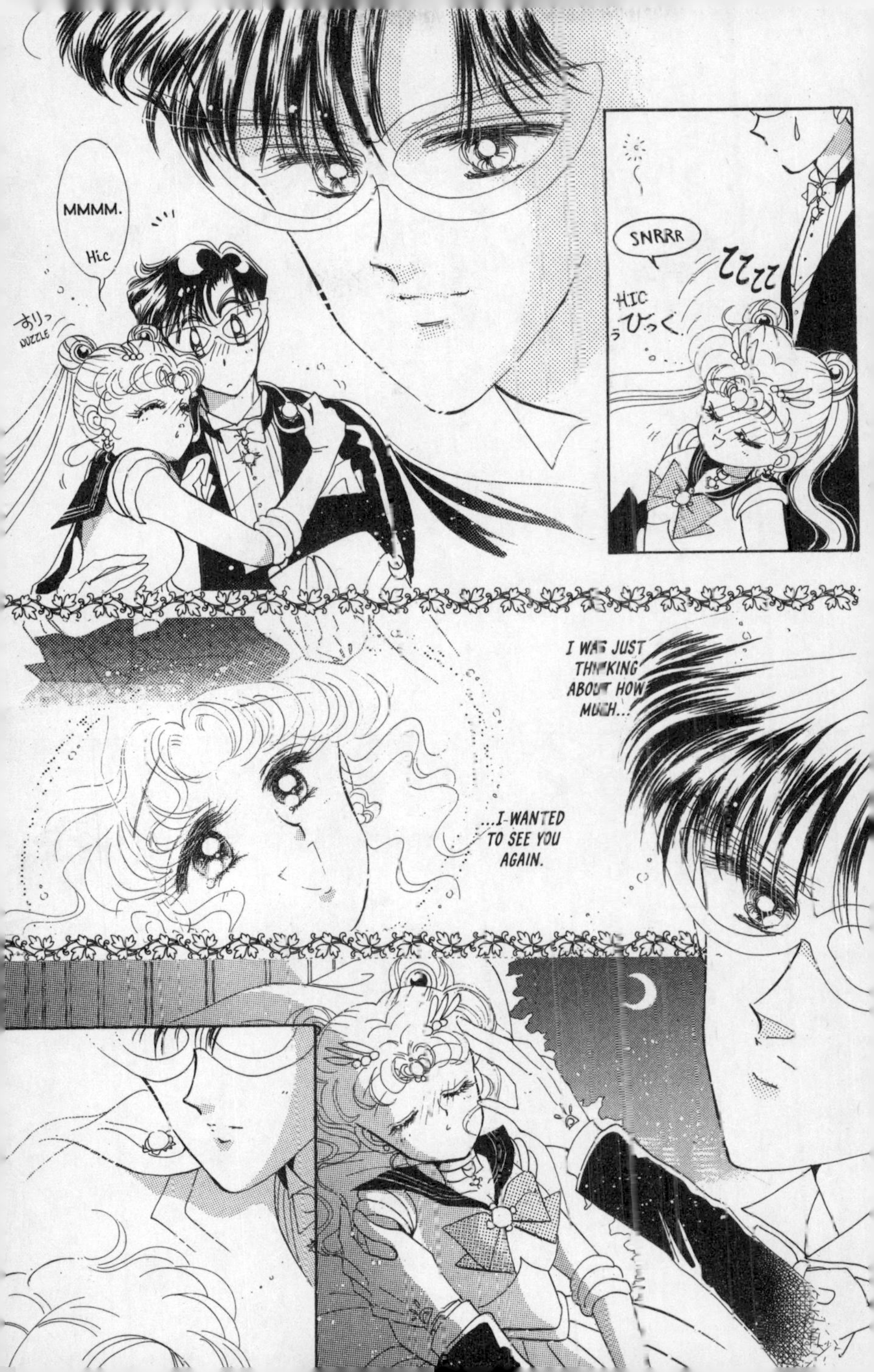
SNRRR
ZZZZ
HIC
ひっく
MMMM.
Hic
すりっ
NUZZLE
I WAS JUST THINKING ABOUT HOW MUCH...
...I-WANTED TO SEE YOU AGAIN.

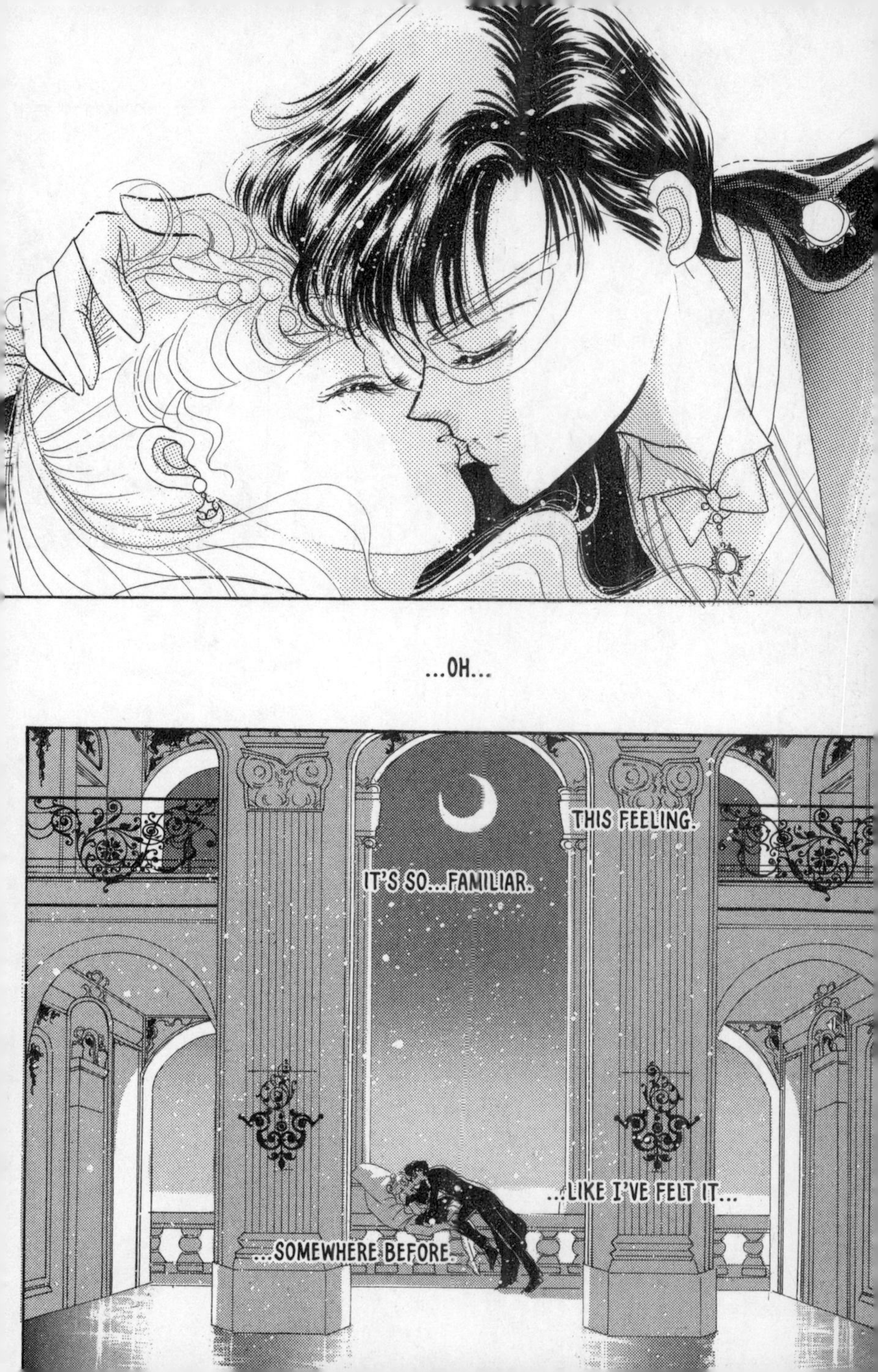
...OH...
THIS FEELING.
IT'S SO...FAMILIAR.
...LIKE I'VE FELT IT...
...SOMEWHERE BEFORE.

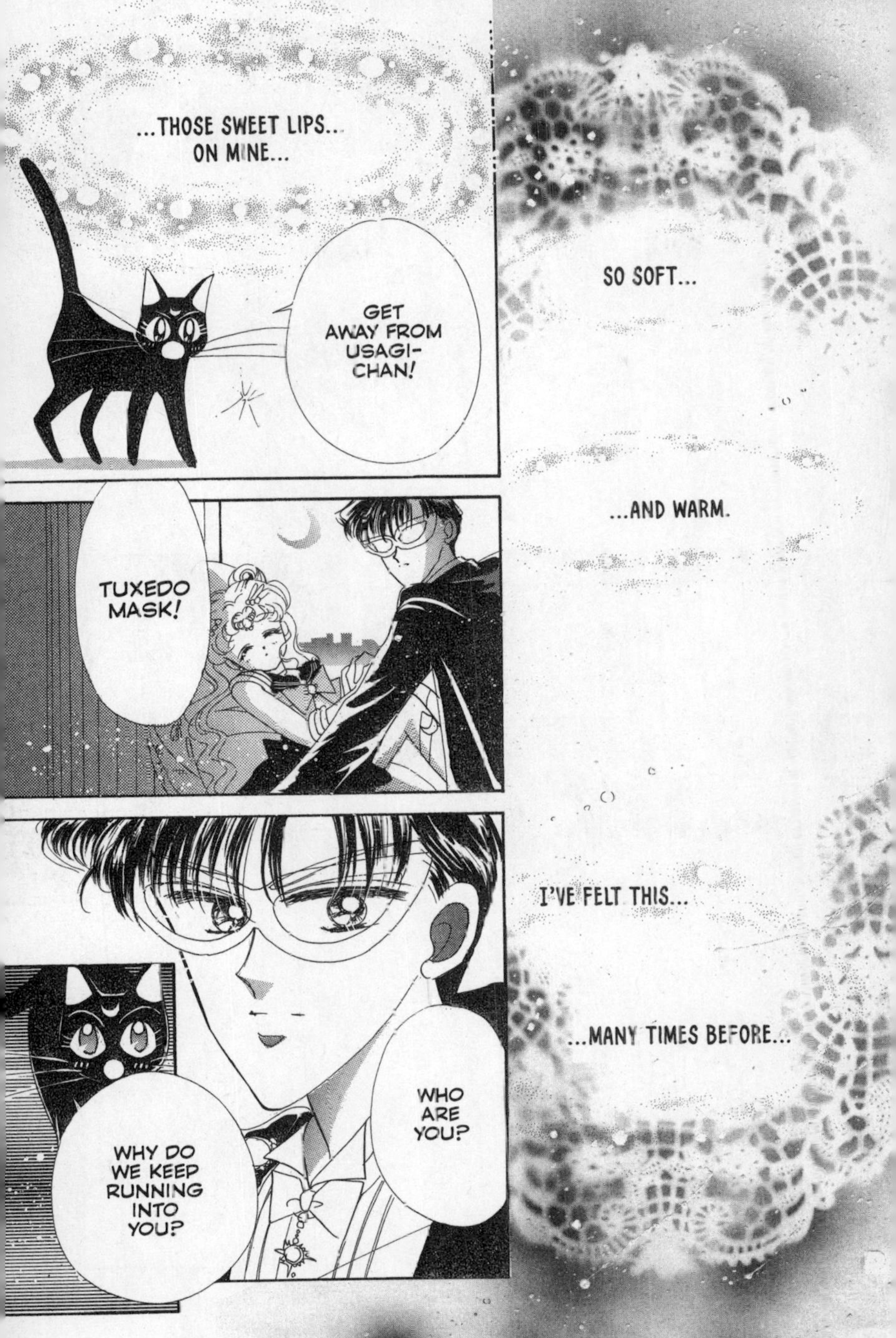
SO SOFT...
...AND WARM.
I'VE FELT THIS...
...MANY TIMES BEFORE...
...THOSE SWEET LIPS... ON MINE...
GET AWAY FROM USAGI-CHAN!
TUXEDO MASK!
WHO ARE YOU?
WHY DO WE KEEP RUNNING INTO YOU?

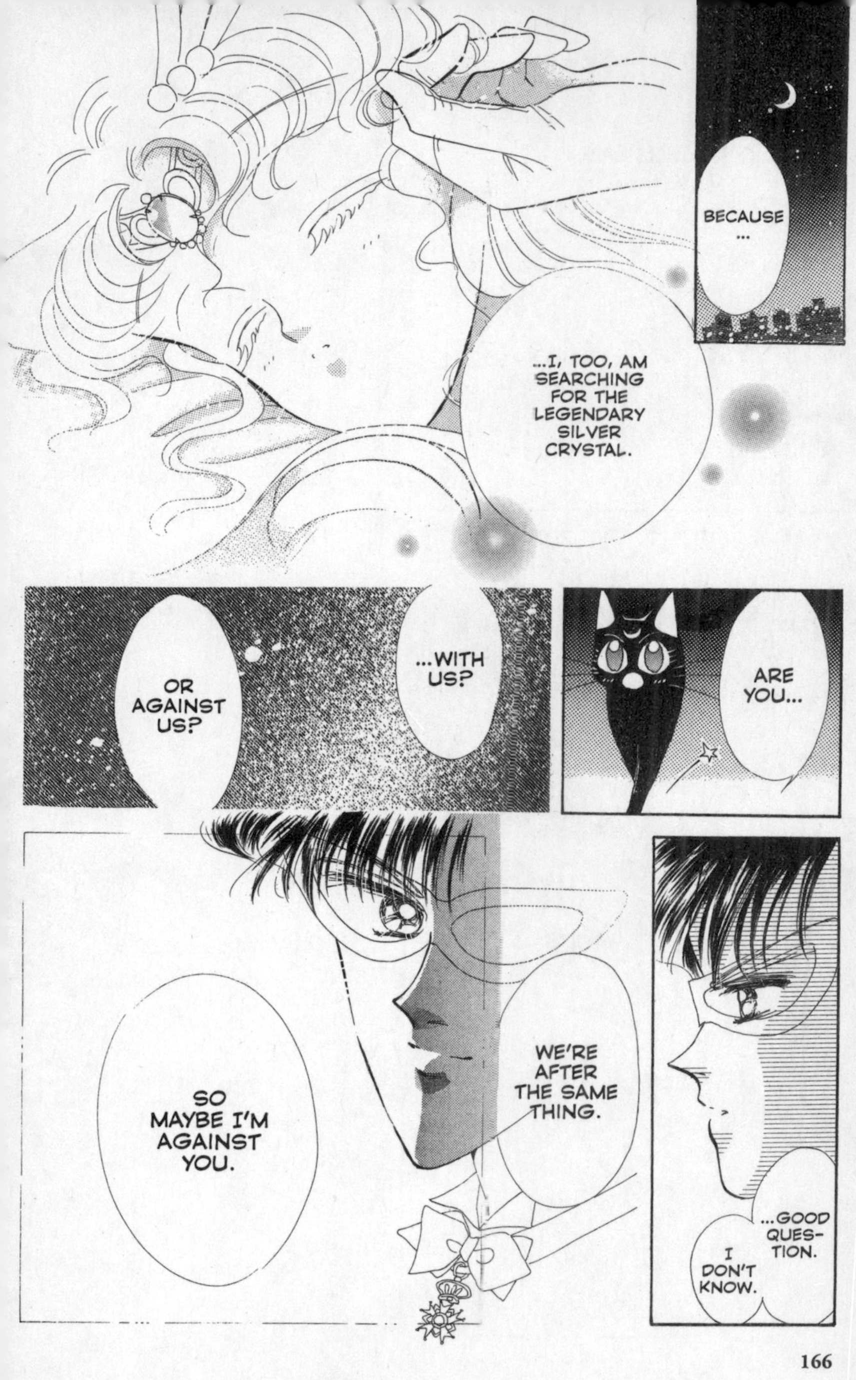
BECAUSE ...
...I, TOO, AM SEARCHING FOR THE LEGENDARY SILVER CRYSTAL.
ARE YOU...
...WITH US?
OR AGAINST US?
...GOOD QUES-TION.
I DON'T KNOW.
WE'RE AFTER THE SAME THING.
SO MAYBE I'M AGAINST YOU.

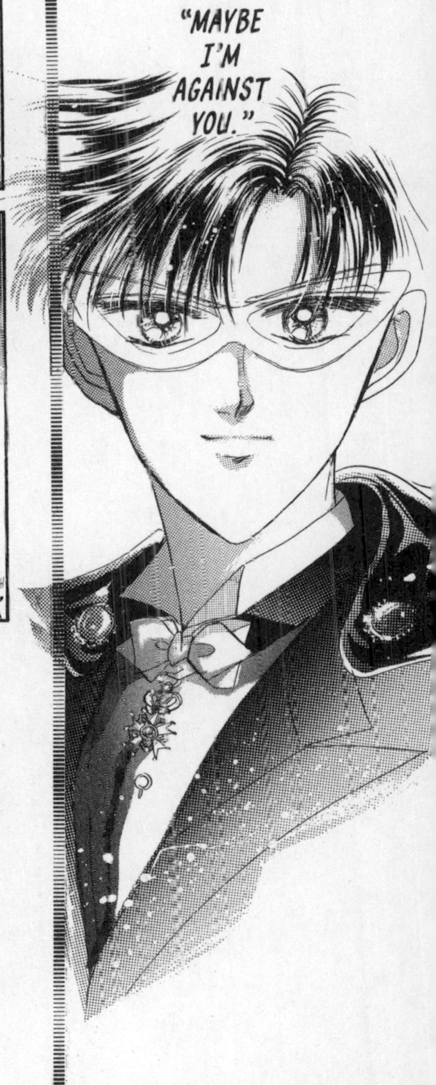
"MAYBE I'M AGAINST YOU."

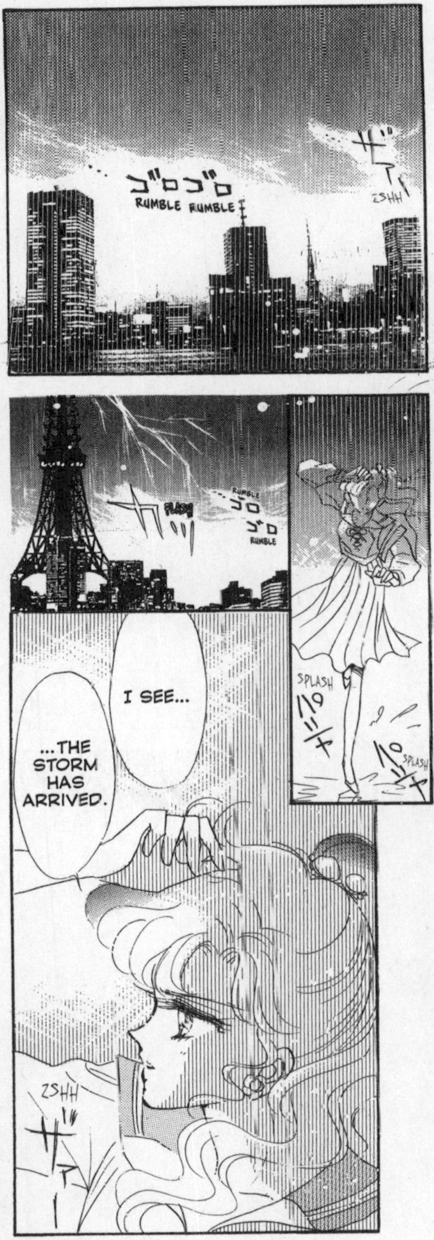
ZSHH
RUMBLE RUMBLE
SPLASH
SPLASH
RUMBLE
RUMBLE
FLASH
I SEE...
...THE STORM HAS ARRIVED.
ZSHH

Pretty Guardian Sailor Moon

Act.5 Makoto: Sailor Jupiter

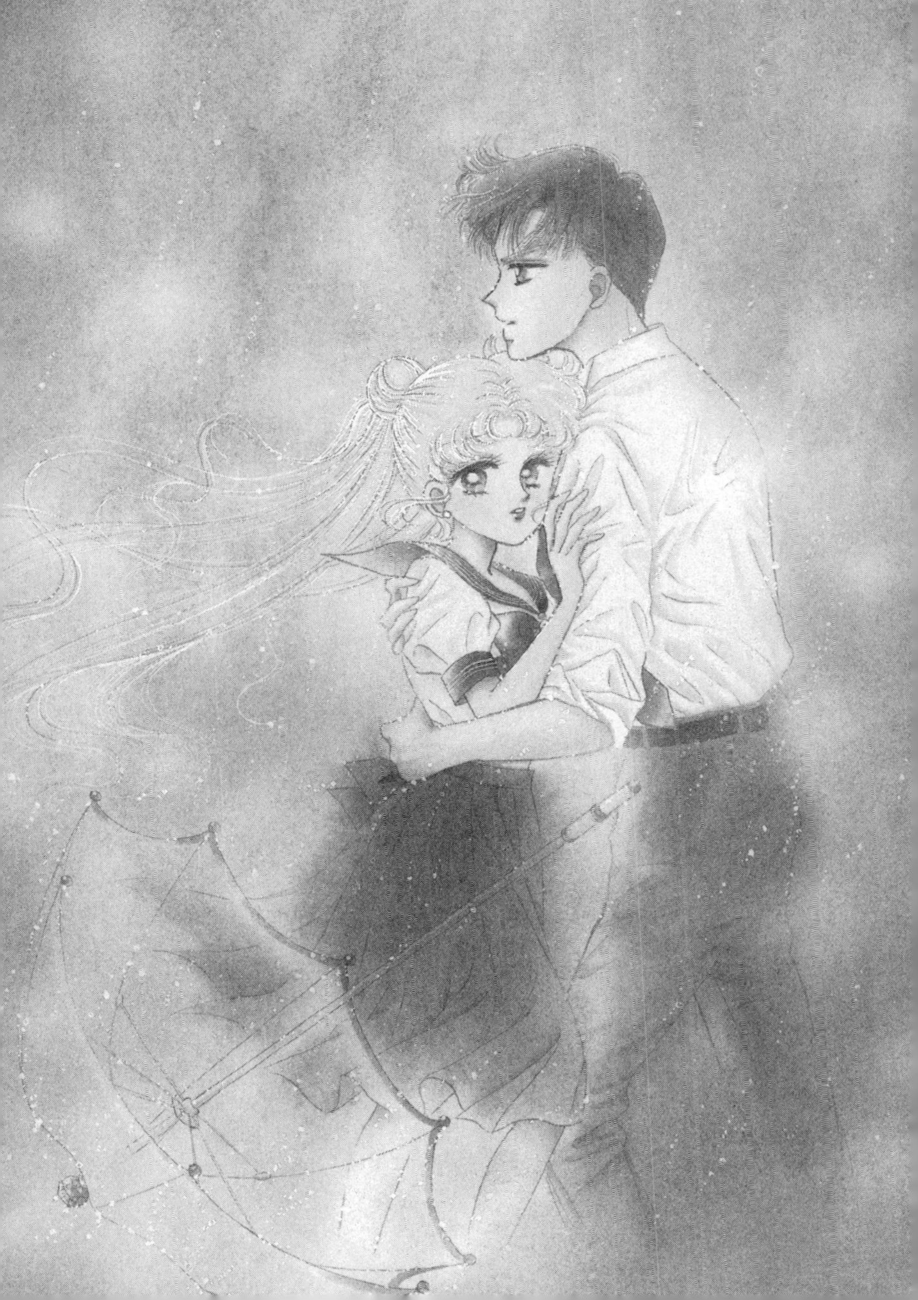

Pretty Guardian Sailor Moon

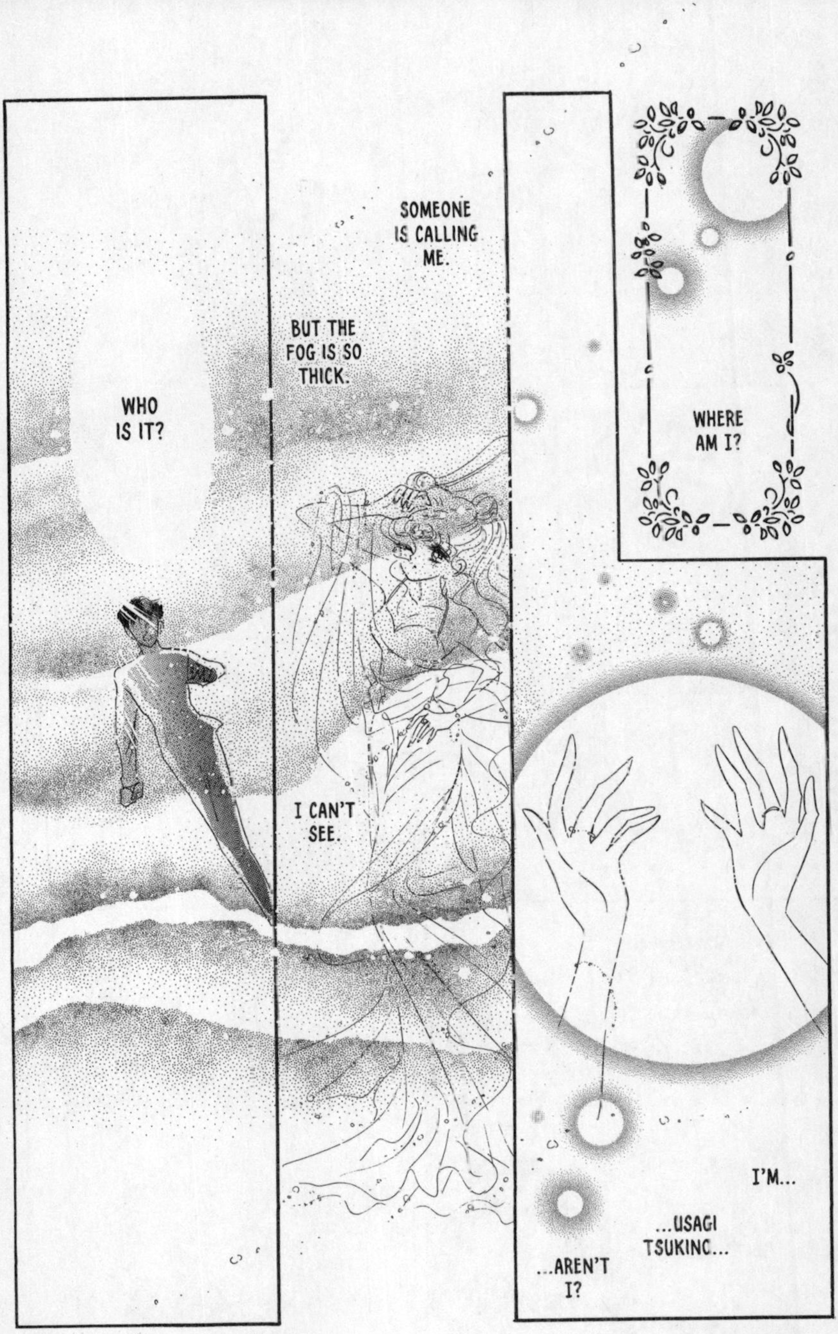
WHERE AM I?
I'M...
...USAGI TSUKINC...
...AREN'T I?
SOMEONE IS CALLING ME.
BUT THE FOG IS SO THICK.
I CAN'T SEE.
WHO IS IT?

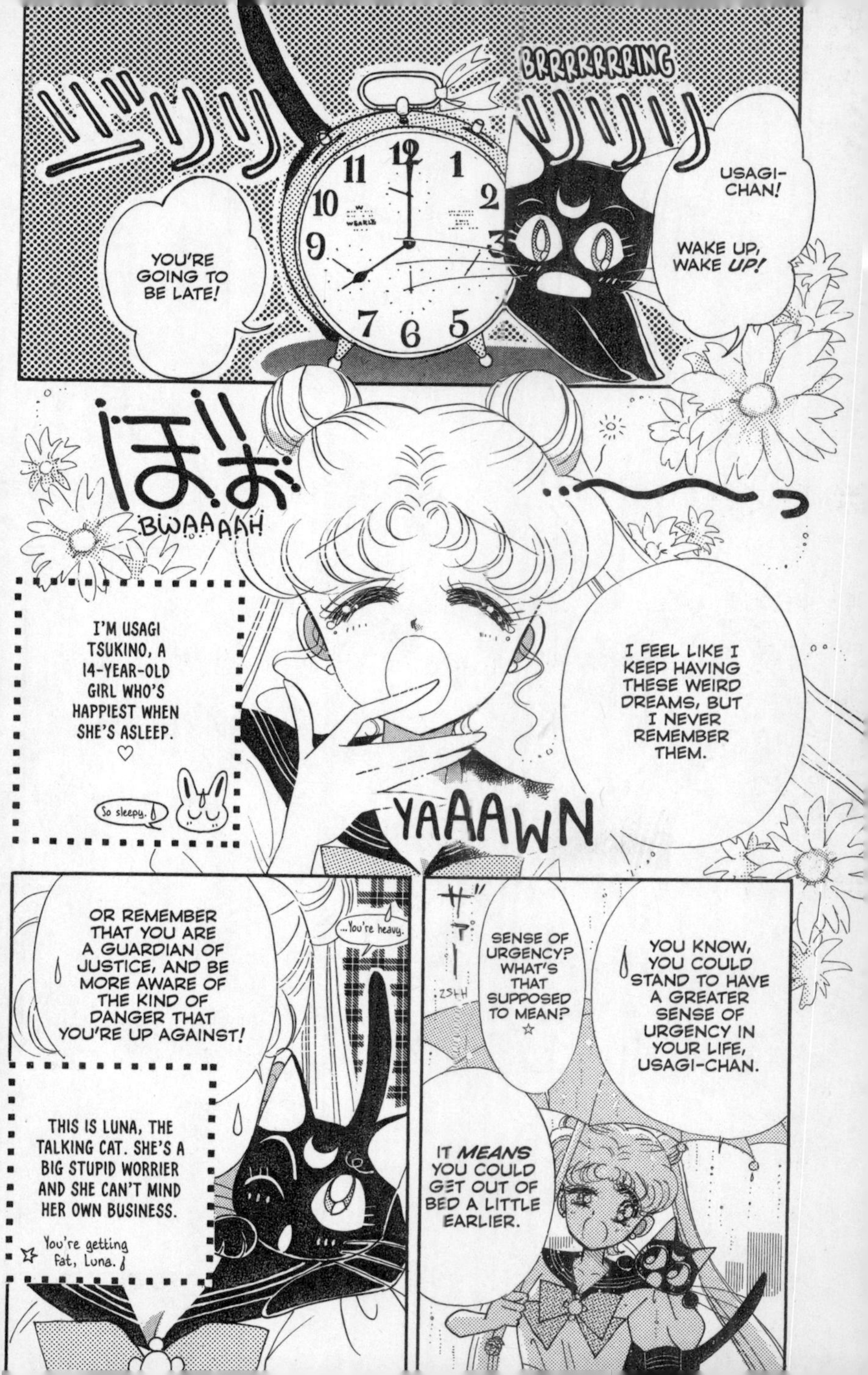
BRRRRRRRING
USAGI-CHAN! WAKE UP, WAKE *UP*!
YOU'RE GOING TO BE LATE!
BWAAAAH
I FEEL LIKE I KEEP HAVING THESE WEIRD DREAMS, BUT I NEVER REMEMBER THEM.
YAAAWN
I'M USAGI TSUKINO, A 14-YEAR-OLD GIRL WHO'S HAPPIEST WHEN SHE'S ASLEEP. ♡
So sleepy.
YOU KNOW, YOU COULD STAND TO HAVE A GREATER SENSE OF URGENCY IN YOUR LIFE, USAGI-CHAN.
SENSE OF URGENCY? WHAT'S THAT SUPPOSED TO MEAN? ☆
ZSHH
IT *MEANS* YOU COULD GET OUT OF BED A LITTLE EARLIER.
...You're heavy.
OR REMEMBER THAT YOU ARE A GUARDIAN OF JUSTICE, AND BE MORE AWARE OF THE KIND OF DANGER THAT YOU'RE UP AGAINST!
THIS IS LUNA, THE TALKING CAT. SHE'S A BIG STUPID WORRIER AND SHE CAN'T MIND HER OWN BUSINESS.
☆ You're getting fat, Luna.

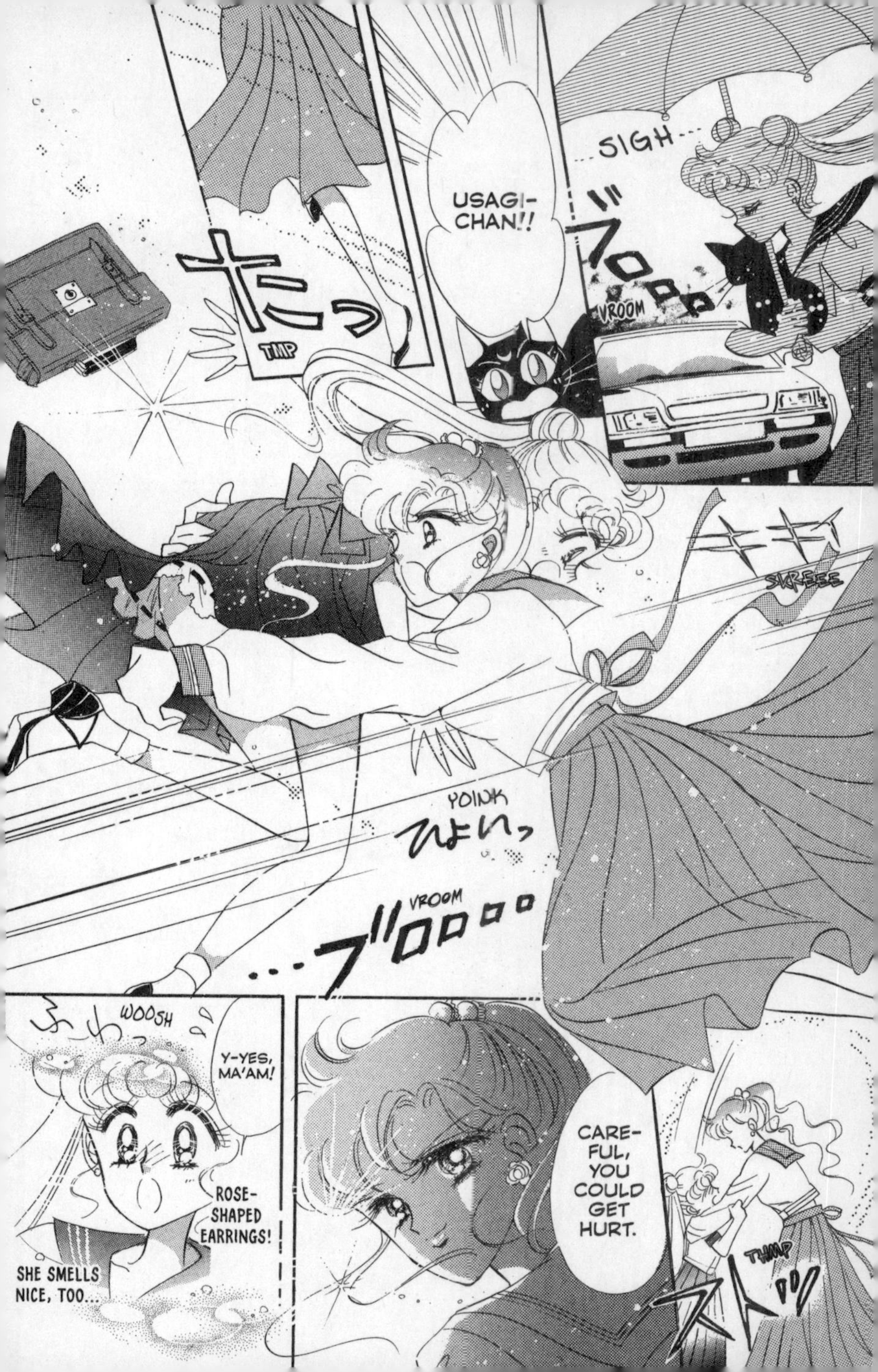
SIGH
VROOM
USAGI-CHAN!!
TMP
SKREEEE
YOINK
VROOM
CARE-FUL, YOU COULD GET HURT.
THMP
WOOSH
Y-YES, MA'AM!
ROSE-SHAPED EARRINGS!
SHE SMELLS NICE, TOO...

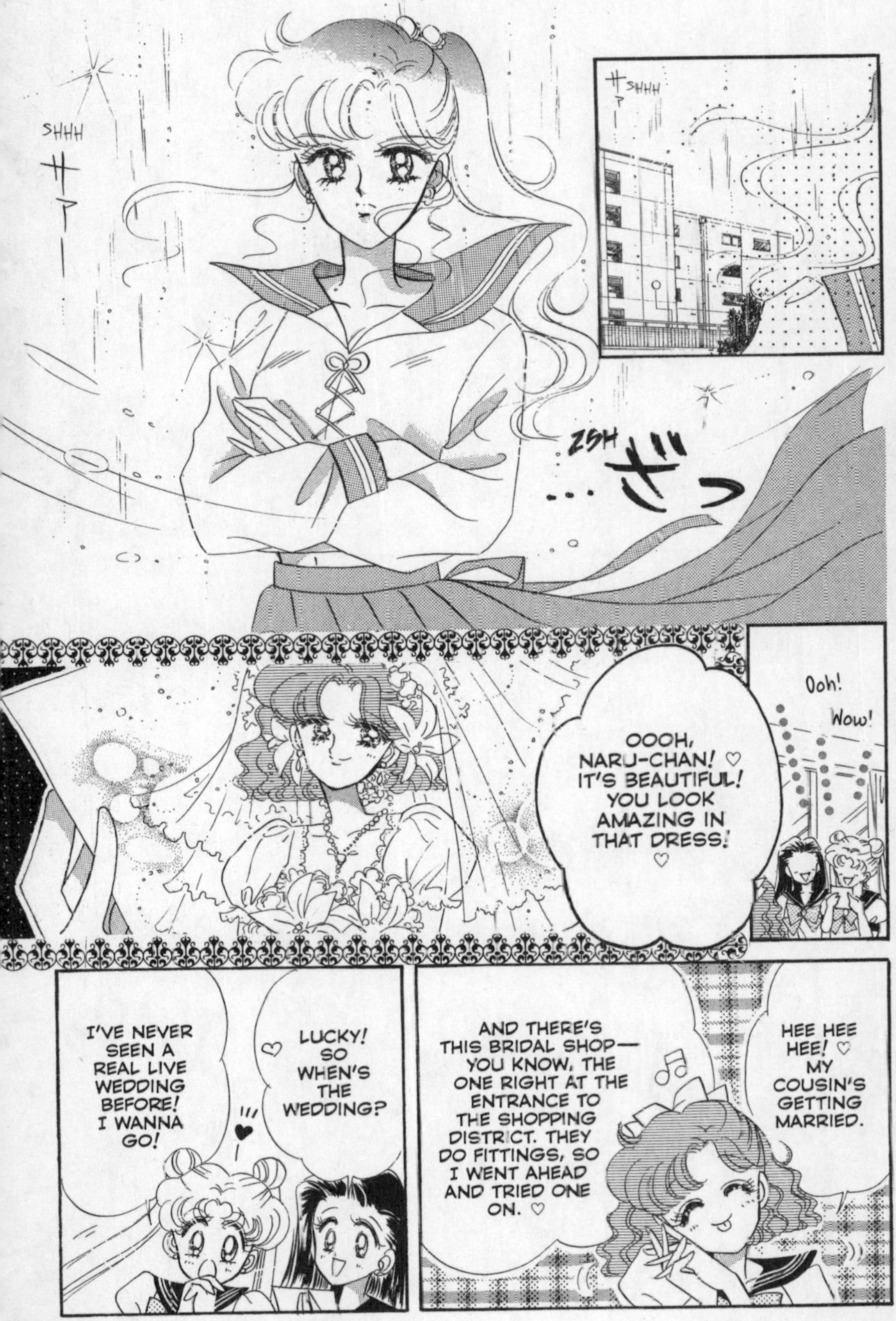
SHHH
SHHH
ZSH
...
Ooh!
Wow!
OOOH, NARU-CHAN! ♡ IT'S BEAUTIFUL! YOU LOOK AMAZING IN THAT DRESS! ♡
HEE HEE HEE! ♡ MY COUSIN'S GETTING MARRIED.
AND THERE'S THIS BRIDAL SHOP— YOU KNOW, THE ONE RIGHT AT THE ENTRANCE TO THE SHOPPING DISTRICT. THEY DO FITTINGS, SO I WENT AHEAD AND TRIED ONE ON. ♡
LUCKY! SO WHEN'S THE WEDDING?
I'VE NEVER SEEN A REAL LIVE WEDDING BEFORE! I WANNA GO!

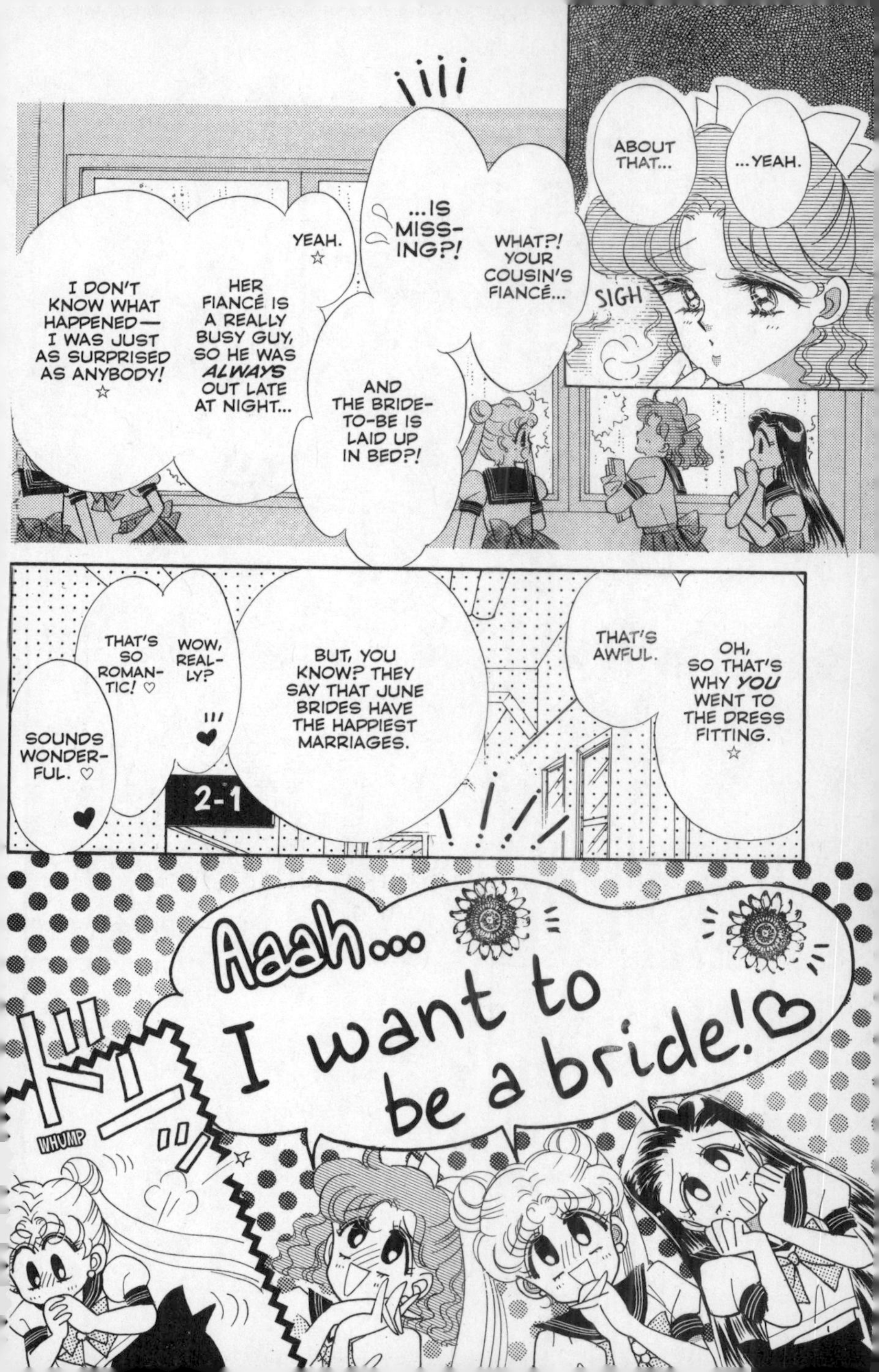
...YEAH.
ABOUT THAT...
SIGH
¡¡¡¡
WHAT?! YOUR COUSIN'S FIANCÉ...
...IS MISSING?!
YEAH. ☆
AND THE BRIDE-TO-BE IS LAID UP IN BED?!
HER FIANCÉ IS A REALLY BUSY GUY, SO HE WAS *ALWAYS* OUT LATE AT NIGHT...
I DON'T KNOW WHAT HAPPENED— I WAS JUST AS SURPRISED AS ANYBODY! ☆
OH, SO THAT'S WHY *YOU* WENT TO THE DRESS FITTING. ☆
THAT'S AWFUL.
BUT, YOU KNOW? THEY SAY THAT JUNE BRIDES HAVE THE HAPPIEST MARRIAGES.
WOW, REALLY?
THAT'S SO ROMANTIC! ♡
SOUNDS WONDERFUL. ♡
2-1
Aaah... I want to be a bride!
WHUMP

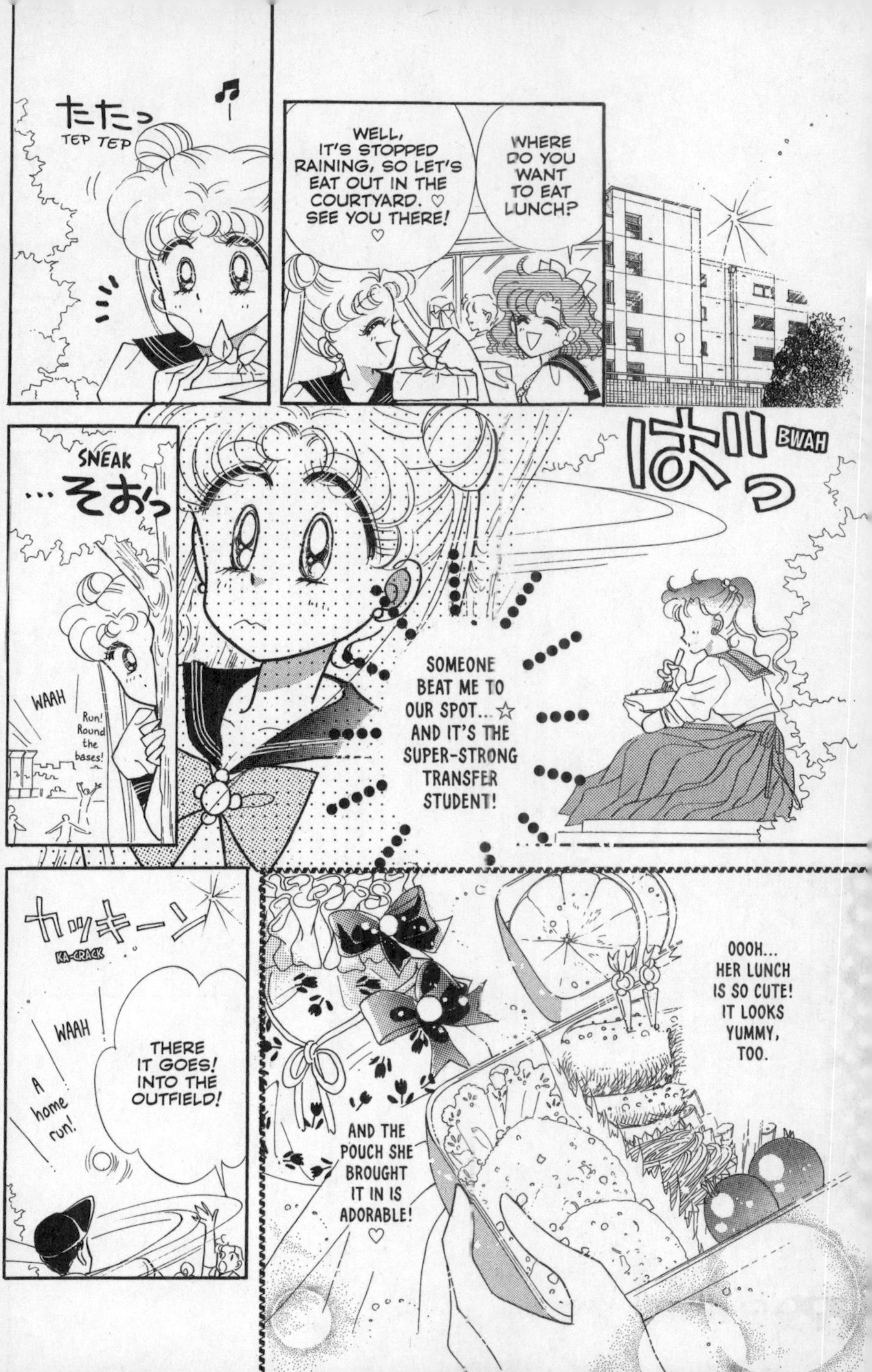
WHERE DO YOU WANT TO EAT LUNCH?
WELL, IT'S STOPPED RAINING, SO LET'S EAT OUT IN THE COURTYARD. ♡ SEE YOU THERE! ♡
たたっ
TEP TEP
はっ
BWAH
SOMEONE BEAT ME TO OUR SPOT... ☆ AND IT'S THE SUPER-STRONG TRANSFER STUDENT!
SNEAK
…そおっ
WAAH
Run! Round the bases!
OOOH... HER LUNCH IS SO CUTE! IT LOOKS YUMMY, TOO.
AND THE POUCH SHE BROUGHT IT IN IS ADORABLE! ♡
カッキーン
KA-CRACK
WAAH
THERE IT GOES! INTO THE OUTFIELD!
A home run!

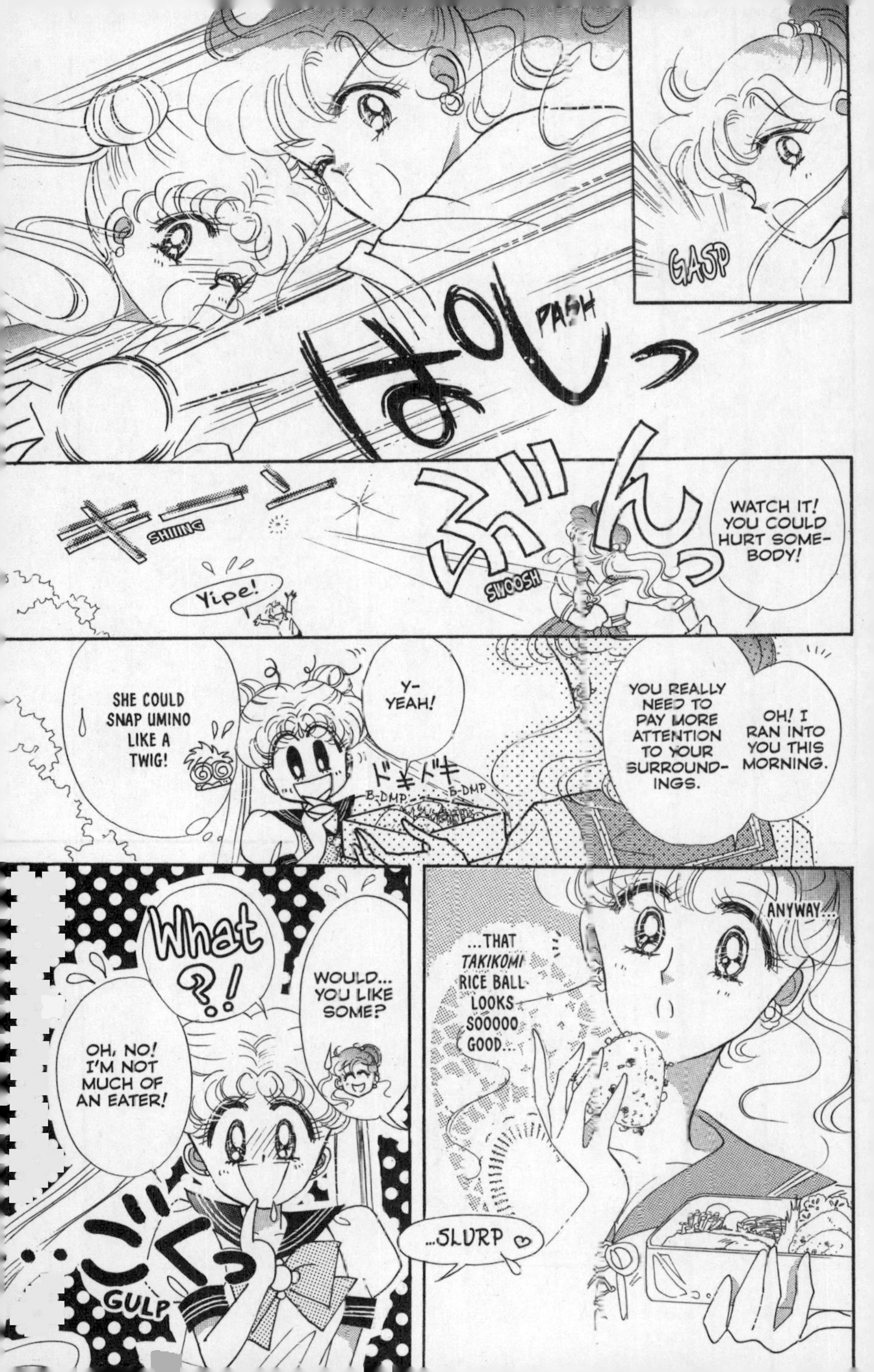
GASP
ぱしっ
PASH
WATCH IT! YOU COULD HURT SOMEBODY!
ぶんっ
SWOOSH
Yipe!
キーン
SHIIING
OH! I RAN INTO YOU THIS MORNING.
YOU REALLY NEED TO PAY MORE ATTENTION TO YOUR SURROUNDINGS.
ドキドキ
B-DMP B-DMP
Y-YEAH!
SHE COULD SNAP UMINO LIKE A TWIG!
ANYWAY...
...THAT *TAKIKOMI* RICE BALL LOOKS SOOOOO GOOD...
...SLURP ♡
WOULD... YOU LIKE SOME?
What?!
OH, NO! I'M NOT MUCH OF AN EATER!
ごくっ
GULP

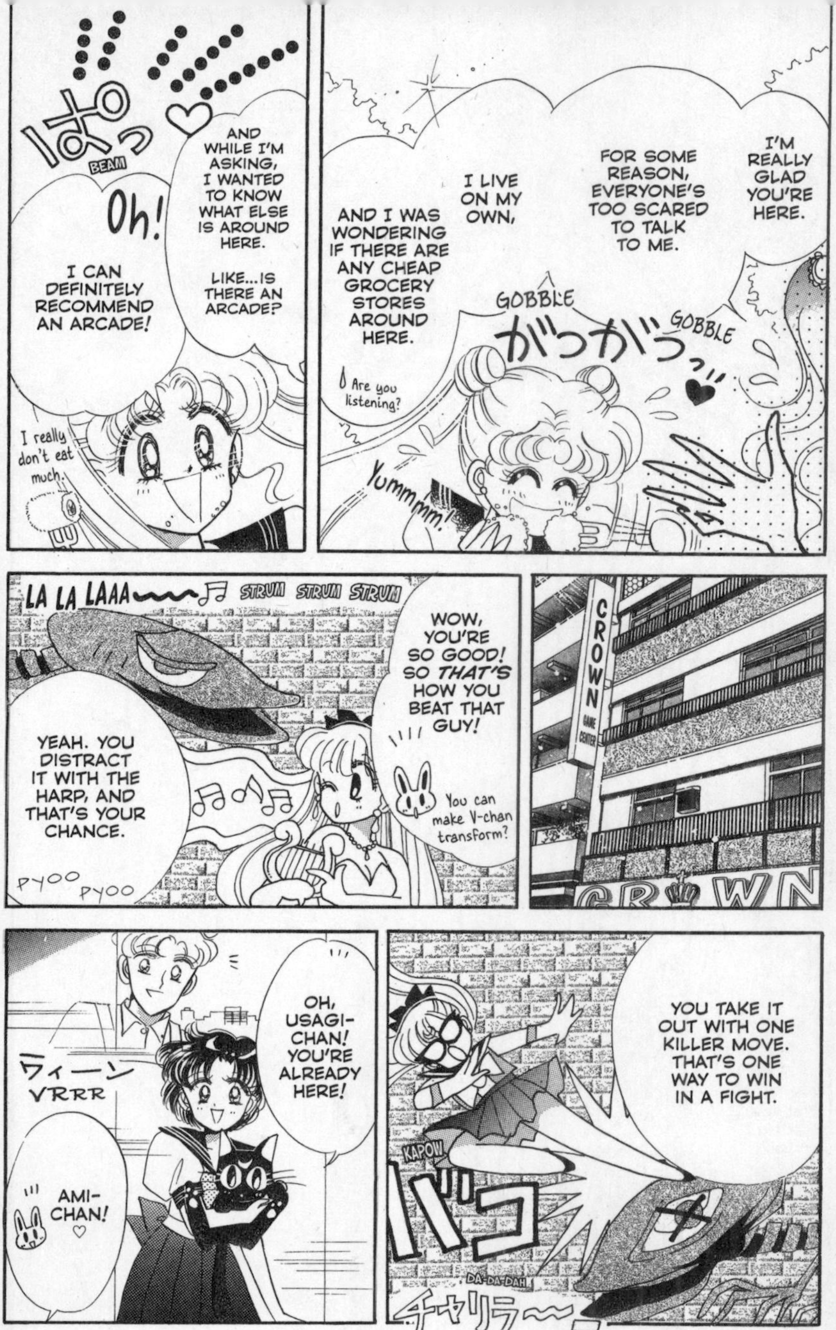
I'M REALLY GLAD YOU'RE HERE.
FOR SOME REASON, EVERYONE'S TOO SCARED TO TALK TO ME.
I LIVE ON MY OWN,
AND I WAS WONDERING IF THERE ARE ANY CHEAP GROCERY STORES AROUND HERE.
GOBBLE
がつがつっ
GOBBLE
Are you listening?
Yummmm!
ぱっ
BEAM
AND WHILE I'M ASKING, I WANTED TO KNOW WHAT ELSE IS AROUND HERE.
LIKE...IS THERE AN ARCADE?
Oh!
I CAN DEFINITELY RECOMMEND AN ARCADE!
I really don't eat much.
CROWN
GAME CENTER
LA LA LAAA
STRUM STRUM STRUM
WOW, YOU'RE SO GOOD! SO *THAT'S* HOW YOU BEAT THAT GUY!
YEAH. YOU DISTRACT IT WITH THE HARP, AND THAT'S YOUR CHANCE.
You can make V-chan transform?
PYOO PYOO
YOU TAKE IT OUT WITH ONE KILLER MOVE. THAT'S ONE WAY TO WIN IN A FIGHT.
KAPOW
バコ
DA-DA-DAH
チャリラ〜
OH, USAGI-CHAN! YOU'RE ALREADY HERE!
ウィーン
VRRR
AMI-CHAN!

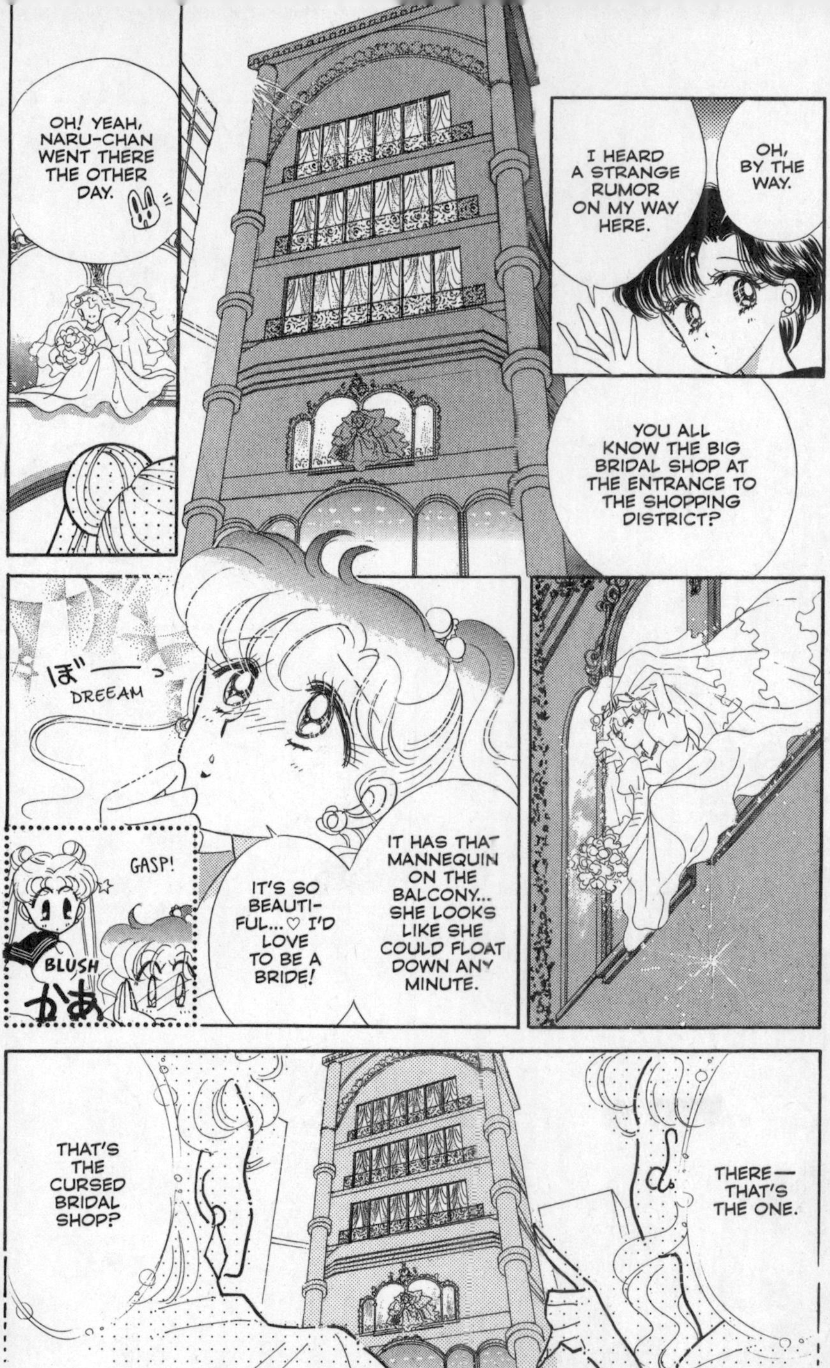
OH, BY THE WAY.
I HEARD A STRANGE RUMOR ON MY WAY HERE.
YOU ALL KNOW THE BIG BRIDAL SHOP AT THE ENTRANCE TO THE SHOPPING DISTRICT?
OH! YEAH, NARU-CHAN WENT THERE THE OTHER DAY.
IT HAS THAT MANNEQUIN ON THE BALCONY... SHE LOOKS LIKE SHE COULD FLOAT DOWN ANY MINUTE.
IT'S SO BEAUTI-FUL...♡ I'D LOVE TO BE A BRIDE!
ぼーーっ
DREEAM
GASP!
BLUSH
かあ
THERE—THAT'S THE ONE.
THAT'S THE CURSED BRIDAL SHOP?

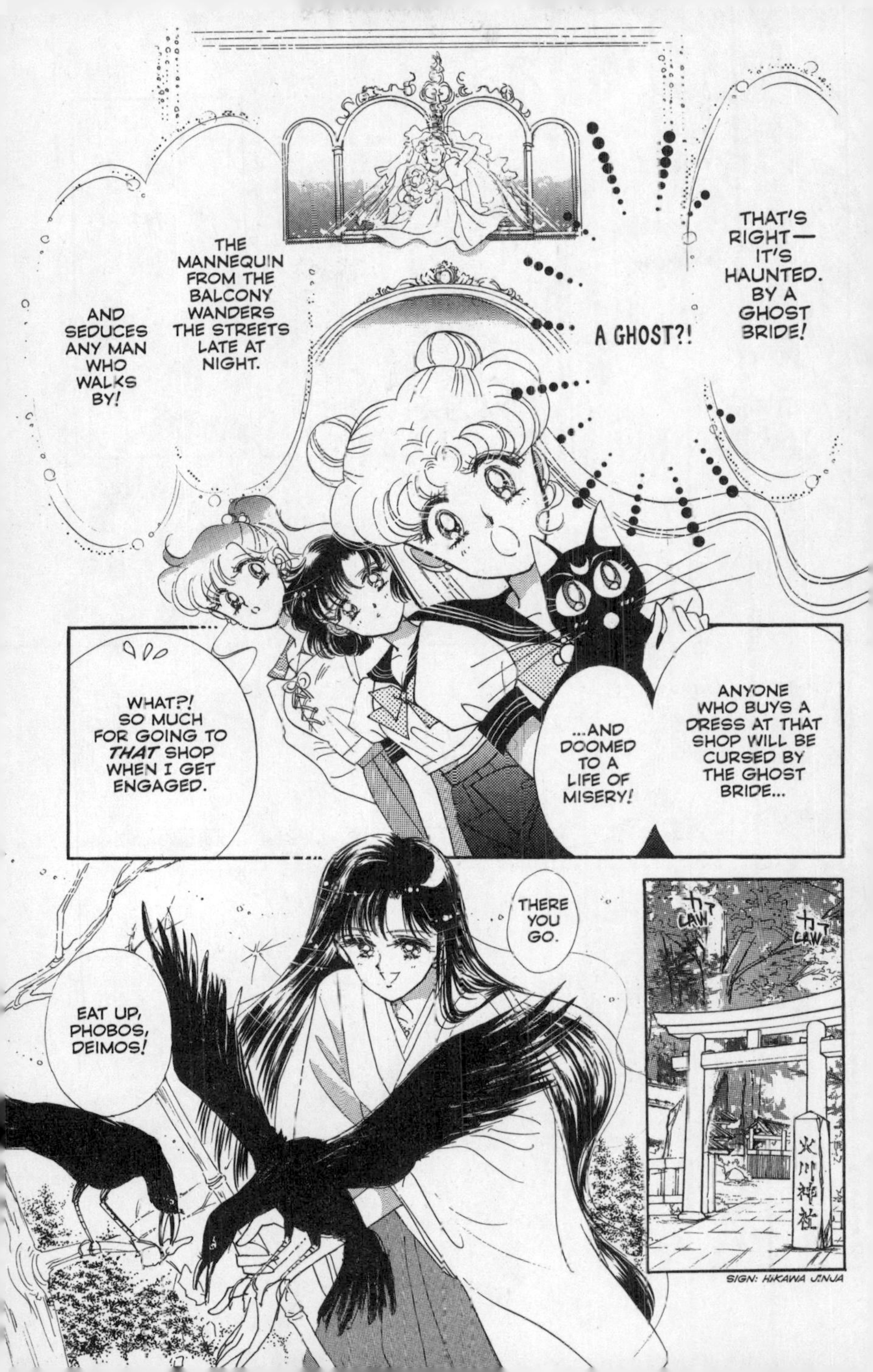
THAT'S RIGHT— IT'S HAUNTED. BY A GHOST BRIDE!
A GHOST?!
THE MANNEQUIN FROM THE BALCONY WANDERS THE STREETS LATE AT NIGHT.
AND SEDUCES ANY MAN WHO WALKS BY!
ANYONE WHO BUYS A DRESS AT THAT SHOP WILL BE CURSED BY THE GHOST BRIDE...
...AND DOOMED TO A LIFE OF MISERY!
WHAT?! SO MUCH FOR GOING TO *THAT* SHOP WHEN I GET ENGAGED.
カァ CAW!
カァ CAW!
火川神社
SIGN: HIKAWA JINJA
THERE YOU GO.
EAT UP, PHOBOS, DEIMOS!

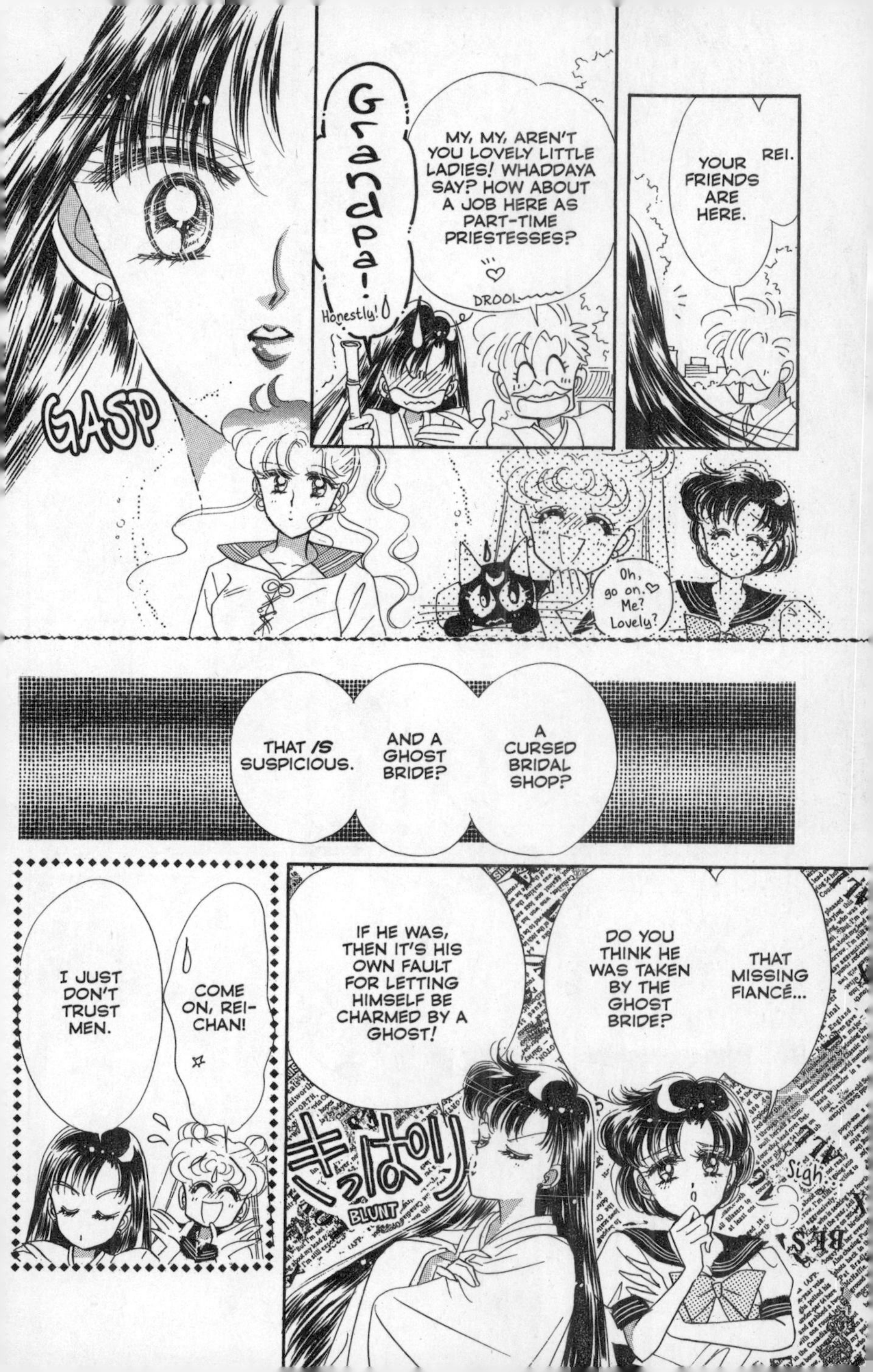

REI. YOUR FRIENDS ARE HERE.
MY, MY, AREN'T YOU LOVELY LITTLE LADIES! WHADDAYA SAY? HOW ABOUT A JOB HERE AS PART-TIME PRIESTESSES?
DROOL
Grandpa!
Honestly!
Oh, go on. Me? Lovely?
GASP
A CURSED BRIDAL SHOP?
AND A GHOST BRIDE?
THAT *IS* SUSPICIOUS.
THAT MISSING FIANCÉ...
Sigh
DO YOU THINK HE WAS TAKEN BY THE GHOST BRIDE?
IF HE WAS, THEN IT'S HIS OWN FAULT FOR LETTING HIMSELF BE CHARMED BY A GHOST!
きっぱり
BLUNT
COME ON, REI-CHAN!
I JUST DON'T TRUST MEN.

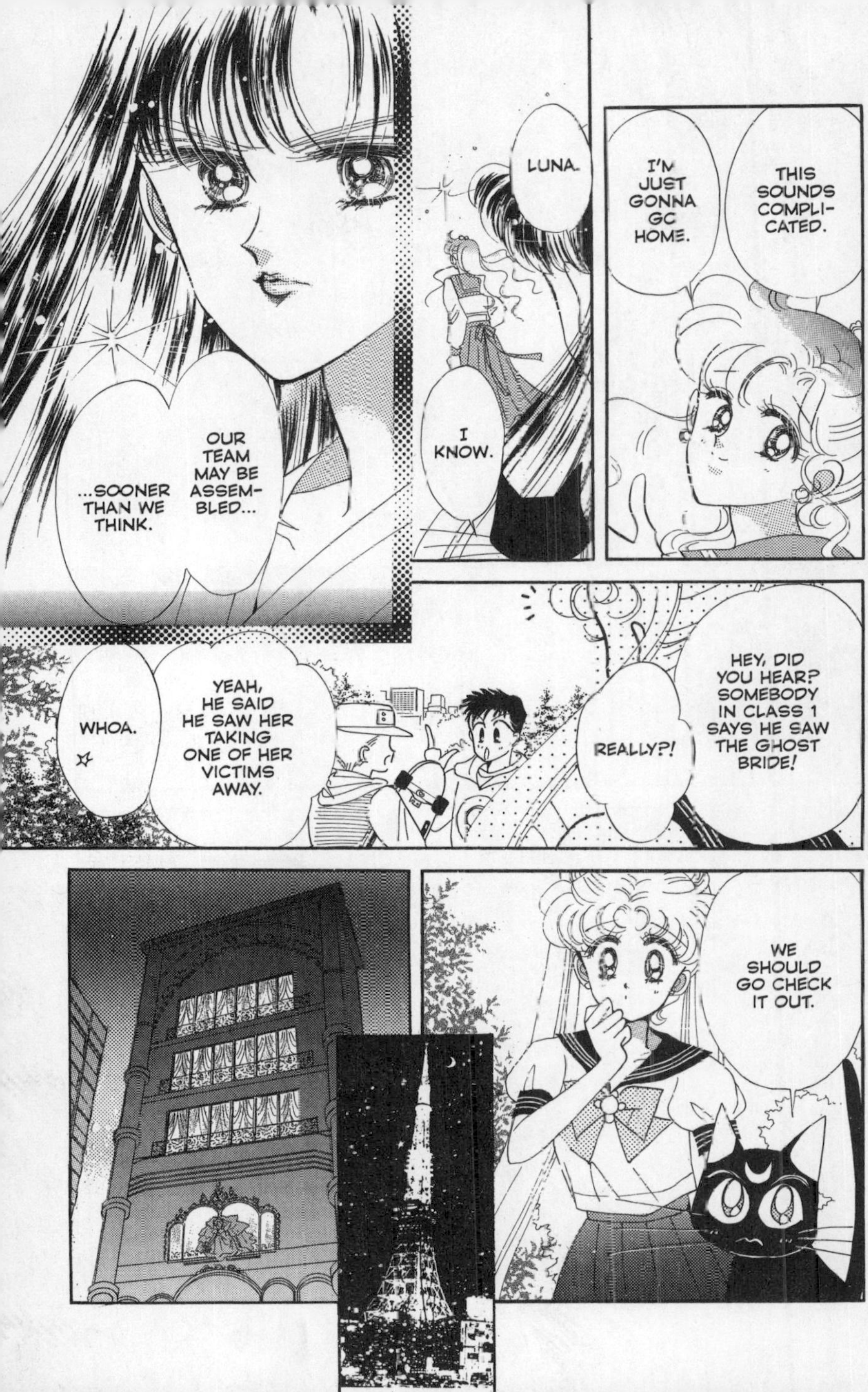
THIS SOUNDS COMPLICATED.
I'M JUST GONNA GO HOME.
LUNA.
I KNOW.
OUR TEAM MAY BE ASSEMBLED...
...SOONER THAN WE THINK.
HEY, DID YOU HEAR? SOMEBODY IN CLASS 1 SAYS HE SAW THE GHOST BRIDE!
REALLY?!
YEAH, HE SAID HE SAW HER TAKING ONE OF HER VICTIMS AWAY.
WHOA.
WE SHOULD GO CHECK IT OUT.

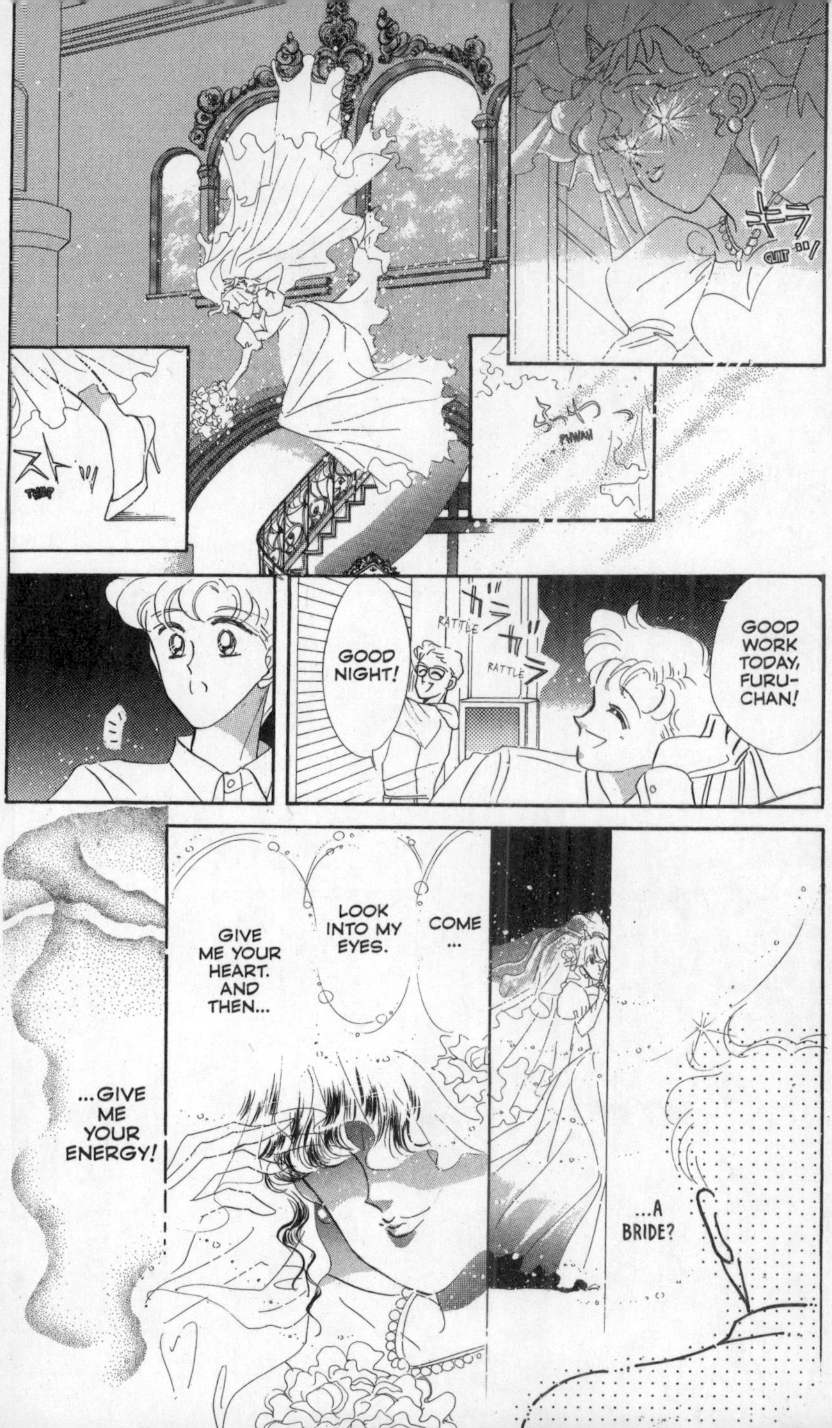
RATTLE
RATTLE
GOOD WORK TODAY, FURU-CHAN!
GOOD NIGHT!
...A BRIDE?
COME ...
LOOK INTO MY EYES.
GIVE ME YOUR HEART. AND THEN...
...GIVE ME YOUR ENERGY!

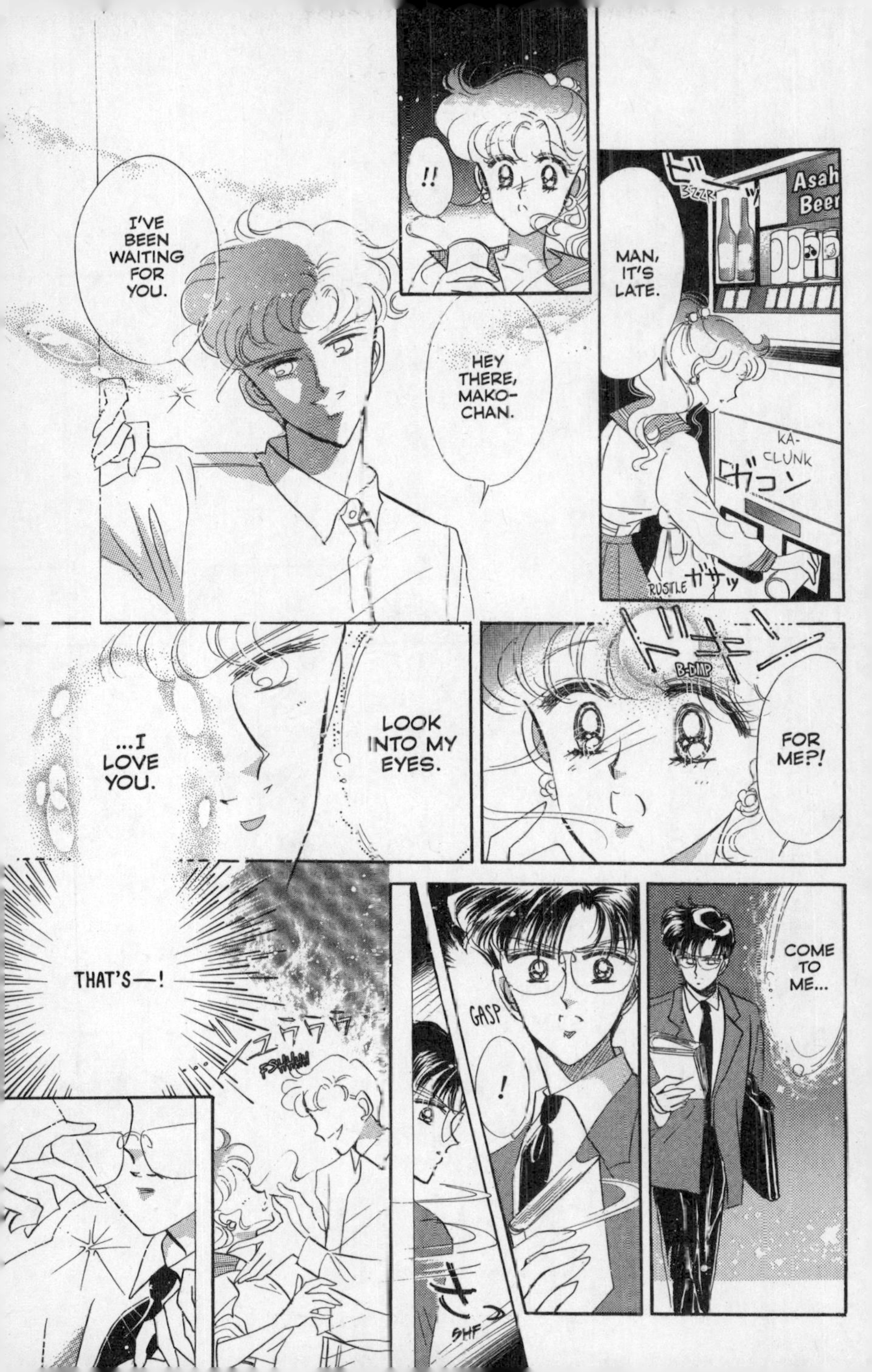

Asah
Beer
MAN, IT'S LATE.
KA-CLUNK
ガコン
RUSTLE
ガサッ
!!
HEY THERE, MAKO-CHAN.
I'VE BEEN WAITING FOR YOU.
B-DMP
FOR ME?!
LOOK INTO MY EYES.
...I LOVE YOU.
COME TO ME...
GASP
!
SHF
THAT'S—!
FSHHH

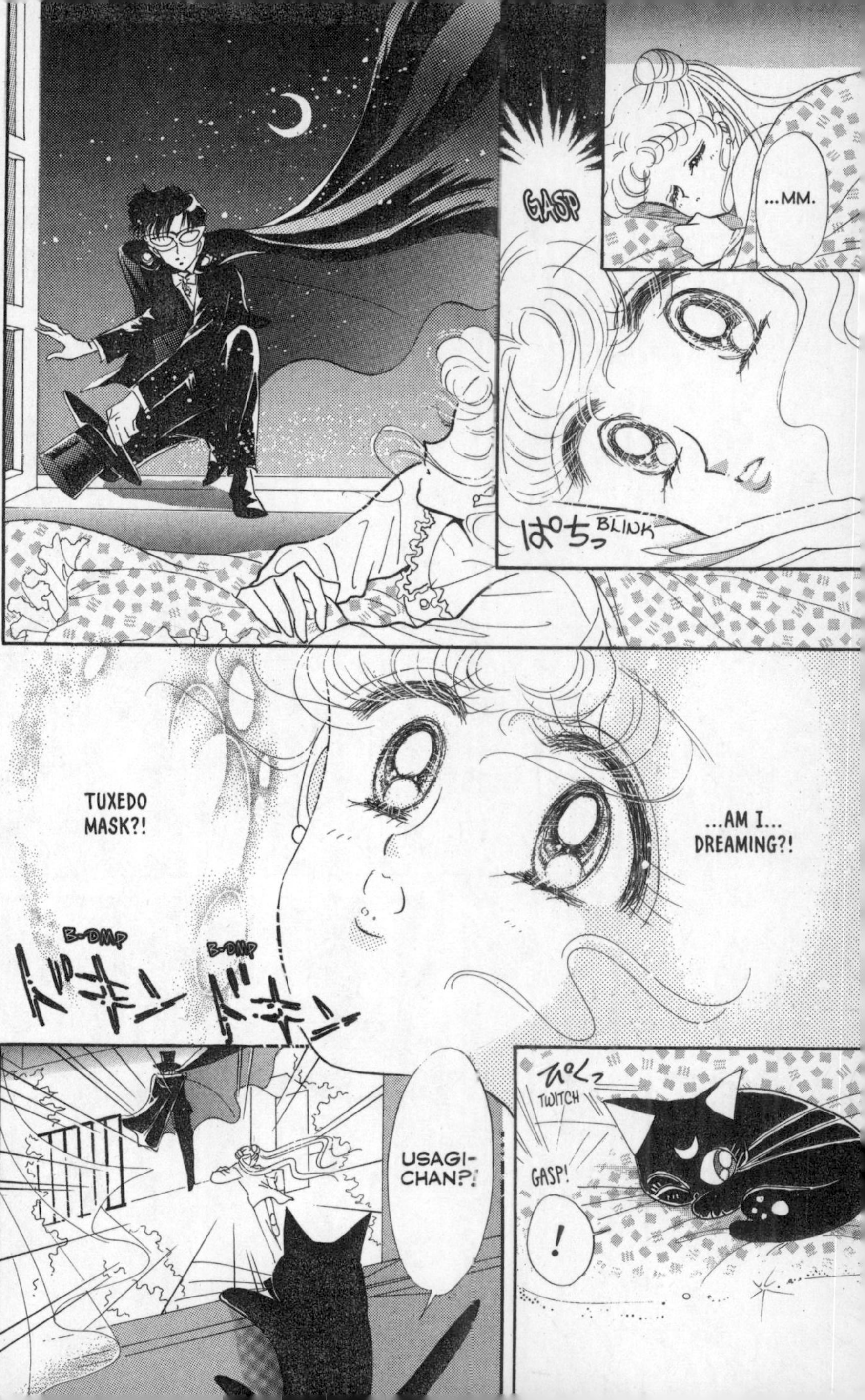

...MM.
GASP
ぱちっ BLINK
...AM I...
DREAMING?!
TUXEDO
MASK?!
B-DMP
B-DMP
ぴくっ
TWITCH
GASP!
!
USAGI-
CHAN?!

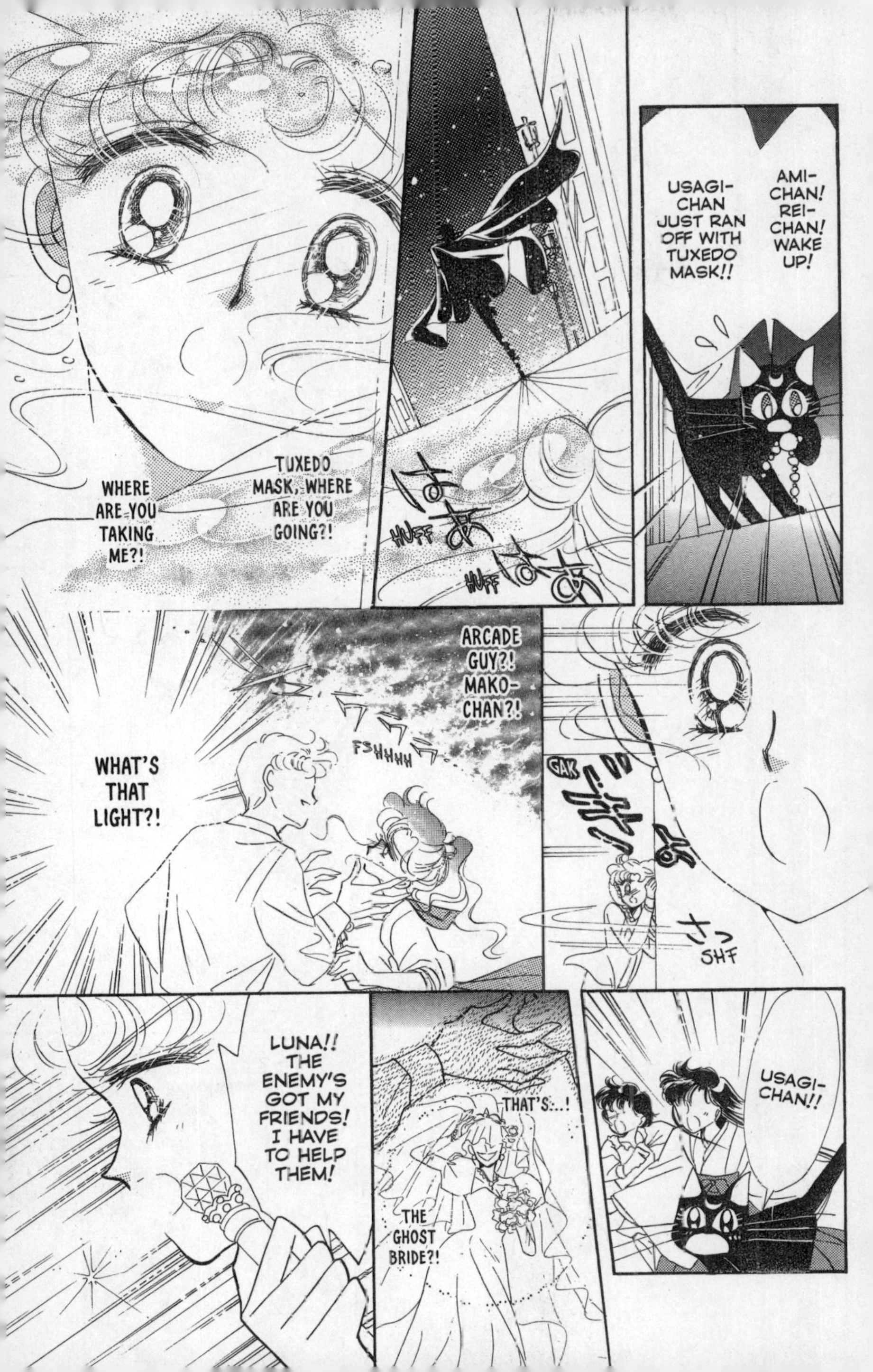
AMI-CHAN! REI-CHAN! WAKE UP!
USAGI-CHAN JUST RAN OFF WITH TUXEDO MASK!!
HUFF
HUFF
TUXEDO MASK, WHERE ARE YOU GOING?!
WHERE ARE YOU TAKING ME?!
GAK
SHF
ARCADE GUY?! MAKO-CHAN?!
FSHHHH
WHAT'S THAT LIGHT?!
USAGI-CHAN!!
THAT'S...!
THE GHOST BRIDE?!
LUNA!! THE ENEMY'S GOT MY FRIENDS! I HAVE TO HELP THEM!

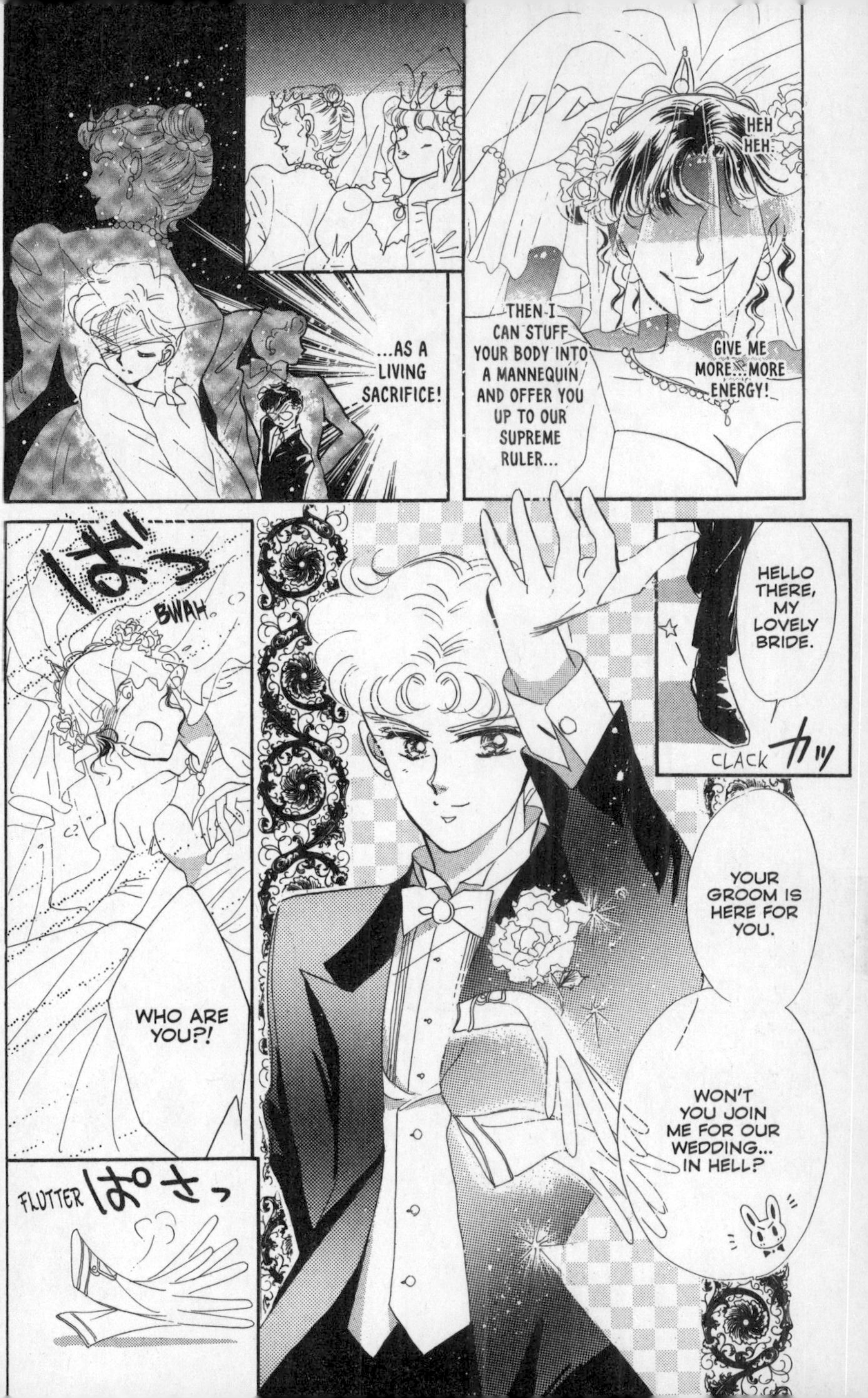
HEH HEH.
GIVE ME MORE... MORE ENERGY!
THEN I CAN STUFF YOUR BODY INTO A MANNEQUIN AND OFFER YOU UP TO OUR SUPREME RULER...
...AS A LIVING SACRIFICE!
HELLO THERE, MY LOVELY BRIDE.
CLACK カッ
YOUR GROOM IS HERE FOR YOU.
WON'T YOU JOIN ME FOR OUR WEDDING... IN HELL?
BWAH
WHO ARE YOU?!
FLUTTER ぱさっ

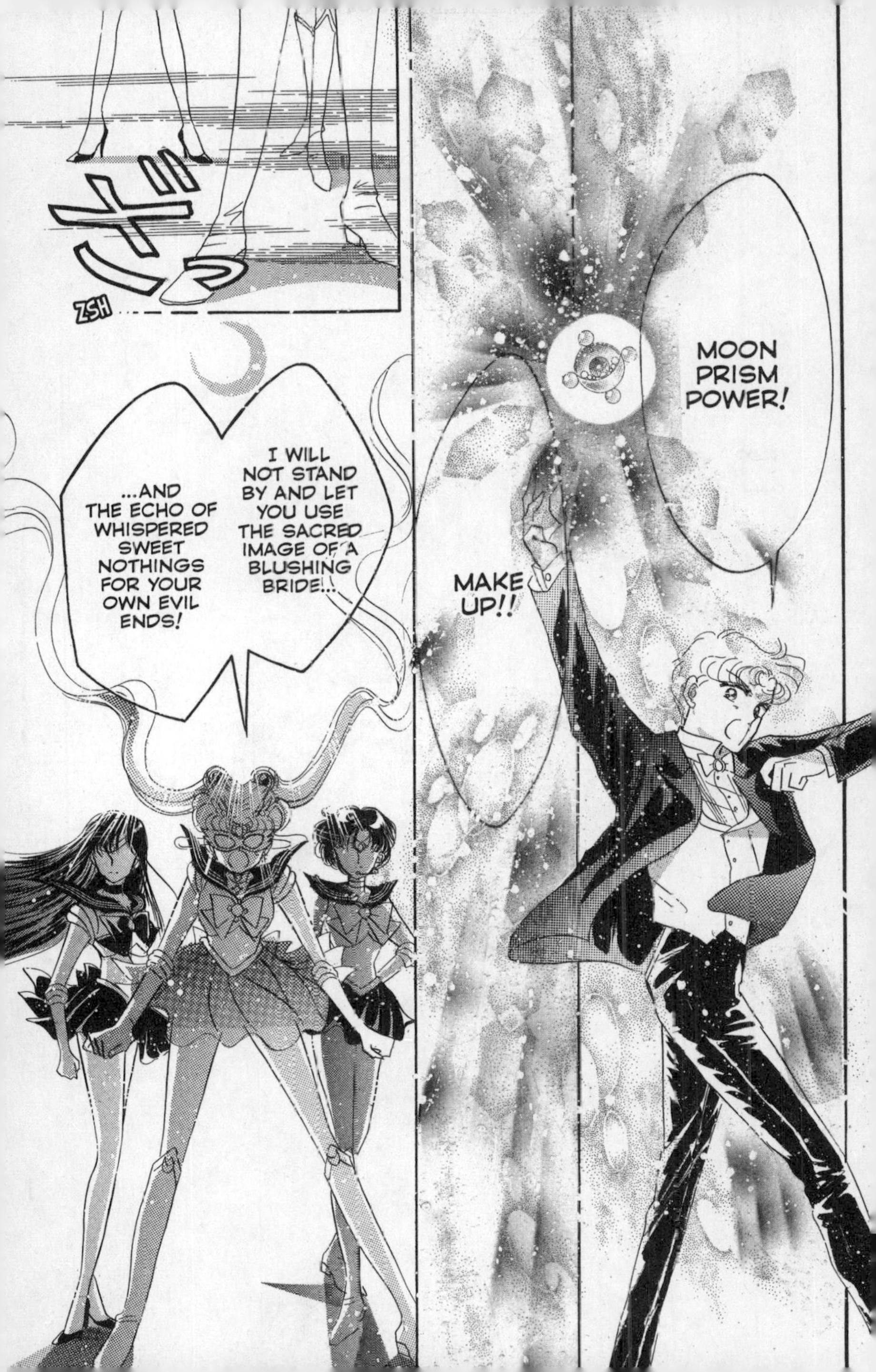
MOON PRISM POWER!
MAKE UP!!
ZSH
I WILL NOT STAND BY AND LET YOU USE THE SACRED IMAGE OF A BLUSHING BRIDE...
...AND THE ECHO OF WHISPERED SWEET NOTHINGS FOR YOUR OWN EVIL ENDS!

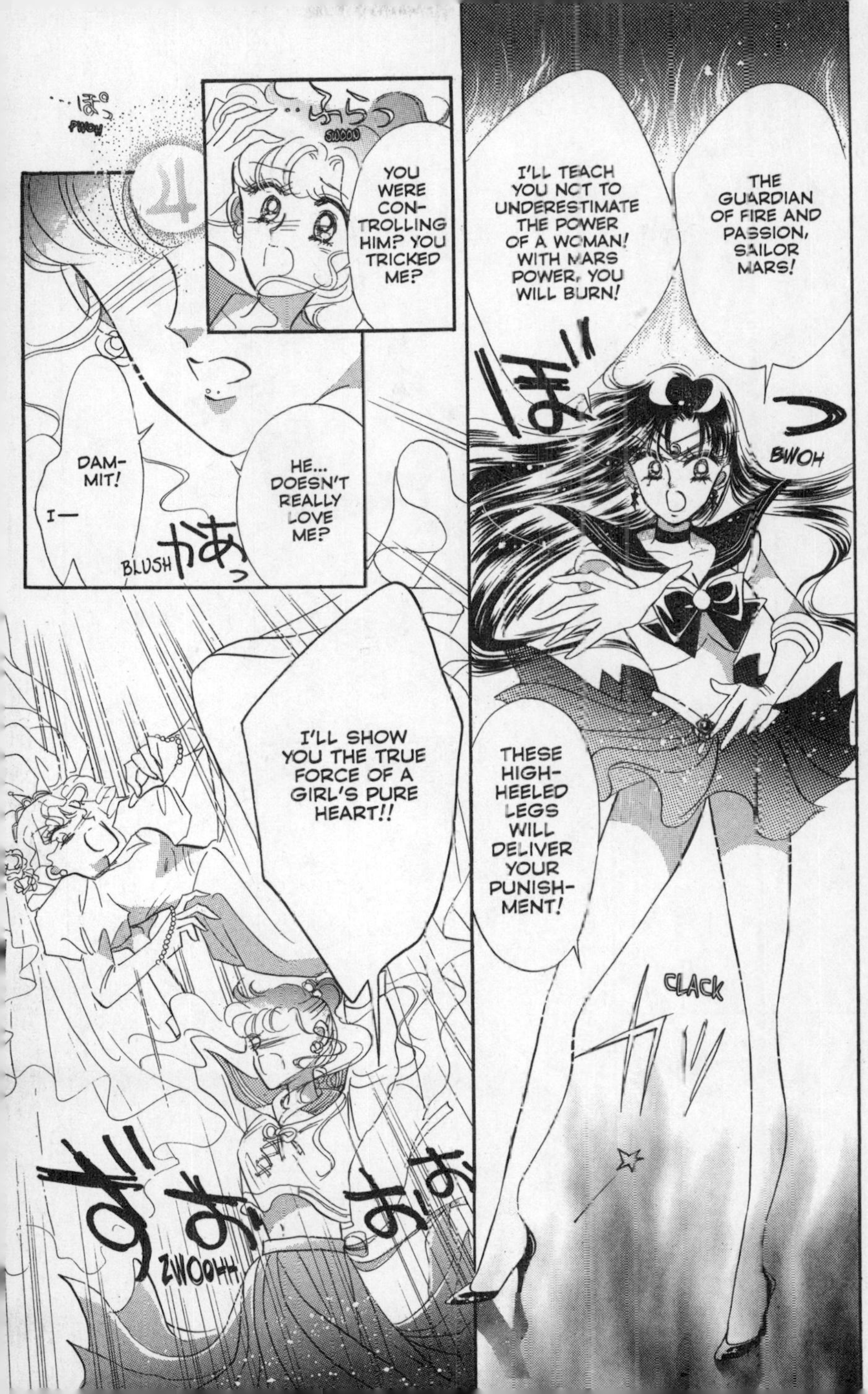

THE GUARDIAN OF FIRE AND PASSION, SAILOR MARS!
I'LL TEACH YOU NOT TO UNDERESTIMATE THE POWER OF A WOMAN! WITH MARS POWER, YOU WILL BURN!
ぼっ
BWOH
THESE HIGH-HEELED LEGS WILL DELIVER YOUR PUNISHMENT!
カッ
CLACK
…ふらっ
SWOON
YOU WERE CON-TROLLING HIM? YOU TRICKED ME?
…ぽっ
PWOH
HE... DOESN'T REALLY LOVE ME?
DAM-MIT!
I—
かあっ
BLUSH
I'LL SHOW YOU THE TRUE FORCE OF A GIRL'S PURE HEART!!
ずおおお
ZWOOHH

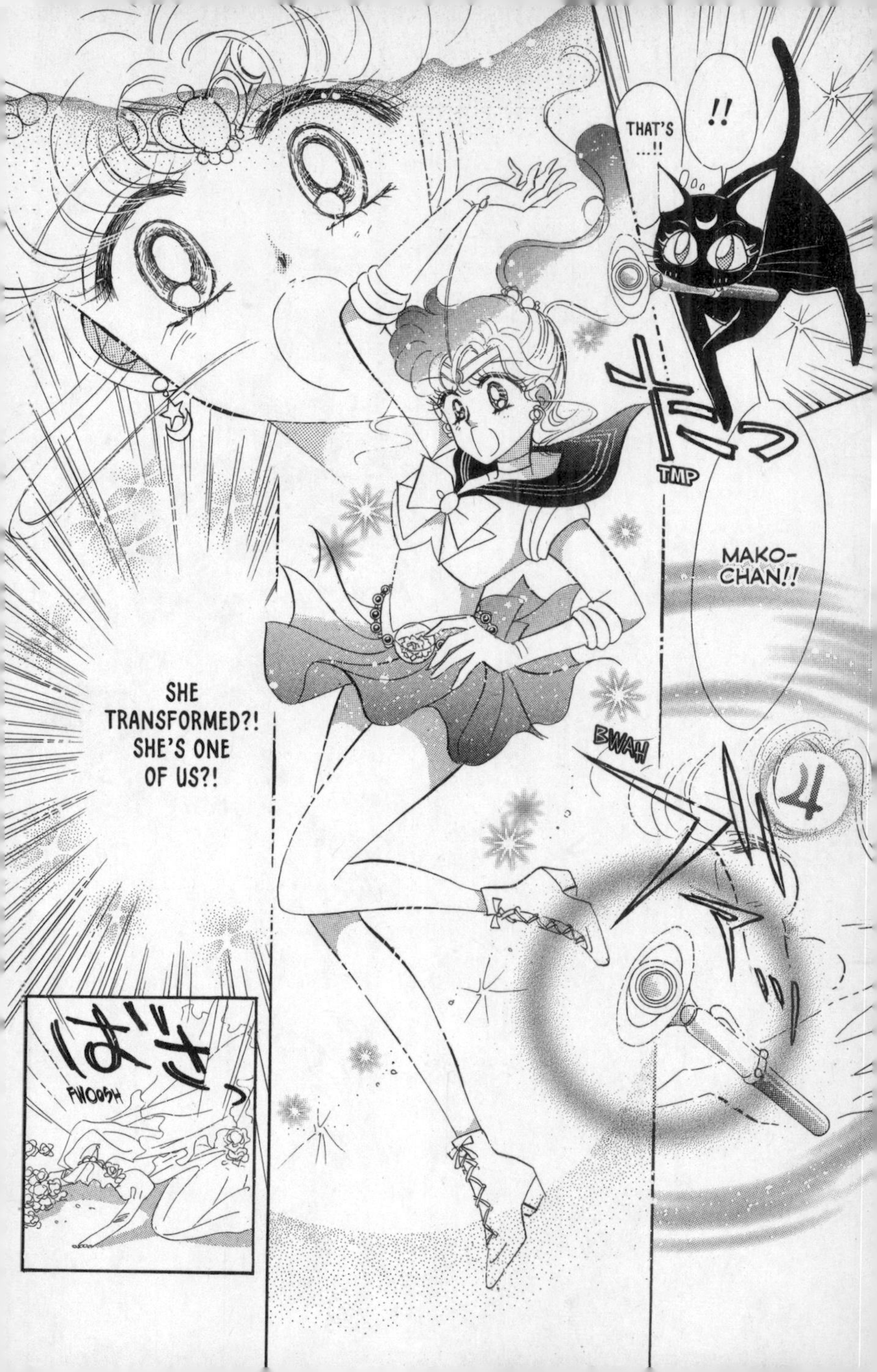
!!
THAT'S ...!!
TMP
MAKO-CHAN!!
BWAH
SHE TRANSFORMED?! SHE'S ONE OF US?!
FWOOSH

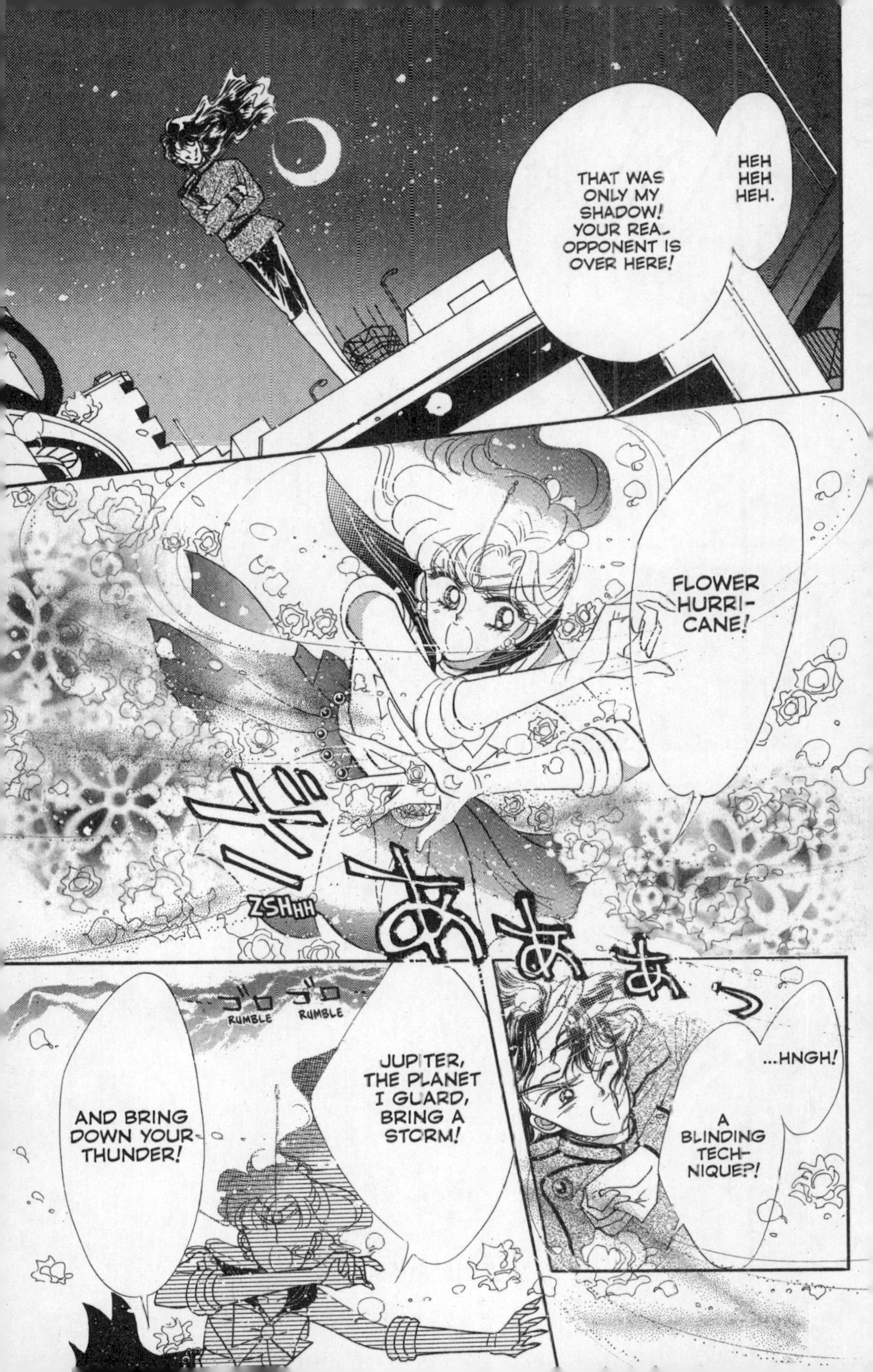
HEH HEH HEH.
THAT WAS ONLY MY SHADOW! YOUR REAL OPPONENT IS OVER HERE!
FLOWER HURRI-CANE!
ZSHHH
...HNGH!
A BLINDING TECH-NIQUE?!
ゴロゴロ
RUMBLE RUMBLE
JUPITER, THE PLANET I GUARD, BRING A STORM!
AND BRING DOWN YOUR THUNDER!

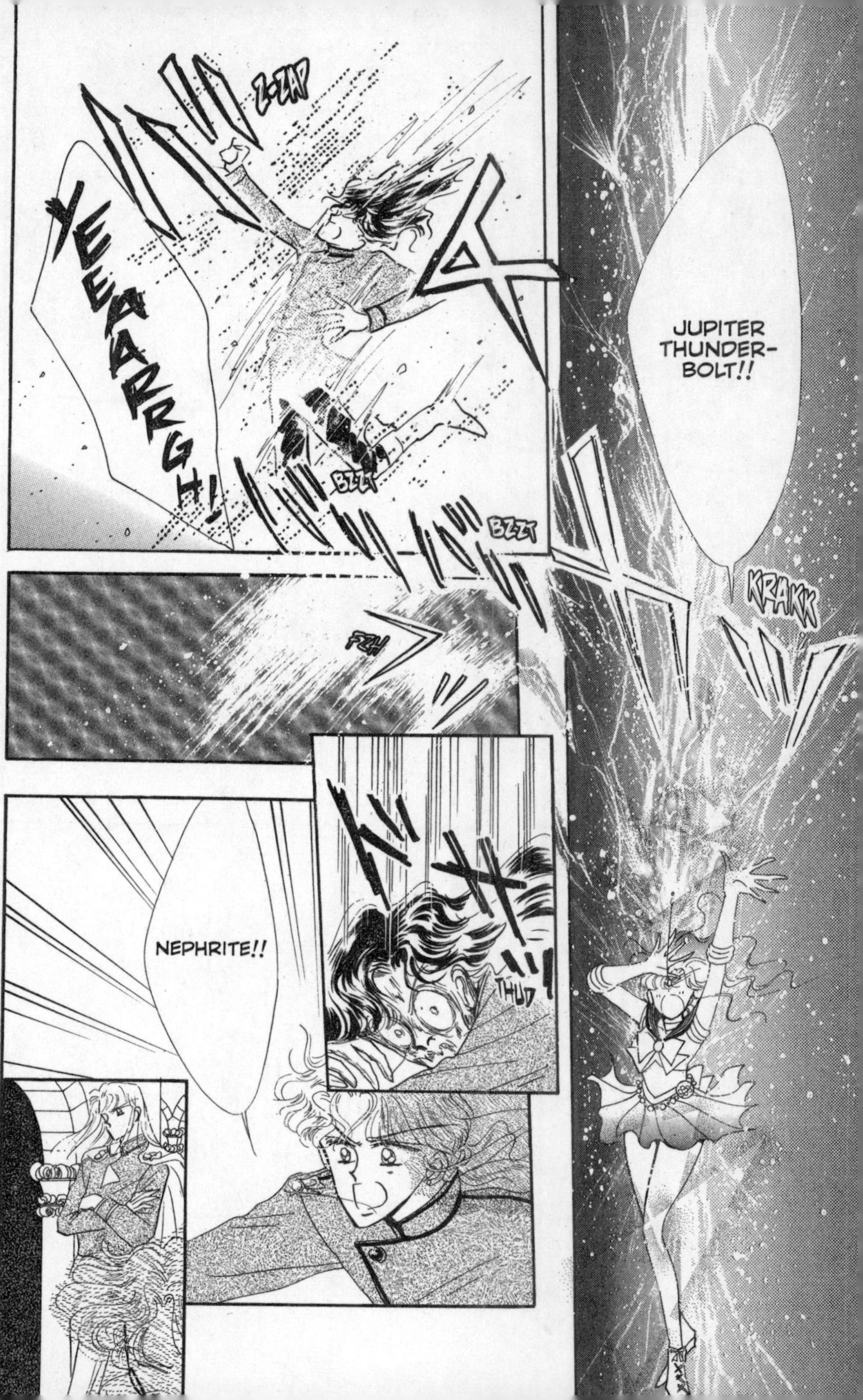
JUPITER THUNDER-BOLT!!
KRAKK
Z-ZAP
YEAARRGH!
BZZT
BZZT
FZH
THUD
NEPHRITE!!

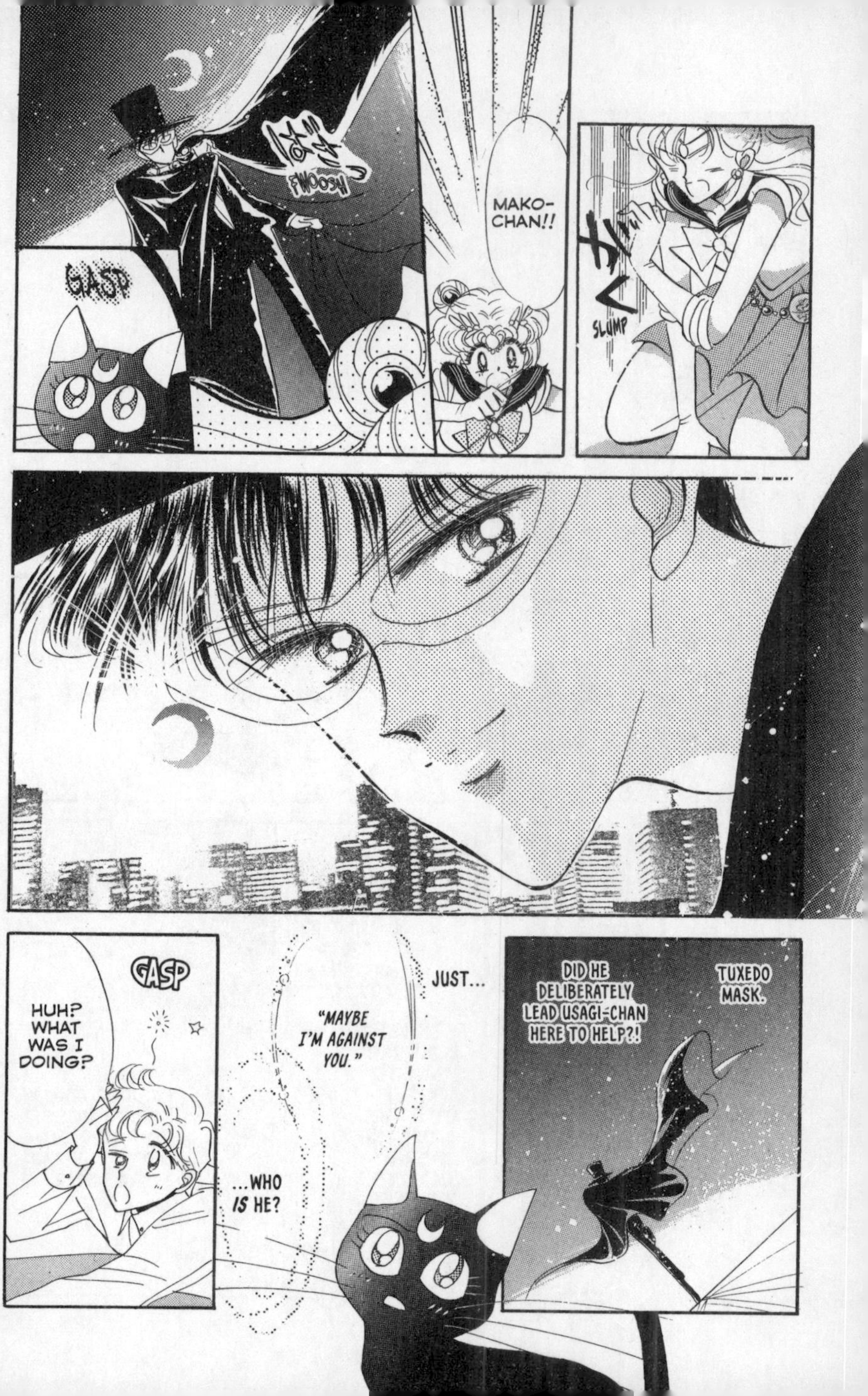
SLUMP
MAKO-CHAN!!
FWOOSH
GASP
TUXEDO MASK.
DID HE DELIBERATELY LEAD USAGI-CHAN HERE TO HELP?!
JUST...
"MAYBE I'M AGAINST YOU."
...WHO *IS* HE?
GASP
HUH? WHAT WAS I DOING?

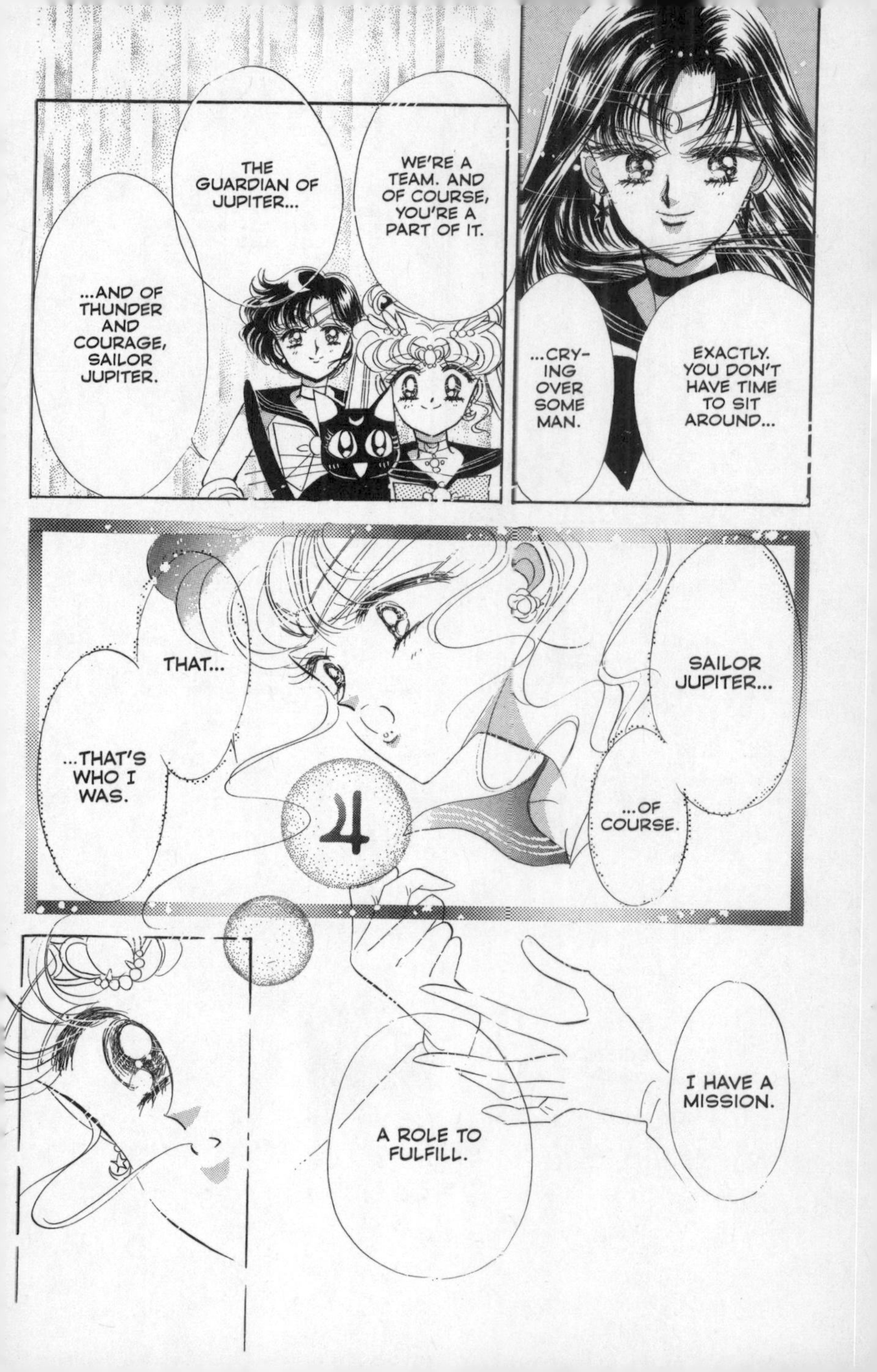
EXACTLY. YOU DON'T HAVE TIME TO SIT AROUND...
...CRY-ING OVER SOME MAN.
WE'RE A TEAM. AND OF COURSE, YOU'RE A PART OF IT.
THE GUARDIAN OF JUPITER...
...AND OF THUNDER AND COURAGE, SAILOR JUPITER.
SAILOR JUPITER...
...OF COURSE.
THAT...
...THAT'S WHO I WAS.
I HAVE A MISSION.
A ROLE TO FULFILL.

Pretty Guardian
Sailor Moon

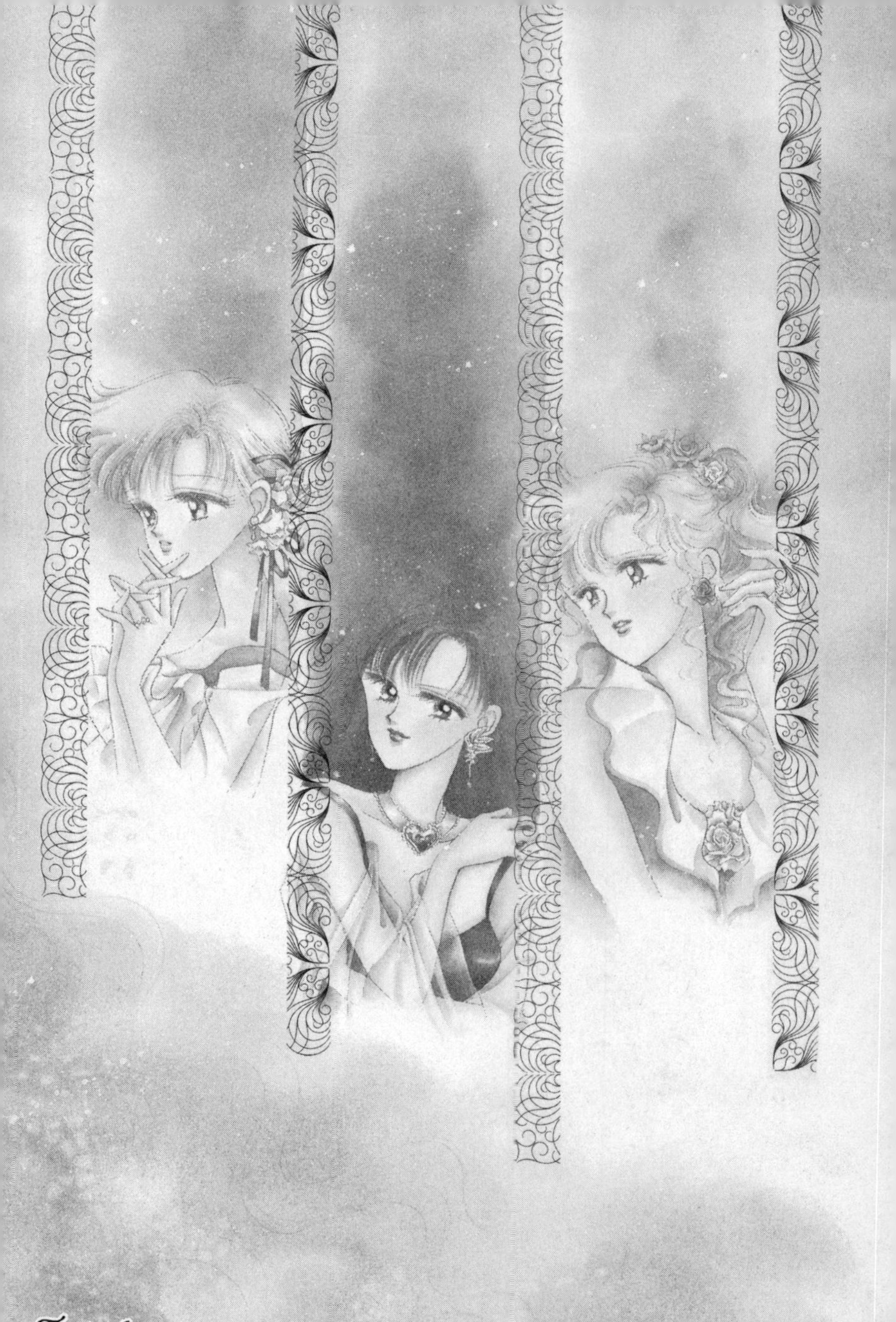

Act. 6 Tuxedo Kamen: Tuxedo Mask

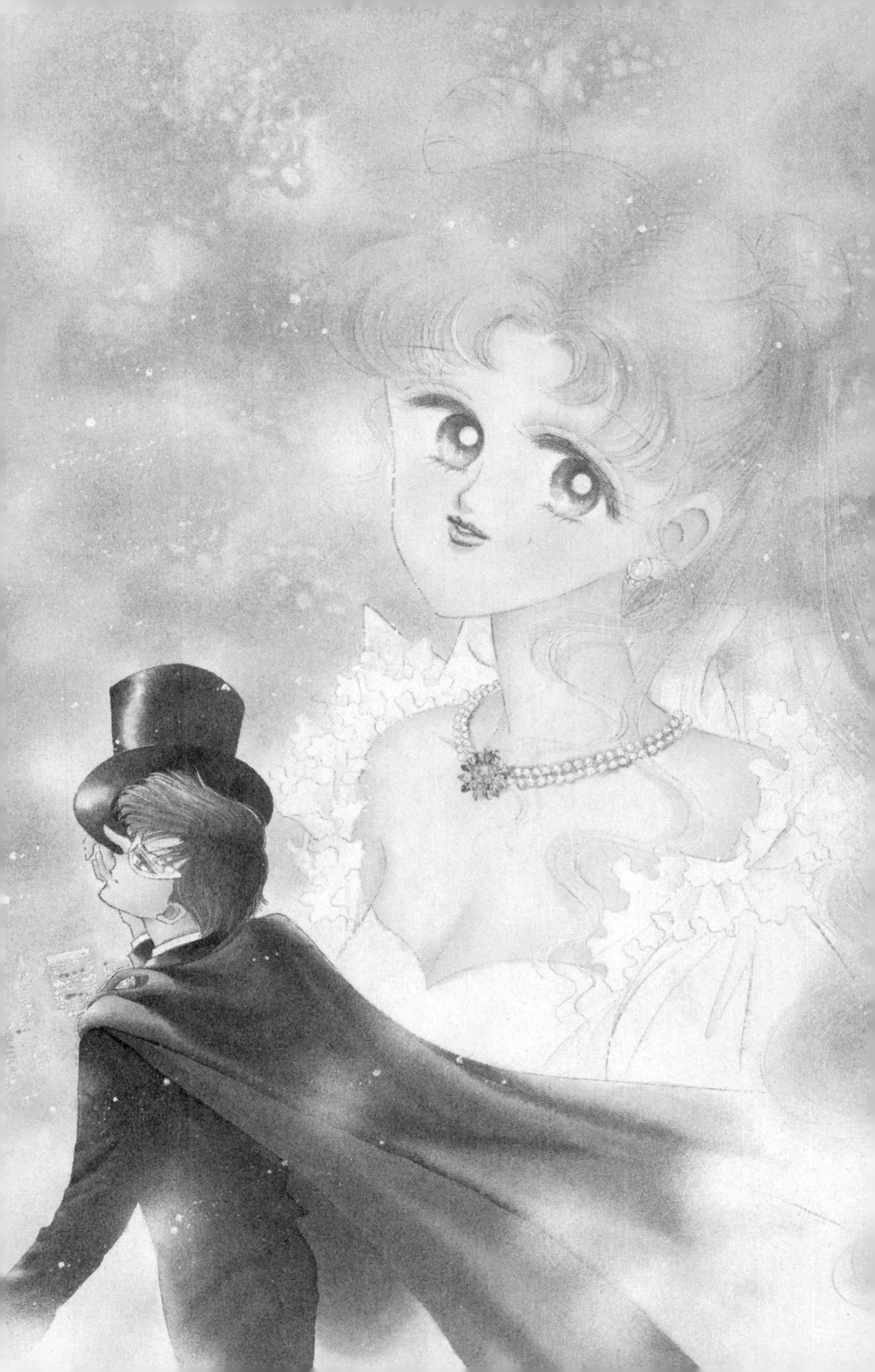

Pretty Guardian Sailor Moon

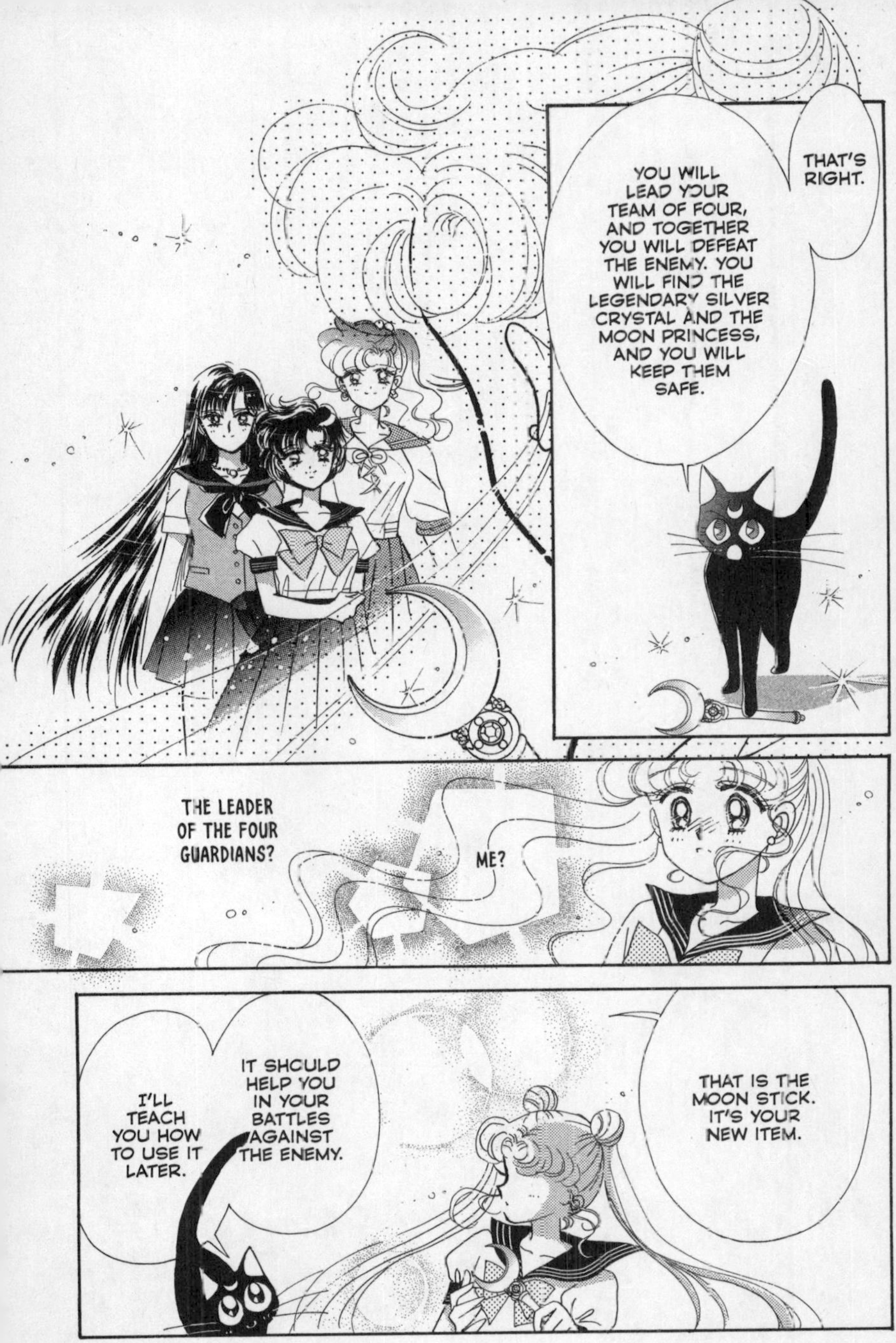
THAT'S RIGHT.
YOU WILL LEAD YOUR TEAM OF FOUR, AND TOGETHER YOU WILL DEFEAT THE ENEMY. YOU WILL FIND THE LEGENDARY SILVER CRYSTAL AND THE MOON PRINCESS, AND YOU WILL KEEP THEM SAFE.
THE LEADER OF THE FOUR GUARDIANS?
ME?
THAT IS THE MOON STICK. IT'S YOUR NEW ITEM.
IT SHOULD HELP YOU IN YOUR BATTLES AGAINST THE ENEMY.
I'LL TEACH YOU HOW TO USE IT LATER.

SAILOR
MERCURY.

AMI-CHAN,
THE BRAINS
OF THE TEAM,
A GIRL GENIUS
WITH AN IQ
OF 300.

THE FOUR
OF US
TOGETHER.

REI-CHAN, THE
BEAUTIFUL PRIESTESS
WHO CONTROLS FIRE
AND SEES THE FUTURE,
AND IS A LITTLE SCARY
WHEN SHE'S MAD.

SAILOR MARS.

GASP

THE LEGENDARY SILVER CRYSTAL...

THAT DREAM AGAIN!...

"THE LEGENDARY SILVER CRYSTAL"...

ALWAYS THE SAME PHRASE:

SHE WHISPERS TO ME,

IN MY DREAM, SOMEONE IS CALLING TO ME.

A WOMAN WITH LONG HAIR...

...I WAKE UP. EVERY TIME.

AND JUST WHEN I'M ABOUT TO SEE HER FACE...

BUT...

...WHO IS SHE?

...SIX O'CLOCK.

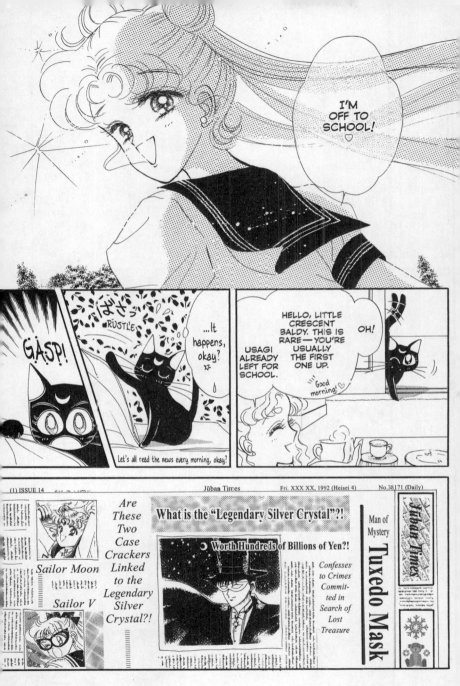

I'M OFF TO SCHOOL! ♡

GASP!

RUSTLE

...It happens, okay? ✗

Let's all read the news every morning, okay?

HELLO, LITTLE CRESCENT BALDY. THIS IS RARE— YOU'RE USUALLY THE FIRST ONE UP.

USAGI ALREADY LEFT FOR SCHOOL.

Good morning! ♡

OH!

(1) ISSUE 14   Jūban Times   Fri. XXX XX, 1992 (Heisei 4)   No.38171 (Daily)

Are These Two Case Crackers Linked to the Legendary Silver Crystal?!

Sailor Moon

Sailor V

What is the "Legendary Silver Crystal"?!

Worth Hundreds of Billions of Yen?!

Man of Mystery

Tuxedo Mask

Confesses to Crimes Committed in Search of Lost Treasure

Jūban Times

211

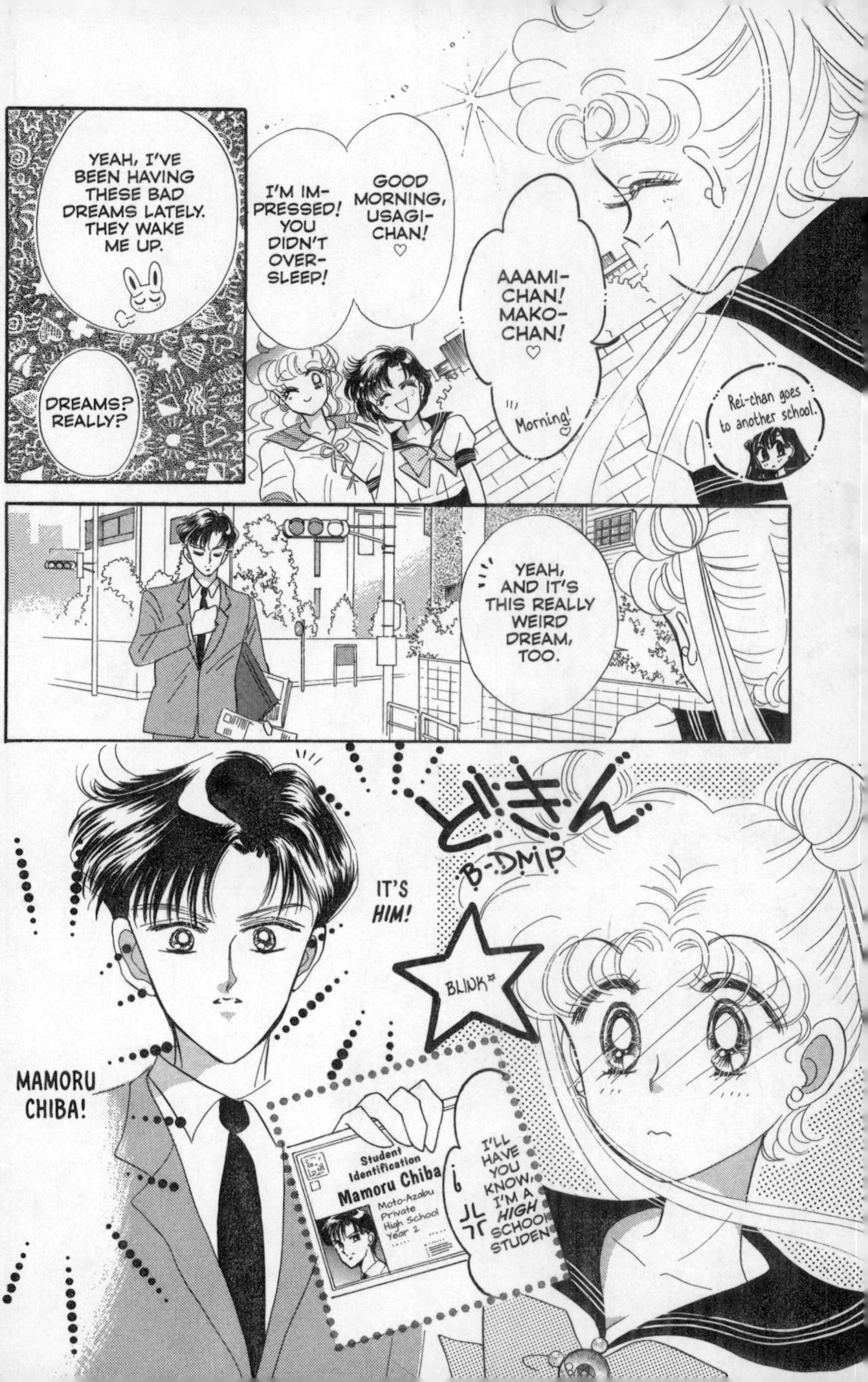
AAAMI-CHAN! MAKO-CHAN! ♡
GOOD MORNING, USAGI-CHAN! ♡
I'M IM-PRESSED! YOU DIDN'T OVER-SLEEP!
Morning! ♡
Rei-chan goes to another school.
YEAH, I'VE BEEN HAVING THESE BAD DREAMS LATELY. THEY WAKE ME UP.
DREAMS? REALLY?
YEAH, AND IT'S THIS REALLY WEIRD DREAM, TOO.
どきん
B-DMP
IT'S HIM!
BLINK
MAMORU CHIBA!
Student Identification
Mamoru Chiba
Moto-Azabu Private High School Year 2
I'LL HAVE YOU KNOW, I'M A HIGH SCHOO STUDEN

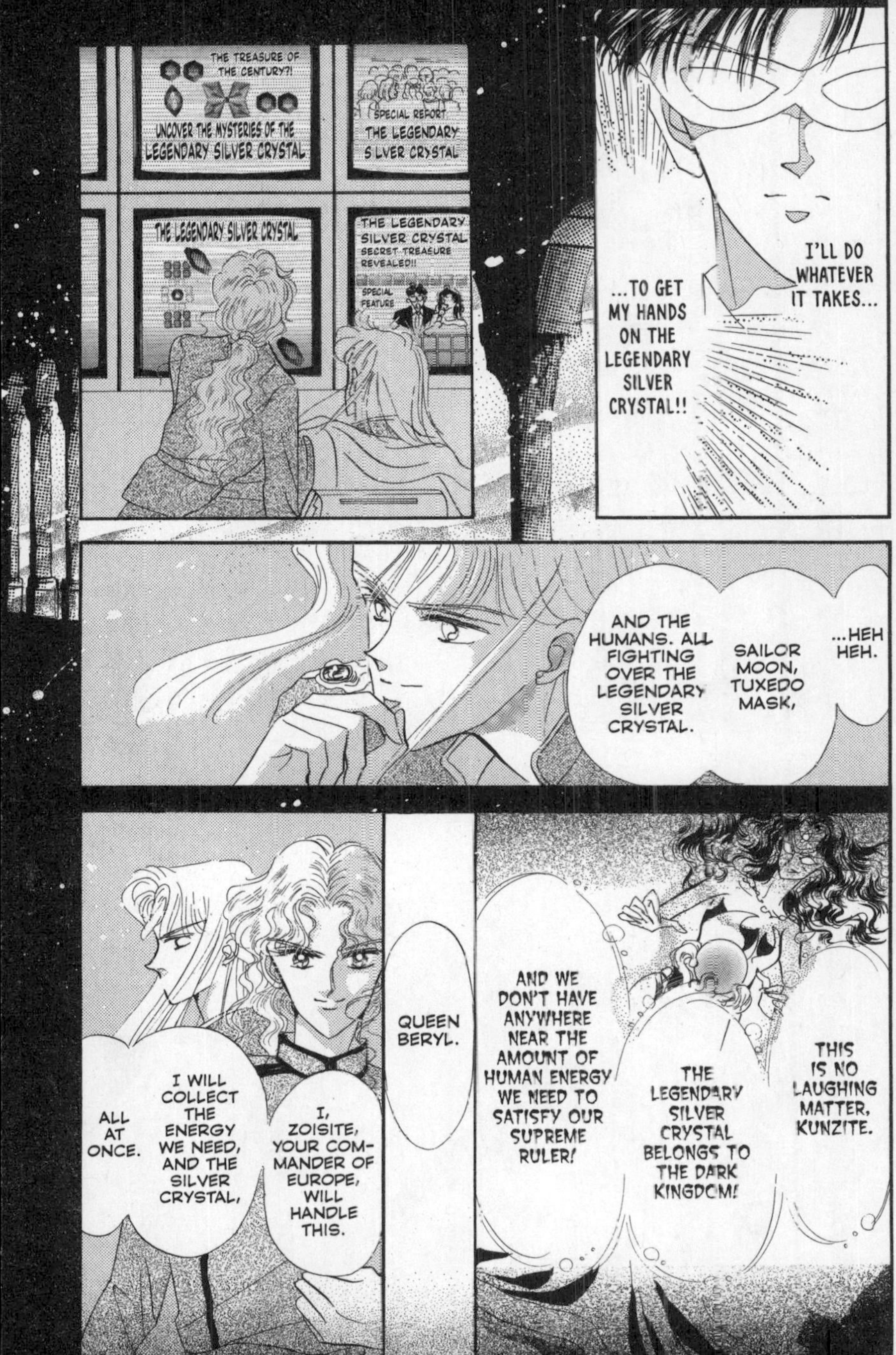
I'LL DO WHATEVER IT TAKES...
...TO GET MY HANDS ON THE LEGENDARY SILVER CRYSTAL!!
SPECIAL REPORT THE LEGENDARY SILVER CRYSTAL
THE TREASURE OF THE CENTURY?!
UNCOVER THE MYSTERIES OF THE LEGENDARY SILVER CRYSTAL
THE LEGENDARY SILVER CRYSTAL SECRET TREASURE REVEALED!!
SPECIAL FEATURE
THE LEGENDARY SILVER CRYSTAL
...HEH HEH.
SAILOR MOON, TUXEDO MASK,
AND THE HUMANS. ALL FIGHTING OVER THE LEGENDARY SILVER CRYSTAL.
THIS IS NO LAUGHING MATTER, KUNZITE.
THE LEGENDARY SILVER CRYSTAL BELONGS TO THE DARK KINGDOM!
AND WE DON'T HAVE ANYWHERE NEAR THE AMOUNT OF HUMAN ENERGY WE NEED TO SATISFY OUR SUPREME RULER!
QUEEN BERYL.
I, ZOISITE, YOUR COMMANDER OF EUROPE, WILL HANDLE THIS.
I WILL COLLECT THE ENERGY WE NEED, AND THE SILVER CRYSTAL,
ALL AT ONCE.

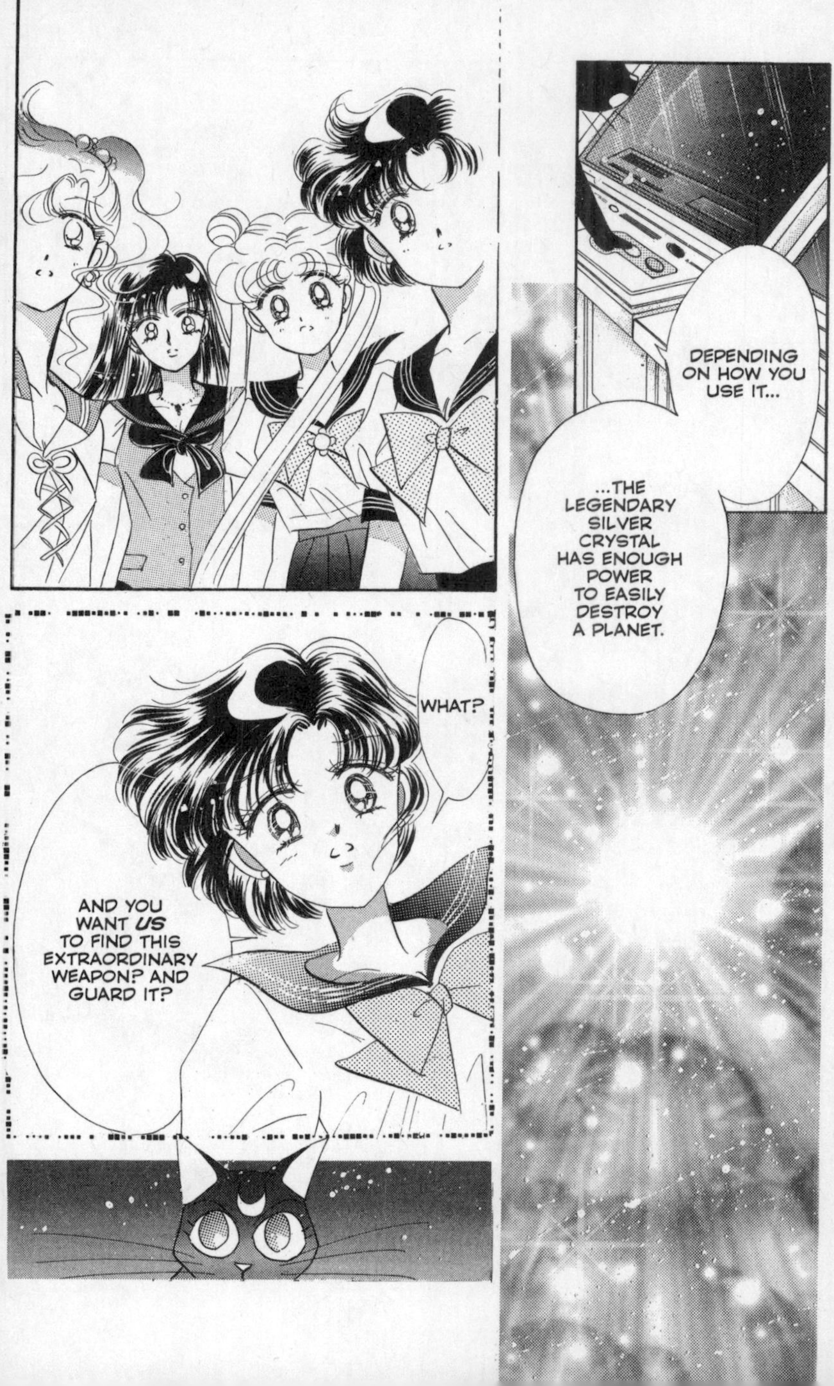
DEPENDING ON HOW YOU USE IT...
...THE LEGENDARY SILVER CRYSTAL HAS ENOUGH POWER TO EASILY DESTROY A PLANET.
WHAT?
AND YOU WANT *US* TO FIND THIS EXTRAORDINARY WEAPON? AND GUARD IT?

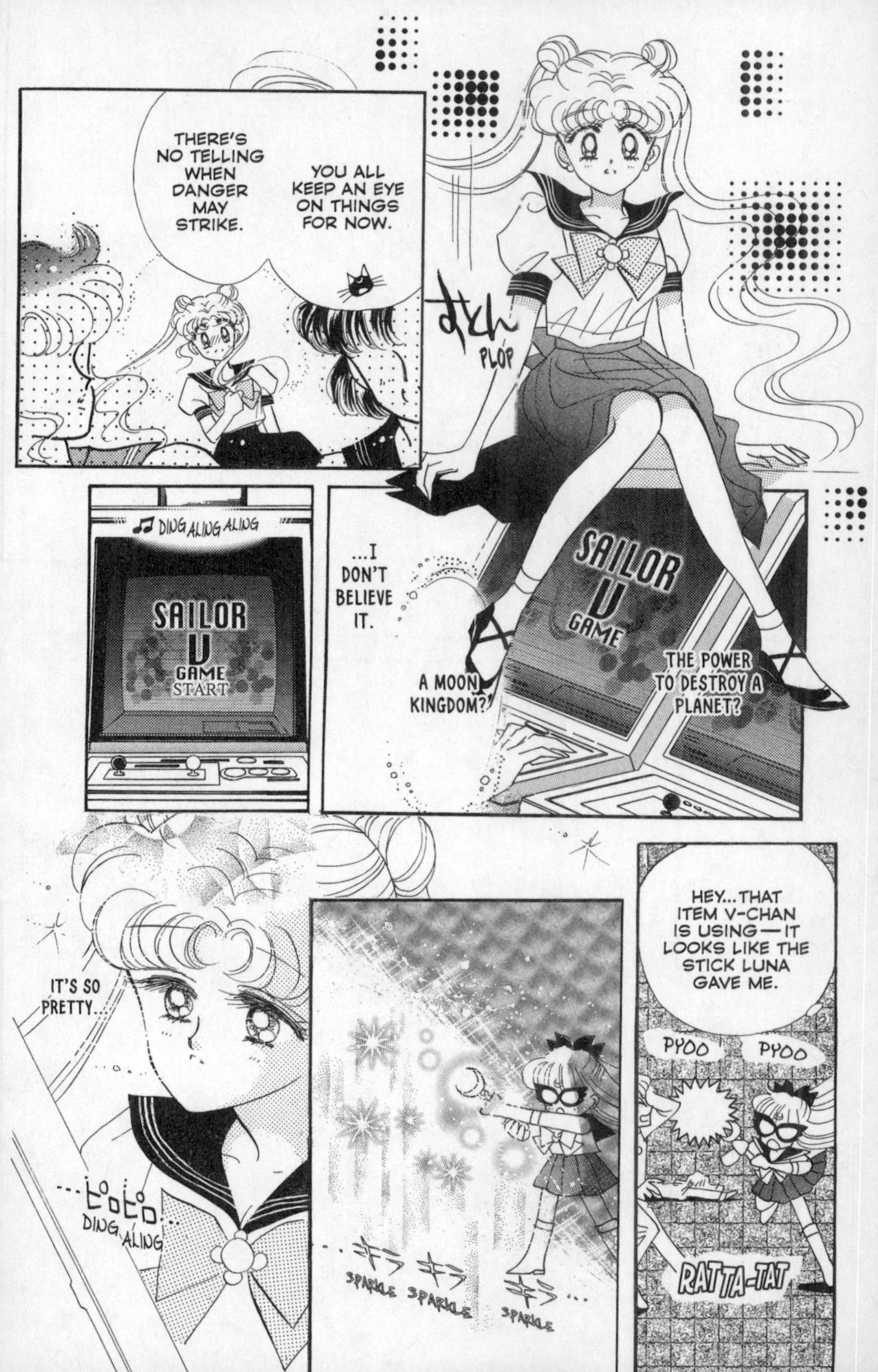
THERE'S NO TELLING WHEN DANGER MAY STRIKE.
YOU ALL KEEP AN EYE ON THINGS FOR NOW.
PLOP
SAILOR V GAME
...I DON'T BELIEVE IT.
THE POWER TO DESTROY A PLANET?
A MOON KINGDOM?
♫ DING ALING ALING
SAILOR V GAME START
HEY... THAT ITEM V-CHAN IS USING—IT LOOKS LIKE THE STICK LUNA GAVE ME.
PYOO PYOO
RATTA-TAT
...キラ キラ
SPARKLE SPARKLE
キラ...
SPARKLE
IT'S SO PRETTY...
...ピロピロ...
DING ALING

I USED TO SEE HER IN THE NEWS A LOT, BUT SHE HASN'T APPEARED IN PUBLIC FOR A WHILE NOW.

PYOO
BEE-BOP ビーー
BEE-BOP ピッン ピッン

DO YOU THINK SHE'S ONE OF US? MAYBE SHE'S JUST A NORMAL GIRL, TOO.

SAILOR V-CHAN IS A GUARDIAN OF JUSTICE, TOO, RIGHT?

...WAIT.

THIS V-CHAN GAME IS SO MYSTERIOUS...

MAYBE IT'S BECAUSE I'VE BEEN SO HOOKED ON THE GAME.

SUDDENLY I'M REALLY CURIOUS ABOUT THIS GAME...AND ABOUT SAILOR V-CHAN.

LEGENDARY TREASURE!
THE LEGENDARY SILVER CRYSTAL

Yomiuri Shimbun

Silver Crystal Amulets Guaranteed to Work!!

Wondrous Power

On Sale Now

DIVE INTO THE MYSTERIES:
THE LEGENDARY SILVER CRYSTAL!!

MAYBE I'LL LOOK INTO IT.

GOOD POINT. THE GAME ASIDE, IF YOU'RE THAT CURIOUS ABOUT HER, USAGI-CHAN,

224

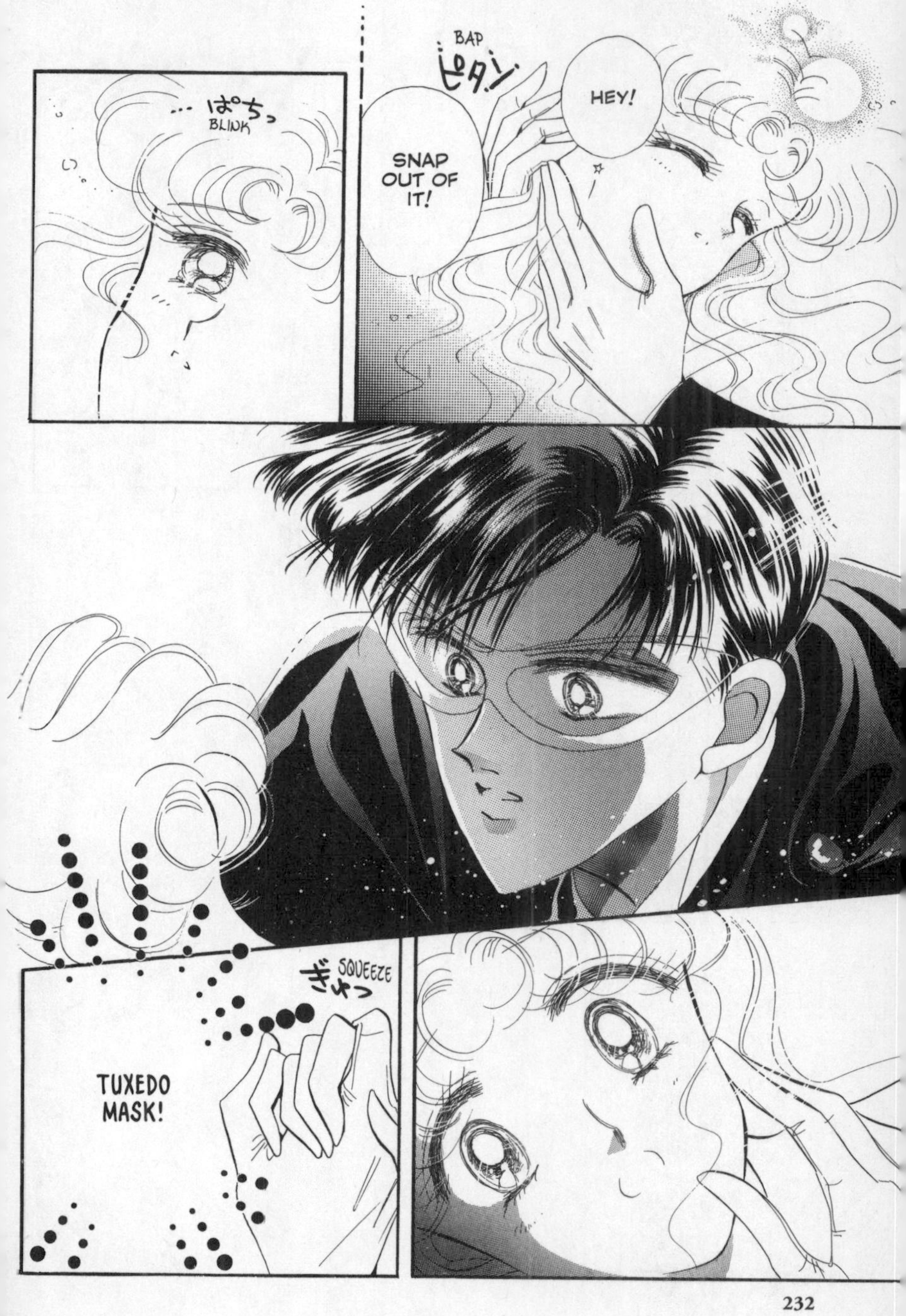
HEY!
BAP
ピタン
SNAP OUT OF IT!
…ぱちっ
BLINK
ぎゅっ
SQUEEZE
TUXEDO MASK!

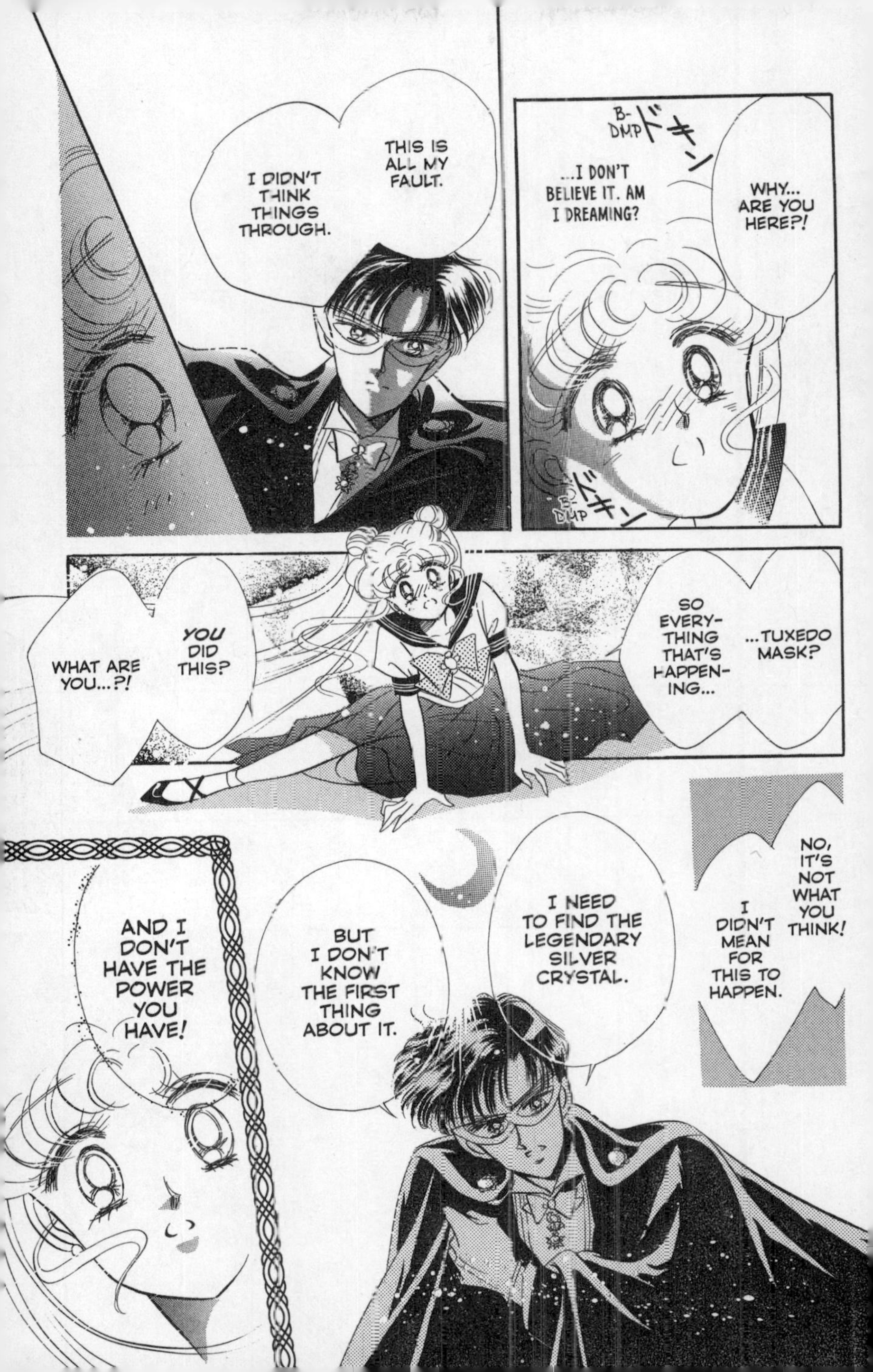
B-DMP ドキン
WHY... ARE YOU HERE?!
...I DON'T BELIEVE IT. AM I DREAMING?
B-DMP ドキン
THIS IS ALL MY FAULT.
I DIDN'T THINK THINGS THROUGH.
...TUXEDO MASK?
SO EVERYTHING THAT'S HAPPEN-ING...
YOU DID THIS?
WHAT ARE YOU...?!
NO, IT'S NOT WHAT YOU THINK!
I DIDN'T MEAN FOR THIS TO HAPPEN.
I NEED TO FIND THE LEGENDARY SILVER CRYSTAL.
BUT I DON'T KNOW THE FIRST THING ABOUT IT.
AND I DON'T HAVE THE POWER YOU HAVE!

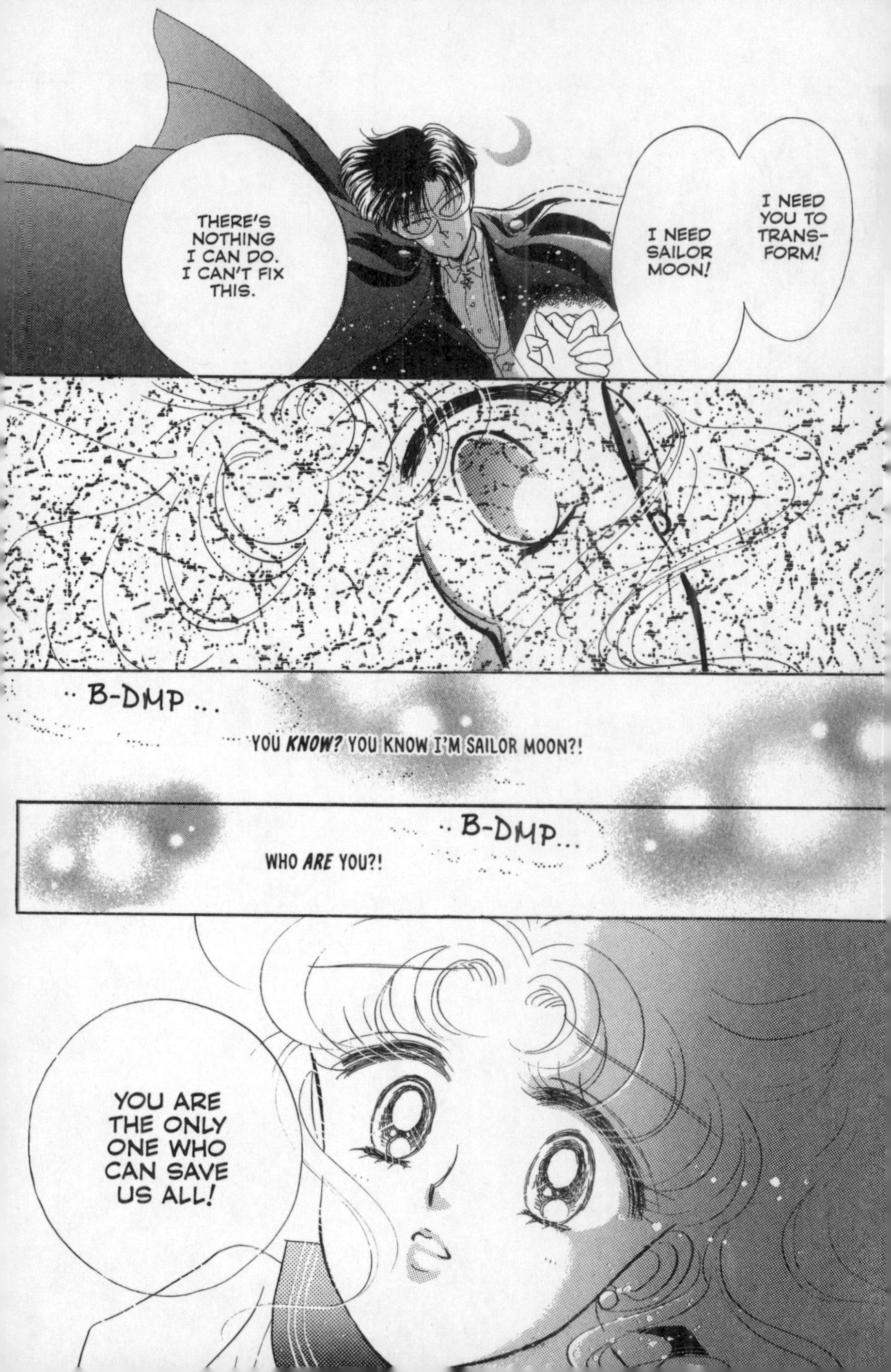
I NEED YOU TO TRANSFORM!
I NEED SAILOR MOON!
THERE'S NOTHING I CAN DO. I CAN'T FIX THIS.
.. B-DMP ...
YOU KNOW? YOU KNOW I'M SAILOR MOON?!
.. B-DMP...
WHO ARE YOU?!
YOU ARE THE ONLY ONE WHO CAN SAVE US ALL!

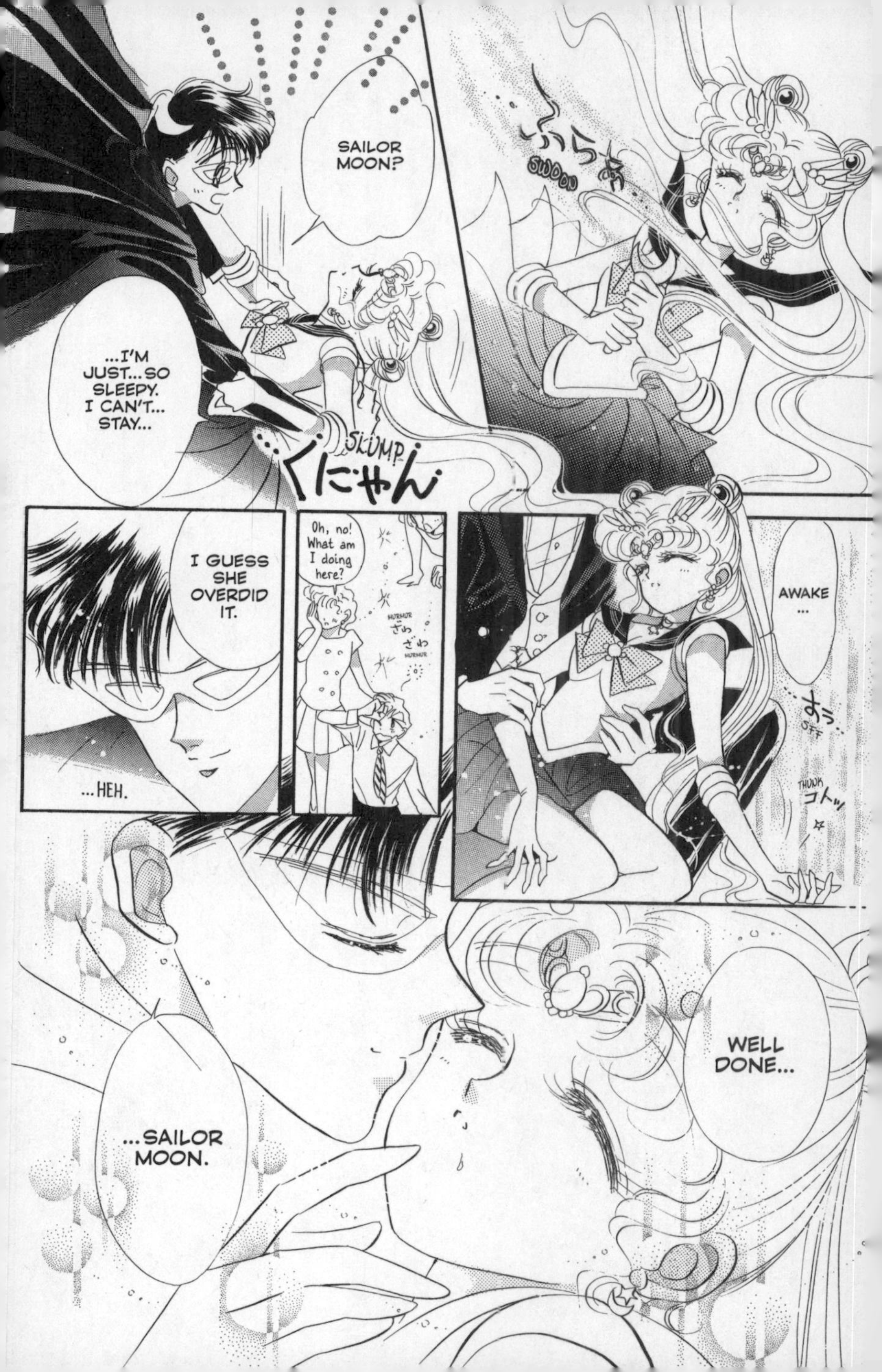
ふらぁ
SWOON
SAILOR MOON?
...I'M JUST...SO SLEEPY. I CAN'T... STAY...
SLUMP
ぐにゃん
AWAKE...
すう
SFF
THUNK
コトッ
Oh, no! What am I doing here?
MURMUR
ざわ
ざわ
MURMUR
I GUESS SHE OVERDID IT.
...HEH.
WELL DONE...
...SAILOR MOON.

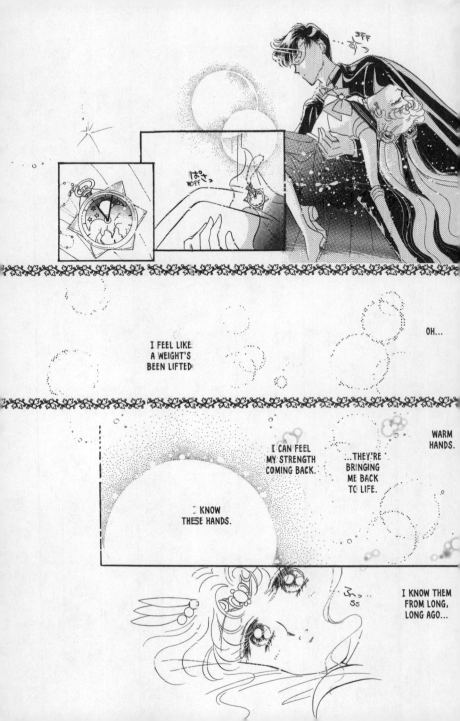

OH...

I FEEL LIKE
A WEIGHT'S
BEEN LIFTED

WARM
HANDS.

I CAN FEEL
MY STRENGTH
COMING BACK.

...THEY'RE
BRINGING
ME BACK
TO LIFE.

I KNOW
THESE HANDS.

I KNOW THEM
FROM LONG,
LONG AGO...

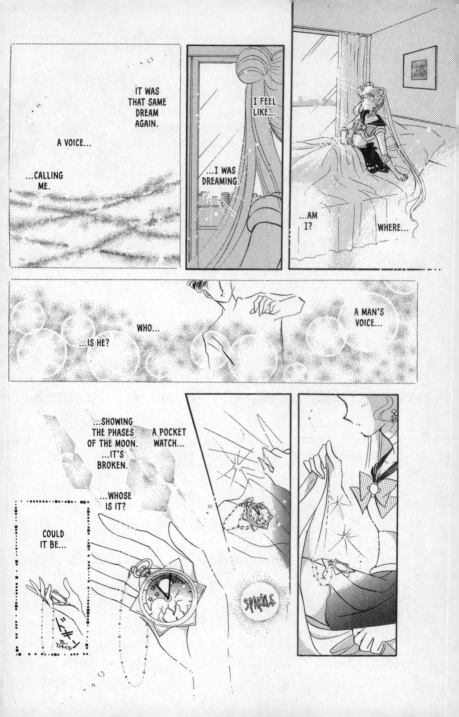

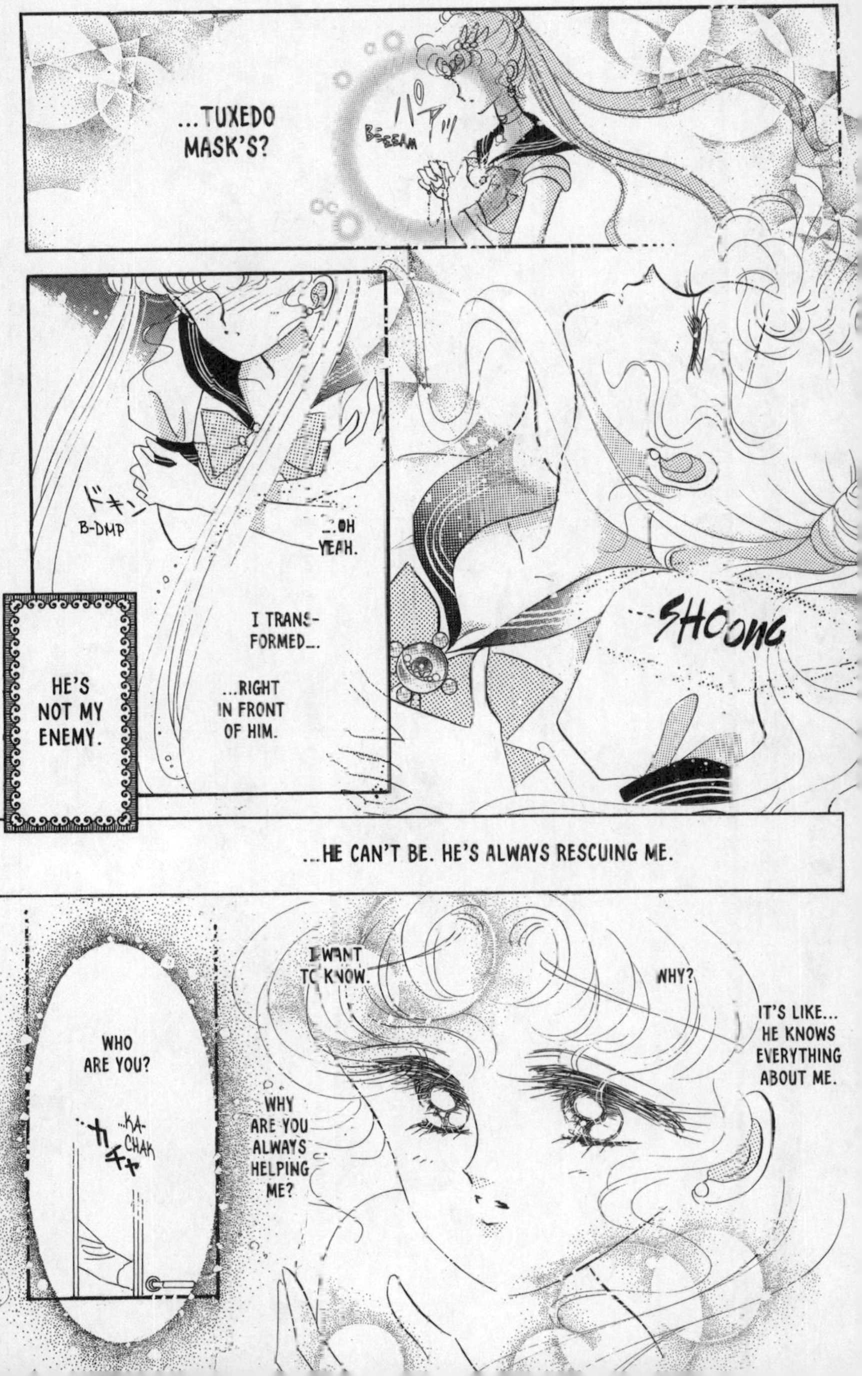
パアッ
B-BEAM
...TUXEDO MASK'S?
SHOONG
...OH YEAH.
ドキン
B-DMP
I TRANSFORMED...
...RIGHT IN FRONT OF HIM.
HE'S NOT MY ENEMY.
...HE CAN'T BE. HE'S ALWAYS RESCUING ME.
IT'S LIKE... HE KNOWS EVERYTHING ABOUT ME.
WHY?
I WANT TO KNOW.
WHY ARE YOU ALWAYS HELPING ME?
WHO ARE YOU?
カチャ
...KA-CHAK

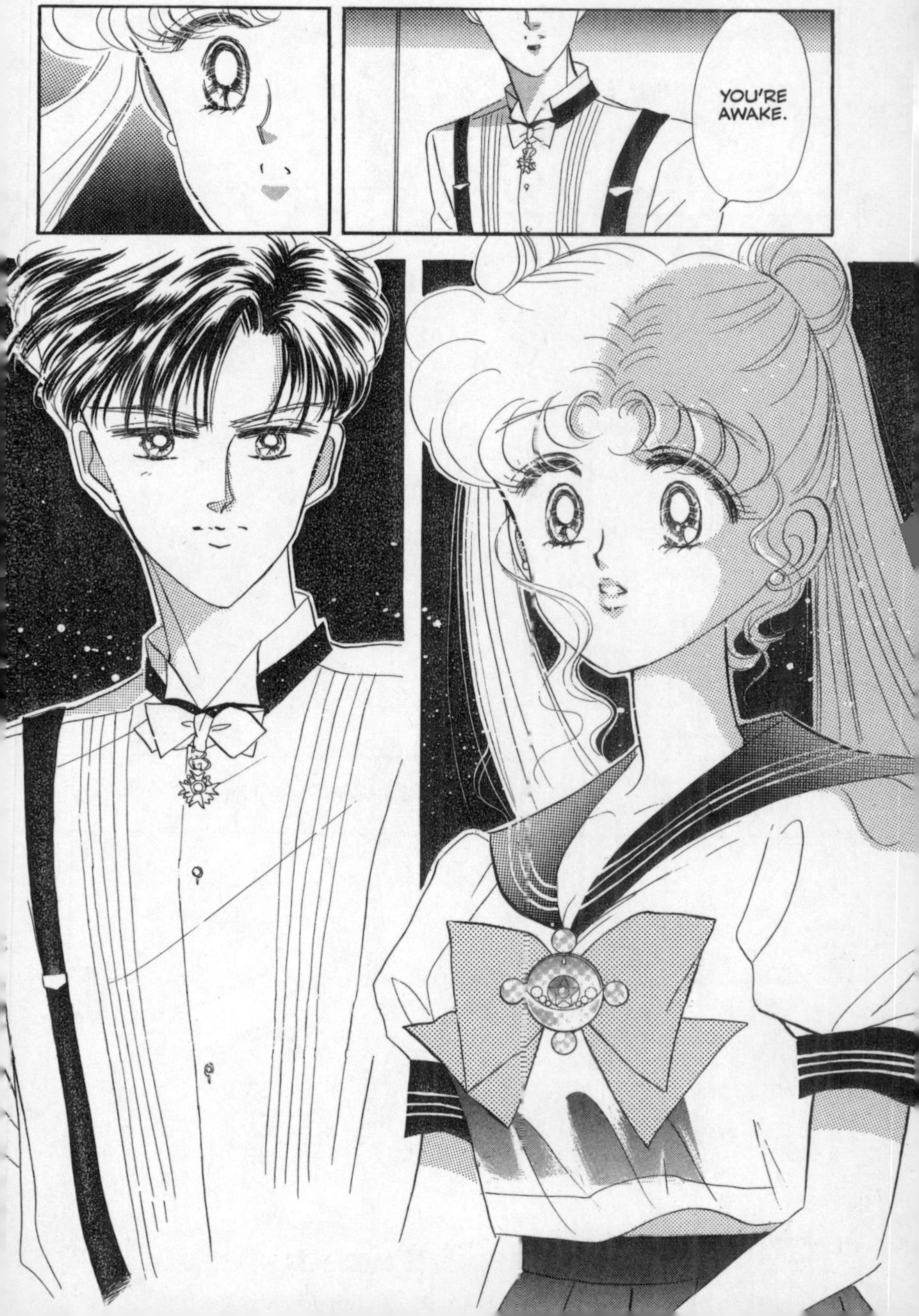
YOU'RE AWAKE.

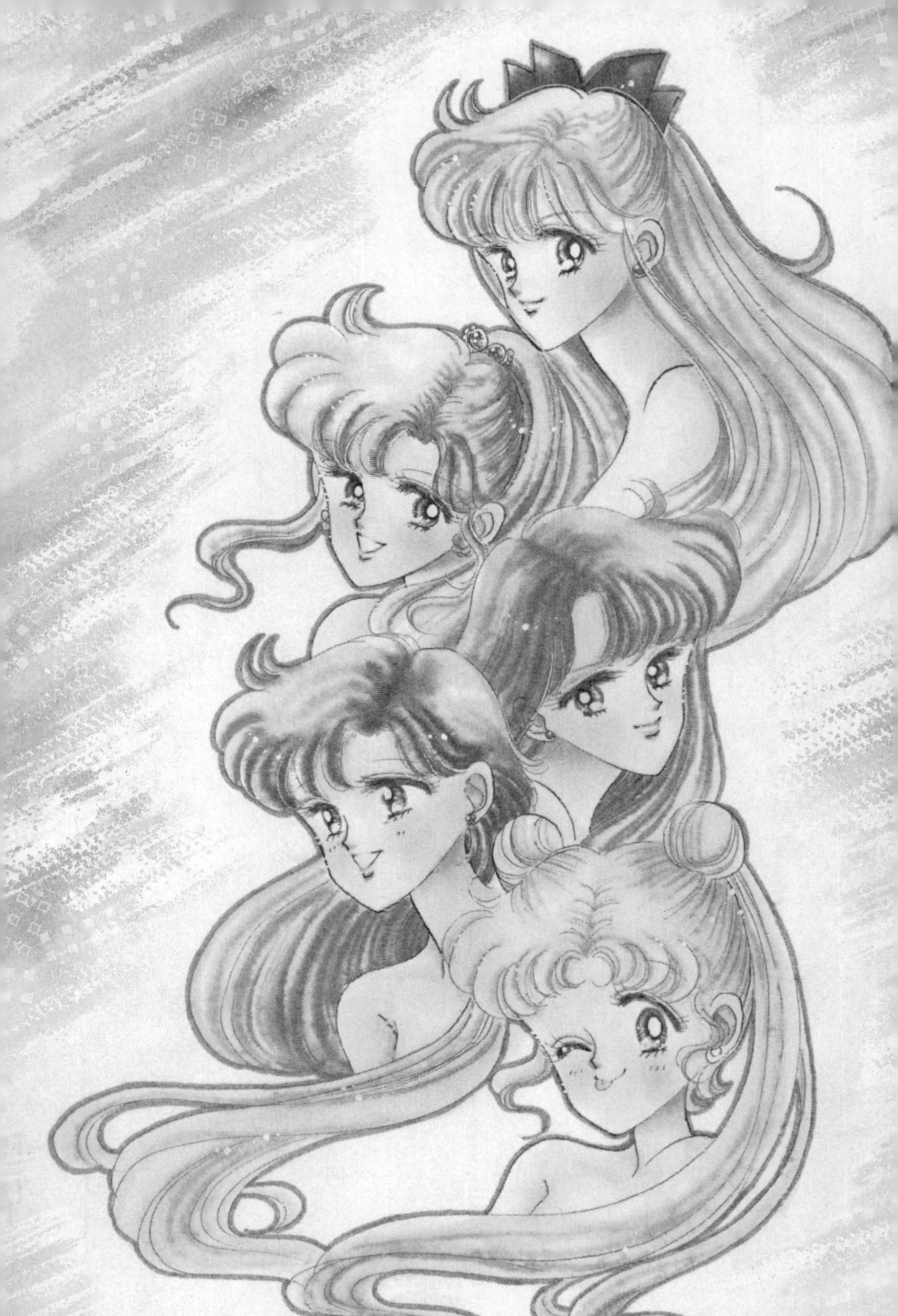

Act. 7 Mamoru Chiba: Tuxedo Mask

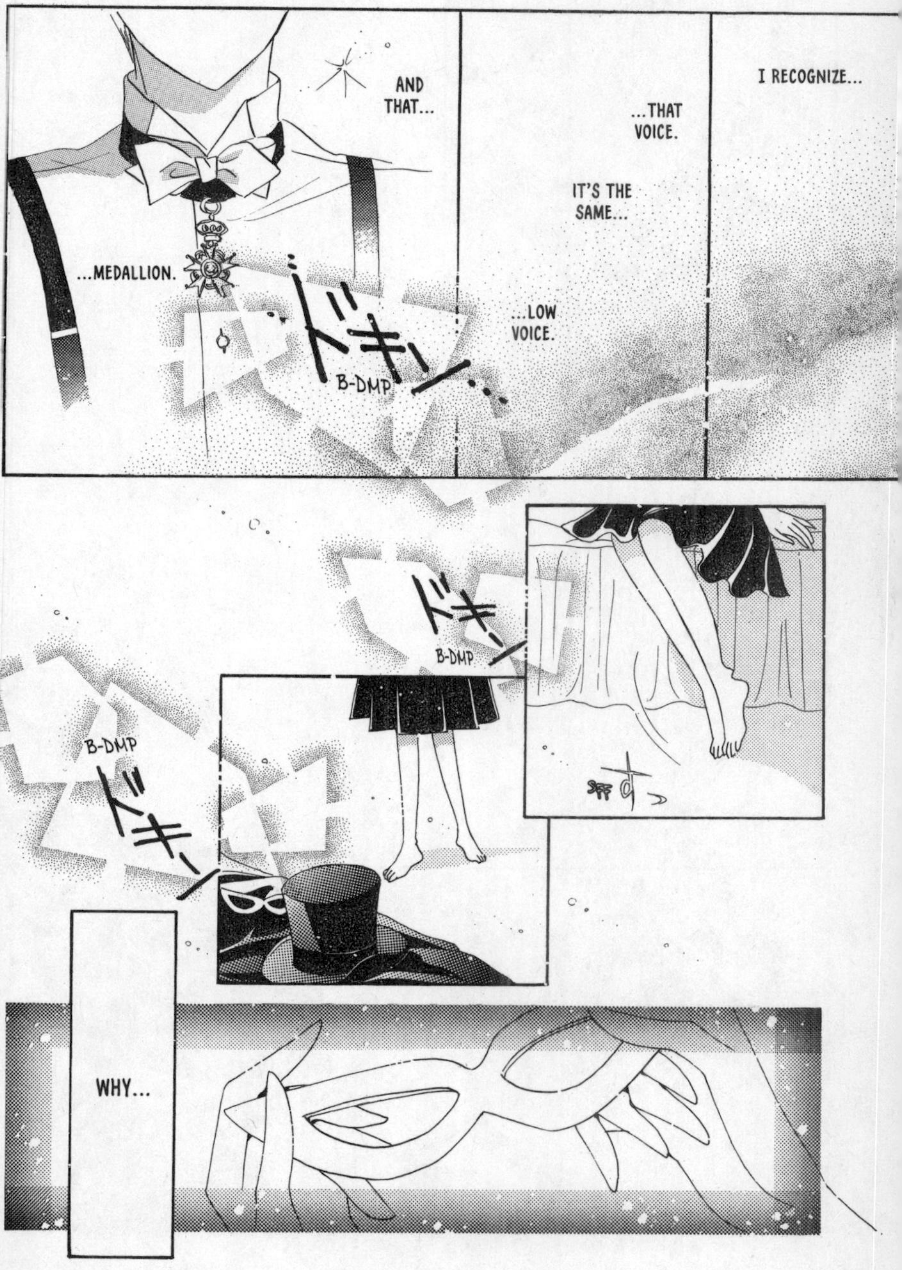
I RECOGNIZE...
...THAT VOICE.
IT'S THE SAME...
...LOW VOICE.
AND THAT...
...MEDALLION.
ドキン
B-DMP
ドキン
B-DMP
SFF
B-DMP
ドキン
WHY...

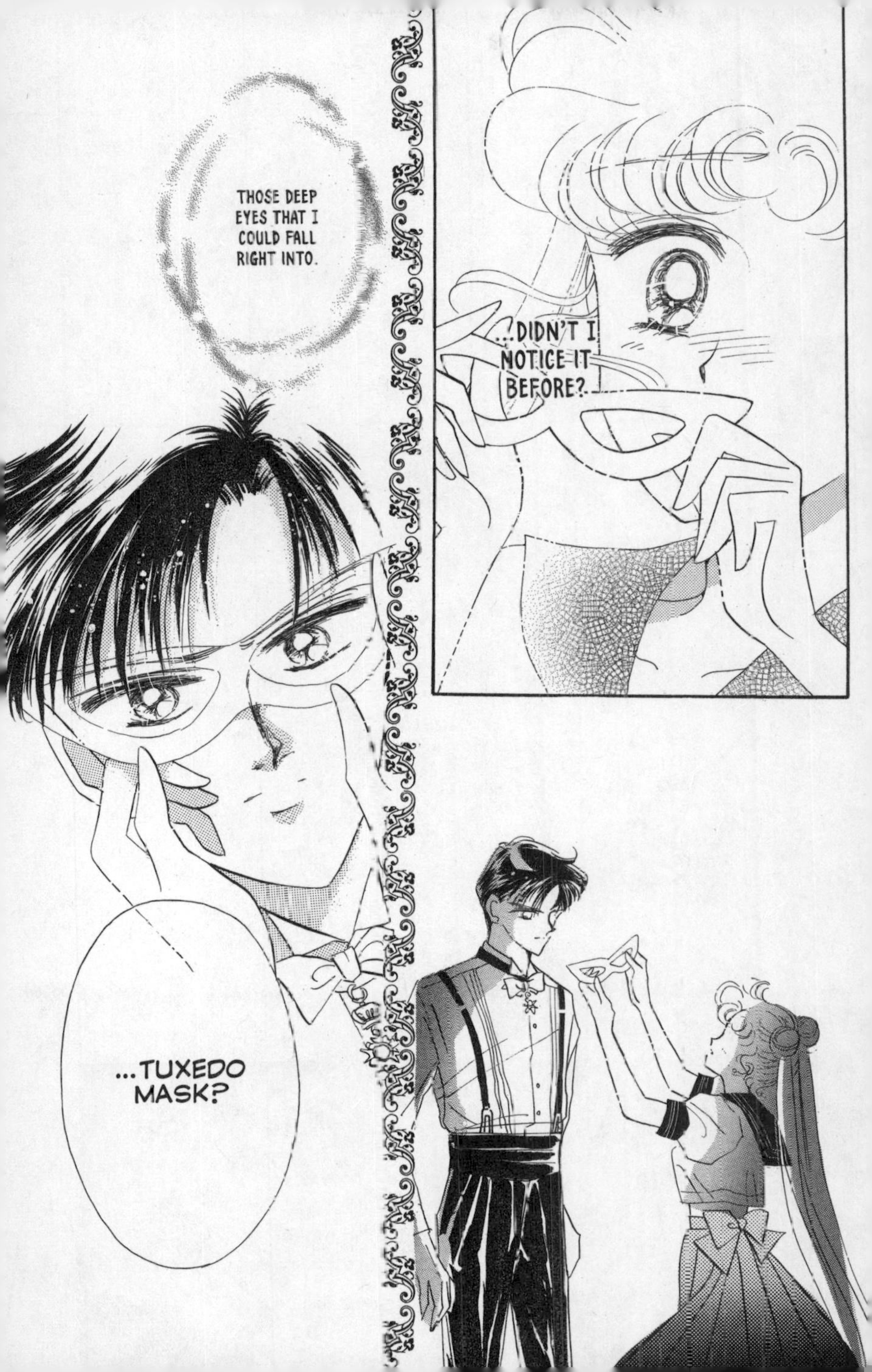
...DIDN'T I NOTICE IT BEFORE?
THOSE DEEP EYES THAT I COULD FALL RIGHT INTO.
...TUXEDO MASK?

AM I REALLY MAMORU CHIBA? OR...

...AM I SOMEONE ELSE? FOR YEARS, I HAD NO WAY OF KNOWING.

I WOKE UP IN THE HOSPITAL, AND THEY TOLD ME MY NAME...BUT I DIDN'T REMEMBER.

"YOUR NAME IS MAMORU CHIBA."

I LOST MY PARENTS, AND ALL OF MY MEMORIES.

I WAS IN AN ACCIDENT ON MY SIXTH BIRTHDAY.

"THE LEGENDARY SILVER CRYSTAL"... JUST THAT ONE PHRASE.

AND THAT'S ALL SHE SAYS, EVERY NIGHT.

"PLEASE... THE LEGENDARY SILVER CRYSTAL..."

THEN I STARTED HAVING THIS DREAM— THE SAME DREAM OVER AND OVER.

SEARCHING FOR THE ONLY CLUE TO MY IDENTITY.

AND I WAS DRESSED IN A TUXEDO, LIKE A PHANTOM THIEF.

THE NEXT THING I KNEW...

...I WAS WANDERING THE STREETS AT NIGHT, LIKE SOME KIND OF SLEEP WALKER.

B-DMP

THE LEGENDARY SILVER CRYSTAL.

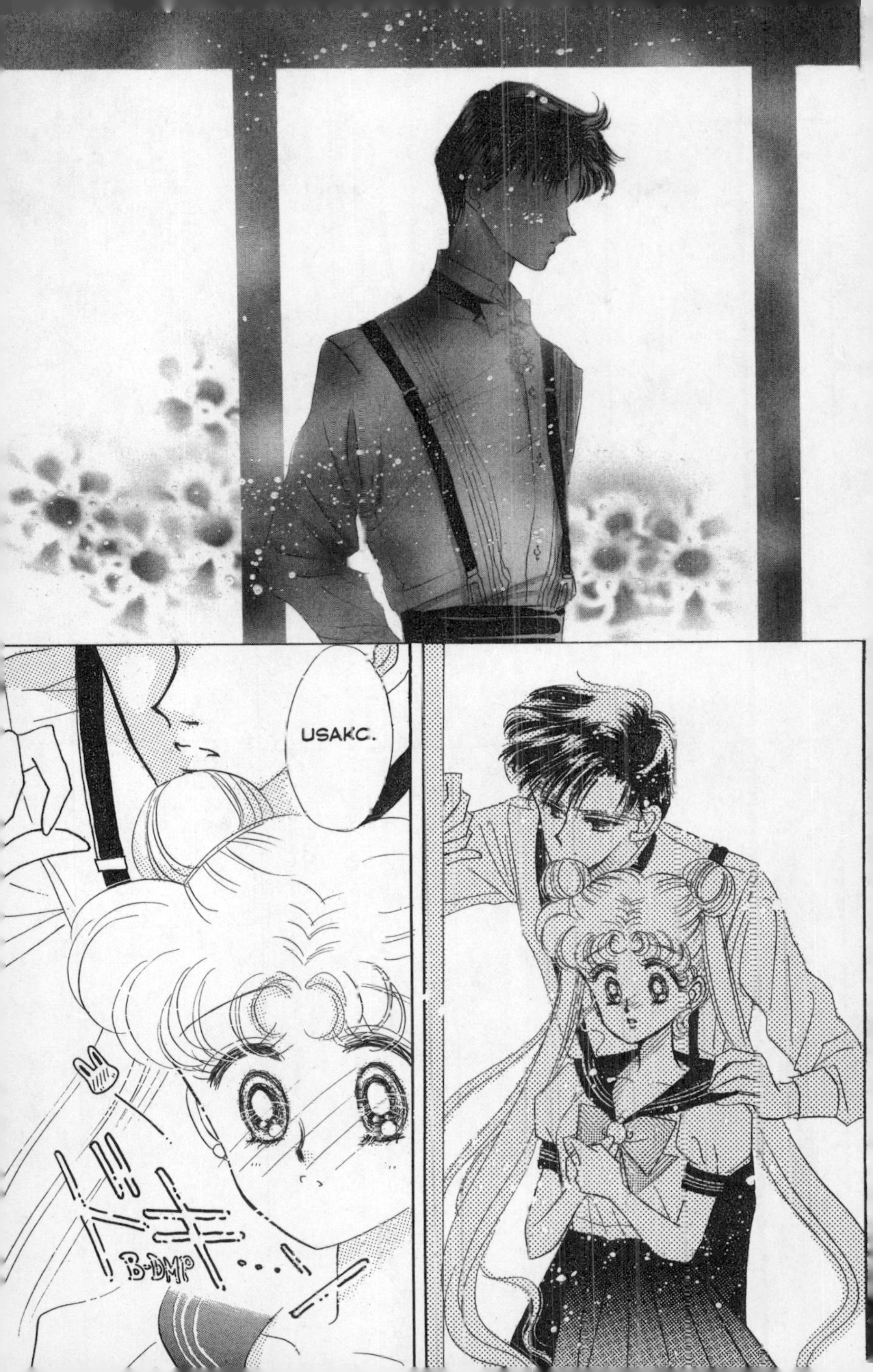
USAKC.
B-DMP

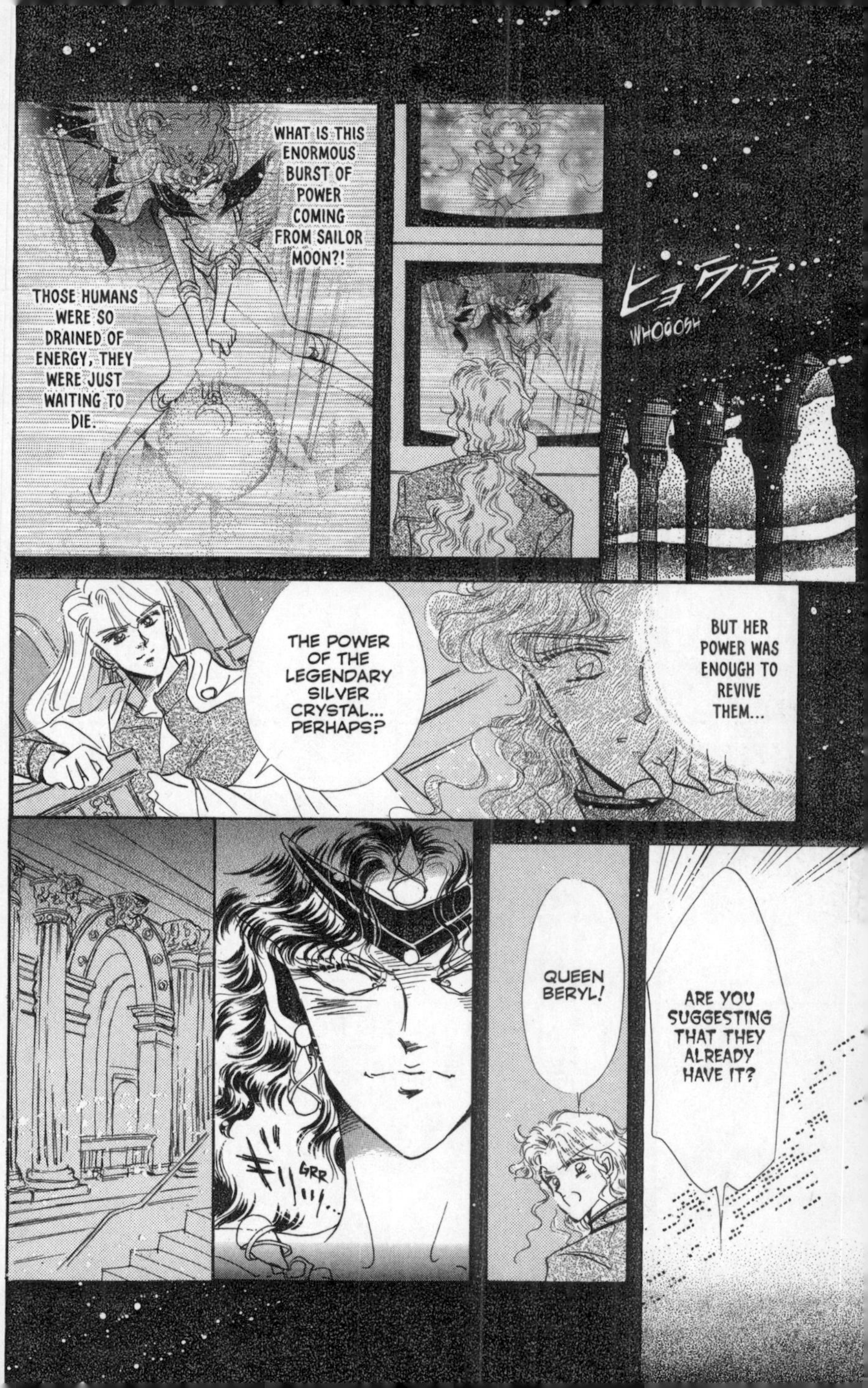
WHAT IS THIS ENORMOUS BURST OF POWER COMING FROM SAILOR MOON?!
THOSE HUMANS WERE SO DRAINED OF ENERGY, THEY WERE JUST WAITING TO DIE.
ヒョウウ…
WHOOOSH
BUT HER POWER WAS ENOUGH TO REVIVE THEM...
THE POWER OF THE LEGENDARY SILVER CRYSTAL... PERHAPS?
ARE YOU SUGGESTING THAT THEY ALREADY HAVE IT?
QUEEN BERYL!
GRR

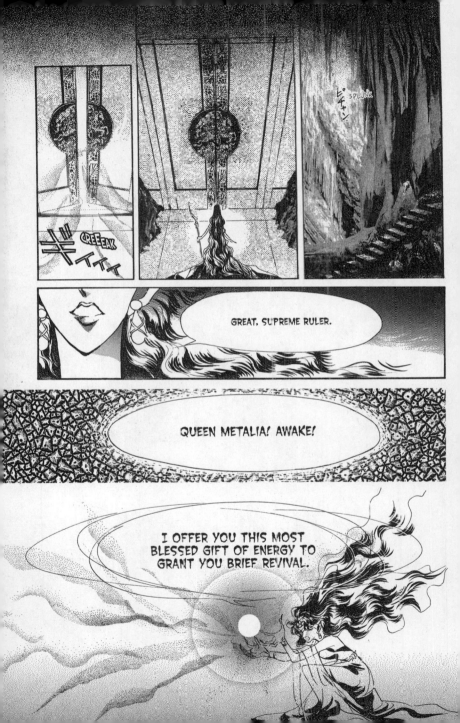

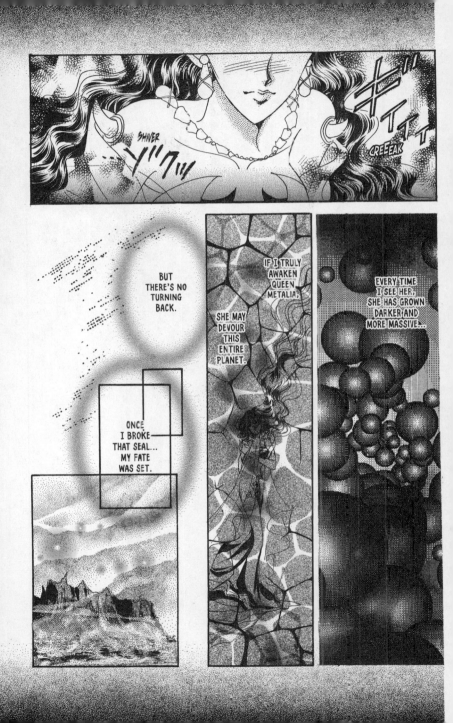

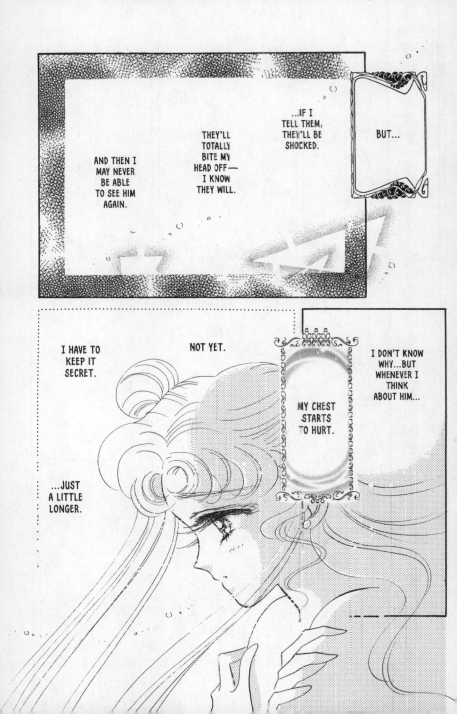

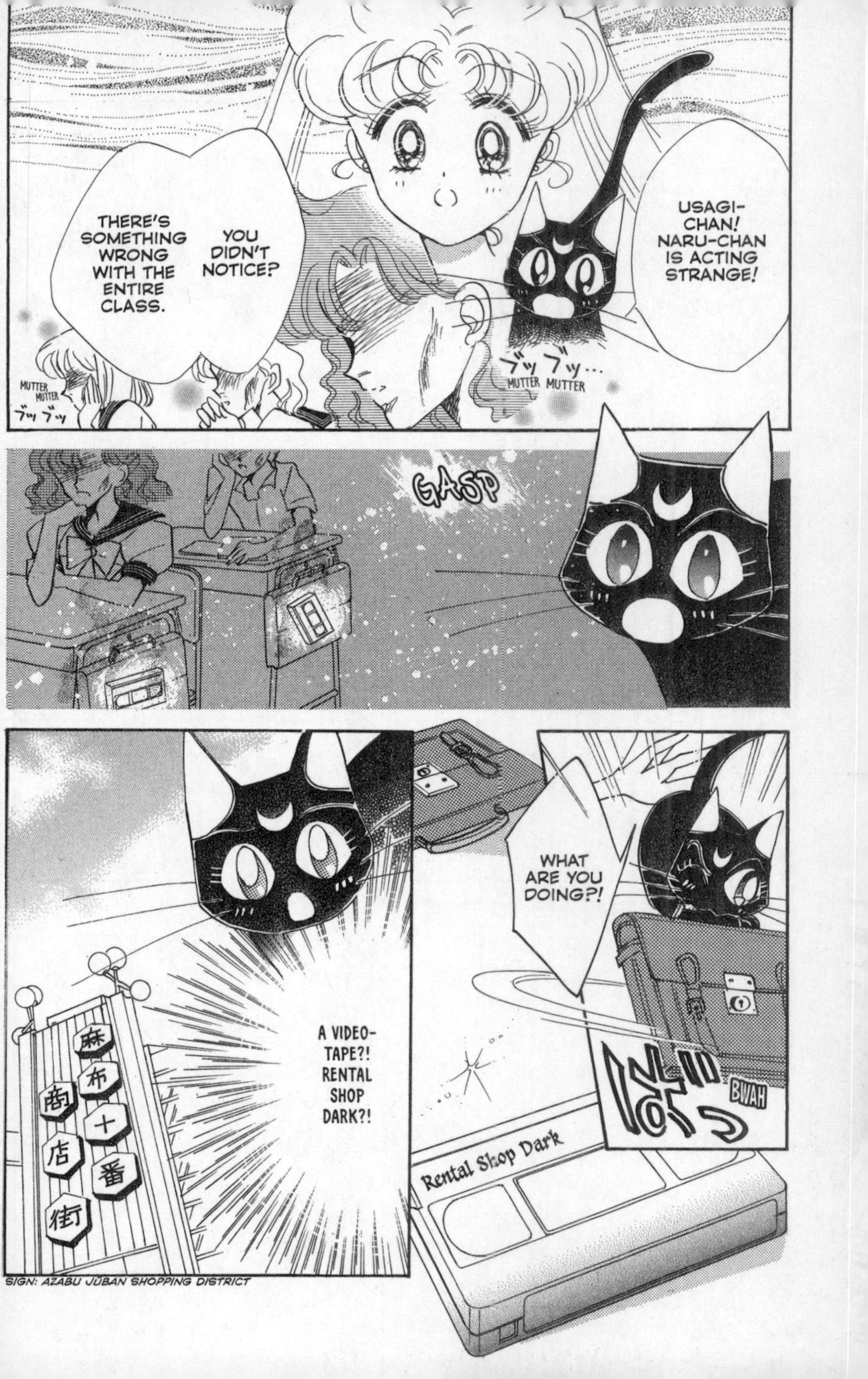
USAGI-CHAN! NARU-CHAN IS ACTING STRANGE!
ブツブツ…
MUTTER MUTTER
YOU DIDN'T NOTICE?
THERE'S SOMETHING WRONG WITH THE ENTIRE CLASS.
MUTTER MUTTER
ブツブツ
GASP
WHAT ARE YOU DOING?!
BWAH
Rental Shop Dark
A VIDEO-TAPE?! RENTAL SHOP DARK?!
麻布十番商店街

SIGN: AZABU JŪBAN SHOPPING DISTRICT

SAILOR V?!

THE GAME IS TALKING TO ME?!

USAGI-CHAN, GO!! I'LL TAKE THIS TO THE UNDERGROUND COMMAND CENTER!!

OH...!

FZH

NO WAY!

FIND SAILOR MOON.

SHE KNOWS THE SECRET OF THE LEGENDARY SILVER CRYSTAL! CAPTURE HER!

BRING HER TO US! ALIVE!

IS THIS SUBLIMINAL MESSAGING?!

!!

GIVE SAILOR MOON TO THE DARK KINGDOM!!

...WHAT'S HAPPENING? IT'S DRAINING MY ENERGY!!

?!

FSHHH

HFF

DID IT SAY DARK KING-DOM?!

BRING US SAILOR MOON!!

THEY KEEP USING PEOPLE FOR ONE EVIL PLOT AFTER ANOTHER... WHO ARE THEY?! WHAT DO THEY WANT?!

WHAT IS THE DARK KINGDOM, LUNA?!

WHERE IS SHE?! WHERE...

KA-CRASH

FIND HER!

I'M RIGHT HERE!!

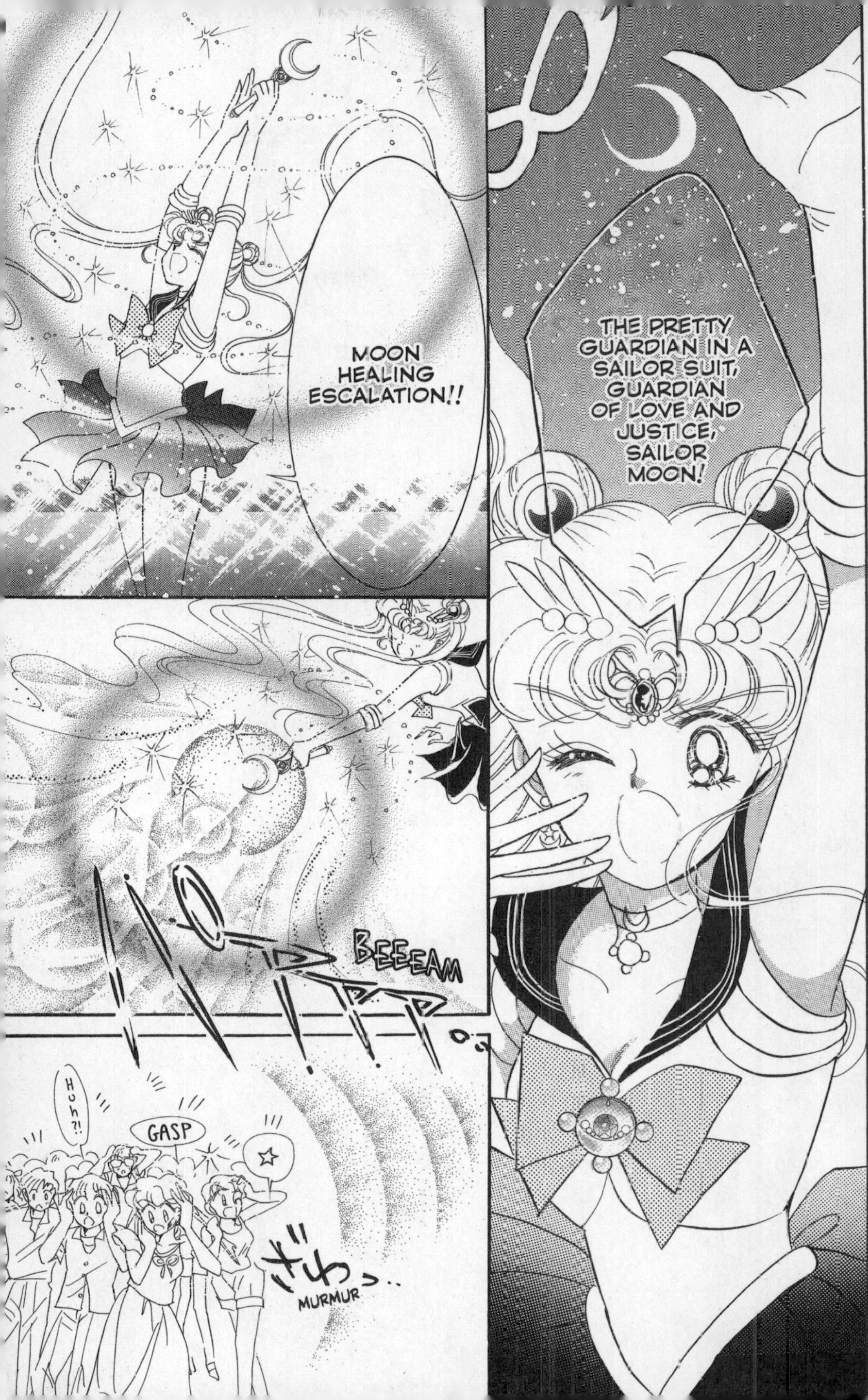
THE PRETTY GUARDIAN IN A SAILOR SUIT, GUARDIAN OF LOVE AND JUSTICE, SAILOR MOON!
MOON HEALING ESCALATION!!
BEEEAM
GASP
Huh?!
ざわっ..
MURMUR

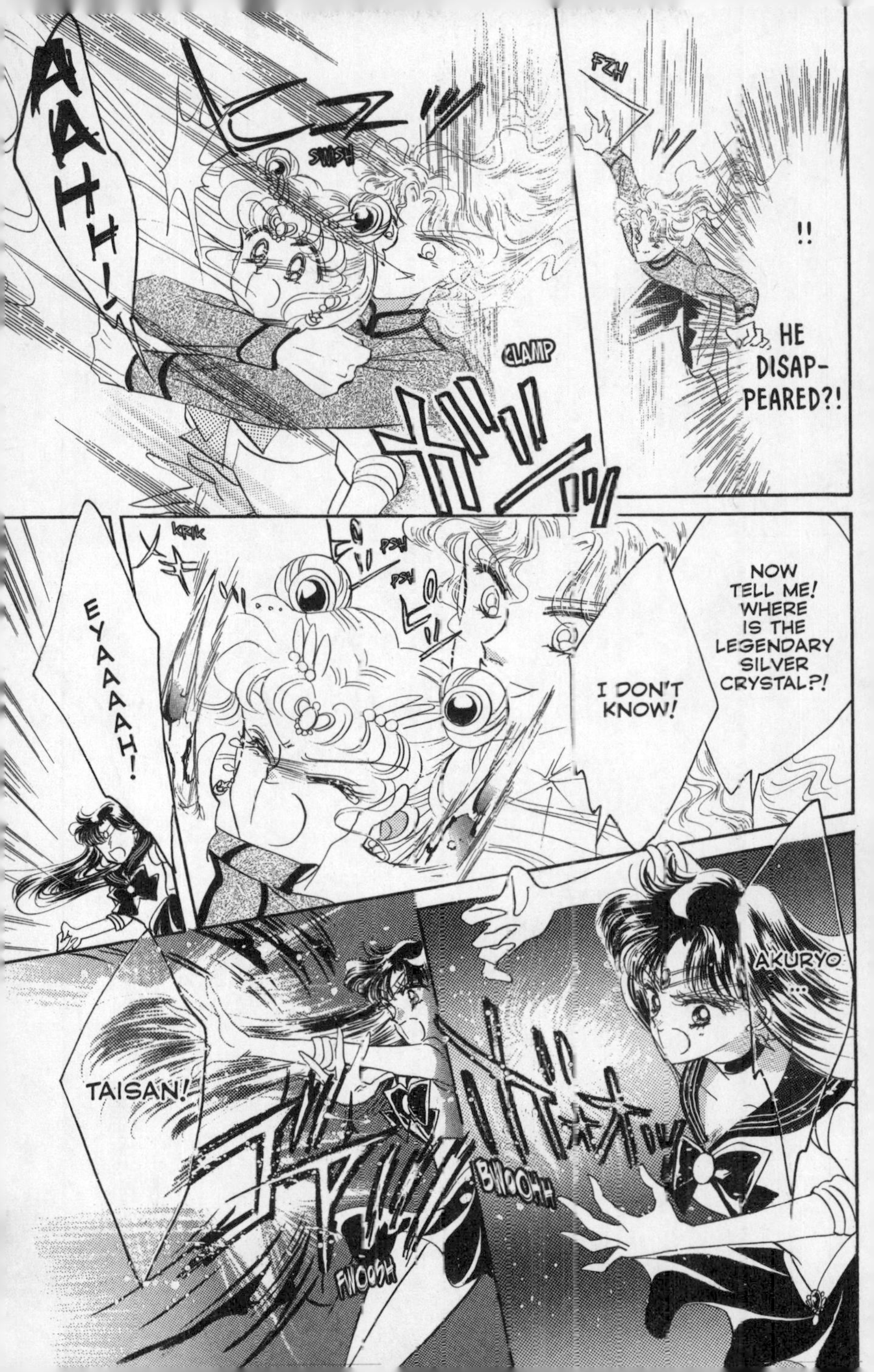
FZH
!!
HE DISAPPEARED?!
AAHH!!
SWISH
CLAMP
NOW TELL ME! WHERE IS THE LEGENDARY SILVER CRYSTAL?!
I DON'T KNOW!
PSH
PSH
KRIK
EYAAAAAH!
AKURYO...
TAISAN!
BHOOHH
FWOOSH

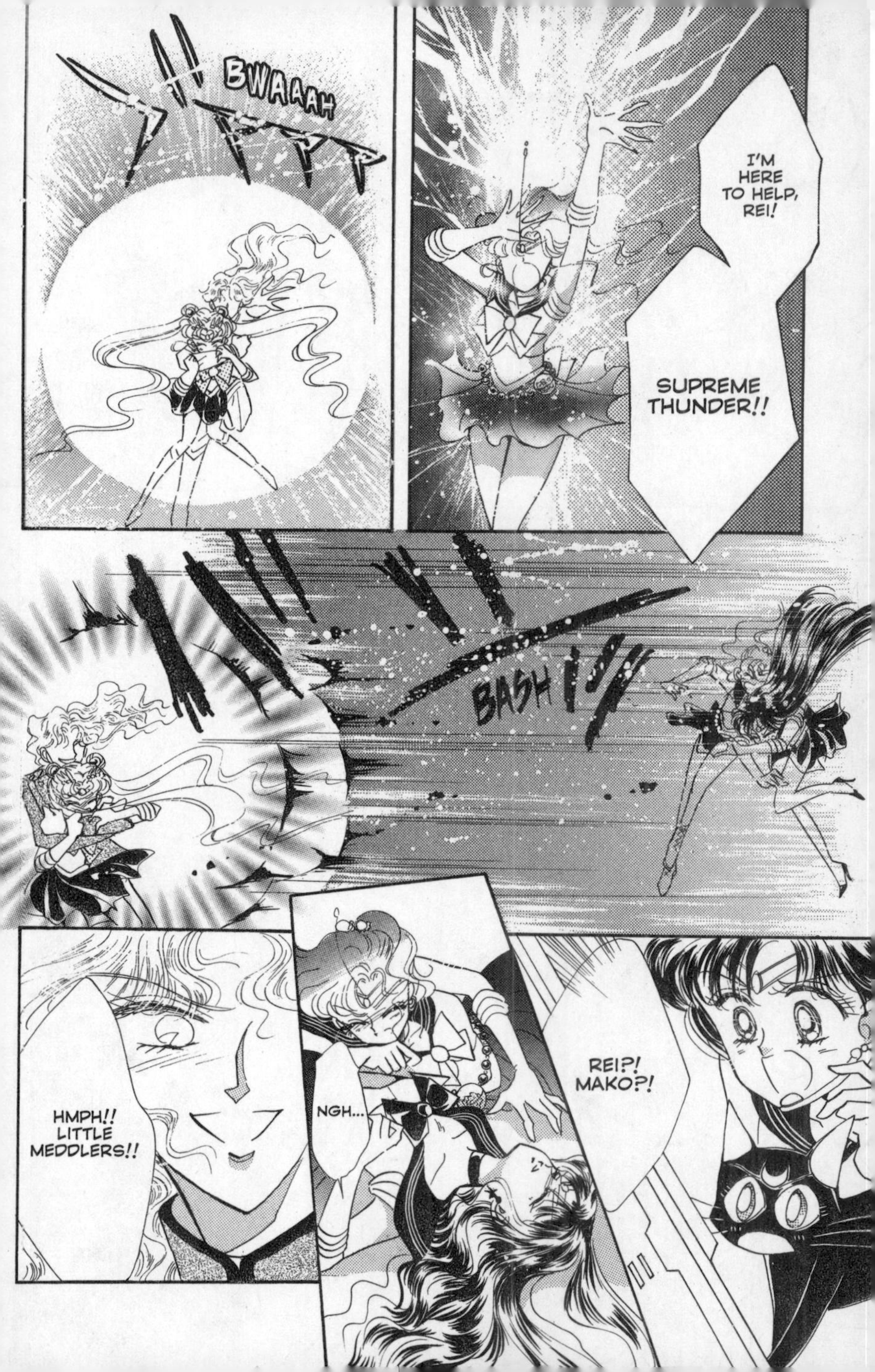
I'M HERE TO HELP, REI!
SUPREME THUNDER!!
BWAAAAH
BASH
REI?! MAKO?!
NGH...
HMPH!! LITTLE MEDDLERS!!

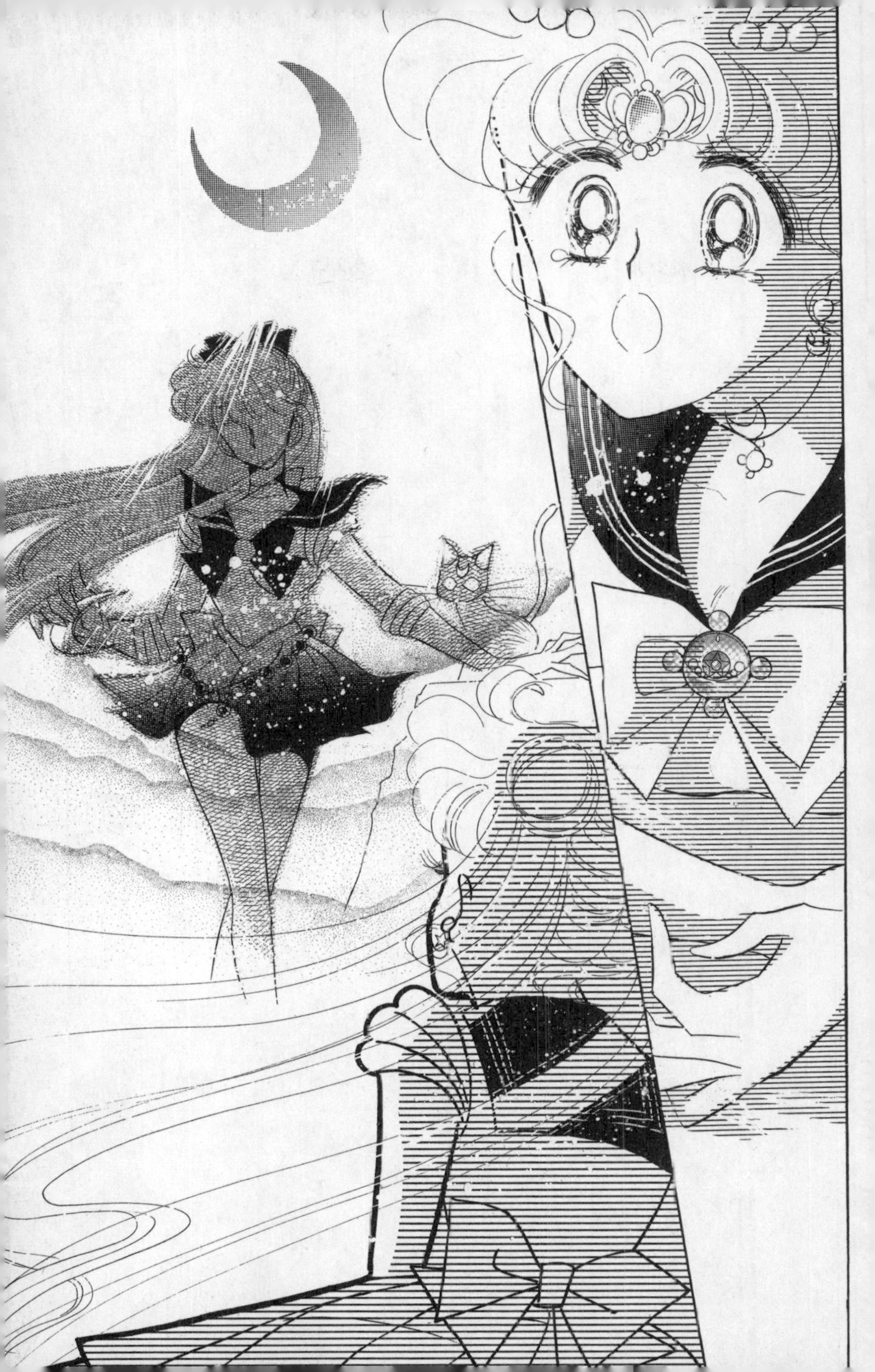

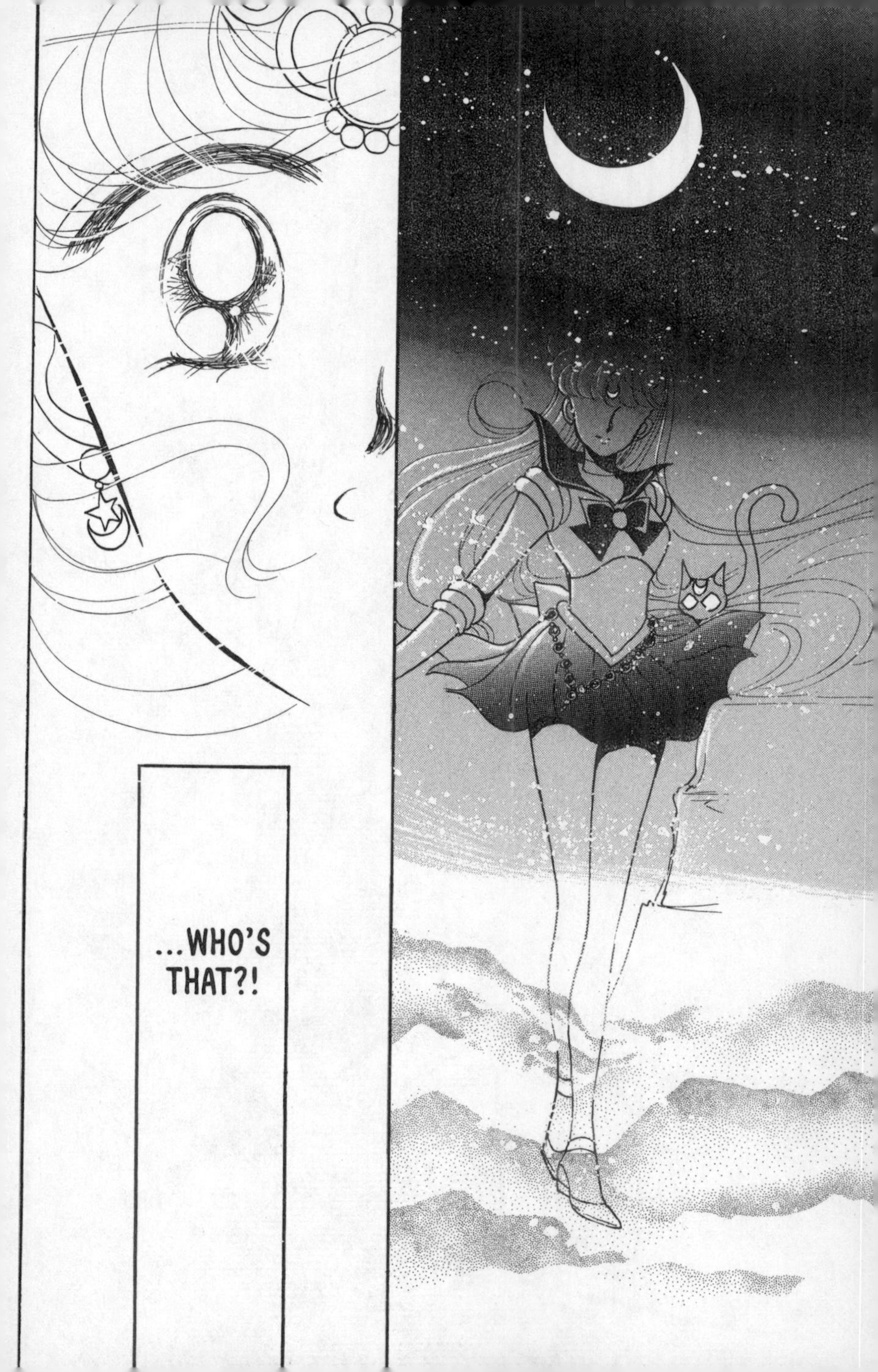
...WHO'S THAT?!

Pretty Guardian
Sailor Moon

Translation Notes

Jūban Sports, page 3
Don't be fooled by the name—Usagi's mother is most likely not reading this paper for local sports news. While Japanese "sports newspapers" do cover athletic events, they also cover some news, leisure and entertainment, and, perhaps most importantly, they're a good source of celebrity gossip.

V-chan, page 3
Usagi's mother tends to add -chan to the name of every young girl she comes across. Attaching -chan to a person's name is a way to express the fact that the speaker thinks of them as a friend, as opposed to using the more distant -san. For more on honorifics, see "Call me Usagi."

Usagi Tsukino, page 7
The reader will find that the names of the main characters of this series were not chosen at random. *Usagi* means "rabbit"—hence the frequent appearance of bunnies in speech bubbles to indicate that Usagi is the one speaking. "*Tsuki no*" means "of the moon," so Usagi's full name means "rabbit of the moon," or "moon rabbit." This is a reference to the Japanese folklore tradition that the image formed on the moon's surface by its topography is that of a rabbit making *mochi* (rice cake).

Stepped on a cat, page 8
It may or may not be interesting to note that Usagi has reenacted the Japanese name of a popular piece of music to teach beginning piano students. Known in the United States as "*Der Flohwalzer*," or "The Flea Waltz," in Japan it's called "*Neko Funjatta*," or "I Stepped on a Cat." The translators recommend looking it up, as it does indeed sound like stepping on a cat (but please refrain from trying to recreate the real sound).

Haruda, page 11

The nickname Haruda may simply be a combination of Sakurada-sensei's given name and surname, but it may also be a play on words. First, the translators must point out that in Japan, names are listed in the order of surname first and given name second, so her full name would be said "Sakurada Haruna." "*Sakura da*" can be roughly translated as, "Look, cherry blossoms!" Cherry blossoms are a symbol of spring, so when someone looks and sees cherry blossoms, their next thought could reasonably be, "It's springtime!", which, in Japanese, is "*Haru da!*" It should also be pointed out that if the students are addressing their teacher by her given name, either they are on friendly terms with her, or they don't respect her at all. Incidentally, Sakurada-sensei first appeared in Naoko Takeuchi's earlier series, *The Cherry Project*.

Azabu Jūban Shopping District, page 16

Also known as Azabu Jūban Shopping Street, this shopping district has an old Edo feel to it, and mix of new and old shops, which make it a popular spot among young people and foreign tourists. The nearby residential area is also highly sought after, due in part to its proximity to other high-end shopping and residential areas. Azabu Jūban is also where the first United States legation (home to a foreign diplomat) was established in the 19th century, and today is home to more than 20 foreign embassies.

They're called buns, page 16

Mamoru has had several different nicknames for Usagi throughout the different incarnations of English-language *Sailor Moon*. While these translators will always have a fondness for the first English dub's "Meatball Head," names relating to buns are really more appropriate. In the original Japanese exchange, Mamoru calls her a "*tankobu* head," suggesting that she has large bumps, possibly caused by some sort of blunt impact. She informs him that the proper name for the bundles

of hair on the sides of her head is not *tankobu* but *odango*. It's a bit of a play on words, because *tanko* and *dango* sound similar. An *odango* is a sweet dumpling that comes in a variety of flavors, but *odango* is also the correct Japanese name for hair buns. So not only is "bun" the correct term for her hair, but it also fits the wordplay, because it sounds like "bump." Buns and *odango* are both types of hair and types of food, so either way, Usagi has an appetizing hairstyle.

Still in uniform again, page 19
In Japan, most high schools and junior high schools require their students to wear uniforms. It is generally encouraged to at least go home and change clothes, and perhaps finish one's homework, before indulging in such frivolities as goofing off at the arcade.

Lupin, the gentleman thief, page 42
Usagi is speaking of Arsène Lupin, the gentleman thief and master of disguise. He first appeared in 1905 as a response to the popular detective literature of the time. Like Sherlock Holmes, he has appeared in several forms of media, including anime and manga, which is no doubt how Usagi learned of his existence. Although he doesn't have a uniform, usually wearing clothes suitable to the task at hand, he is often depicted wearing a top hat and cape, just like Tuxedo Mask.

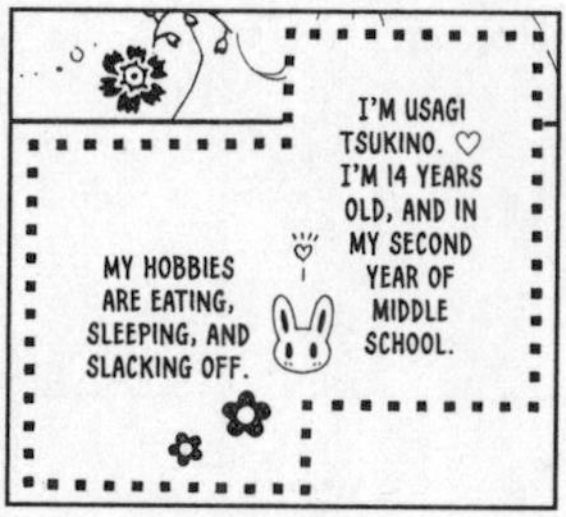

I'm Usagi Tsukino, page 51
It may seem strange that Usagi is introducing herself again, when we've all gotten to know her fairly well from the first chapter. The reason she needs to reintroduce herself is that when this story first showed up, it was published one chapter at a time in a monthly magazine. By introducing herself again, Usagi is helping readers who may have missed the previous issue for whatever reason, or who may not remember her very well after an entire month.

Pudding, page 53
Although it sounds strange that Usagi would suddenly think of pudding, in the original Japanese, she was thinking of Flan. When describing Sailor Moon's mission, Luna uses the English word for princess, which is phonetically written in Japanese as *purinsesu*. Constantly hungry Usagi immediately thinks of food—in this case, *purin*, the Japanese word for flan.

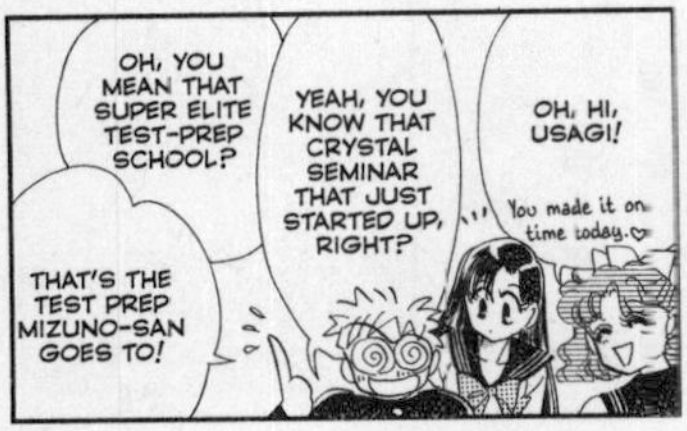
OH, HI, USAGI!
You made it on time today.♡
YEAH, YOU KNOW THAT CRYSTAL SEMINAR THAT JUST STARTED UP, RIGHT?
OH, YOU MEAN THAT SUPER ELITE TEST-PREP SCHOOL?
THAT'S THE TEST PREP MIZUNO-SAN GOES TO!

Test-prep school, page 55

In Japan, many high schools require their potential students to pass an entrance exam before they can enroll. The more elite the school, the harder the exam. To prepare for these tests, students can attend *juku*, a type of supplementary school specifically geared to help them get into the high school, and eventually college, of their choice.

I'm out of 100 yen coins, page 59

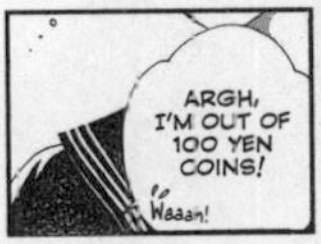
ARGH, I'M OUT OF 100 YEN COINS!
Waaah!

Like in America, game machines in Japan require the player to insert coins. Unlike in America, the most common coin accepted is not the quarter, but the 100 yen coin, which is worth approximately one US dollar.

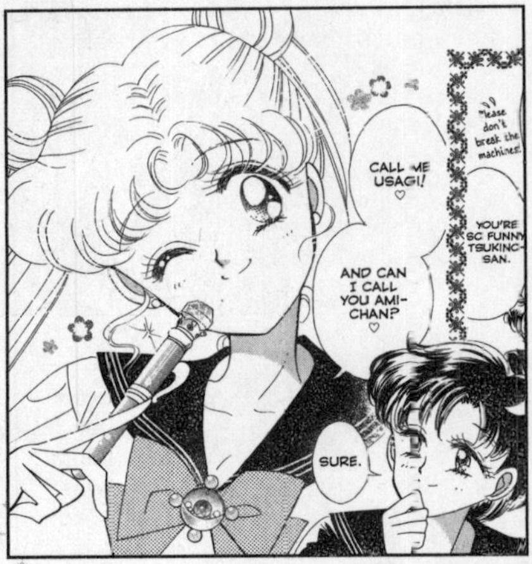
don't break the machines!
YOU'RE SO FUNNY TSUKINO-SAN.
CALL ME USAGI! ♡
AND CAN I CALL YOU AMI-CHAN? ♡
SURE.

Call me Usagi, page 61

In Japan, when you're just getting to know someone, it can be very rude to address them by their given name. Sometimes it's appropriate to ask someone how they prefer to be addressed, but when that's not feasible, the safest bet in most circumstances is to call them by their surname and add the honorific -san (similar to the English "Mr." or "Miss"), as Ami did when she called Usagi "Tsukino-san." But Usagi isn't one to stand on formality, and she's happy to have her friends—even brand new ones—call her by name. However, it's still bad manners to call someone simply by name unless you're very close (and can sometimes even be a sign of enmity), so she adds -chan to Ami's name, because it is a suffix that expresses closeness and friendship. Another suffix the reader will see attached to characters' names is -kun, which is generally attached to boys' names, especially boys who are the speaker's age or younger. It is a suffix that expresses closeness and respect. The suffix -shi (seen on page 274) is somewhat more formal than -san.

Crystal Seminar disks, page 63

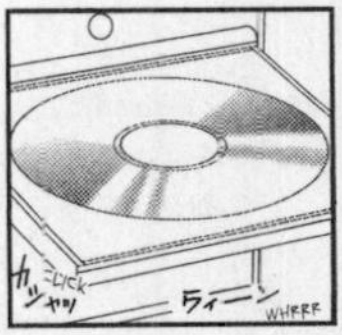
CLICK
WHRRR

Before the magical days when the internet made it possible to share information instantly, if someone wanted to transfer data from one computer to another, they had to save it on what was called a "disk." You may have seen one of these old-fashioned disks in the form of a music CD or video game disk, but in the case of the Crystal Seminar, it contains a learning program.

Fauchon, page 62

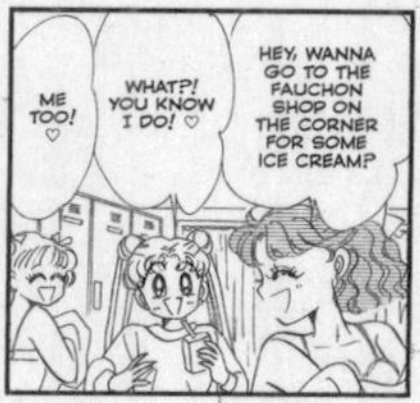
HEY, WANNA GO TO THE FAUCHON SHOP ON THE CORNER FOR SOME ICE CREAM?
WHAT?! YOU KNOW I DO! ♡
ME TOO! ♡

Although the name may not be so well-known in the United States, Fauchon (pronounced "foe-shone") is a world-famous luxury food brand originating in France. It made a name for itself in Japan with its fruit-flavored teas in the 1960s, and opened its first retail store there in 1972.

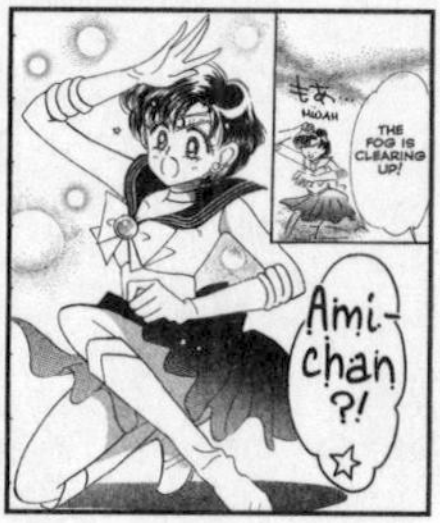
THE FOG IS CLEARING UP!
もあ…
HUOAH
Ami-chan?!

The guardian of water, page 79

Because people in East Asia didn't worship the same gods as the Romans, their astronomers came up with different names for the planets, and each of the five planets closest to the sun (excepting Earth) is associated with one of the five elements: wood, fire, earth, metal, and water. In Japanese, Mercury is *suisei*, which literally means "water star." That being the case, Sailor Mercury naturally is the guardian of water and has water powers. Fittingly, her alter-ego's surname "Mizuno" means "of water."

Hikawa Shrine, page 86

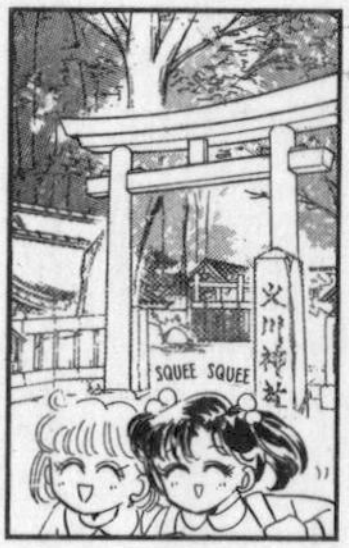
SQUEE SQUEE

This particular shrine's name means "fire river shrine," which is fitting because the priestess there uses fire for divination. Readers may be interested to know that this shrine is modeled after a real shrine in the real Minato Ward of Tokyo, also named Hikawa, but with different characters that mean "ice river."

Akuryo-Taisan, page 95

This is a phrase that means something to the effect of "evil spirit, be exorcised!"

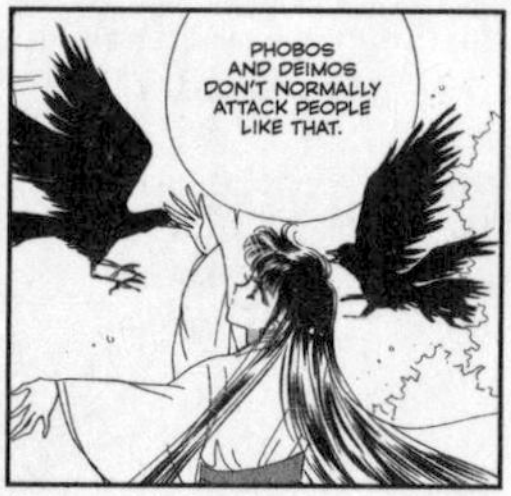
PHOBOS AND DEIMOS DON'T NORMALLY ATTACK PEOPLE LIKE THAT.

Phobos and Deimos, page 96

While Rei asserts that her pet crows are usually harmless, their names are rather intimidating. Greek for "fear" and "terror," these are also the names of the two moons of Mars, named for the sons of Ares, god of war.

Worship at a Shinto shrine, page 97

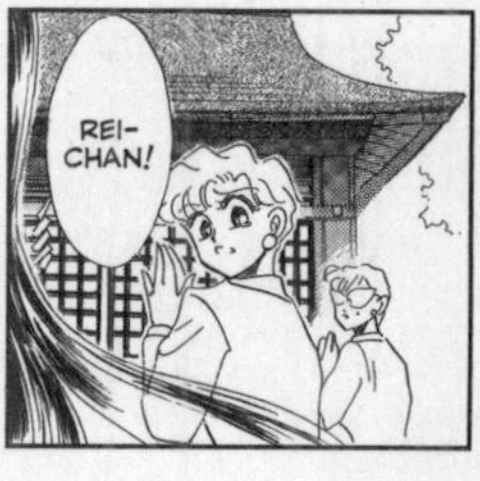
REI-CHAN!

The people who have come to pray for their daughters' safe return are shown here following the procedure for worship at a Shinto shrine. This is done by bowing twice, clapping twice, then bowing again. The first bows show respect, the clapping invites the deity to you, and the last bow is to respectfully send the deity off after offering your prayer.

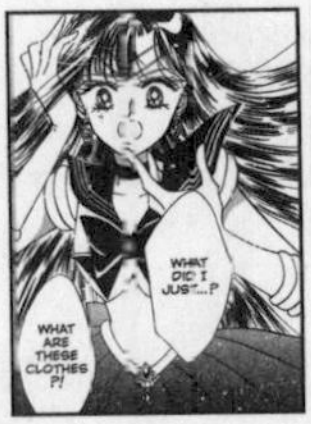
WHAT DID I JUST...?
WHAT ARE THESE CLOTHES ?!

Guardian of fire, page 122

As the red planet, it stands to reason that the planet Mars's Japanese name would be *kasei,* or "fire star." Sailor Mars's name in the Japanese name order, Hino Rei, fittingly means "spirit of fire."

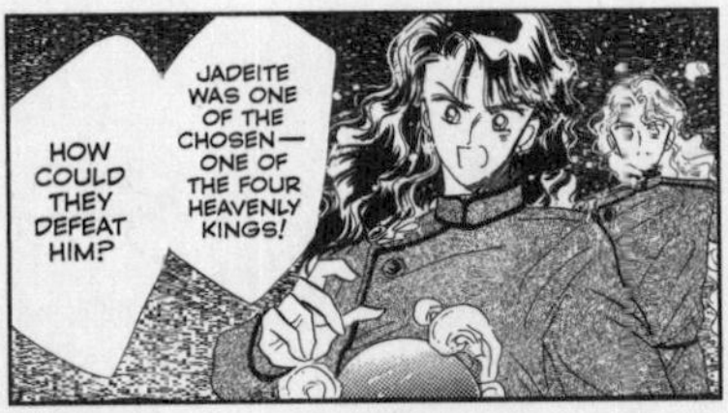
JADEITE WAS ONE OF THE CHOSEN— ONE OF THE FOUR HEAVENLY KINGS!
HOW COULD THEY DEFEAT HIM?

Four Heavenly Kings, page 123

The reader may be wondering why the commanders of the underground Dark Kingdom would be calling themselves "heavenly" kings. The name is a direct translation of the word *Shitennō,* which is the name of a set of four Buddhist deities. The Sanskrit name of these deities simply means "four great kings," or "guardians of the world." They include Vaiśravaṇa, Virūḍhaka, Dhṛtarāṣṭra, and Virūpāksa, who have been charged with guarding the cardinal directions of the Earth. In other words, Jadeite and the others are four men who have been chosen to be in charge of certain regions of the map.

The reader may be interested to know that, while the Four Heavenly Kings of the Dark Kingdom do have stewardships to watch over like the original Four Heavenly Kings, in modern Japan, the term *Shitennō* has come to be associated with any set of four people who are particularly well-known or powerful, especially in video games. If the reader should come across a video game with an "elite four" or "four champions," there is a good chance that set of four is also *Shitennō.*

The guardians' zodiac signs, page 125

It may seem odd to include a person's zodiac sign in their dossier, but when dealing with mystical planetary powers, it makes perfect sense. According to astrology, each zodiac sign is ruled by a celestial body. As the reader may guess, Cancer is ruled by the moon, Virgo is ruled by Mercury, and Aries is ruled by Mars.

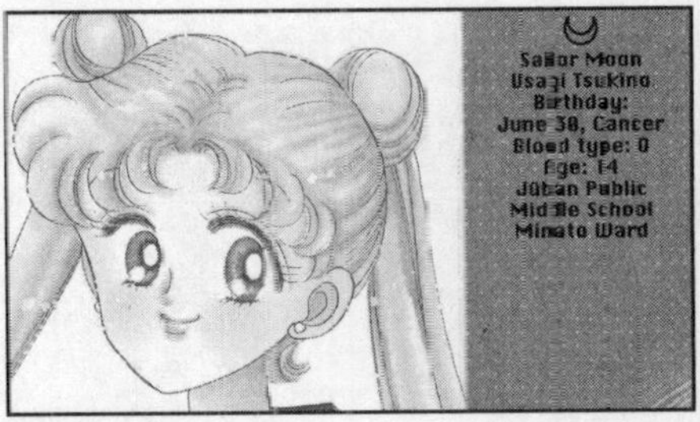
Sailor Moon
Usagi Tsukino
Birthday:
June 30, Cancer
Blood type: O
Age: 14
Jūban Public
Middle School
Minato Ward

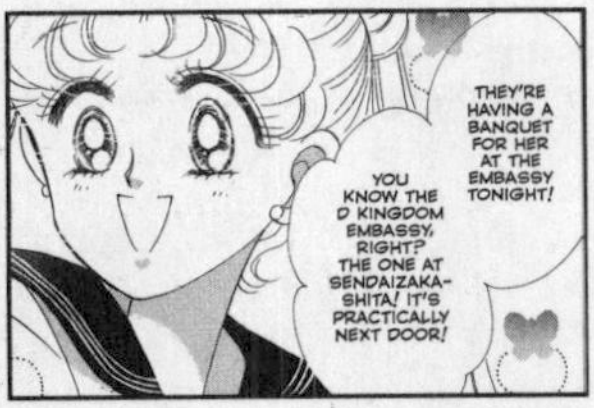
THEY'RE HAVING A BANQUET FOR HER AT THE EMBASSY TONIGHT!
YOU KNOW THE D KINGDOM EMBASSY, RIGHT? THE ONE AT SENDAIZAKA-SHITA! IT'S PRACTICALLY NEXT DOOR!

Sendaizaka-shita, page 132

The reader will no doubt recognize Sendaizaka as the place of mysterious disappearances in the previous chapter. No need to worry about the safety of Princess D in Sendaizaka-shita, however, because not only has Sailor Moon thwarted Jadeite's evil bus plot, but the place where five slopes meet is at Sendaizaka-ue, at the top of Sendaizaka Slope (*ue* means "up" or "top"). The D Kingdom Embassy is in Sendaizaka-shita, at the bottom of the slope (*shita* means "down" or "bottom"). Of course, if D Kingdom is in any way related to the Dark Kingdom, the proximity may not be a coincidence...

June brides, page 176
June is named after the Roman goddess Juno, who happens to be the patroness of marriage. That being the case, it's easy to believe that she would smile on anyone who gets married in the month named for her.

Takikomi rice ball, page 179
Takikomi gohan is rice (*gohan*) with ingredients cooked in (*takikomi*), as opposed to cooking the rice alone and eating it alongside other dishes. Common ingredients in this dish include dashi broth, soy sauce, vegetables, mushrooms, meat, fish, etc. Here, Makoto has packed her *takikomi gohan* into rice balls for easier portability.

Part-time priestess, page 184
Although Rei has a sixth sense that perhaps gives her an edge in spiritual professions, in modern-day Japan there are no specific qualifications required to serve as a priestess, or *miko*, at a Shinto shrine, as the part-time priestess's duties consist mainly of reception work and selling good luck charms and fortunes. Often the girls hired are attending vocational school, training to be full-time priestesses, but it would appear that Old Man Hino's only requirement is that the girls be pretty enough.

Guardian of thunder, page 200
Jupiter is the god of sky and thunder, so naturally a guardian under his protection would have thunder powers. However, the Japanese name of the planet is *mokusei*, or "wood star," which is why Sailor Jupiter also has plant-based attacks, and why her alter ego is named Kino, or "of wood." In fact, wood and thunder are related, as the eight trigrams of Daoist cosmology divide the five elements into eight, with lightning and wind being part of the wood element.

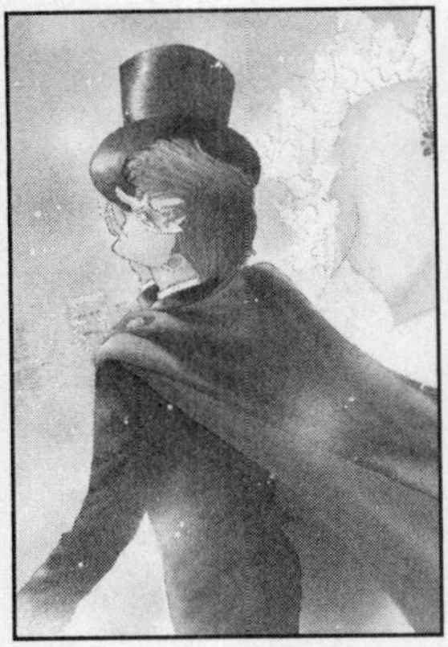

Tuxedo Kamen, page 204
Kamen is the Japanese word for "mask," and Tuxedo Kamen is the name of this well-dressed character in Japanese. The original Japanese title of this chapter is, "*Takshiido Kamen:* Tuxedo Mask," which translates to, "Tuxedo Mask: Tuxedo Mask," but mirrors the Japanese/English format of previous chapter titles (which originally left all the Sailor Guardian titles in English). Masked warriors and/or superheroes are not uncommon in greater Japanese pop culture, including the classic *Power Rangers*-esque morning children's show, *Kamen Rider.*

Moon Stick, page 207
"Stick" was the en-vogue word for magic wands in Japanese magical girl anime of the 1980s and '90s, and *Pretty Guardian Sailor Moon* made no exception. "Stick" is an English translation of the word *tsue,* which, in turn, is the Japanese translation of "wand." It seems likely that "stick" was the word of choice where magical girls were concerned because "stick" sounds similar to *suteki,* a Japanese adjective describing things that are "wonderful," "beautiful," "dreamy," etc.

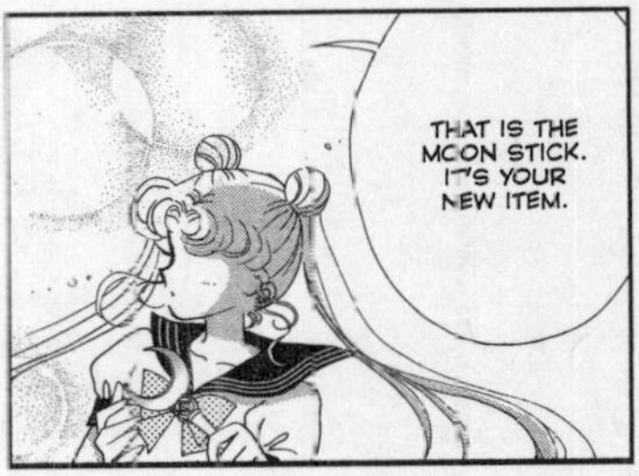
THAT IS THE MOON STICK. IT'S YOUR NEW ITEM.

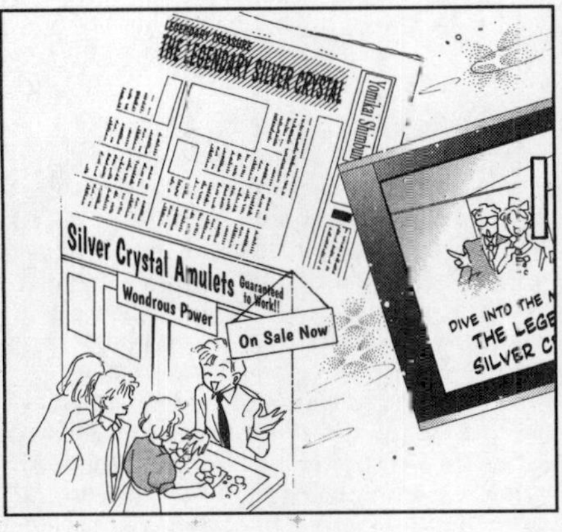
THE LEGENDARY SILVER CRYSTAL
Yomikai Shimbun
Silver Crystal Amulets
Guaranteed to Work!!
Wondrous Power
On Sale Now

***Yomikai Shimbun*, page 223**
We've seen the local paper in Usagi's world before, and now we're seeing a national newspaper, showing just how much of a sensation Tuxedo Mask has caused. The name of this paper is a play on the famous real-world paper the *Yomiuri Shimbun. Yomiuri* means "read-sell," and comes from one of the names for the people in the Edo era who would walk the streets reading the news in a loud voice and selling fliers with the news printed on them. *Yomikai,* on the other hand, means "read-buy," perhaps in the hopes that the public will read the headlines and buy the paper, but mostly just as a parody.

Usako, page 257

Mamoru's nickname for Usagi is a combination of her real name with the suffix -ko, which is commonly found in Japanese girls' names. The reason he does this instead of calling her Usagi-chan is unclear, but there are a few possibilities. First, he likely would want a name for her that is unique to him, and so used something more original. (It may not be entirely original, though, as it is also the Japanese name for the famous Dutch rabbit character Miffy.) It's also possible that by adding the -ko he is deliberately making her name more feminine, which could be a subtle way of suggesting that he sees her as someone he would like to have a romantic relationship with, or has strong, fond feelings for.

USAKO.
B-DMP

MAYBE I'LL CALL HIM...
...MAMO-CHAN.
B-DMP
B-DMP

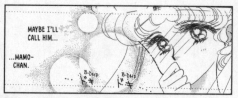

Mamo-chan, page 258

Adding -chan after the first two syllables of someone's given name is an unoriginal (see: Furu-chan, Mako-chan) but effective way of showing affection for someone. But the important thing is that it gives the translators the opportunity to talk about Mamoru's name. *Mamoru* is the word that Luna constantly repeats to the sailor guardians in reference to their mission regarding the princess and the Silver Crystal; it means "to defend or protect." *Chiba* is a word that means "place" or "locality." In other words, his name means "to protect the area." (Also, since *chi* is the same *chi* used in the word for the planet Earth, it can refer to defending the earth.)

HEY, NARU-CHAN! ARE YOU HERE TO RENT A VIDEO, TOO?
Yumiko
Kuri

Rent a video, page 268

Long, long ago, before the magic of Netflix, before even DVDs, mankind recorded movies on little boxes with magnetic tape inside called "videocassettes," or "videos" for short. These videocassettes could only be viewed with an ancient machine called a VCR, and to obtain more videos, one had to set out into brick-and-mortar shops to buy them. Alternatively, if someone wanted to watch a videocassette but not necessarily own it, they could go to a rental shop, where a customer could borrow a video for a fee. Because one had to have the physical cassette in order to view the video contained thereon, if all cassettes for a certain movie were already rented out, a customer looking for that movie would be out of luck, and their only recourse would be to choose a different movie or drive across town to a different rental shop.

A Kodansha Trade Paperback Original

Pretty Guardian Sailor Moon Naoko Takeuchi Collection 1 copyright © Naoko Takeuchi
English translation copyright © Naoko Takeuchi

Published in the United States by
Kodansha USA Publishing, LLC, New York.

Publication rights for this English edition arranged through
Kodansha Ltd., Tokyo.

First published in Japan in 2018 by Kodansha Ltd., Tokyo.

ISBN 978-1-64651-201-0

Printed in the United States of America.

1st Printing

Translation: Alethea Nibley & Athena Nibley
Lettering: Lys Blakeslee
Additional lettering and layout: Sara Linsley
Naoko Takeuchi Collection editing: Vanessa Tenazas
Kodansha USA Publishing edition cover design by Phil Balsman

Publisher: Kiichiro Sugawara

Director of Publishing Services: Ben Applegate
Associate Director of Operations: Stephen Pakula
Publishing Services Managing Editors: Alanna Ruse, Madison Salters
Production Managers: Emi Lotto, Angela Zurlo

KODANSHA.US

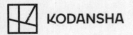